THE SOCIAL ROOTS OF
BIBLICAL YAHWISM

Society of Biblical Literature

Studies in Biblical Literature

General Acquisitions Editors

Dennis T. Olson,
Old Testament/Hebrew Bible

Sharon H. Ringe,
New Testament

Number 8

THE SOCIAL ROOTS OF
BIBLICAL YAHWISM

THE SOCIAL ROOTS OF
BIBLICAL YAHWISM

by
Stephen L. Cook

Society of Biblical Literature
Atlanta

THE SOCIAL ROOTS OF BIBLICAL YAHWISM

Library of Congress Cataloging-in-Publication Data

Cook, Stephen L., 1962–
   The social roots of biblical Yahwism / by Stephen L. Cook.
       p. cm. — (Society of Biblical literature Studies in biblical literature ; no. 8)
   Includes bibliographical references and indexes.
   ISBN 1-58983-098-9 (paper binding : alk. paper)
       1. Judaism—History—To 70 A.D. 2. Covenants—Religious aspects—Judaism—History of doctrines. 3. Bible. O.T. Hosea—Social scientific criticism. 4. Bible. O.T. Micah—Social scientific criticism. I. Title. II. Series: Studies in biblical literature (Society of Biblical Literature) ; 8.
   BM170.C66 2004
   296.3'09'01—dc22   2004021015

                    12 11 10 09 08 07 06 05 04   5 4 3 2 1

Printed in the United States of America on acid-free, recycled paper conforming to ANSI/NISO Z39.48-1992 (R1997) and ISO 9706:1994 standards for paper permanence.

CONTENTS

ACKNOWLEDGMENTS

As I have worked for the past decade to unearth the social roots of the Bible, numerous people have provided inspiration and help. I gratefully acknowledge my former teacher, Robert R. Wilson, Yale University, for introducing me to many of the stimulating theories at the heart of this project. My colleagues on the steering committee of the Social Sciences and the Interpretation of the Hebrew Scriptures Section of the Society of Biblical Literature also deserve thanks. The discussions and publications of the section allowed me to air and test my work before synthesizing it as a monograph.

I was further aided by the comments and suggestions of scholars who read my manuscript, or portions of it, including Gregory L. Glover, Andrew G. Vaughn, and several anonymous peers. Of course, I take full responsibility for the monograph as it now stands. I extend my thanks as well to John Schneider, New Haven, CT, for his expert assistance with writing and style.

I am most grateful to my home institution, Virginia Theological Seminary, and The Very Rev. Martha J. Horne, Dean and President, for encouraging and funding my scholarship and for supporting it with warm collegiality. The seminary staff at the Bishop Payne Library was especially helpful in supplying my many bibliographic needs. My work was partially funded by a generous Conant Fund Grant, awarded by the Episcopal Church, the Standing Commission on Ministry Development.

My editors at the Society of Biblical Literature have been superb to work with. I am deeply grateful for the encouragement and support of Dennis T. Olson and Rex D. Matthews. Bob Buller, Editorial Director at the Society, brought everything together wonderfully through hours of hard work.

As always, I am indebted to my wife, Catherine Elizabeth Cook, M.Div., M.A. My deepest love and appreciation go to her for her confidence in me and for her unfailing inspiration and encouragement. Catherine and I together would like to dedicate this book to our new nephew, William Arthur R. Jacobs IV. We wholeheartedly pray that in his life he will experience the ideal of Mic 4:4: "Everyone will live quietly in their own homes in peace and prosperity, for there will be nothing to fear. The LORD Almighty has promised this!" (NLT).

ABBREVIATIONS

AB	Anchor Bible
ABD	*Anchor Bible Dictionary.* Edited by D. N. Freedman. 6 vols. New York: Doubleday, 1992.
AnBib	Analecta biblica
ANET	*Ancient Near Eastern Texts Relating to the Old Testament.* Edited by J. B. Pritchard. 3rd ed. Princeton: Princeton University Press, 1969.
AOAT	Alter Orient und Altes Testament
ARM	Archives royales de Mari
ASOR	American Schools of Oriental Research
B	"B" (or second) source of the books of Samuel
BA	*Biblical Archaeologist*
BAR	*Biblical Archaeology Review*
BARead	*Biblical Archaeologist Reader*
BASOR	*Bulletin of the American Schools of Oriental Research*
BDB	Brown, F., S. R. Driver, and C. A. Briggs. *A Hebrew and English Lexicon of the Old Testament.* Oxford: Oxford University Press, 1907.
BETL	Bibliotheca ephemeridum theologicarum lovaniensium
BHS	*Biblia Hebraica Stuttgartensia.* Edited by K. Elliger and W. Rudolph. Stuttgart: Deutsche Bibelgesellschaft, 1983.
BibOr	Biblica et orientalia
BJRL	*Bulletin of the John Rylands University Library of Manchester*
BWANT	Beiträge zur Wissenschaft vom Alten und Neuen Testament
BZ	*Biblische Zeitschrift*
BZAW	Beihefte zur Zeitschrift für die alttestamentliche Wissenschaft
C	"C" (or Deuteronomistic) editorial stratum of Jeremiah

CBC	Cambridge Bible Commentary
CBQ	*Catholic Biblical Quarterly*
CC	Continental Commentaries
ConBOT	Coniectanea biblica: Old Testament Series
CTA	*Corpus des tablettes en cunéiformes alphabétiques découvertes à Ras Shamra-Ugarit de 1929 à 1939.* Edited by A. Herdner. Mission de Ras Shamra 10. Paris: Geuthner, 1963.
D	Deuteronomist source (of the Pentateuch)
E	Elohist source (of the Pentateuch)
EA	Amarna letter, as found in *Die el-Amarna Tafeln.* Edited by J. A. Knudtzon. Leipzig: Hinrichs, 1915.
EBib	Etudes bibliques
ErIsr	*Eretz-Israel*
FRLANT	Forschungen zur Religion und Literatur des Alten und Neuen Testaments
GBS	Guides to Biblical Scholarship
H	Holiness School source (of the Pentateuch)
HSM	Harvard Semitic Monographs
HSS	Harvard Semitic Studies
HTR	*Harvard Theological Review*
HUCA	*Hebrew Union College Annual*
ICC	International Critical Commentary
IDBSup	*Interpreter's Dictionary of the Bible: Supplementary Volume.* Edited by K. Crim. Nashville: Abingdon, 1976.
IEJ	*Israel Exploration Journal*
IESS	*International Encyclopedia of the Social Sciences.* Edited by D. L. Sills. New York: Macmillan, 1968–.
J	Jahwist or Yahwist source (of the Pentateuch)
JAAR	*Journal of the American Academy of Religion*
JBL	*Journal of Biblical Literature*
JCS	*Journal of Cuneiform Studies*
JESHO	*Journal of the Economic and Social History of the Orient*
JPSTC	Jewish Publication Society Torah Commentary
JQR	*Jewish Quarterly Review*
JSOT	*Journal for the Study of the Old Testament*
JSOTSup	Journal for the Study of the Old Testament Supplement Series
JSS	*Journal of Semitic Studies*
JSSEA	*Journal of the Society for the Study of Egyptian Antiquities*
JTS	*Journal of Theological Studies*
KAI	*Kanaanäische und aramäische Inschriften.* H. Donner and W. Röllig. 2nd ed. Wiesbaden: Harrassowitz, 1966–69.
KAT	Kommentar zum Alten Testament

KTU	*Die keilalphabetischen Texte aus Ugarit.* Edited by M. Dietrich, O. Loretz, and J. Sanmartín. AOAT 24/1. Neukirchen-Vluyn: Neukirchener Verlag, 1976.
LXX	Septuagint
MT	Masoretic Text
NAB	New American Bible
NASB	New American Standard Bible
NCBC	New Century Bible Comentary
NEB	New English Bible
NedTT	*Nederlands theologisch tijdschrift*
NICOT	New International Commentary on the Old Testament
NIV	New International Version
NJB	New Jerusalem Bible
NLT	New Living Translation
NRSV	New Revised Standard Version
OBT	Overtures to Biblical Theology
OTG	Old Testament Guides
OTL	Old Testament Library
P	Priestly source (of the Pentateuch)
PEQ	*Palestine Exploration Quarterly*
REB	Revised English Bible
RelSRev	*Religious Studies Review*
RS	Ras Shamra
SBLABS	Society of Biblical Literature Archaeology and Biblical Studies
SBLDS	Society of Biblical Literature Dissertation Series
SBLMS	Society of Biblical Literature Monograph Series
SBT	Studies in Biblical Theology
SHANE	Studies in the History of the Ancient Near East
SJOT	*Scandinavian Journal of the Old Testament*
SPAW	Sitzungsberichte der preussischen Akademie der Wissenschaften
SWBA	Social World of Biblical Antiquity
TA	*Tel Aviv*
TDOT	*Theological Dictionary of the Old Testament.* Edited by G. J. Botterweck and H. Ringgren. Translated by J. T. Willis, G. W. Bromiley, and D. E. Green. 8 vols. Grand Rapids: Eerdmans, 1974–.
ThT	*Theologisch tijdschrift*
TRE	*Theologische Realenzyklopädie.* Edited by G. Krause and G. Müller. Berlin: de Gruyter, 1977–.
UF	*Ugarit-Forschungen*
VT	*Vetus Testamentum*

VTSup   Supplements to Vetus Testamentum
WBC   Word Biblical Commentary
WMANT   Wissenschaftliche Monographien zum Alten und Neuen
             Testament
ZAW   *Zeitschrift für die alttestamentliche Wissenschaft*
ZDMG   *Zeitschrift der deutschen morgenländischen Gesellschaft*

1

INTRODUCTION

SCHOLARLY REVISIONISTS AND CHALLENGERS NOW QUESTION THE historical roots of Israel's traditional covenantal faith, rocking the foundations of Judaism and Christianity. Raising these challenges, based in part on new archaeological finds, they argue that the central religious understandings now found in the Hebrew Bible emerged historically only at a relatively late point in Israel. The beliefs and practices that the Bible advocates, these scholars contend, lack a legitimate pedigree. They evolved as a religious breakthrough or an ideological polemic around the time of the Babylonian exile in the sixth century B.C.E.

In this book, I take on this present-day, revisionist scholarship. I go behind the texts of the Hebrew Bible to explore the actual social roots of what Scripture describes as Israel's ancient covenant beliefs, revealed at Mount Sinai. I show that they are not the product of a long history of Israelite religious and cultural development, but an early, minority perspective from outside of Israel's and Judah's central state culture.

What is at stake is the provenance and time of origin of the Hebrew Bible's *dominant beliefs.* By dominant beliefs, I mean the overt religious points of view that the Bible presents and supports—viewpoints that Jews and Christians will instantly recognize.

I shall call these dominant, scriptural beliefs *biblical Yahwism.* This term, though susceptible to multiple interpretation and misunderstanding, serves to distinguish the religious perspective of which I shall speak from other patterns of belief that include worship of Yahweh, the God of the Bible. A term such as *canonical, covenantal, Sinai Yahwism* would be more appropriate for my subject matter, but it would be cumbersome.[1]

---

1. As I discuss in chapter 2, I use the term Sinai as shorthand for the broad covenantal theology of Deuteronomy and related biblical texts. I do not make any claims about actual

At least three clarifications of my terminology are in order. First, the term *biblical* is an important qualifier. There is much evidence in the Bible, and in extrabiblical sources, that the various populations and groups within ancient Israelite culture held to a wider range of beliefs and practices in worshiping Yahweh than those that the Hebrew Bible supports. This wider range of Israelite religious activity is interesting, but it is not the focus of this book.

Second, even the religion of Yahweh within the Bible has several forms, all of which can legitimately claim the name Yahwism. In using the term biblical Yahwism for the Bible's dominant claims, I do not mean to deny this innerbiblical plurality of perspectives or to downplay these perspectives' real, distinctive contributions.

Third, in arguing that biblical Yahwism was no exilic-era, evolutionary breakthrough or innovation, I do not mean to suggest that the Bible's religious claims emerged in old Israel fully formed and inert. I simply mean that they had a long history, separate from polytheistic, Canaanite forms of Yahwism. There is no doubt that the Bible's theological traditions grew over time and responded to changing events. There was imagination, ingenuity, and political activism along the way.

The Hebrew Bible contains a blend of voices; these voices developed in clarity and expression over time. Having acknowledged this, I intend to focus on one of the Bible's religious perspectives and argue that it had stable, enduring emphases: the perspective seen in the book of Deuteronomy and in many related texts. This perspective eventually earned a dominating position among biblical traditions and played a major role in the editorial shaping of the Bible. It now characterizes the overall form of our canonical Scriptures. I believe it is possible to demonstrate that its roots run early and deep within Israelite tradition.

Biblical Yahwism is as good a designation for this religious perspective as any other rubric. It is this scriptural, canonical understanding of Yahwistic faith that the present-day revisionists of Israelite religion hold to lack ancient roots and to be a late, tendentious development.

Modern suspicions about the authentic pedigree of biblical Yahwism have many scholarly antecedents. Since the seventeenth century critics have questioned the Bible's presentation of history and classical interpretations of biblical religion. Using scientific, objective tools and methods to better understand Israel's *real* history in terms of modern knowledge and frameworks of thought, they have constructed a new, critical history of

---

historical events in the wilderness at Mount Sinai after the Hebrew exodus from Egypt. Our literary sources for understanding biblical Yahwism associate this historically dubious place and time with the forging of God's vassal covenant with Israel.

Israel and its religion and then fitted the narratives and religious beliefs of the Bible into various niches along the new timeline.

The modern critics saw that biblical religion was not unified and static, that there was variety and change within Israelite religion. Nineteenth-century critics, in particular, stressed the idea that religious change over time specifically involved evolutionary development. Theories of evolutionary development in Israelite religion have long enjoyed widespread acceptance. Since the beginning of historical criticism, the thesis that monotheism evolved slowly out of primitive Israelite religious beliefs has been very popular. The theory of the evolution of Israelite religion from polytheism to monotheism has been a keystone of classic liberal criticism of the Bible.

There is no sense in trying to turn back the clock to a premodern view of biblical religion. The Bible itself affirms that the beliefs and practices of the Israelite people changed over time. At many points in history, furthermore, biblical religion was not what most Israelites were practicing in the larger culture. According to the biblical account, Elijah despaired that he alone in Israel had not forsaken Yahweh's covenant and bowed to Baal (1 Kgs 19:14).

Archaeology and biblical criticism yield much fascinating, unassailable evidence about religious beliefs and practices in the larger Israelite culture that clash with the faith of the Bible. Biblical Yahwism must have often been in the minority in ancient times. It would be foolish to disregard or downplay this new knowledge.[2]

It is equally misguided, I argue, to view *biblical* religion as inauthentic, secondary, and revisionist. Considering what the newer reconstructions tell us was ancient Israel's wide-ranging religious practice, biblical Yahwism could have been one viable alternative among many from very early times. It is particularly simplistic to view biblical Yahwism as a belated product of general, cultural evolution in Israel.

Now, I shall briefly sketch the rise of the developmental hypothesis in biblical scholarship and summarize its current forms. I shall then suggest a basis upon which this book can provide an alternative, more critical understanding of the roots of biblical Yahwism.

Julius Wellhausen, the great nineteenth-century founder of historical criticism of the Bible, asserted that before the time of the prophets the God of Israel was a tribal deity. It was only through the prophets' work

---

2. For accessible and fair-minded surveys of ancient Israelite religion, see Susan Niditch, *Ancient Israelite Religion* (New York: Oxford University Press, 1997); and Patrick D. Miller, *The Religion of Ancient Israel* (Library of Ancient Israel; Louisville: Westminster John Knox, 2000).

that the distinctive faith of Israel developed from its earlier religions of animism, polytheism, and monolatry. (*Monolatry* is devotion to one god among many. *Henotheism* is a synonym.)

As G. Ernest Wright aptly summarizes, "The Graf-Wellhausen reconstruction of the history of Israel's religion was, in effect, an assertion that within the pages of the Old Testament we have a perfect example of the evolution of religion from animism in patriarchal times through henotheism to monotheism.... It was the prophets who were the true innovators and who produced most, if not all, of that which was truly distinctive in Israel.... [T]he grand culmination [came] with the universalism of II Isaiah [during the Babylonian exile in the sixth century B.C.E.]."[3]

The Dutch scholar Abraham Kuenen anticipated Wellhausen's claims about the evolutionary development of Israel's religion. Kuenen committed himself to approaching and understanding Israelite religion as one would assess its neighbors' ancient religions. He assumed that Israelite religion must have changed over time in accordance with humanity's natural anthropological development. "To what we might call the universal, or at least the common rule, that religion begins with fetishism, then develops into polytheism, and then, but not before, ascends to monotheism—that is to say, if this highest stage be reached— to this rule the Israelites are no exception."[4]

Prophets such as Hosea moved Israel toward worship of Yahweh alone. But true monotheism, which denies the existence of other gods, only emerged at the time of the Babylonian exile. In one representative statement, Wellhausen writes: "Monotheism was unknown to ancient Israel.... It would only be from the time of the Babylonian exile that the concept was alive. Around that time, it suddenly [*plötzlich*] emerges that he [Yahweh] not only controls but also created the lands and seas, with all their abundance, the heavens and their host."[5]

Many scholars who followed Wellhausen continued his developmental approach to Israel's religion. In the late nineteenth century and first decades of the twentieth century, historians of Israelite religion relied

---

3. G. Ernest Wright, "The Present State of Biblical Archaeology," in *The Study of the Bible Today and Tomorrow* (ed. H. Willoughby; Chicago: University of Chicago Press, 1947), 89–90. See also, e.g., E. W. Nicholson, *Deuteronomy and Tradition* (Oxford: Basil Blackwell, 1967), xi.
4. Abraham Kuenen, *The Religion of Israel* (trans. A. H. May; Edinburgh: Williams & Norgate, 1874), 225. On Kuenen's view of the prophets as the innovators of ethical monotheism in Israel, see his Dutch volume: *De Profeten en de Profetie onder Israël: Historisch-Dogmatisch Studie* (2 vols. in 1; Leiden: Engels, 1875), 361–68.
5. Julius Wellhausen, *Israelitische und Jüdische Geschichte* (9th ed.; Berlin: de Gruyter, 1958), 29–30.

heavily on evolutionary philosophical principles. These scholars, members of the "history of religions school," described Israel's religion as evolving from nature religion to ethical monotheism. The philosophical idealism of earlier scholars prepared the way for this trend.

Even after this period, developmental approaches to Israelite religion remained popular. For example, in the 1930s, Otto Eissfeldt argued that, despite the biblical protests against it, child sacrifice was an original, lawful part of Yahwism.[6] Only with time was Israel able to advance beyond this inhumane practice.

Wellhausen believed that the concept of the Sinai covenant, which demanded the people's exclusive allegiance to Yahweh, only developed in Israel after the time of the earlier prophets.[7] The lateness of covenant theology was, in fact, a cornerstone of Wellhausen's understanding of the development of Israelite religion. The prophets were thus not the inheritors and guardians of the covenant and its laws, he concluded, as classical views of Israel's religion held. Rather, they were the true religious innovators in Israel. For Wellhausen, the prophets were not reactionaries who opposed covenant apostasy but Israel's primary catalysts for religious and ethical progress.

Although the scholarly pendulum has swung back and forth on the question of the origin of the covenant idea in Israel, scholars such as Lothar Perlitt have advanced Wellhausen's skeptical view.[8] They argue

---

6. Otto Eissfeldt, *Molk als Opferbegriff im Punischen und Hebräischen und das ende des Gottes Moloch* (Beiträge zur Religionsgeschichte des Altertums 3; Halle: Niemeyer, 1935).

7. Wellhausen states: "The relation of Yahweh to Israel was in its nature and origin a natural one; there was no interval between him and his people to call for thought or question. Only when the existence of Israel had come to be threatened by the Syrians and Assyrians, did such prophets as Elijah and Amos raise the deity high above the people, sever the natural bond between them, and put in its place a relation depending on conditions, conditions of a moral character.... In this way arose..., as an entirely new thing, the substance of the notion of covenant or treaty. The name Berith ['covenant'], however, does not occur in the old prophets, not even in Hosea." He goes on, "After the solemn and far-reaching act by which [King] Josiah introduced [the Deuteronomic] law [in the seventh century B.C.E., six hundred years after Moses' death], the notion of covenant-making between Yahweh and Israel appears to have occupied the central position in religious thought." See Julius Wellhausen, *Prolegomena to the History of Ancient Israel* (trans. W. Robertson Smith; New York: Meridan, 1957), 417–19; first published in German in 1883.

8. Lothar Perlitt, *Bundestheologie im Alten Testament* (WMANT 36; Neukirchen: Neukirchen-Vluyn, 1969). Perlitt's views have been furthered by Ernst Kutsch, *Verheissung und Gesetz: Untersuchungen zum sogenannten Bund im Alten Testament* (BZAW 131; Berlin, New York: de Gruyter, 1973). For a good, brief discussion of major critical reactions to the work of Perlitt and Kutsch, see Jon D. Levenson, *Sinai and Zion: An Entry into the Jewish Bible* (San Francisco: Harper, 1985), 25–26 n. 10.

that the Hebrew term for covenant is absent or scarce in the earlier writings of the Bible and that the idea of the covenant only becomes clear in our evidence after the time of the publication of the book of Deuteronomy (no earlier than the seventh century). Many contemporary scholars agree.

The events of the mid-to-late twentieth century tended to shake people's confidence in evolutionary development and human moral progress. The two world wars, as well as the Holocaust and other catastrophes of genocide and ethnic cleansing, caused a loss of faith in the religious ascent of humankind.

As the twenty-first century begins, new views, especially postmodernism, seem to question grand visions of evolutionary progress. Nevertheless, contemporary historians of Israelite religion remain largely wedded to notions of progressive development within religion. Present-day theologians and religious thinkers no longer attempt to articulate and define God completely after the manner of nineteenth-century thinkers. All the same, biblical historians often look as if they are trying to thoroughly account for the identity of God. But as Ludwig Feuerbach observed, to succeed at this is to assure that God is a mere human construct.

The idea of an evolutionary development of biblical monotheism received a boost when archaeological discoveries and new approaches to Israel's settlement of the land of Canaan questioned the idea of a military conquest of the Canaanites by Israel. Critical scholars had always been skeptical about the account given by the book of Joshua that a united Israel conquered Palestine rapidly by force. Up until the 1920s, however, they had generally accepted the idea of some sort of invasion (or invasions) by Israel into the land. This changed by the middle of the twentieth century, when scholars were grappling hard with the problem of Israel's origins in the land. Doubts about a military conquest led to alternative theories of Israel's settlement.

Eventually, by the 1960s and 1970s, George Mendenhall and Norman Gottwald had advanced theories that Israel arose as a people entirely from within the borders of Palestine (autochthonously).[9] They argued that Israel did not enter the land from outside of it, but emerged and developed as a people directly out of Palestine's Canaanite population.

This model of Israel's emergence from within Canaan has led recent historians of Israelite religion to suppose that at first there must have been a great deal of continuity between the religions of Israel and

9. George E. Mendenhall, *The Tenth Generation: The Origins of the Biblical Tradition* (Baltimore: John Hopkins University Press, 1973); Norman K. Gottwald, *The Tribes of Yahweh: A Sociology of the Religion of Liberated Israel 1250–1050 B.C.E.* (Maryknoll, N.Y.: Orbis, 1979).

Canaan. Originally, Israelite religion was much closer to Canaanite religion than to the religion that the Bible now advocates. According to this current view, the religious perspective of the Hebrew Bible developed gradually from a Canaanite background. The contravening picture that the Bible presents is polemical and fundamentally distorted. Obviously, this current scholarship makes biblical Yahwism look more like revisionist history than historical religious tradition associated with real-life lawgivers and prophets in old Israel.

New archaeological finds that attracted enormous attention in the late 1970s further invigorated the efforts of scholars to understand Yahwism as emerging out of Canaanite religion.[10] The discovery, in 1976, of new inscriptions related to the Canaanite fertility goddess, Asherah, particularly captured scholars' imaginations. The inscriptions relate Asherah, or at least her cult symbol, to Israel's God, Yahweh. Most notably, inscriptions from Kuntillet ʿAjrûd (in northeast Sinai) refer to "Yahweh and his Asherah." An inscription from Khirbet el-Qom, another site (near Hebron), also refers to Yahweh's Asherah. Based on the new inscriptions, scholars concluded that some ancient Israelites understood Asherah to be in partnership with Yahweh, perhaps as his consort.

At first glance, the new inscriptions seem to confirm that biblical Yahwism is secondary and revisionist. The religious understandings of the inscriptions stood in clear tension with the understandings that the Hebrew Bible authorizes. Scholars reasoned that in its early stages, Yahwism must have had the polytheistic, Canaanite form that the new inscriptions depict.

Saul Olyan, in his 1988 book *Asherah and the Cult of Yahweh in Israel,* brought scholars' thinking about Israelite religion directly into step with the latest theories about Israel's indigenous origins in Palestine.[11] Based on a thorough study of both new and old evidence, Olyan argued that Asherah was a legitimate part of the cult of Yahweh in Israel's state and popular religion. Texts within the Bible arguing otherwise were polemical distortions of the truth. Canaanite religious traditions and practices were a living part of Israelite religion from the start, and this fact was not due to apostasy, the falling away from a pure faith, or to syncretism, the mixing and blending of originally separate religious beliefs and practices. Rather, having emerged out of Canaanite religion, Yahwism had

---

10. See, for example, J. A. Emerton, "New Light on Israelite Religion: the Implications of the Inscriptions from Kuntillet 'Ajrud," *ZAW* 94 (1982): 2–20; John Day, "Asherah in the Hebrew Bible and Northwest Semitic Literature," *JBL* 105 (1986): 385–408.

11. Saul M. Olyan, *Asherah and the Cult of Yahweh in Israel* (SBLMS 34; Atlanta: Scholars Press, 1988).

gradually differentiated itself from its own Canaanite cultic and historical origins.

Other publications taking a similar approach to Israelite religion soon followed Olyan's book.[12] These advance the thesis that biblical Yahwism evolved out of the general Canaanite culture of the late Bronze Age. Many of these publications have been articles and studies with a narrow focus. However, some have been attempts at a larger synthesis.

One year before Olyan's book appeared, a group of Frank Moore Cross's students edited and published a major collection of studies on Israelite religion in honor of the famous Harvard University scholar of Israelite religion. The collection, appropriately entitled *Ancient Israelite Religion: Essays in Honor of Frank Moore Cross* (1987), contained a number of essays by senior scholars in the field reflecting a consensus that true monotheism developed only late in Israel's history, probably after the exile.[13]

Michael Coogan's contribution to the volume argued that emergent Israelite monotheism had "Canaanite Origins and Lineage."[14] Drawing in part on the evidence from Kuntillet ʿAjrûd, Coogan defends the thesis that Israelite religion was in direct cultural continuity with the religion of its West Semitic neighbors and that the living Canaanite tradition within Israel included belief in Asherah as the consort of Yahweh. Ezekiel's genealogy of Jerusalem is accurate, according to Coogan: "By origin and by birth you [Jerusalem] are of the land of the Canaanites" (Ezek 16:3).

Mark Smith's *The Early History of God* (1990) is an excellent attempt to synthesize a scholarly model of the emergence of biblical Yahwism out of earlier Canaanite religious forms.[15] Smith surveys a great variety of archaeological, inscriptional, and textual data. He uses this data to show the evolution of Yahwistic monotheism through dual processes of "convergence" and "differentiation." On the one hand, according to Smith, preexilic Yahwism took shape as some Canaanite deities, or at

12. For one good survey of late twentieth-century approaches to Israelite religion that take an evolutionary approach, see Robert Gnuse, "New Directions in Biblical Theology: The Impact of Contemporary Scholarship in the Hebrew Bible," *JAAR* 62/3 (1994): 893–918, especially pp. 898ff.

13. Patrick D. Miller, Paul D. Hanson, and S. D. McBride, eds., *Ancient Israelite Religion: Essays in Honor of Frank Moore Cross* (Philadelphia: Fortress, 1987).

14. Michael D. Coogan, "Canaanite Origins and Lineage: Reflections on the Religion of Ancient Israel," in *Ancient Israelite Religion: Essays in Honor of Frank Moore Cross* (ed. Patrick D. Miller; Paul D. Hanson, and S. D. McBride; Philadelphia: Fortress, 1987), 115–24.

15. Mark S. Smith, *The Early History of God: Yahweh and the Other Deities in Ancient Israel* (San Francisco: Harper & Row, 1990).

least their features, converged into the figure of Yahweh. On the other hand, as it evolved, Yahwism rejected many other features of its earlier Canaanite heritage. Slowly and gradually, Israelite monotheism developed through the centuries reaching a pinnacle in the texts of Isa 40–55.

Johannes C. de Moor's book, *The Rise of Yahwism: The Roots of Israelite Monotheism* (1990; reissued 1997), is a different example of current thinking among historians of Israelite religion.[16] The book is a creative attempt to reconstruct earliest Israel and its religion against the backdrop of the psychological moods of ancient Near Eastern cultures. Based largely on data from outside biblical texts, de Moor traces a broad, linear development of Israelite monotheism out of Canaanite religion. He argues that a major factor in this development was a psychological crisis of polytheism in Canaan.

A third example of the new approach to Israel's religion is provided by Robert Gnuse's 1997 book, *No Other Gods: Emergent Monotheism in Israel*.[17] This work aims to demonstrate to a general audience that Yahwism evolved through a series of developmental stages. Gnuse argues that Israelite monotheism developed over time, throughout the first six centuries of Israel's history. This evolution often occurred through breakthroughs or "bursts" in response to particular social and religious crises. Monotheism reached full expression in Israel only in response to the social and religious crisis of the Judean's exile to Babylon in the sixth century B.C.E.

Even in this brief review of selected current scholarly models of Yahwism's developmental history, it is hard to miss a strong resemblance to comparable approaches of the nineteenth century. As noted above, a major distinctive of the history of religions school of this period was the thesis of Yahwism's evolutionary development.

One can defend nineteenth-century scholars' embrace of the developmental thesis as appropriate to their times, because of the contemporary dominance of Hegel's and Darwin's ideas of progress, evolution, and *becoming*. It is harder to view the current espousal of this thesis charitably, given the atrocities of the twentieth century and late-modern critiques of the idea of humanity's general religious ascent.

Note further that current scholarly proponents of Yahwism's developmental history agree that the various evidence of polytheism in Israel, such as the inscriptions about Asherah, depicts the early history

16. Johannes C. de Moor, *The Rise of Yahwism: The Roots of Israelite Monotheism* (Leuven: Uitgeverij Peeters, 1990, 1997).
17. Robert Karl Gnuse, *No Other Gods: Emergent Monotheism in Israel* (JSOTSup 241; Sheffield: Sheffield Academic Press, 1997).

of biblical Yahwism, not its external milieu. It seems not to have occurred to these scholars to consider that the polytheistic inscriptions and other data depict elements of the broader religious and cultic setting with which biblical Yahwism interacted and struggled. Many have rightly questioned similar assumptions when researchers have applied them in other contexts.

Some scholars writing about the Dead Sea Scrolls have argued, for example, that the commonalities between the Qumran group and primitive Christianity suggest that Christianity must have grown out of the movement that treasured the scrolls. Most Dead Sea Scrolls scholars find this view untenable. They believe that the scrolls display elements of the larger milieu in which early Christians understood and preached the unique life and teachings of Jesus of Nazareth.

Recent theories about Israelite religion and history seem to outdo their predecessors in radicalness. Over the past several years, so-called minimalist historians of the Bible have pushed the view that biblical history and religion is revisionist to an extreme.[18] The minimalist historians hold that the Bible has little or no historical connection to the events that it depicts. Rather, it reflects an ideological and social setting of a much later time. The minimalists date the composition of the Bible to long after the exilic and postexilic period (the usual sixth–fifth century date of the Bible's main compilation), giving it an origin in Hellenistic times (332–167 B.C.E.). Even more radically, they have called into question major elements of the biblical history, such as the united monarchy of David and Solomon.

Although these new views have caused some current turmoil, they seem unlikely to stand the test of time. They cannot account, for example, for the accuracy of historical and cultural details in the biblical texts, which would not have been known to Hellenistic writers. And recent archaeological discoveries reconfirm the historical existence of biblical entities such as the state of Judah and the dynasty of David, which the minimalists had questioned. Nevertheless, despite increasing erosion of the minimalists' position, their claims still call for a strong reclarification of the antiquity of biblical Yahwism's roots.

In this book, I critique the current, commonplace view that biblical Yahwism is a late development in Israel's history, with only a minimal historical pedigree. In particular, I disagree that biblical Yahwism

---

18. Representative publications taking a minimalist approach include: Philip R. Davies, *In Search of "Ancient Israel"* (JSOTSup 148; Sheffield: JSOT Press, 1992); Niels Peter Lemche, "Is It Still Possible to Write a History of Ancient Israel?" *SJOT* 8 (1994): 165–90; Thomas L. Thompson, *Early History of the Israelite People: From the Written and Archaeological Sources* (SHANE 4; Leiden: Brill, 1992); idem, *The Mythic Past: Biblical Archaeology and the Myth of Israel* (New York: Basic Books, 1999).

evolved out of Canaanite religion and then developed through the work of the prophets and through various reforms and crises into its current form of universal monotheism. In place of this common view, I shall offer a more critical understanding of the roots of biblical Yahwism. I shall show that these roots run deep in ancient Israel's history and society.

My argument relies on approaches from the social sciences. Such approaches have been maturing within the biblical guild in recent decades, and most scholars now recognize their validity and usefulness in interpreting the Bible. I draw on comparisons and parallels from a variety of cultures and settings, many from the traditional peoples of Africa. These cross-cultural comparisons illuminate and clarify the social settings of the biblical texts and the social roots of the religion of the texts. Methods of modern biblical interpretation, that is, exegetical methods, equally aid my efforts. Exegesis tests if cross-cultural comparisons that may illuminate the Bible actually apply to the details of particular biblical texts.

The evolutionary understanding of Israelite religion assumes that Israel's culture and society developed as a whole, over time, towards monotheism. Social-scientific studies of the social world of the Bible over the last twenty-five years show that we cannot view Israel in such a monolithic way. Israel's culture and society were complex and diverse. It exhibited what social scientists call *subcultural diversity.* Within the society, groups with varying beliefs and traditions vied for attention and power. Different groups were active and prominent at different times and in different geographical and social locations.

The complexity and diversity of groups and their religious perspectives within Israel means that the religion advocated by the lawgivers, prophets, and reformers of the Hebrew Bible cannot be equated with the general phenomenon of ancient Israelite religion. The religious norms of the Hebrew Bible and the actual practice of ancient Israelite religion are not synonymous entities or part of one unilinear, evolutionary continuum.

The canonical, covenantal Yahwism found in the Bible was likely only one religious perspective among many in ancient Israel. Biblical Yahwism probably coexisted, as a *coterminous* phenomenon within Israel, alongside of other religious systems and perspectives. Biblical Yahwism did not evolve out of earlier religious forms but existed as a religious option alongside of such other forms of religion in ancient Israel as Canaanite religious practices, syncretistic forms of religion, popular or folk religious practices, and official, state religion.[19]

---

19. As noted above, the Hebrew Bible itself preserves more than one brand of Yahwism. A Sinai-oriented, covenantal Yahwism now predominates in the Hebrew Scriptures,

The Bible itself portrays the religious situation in ancient Israel in exactly this way. In most of the narratives and books of the Bible, the people and their rulers do not follow the religion that the Bible advocates but have fallen into apostasy. Their religious practice fails to square with the beliefs and injunctions of Yahwism presented in the texts. Only small groups of prophets, priests, or families preserve and proclaim biblical Yahwism. For a good illustration of this, see the list of Canaanite and polytheistic cult objects that King Hezekiah orders removed in 2 Kgs 18:4. An even more extensive picture of Israelite polytheistic worship is provided by 2 Kgs 23:4–14, which describes King Josiah's purging of the temple and land.

Most of the chapters of this book examine and interpret passages from the Bible. I want particularly to focus on the Minor Prophets. Several of these books preserve the authentic words of Israel's earliest "writing" prophets (actually a misnomer, since these figures delivered their oracles in oral form, and their disciples collected and preserved them in writing).

Prophets such as Hosea and Micah were relatively early (eighth century) religious believers and advocates of what I have been calling biblical Yahwism (the dominating religious perspective of the Hebrew Bible in its received, canonical form). The tenets of these prophets' beliefs and their special language and diction place them in the stream of tradition that led to the book of Deuteronomy and other programmatic examples of the Sinai-oriented, covenant faith of the Bible.[20]

Examining the texts of these prophets helps us to trace biblical Yahwism back to the prophets' own contemporary period in the eighth century. Since these prophets come both from the northern kingdom and from Judah in the south, studying these texts affords us an understanding of biblical Yahwism in its full geographical sweep. Moreover, these prophets come from various places and circles within Israel's society. When we uncover the social settings of their prophecies, we get a full

---

but other significant theological voices also make themselves heard. Indeed, even within Sinai theology, a variety of distinct traditions comes to expression within the biblical texts. Sinai-oriented Yahwism was not homogeneous, as I shall show.

20. Odil Hannes Steck notes the marks of what he terms a theological stream of tradition: "A breadth in substance and conceptional design, characteristic thought-patterns, leading views, and not least of all a distinctive, stereotyped language which exerts a uniform influence for centuries." See his "Theological Streams of Tradition," in *Tradition and Theology in the Old Testament* (ed. D. Knight; Philadelphia: Fortress, 1977), 202. For further clarification of this concept, see Brevard S. Childs, *Memory and Tradition in Israel* (SBT 37; London: SCM, 1962); Walter E. Rast, *Tradition History and the Old Testament* (GBS; Philadelphia: Fortress, 1972).

sense of the various social locations and groups that nurtured biblical Yahwism in Israel's monarchic period.

The particular methods and tools of this study allow us to penetrate even farther into the roots of biblical Yahwism, however. Careful study of the eighth-century prophets of biblical Yahwism reveals that they were not primarily innovators of the Bible's unique traditions. They were bearers and preservers of these traditions. Furthermore, the biblical prophets were not able to preserve these traditions without also preserving clues about these traditions' older social roots.

Because Israel's society changed over time, some of the outdated social traits of the traditions that the prophets preserve stand out as vestigial. The language of their traditions has anachronistic features from earlier times, and their beliefs repristinate older ways of life that would often have seemed impractical to their contemporary audiences. Such vestigial traits in the traditions of biblical Yahwism allow us to trace these traditions back in time beyond their eighth-century prophetic proponents.

Here it is helpful to bring comparisons from other cultures into the discussion. Cross-cultural comparisons reveal groups similar to those of Israelite society, which fought to preserve older beliefs and ways of life amid changing social situations and fortunes.

THE BASIC FEATURES OF BIBLICAL YAHWISM

A NECESSARY FIRST STEP IN TRACING THE EARLY ROOTS OF BIBLICAL Yahwism is to define the nature and basic characteristics of this type of religion. We must have a solid handle on the nature of biblical Yahwism to successfully trace its cultural and historical roots in ancient Israel.

Biblical Yahwism is a body of traditions that specific groups within Israelite culture passed down over time. It is not the religion of an entire culture but the distinctive traditions of a minority of Israelites, one of many perspectives even within the Bible.

A preliminary task of this chapter, therefore, is to define the specific sources within the Bible directly associated with, and clearly reflecting, the characteristics of biblical Yahwism.

Biblical "sources" are the specific books, passages, and strands within the Bible that advocate a specific perspective and tradition. Critical methods of exegesis, such as source criticism and form criticism, are essential for probing beneath the Bible's surface to isolate some of these sources.

SOURCES FOR DESCRIBING BIBLICAL YAHWISM

Traditional readers of the Bible have always been theologically oriented. They read the Bible to try to understand Israel's *true* religion. Israel's true religion is the one that *Yahweh intended* for the Israelites, not the religion the Israelites actually practiced. It is the religion that the Hebrew Bible commends to its readers.

If asked about this religion, most Bible readers would stress Israel's belief in one God, Yahweh, who chose Israel to be a special people. Yahweh delivered the people from slavery in Egypt, and promised that they would live securely in a land of their own. Yahweh expected a relationship with the people based on these gracious acts. This relationship included the people's sole allegiance to God and their obedience of God's laws for how they should relate to God and each other in community and in the land.

Rather than focusing on the entire literary picture of Israel's religion that the Hebrew Bible provides, we will focus on a smaller group of biblical texts related to the book of Deuteronomy. Deuteronomy and related texts most closely embody the biblical Yahwism most readers envision.

I shall focus on a narrow group of texts within the Bible that share a similar diversity of concerns, a set of particularly loaded concepts, a specific terminology, and characteristic forms of expression. If a group of unconnected biblical books and texts—whose literary features do not depend on one another—share these elements, then these texts must be part of a living body of *tradition* within ancient Israel.

Traditions are more than a faddish political program or an evolutionary stage of development. Traditions are thematically centered associations of religious notions that specific groups within society pass down over time to future generations. If groups possess and bear traditions, then they likely extend over time and have a history of forebears.

Biblical Yahwism is much more deeply rooted in Israel's history and society than developmentally oriented theorists claim. I shall present biblical Yahwism as a *stream of tradition* within ancient Israel, uncovering the bearers and forebears of this theological stream.

Groups of tradition bearers, what scholars call *tradents*, promulgated the tenets of biblical Yahwism in the face of the wider Israelite culture's polytheism, and they passed down these tenets over the course of Israel's history in the land. Psalm 78, one text exemplifying biblical Yahwism, expresses how important it was to the *tradents* to pass down the biblical traditions to each new generation. Verse 4 reads, "We will not conceal them from [our ancestors'] descendants, but tell to the generation to come the praises of the LORD, and his strength and his wondrous works that he has done."

Biblical Yahwism is most closely associated with the family of texts and sources scholars connect with Deuteronomy (or, the D source). Since the time of Martin Noth, scholars have closely linked Deuteronomy to the editing of the books of Joshua through 2 Kings.[1] In fact, they designate the collection of books from Deuteronomy to 2 Kings as the Deuteronomistic History. Sources or strands within the Deuteronomistic History,

---

1. Martin Noth, *The Deuteronomistic History* (JSOTSup 15; Sheffield: JSOT Press, 1981); Richard D. Nelson, *The Double Redaction of the Deuteronomistic History* (JSOTSup 18; Sheffield: JSOT Press, 1981).

such as the strand in Samuel that scholars call the B source, also connect closely to Deuteronomy.

Scholars have also long argued that the books of Hosea, Jeremiah, and Malachi, along with the so-called Elohist, or E, strand of the Pentateuch, have strong affinities with Deuteronomy.[2] At least until recently, many scholars agreed that these biblical works cohere to express the same theological traditions.

In addition, various scholars have made strong arguments that other texts of the Bible share these same traditions. Harry P. Nasuti has argued persuasively in his Yale University dissertation, published as *Tradition History and the Psalms of Asaph* (1988), that these texts should also include the Psalms of Asaph (Pss 50; 73–83).[3] In his 1996 book, Michael D. Goulder builds on the work of Nasuti and others to argue that the Asaphite psalms contain the traditions behind the Deuteronomic parts of the Pentateuch.[4] Various additional scholarly studies have convincingly argued that the book of Micah, or at least a significant body of passages within Micah, also belongs within this circle of texts.[5]

This is not the place to renew or develop the history of interpretation and the exegetical arguments that support taking these books and texts together as a group closely related to Deuteronomy. For now I simply suggest the model that these texts cohere in their common espousal of a biblical Yahwism, and save for later chapters evidence that some eighth-century Minor Prophet books have a strong family resemblance to this unique group of texts. These prophetic books do not have a similar connection with any other text groups.

---

2. On the connections between E and Deuteronomy, see, e.g., Terence E. Fretheim, "Elohist," *IDBSup*, 259–63; Alan W. Jenks, "Elohist," *ABD* 2:478–82.

3. Harry Peter Nasuti, *Tradition History and the Psalms of Asaph* (SBLDS 88; Atlanta: Scholars Press, 1988).

4. Michael Douglas Goulder, *The Psalms of Asaph and the Pentateuch: Studies in the Psalter, III* (JSOTSup 233; Sheffield: JSOT Press, 1996).

5. Jon D. Levenson's work has drawn connections between Micah and "Sinai" traditions related to Deuteronomism. See his *Sinai and Zion: An Entry into the Jewish Bible* (San Francisco: Harper & Row, 1987), 195–200. Levenson's understanding of Micah's traditions draws on Walter Beyerlin's work, *Die Kulttraditionen Israels in der Verkündigung des Propheten Micah* (FRLANT 62; Göttingen: Vandenhoeck & Ruprecht, 1959). Other scholarly studies focusing on particular texts within Micah have linked them closely to Hosea and Deuteronomy. See F. C. Burkitt, "Micah 6 and 7 a Northern Prophecy," *JBL* 45 (1926): 159–61; Otto Eissfeldt, *Der Gott Karmel* (SPAW; Berlin: Akademie Verlag, 1953), 7–8; idem, "Ein Psalm aus Nord-Israel: Micha 7, 7–20," *ZDMG* 112 (1962): 259–68; Adam S. van der Woude, "Deutero-Micha: Ein Prophet aus Nord-Israel?" *NedTT* 25 (1971): 365–78; J. T. Willis, "A Reapplied Prophetic Hope Oracle," in *Studies on Prophecy* (ed. G. W. Anderson et al.; VTSup 26; Leiden: Brill, 1974), 64–76.

Strong family ties exist between some of the eighth-century prophets and Deuteronomy and related writings. These include a common stress on the provisions of the covenant enacted at Sinai, as well as fixed expressions, idioms, and emphases held in common. Emphases include the idea of Moses as a continuing model for prophets, judges and other leaders, an antimonarchic perspective, and a way of talking and preaching about Israel's history that stresses moral exhortation.

My study does not aim to discover the background and sources of the book of Deuteronomy specifically, as previous scholarly work has attempted. Instead, I shall show that a theological stream of tradition in ancient Israel coexisted and struggled with other more polytheistic forms of Israelite religion, before flowering into biblical Yahwism.

Not restricting ourselves to texts that use the specific forms of speech of Deuteronomy gives us some working room. We will be able to discuss fascinating evidence in the Psalms of Asaph, the book of Micah, and other biblical passages usually neglected in the study of the specific phenomenon of Deuteronomism.

I shall use a social-scientific approach to move back *behind* the Yahwism of the eighth-century "writing prophets," to the forebears and spheres of early Israelite society from which they inherited their religious traditions.

This book differs significantly from previous studies in the way I view geography. Biblical scholarship has often used geography to distinguish among biblical traditions. Albrecht Alt, in one of the most venerable versions of this geographical approach in 1953,[6] argued that the traditions of biblical Yahwism we have discussed are the products of a northern geography.

Such a geographical interpretation of Israel's traditions takes God's eternal promises to Israel and to King David's dynasty as southern in origin. Conversely, the covenant traditions associated with Sinai originated in north Israel. In particular, scholars have held that Deuteronomy's major precursors, Hosea and the Elohist strand (E) of the Pentateuch, clearly had their original settings in the northern kingdom. In his 1953 study, Alt concludes, "The program of Deuteronomy is rooted in the same soil as the prophecy of Hosea, thus in the traditions of the northern kingdom."[7]

Contemporary scholars have continued to think of Sinai covenant traditions as northern. Yale's Robert R. Wilson has suggested that the

---

6. Albrecht Alt, "Die Heimat des Deuteronomiums," in *Kleine Schriften zur Geschichte des Volkes Israel* (3 vols.; Munich: Beck, 1953), 2:250–75.

7. Ibid., 268.

term "Ephraimite" is a useful rubric for designating our particular theological stream of tradition.[8] Ephraim was a major tribe of the northern kingdom of Israel, and its name can designate the entire northern state. Since Nasuti's study, which I mentioned above, suggests that the Asaph psalms originated in the north, he is able to continue to use Wilson's term "Ephraimite" in describing the Asaph collection.

The general findings of Wilson and Nasuti represent tremendous breakthroughs, but I disagree with their geographical approach.

Hosea certainly operated in the north, but Micah was a southern prophet. Several of the concerns of the E strand bear on specifically southern issues. The strand is not necessarily northern. A *social-scientific* approach can explain this evidence far better than a *geographical* one. The various streams of tradition of ancient Israel belonged to differing spheres of society rather than to differing geographical locations. The biblical traditions centering on Moses and Sinai, I contend, have their roots in specific societal groups, not geographical locales.

Jon Levenson has argued that established southern literature orients itself specifically towards Sinai and Moses at places. At points, the traditions of the Sinai covenant intermingle with other traditions that emphasize Zion, Jerusalem, and the temple. They coexist peacefully amid southern traditions in avowedly southern texts. Furthermore, analysis reveals that some of this intermingling arose even before the northern kingdom's demise in 722 B.C.E.[9]

Levenson concludes that some traditions oriented towards the Sinai covenant have an authentic southern pedigree that predates the forced emigration south of many of the northern traditions in 722. The evidence is convincing. Geographical locations can harbor more than one body of tradition, even though those traditions may be in tension with or even contradict one another.

It is best, then, to avoid geographic terms to designate the stream of theological tradition that flowered into biblical Yahwism. I instead use the term *Sinai theology* for this tradition stream. Admittedly, this does not solve all the problems.

The term "Sinai" does not appear in Hosea and Micah, which are key texts in the present study. The E strand of the Pentateuch does not use the term "Sinai" for the holy mountain of the wilderness, preferring the term "Horeb" instead. The term *Sinai theology* can serve as a handy rubric for us (i.e., an etic label) nonetheless, a label of convenience.

---

8. Robert R. Wilson, *Prophecy and Society in Ancient Israel* (Philadelphia: Fortress, 1980), 17–18, 135–252.

9. Levenson, *Sinai and Zion*, 194.

This study further differs from some previous work in its focus on the land of Israel. Scholars sometimes neglect the crucial religious role played by Israel's land, partly because modern Western civilization seems to distance most people from the sources of their food. In recent years, however, some scholars have begun to see that the land must have been a major part of most Israelites' daily lives. The covenant would have had to take the land seriously—as the physical, material context for community relationships. Using a social-scientific approach enables us to fully examine the role that the land played in the actual practice of the covenant in ancient society.

BASIC TENETS OF BIBLICAL YAHWISM

Israel as God's Elected Vassals

Using particular, characteristic expressions, our biblical sources about Sinai theology speak of God's election of Israel out of all peoples of the earth. Israel is to be the "special treasure" of God (Exod 19:5 [E]; Deut 7:6; 14:2; [cf. Deut 26:18; Mal 3:17]). No special qualities evoked God's election of Israel. Rather, God freely and mysteriously came to treasure the Israelites as God's own unique people, not to be transferred to anyone else's ownership.

The term "inheritance" (נחלה) appears in several fixed idioms that bind our sources of Sinai theology. The idea is not that God inherited the people from someone else, but that due to God's election of them, the people are now God's "permanent allotment." The people are God's own "inherited people" (Deut 4:20); the "inherited flock" of God (Mic 7:14; cf. Ps 78:71, an Asaphite psalm); God's "inherited tribe" (Jer 10:16; 51:19; Ps 74:2, an Asaphite psalm).[10]

According to the biblical story, before the exodus the people were in bondage in Egypt. To claim and possesses them, God liberated them and brought them up out of that land. Our sources of Sinai theology speak of this liberation out of Egypt as deliverance out of an "iron smelter" (Deut 4:20; 1 Kgs 8:51; Jer 11:4). According to the sources, God brings the people out of Egypt specifically to become God's "inheritance" (Deut 4:20; 9:26; 1 Kgs 8:51, 53; cf. Deut 9:29).

God redeems the people out of Egypt as one tribe, one flock. Sinai theology strongly emphasizes that God rescued the whole tribe of Israel,

---

10. On this phraseology as characteristic of Sinai texts, see Nasuti, *Psalms of Asaph*, 67.

and that the Israelites are to remain one united, holy people. In a programmatic text in the E strand, God addresses Israel after the exodus as a cohesive entity—"my treasured possession out of all the peoples, ... a priestly kingdom and a holy nation" (Exod 19:5–6). The final chapter of Joshua describes a ceremony at Shechem at which all the elders, heads, and people of Israel pause after their occupation of the promised land to affirm their election as a united people of God (Josh 24:1).

During the course of Israel's history, unfortunately, the people split into two kingdoms: Judah in the south and the northern kingdom of Israel. Later, foreign superpowers disperse and exile various parts of the people, further breaking apart their union. Despite these events, those who were committed to Sinai theology firmly clung to its ideal that Israel was one people.

Despite their political separation, in Hos 6:4 God wrestles with the dual fates of Judah and Israel as though they are still one entity. Micah 1:5, 8–9 takes a similar stance, assuming that sin and rebellion in the northern kingdom will affect Judah. Micah sees Judah as the lower part of Israel's body. Although it dates to well after the schism between the two kingdoms, the book of Deuteronomy likewise retains the unity of the whole people of Israel as a major ideal.[11] In a classic text, the book addresses Israel as "A holy people to the LORD your God." "The LORD your God has chosen you to be a people for his own possession out of all the peoples who were on the face of the earth" (Deut 7:6).

In electing the people of Israel, according to Sinai theology, God desires a bilateral, committed relationship with them.[12] Such a mutual relationship would allow the people to respond to God's loving kindness and, in fact, transform them. The E strand, for example, specifies that although it is God's fervent hope that the people remain God's patrimony, the relationship is dependent both on the people's initial consent and on their enduring loyalty. In Exod 19:5 (E) God states, "*If you obey my voice ...* , you shall be my treasured possession out of all the peoples." Similarly, Ps 50:16–21, an Asaphite psalm, states that God's relationship with Israel cannot be taken for granted but should involve an ongoing, disciplined response by the people.

---

11. Gerhard von Rad, *Studies in Deuteronomy* (trans. D. Stalker; SBT 9; Chicago: Regnery, 1953), 62.

12. William L. Moran, "The Ancient Near Eastern Background to the Love of God in Deuteronomy," *CBQ* 25 (1963): 77–87; Moshe Weinfeld, *Deuteronomy and the Deuteronomic School* (Oxford: Clarendon, 1972), 80–81; George E. Mendenhall, "The Suzerainty Treaty Structure: Thirty Years Later," in *Religion and Law: Biblical-Judaic and Islamic Perspectives* (ed. E. B. Firmage, B. G. Weiss, and J. W. Welch; Winona Lake, Ind.: Eisenbrauns, 1990), 85–100; G. Wallis, "אהב," *TDOT* 1:99–118.

The first three chapters of Hosea illustrate this theme using the symbol of marriage to embody the mutuality that should flow from God's election of Israel. The symbolism of marriage reminds the people that God requires both their fidelity and their love as a response to God's grace.

Deuteronomy sums up this ideal. For Deuteronomy, Israel's relationship with God is such that love and obligation are inseparable. "Hear, O Israel! ... You shall love the LORD your God with all your heart and with all your soul and with all your might" (Deut 6:4–5).

Our various source texts of Sinai theology further make clear that for Israel's requited love of God to have real meaning, it needed a concrete structure. A merely emotional basis is inadequate. After the exodus from Egypt, God appeared to Israel in thunder at Sinai (Exod 19:19 [E]; 20:18–21 [E]; Ps 81:7, an Asaphite psalm). Out of this terrifying manifestation, God reveals laws that testify to the nature of God's very person and purpose (e.g., Deut 4:45; Pss 78:5; 81:5, both Asaphite psalms). To enter into their mutual, committed relationship with God, the Israelites had to agree to these laws and swear to obey them (Exod 19:8 [E]; 24:3, 7 [E]; Deut 26:17; Josh 24:22).[13]

Thus far, our source texts have described God and Israel in a binding relationship that involves obligations. They impel us to ask if a binding *covenant* between God and Israel is at the heart of Sinai theology.

Readers familiar with biblical studies know that the question of whether the idea of covenant is central to biblical religion, along with the question of the antiquity of the covenant, has challenged and exercised modern biblical critics for well over a century.[14]

Before we move ahead, let me make several basic observations at this point to ground my approach to this issue. In subsequent chapters, I shall elaborate on Sinai theology's treatment of the covenant. I shall also present my arguments and evidence for the covenant's deep roots in Israelite society and history.

The current lack of confidence in the historicity of the covenant traces back to the work of Lothar Perlitt and Ernst Kutsch. Their revisionist studies of the covenant date to 1969 and 1973, respectively.[15] The vigorous

---

13. The Bible in general views "covenant" and "oath" as complementary concepts. See Deut 29:13; Ezek 16:59; 17:13. In taking an oath, one makes a covenant.

14. See the surveys of scholarship and the bibliographies in R. A. Oden Jr., "The Place of Covenant in the Religion of Israel," in *Ancient Israelite Religion: Essays in Honor of Frank Moore Cross* (ed. Patrick D. Miller; Paul D. Hanson, and S. D. McBride; Philadelphia: Fortress, 1987), 429–47; George E. Mendenhall and Gary A. Herion, "Covenant," *ABD* 1:1179–1202; Moshe Weinfeld, "ברית," *TDOT* 2:253–79.

15. Lothar Perlitt, *Bundestheologie im Alten Testament* (WMANT 36; Neukirchen-Vluyn: Neukirchener Verlag, 1969); Ernst Kutsch, *Verheißung und Gesetz: Untersuchungen zum*

arguments of these studies strongly revive Julius Wellhausen's skeptical view of 1883, as I noted above. Perlitt and Kutsch argue that only in the late monarchic period did Israel develop the notion of a covenant between itself and God. Specifically, the development dates to the seventh century, when Deuteronomy appeared. The impact of this radical criticism has been largely negative, sending many people back to the drawing boards. Nevertheless, it has also had some constructive effect.

Perlitt's and Kutsch's renewed skepticism has caused scholars to rethink our data, advancing and sharpening our understanding of the covenant. Modern skeptics, for example, caution against crediting the covenant with the primary, society-forming work that past scholars envisioned. W. Robertson Smith, Martin Noth, Max Weber, and George Mendenhall have all argued that the covenant was the original and primary basis of social cohesion in Israel. This view cannot be correct.

Knowledge of the covenant, and obedience to it, was a priority among so few Israelites that I doubt the Sinai covenant could have held the Israelites together as a people over the years. What is more, a community based solely on the Sinai covenant, with no preexisting societal organization, would have no viable leadership or means of administration.

The Sinai covenant introduces God's formative oversight, assuming structures are already in place for administering society. A critical, social-scientific interpretation of Israel's covenant distinguishes it from Israel's culture and society. Culture and covenant are distinct entities.

The Sinai covenant did not intend to create a culture for the Israelites.[16] The Hebrew people already had sufficient social glue to hold them together. They already had their own language for communicating with one another, their own economic system for the exchange of goods, their own family and kin structures for relating to one another, and even their own religious practices and rites. This Hebrew culture itself existed within an established, Semitic cultural context. Its specific milieu was the northwestern part of the ancient Near East.

As I shall elaborate in chapter 6, the specific social structure of the Hebrews matched a pattern that anthropologists observe elsewhere among peoples without a centralized state. They organized and governed

---

Sogenannten "Bund" im Alten Testament (BZAW 131; Berlin: de Gruyter, 1973). For previous critiques of Perlitt and Kutsch, see, e.g., Levenson, Sinai and Zion, 25–26 n. 10; J. Barr, "Some Semantic Notes on the Covenant," in Beiträge zur Alttestamentlichen Theologie: Festschrift für Walther Zimmerli zum 70. Geburtstag (ed. H. Donner, R. Hanhart, and R. Smend; Göttingen: Vandenhoeck & Ruprecht, 1977), 37–38.

16. For an excellent discussion, see David A. Fraser and Tony Campolo, Sociology through the Eyes of Faith (San Francisco: HarperCollins, 1992), 180, 196–98, 255–56.

themselves based on their kin relationships, a tribal framework organized and validated by genealogical lineage.

The Sinai covenant's stipulations were not destructive of Israel's ancient cultural patterns. They set boundaries to distinguish Israel from its neighbors, provided a normative framework to regularize and regulate Israel's preexisting culture. The covenant placed Israel's customs under Yahweh's sovereign rule, modified them according to Yahweh's person, purpose, and command.

The covenant legitimized some social patterns, while tempering, reforming, or directly challenging others. Its regulation of culture was firmest in the area of worship and cult, though also penetrating deeply into Israel's social relationships and issues of land ownership, which connected closely with social relationships.

Other aspects of Kautsch's and Perlitt's work on the covenant are more vulnerable to criticism. First, Kautsch took a wrongheaded linguistic approach. He tried to show that the Hebrew term for "covenant" (ברית) at first had a more limited meaning than what Deuteronomy understood by it in the seventh century. Kautsch argued that the term did not originally signify a mutual, bilateral relationship, but that it simply meant "obligation." The more complex understanding of covenant in Deuteronomy is a late development.

Kautsch was correct that the idea of obligation is a common feature in biblical uses of the term "covenant," but these uses display a far broader semantic range as well. The word applies to a whole range of relationships, including agreements, treaties, contracts, marriages, and promises. To limit the term's meaning to a common denominator within this range of use is reductionistic and linguistically faulty.

We can learn from Kautsch's focus on terminology, however. We should not assume that every mention of covenant in our source texts necessarily carries with it all of Deuteronomy's understanding. Nor must every mention reflect elaborate ancient Near Eastern treaties, which sometimes influenced biblical texts about covenant.

Sinai theology originally understood covenant to entail, at a minimum, a binding, mutual relationship with a concrete structure. Nevertheless, it is specious to suppose that all texts about the covenant automatically entail allusions to cosmic witnesses, extended lists of curses, and provisions for safekeeping. The parallel ancient Near Eastern treaties often contain such elements, but the influence of these extrabiblical treaties must have varied over the history of the stream of Sinai tradition.

For his part, Perlitt overlooked important biblical evidence of the Sinai covenant's existence, and its renewal within Israel's liturgy, long before the appearance of Deuteronomy in 630 B.C.E. Perhaps most significantly, he ignored the fact that several of the Psalms of Asaph clearly stress the Sinai covenant between God and Israel. Psalm 50 is set in a northern worship festival, a yearly celebration of the covenant from at least a century before the time of Deuteronomy.[17] Both 50:5 and 16 use the specific term "covenant." Verse 4 even invokes cosmic witnesses to testify if the people have shown fidelity to the agreement. Verses 16–21 mention specific commandments, familiar from texts in the Pentateuch about the covenant.

Psalm 78 also contains pre-Deuteronomic references to the Sinai covenant.[18] Verse 10 refers to the covenant and specifically mentions its stipulations that the people must obey. Verse 37 of the psalm also speaks about the covenant by name and regards it as in place at Israel's beginnings, in the context of the exodus period and the people's rebellions in the wilderness.

Psalm 74 is a third Asaphite psalm referencing the covenant, since 74:20 calls upon God to consider the covenant and to come to Israel's aid at a dark time of oppression.

As a group, the Asaphite psalms stem from liturgical worship within northern Israel. They speak of a sacred sanctuary at Salem/Shechem in the north; they refer to God's people as "Joseph," the patriarch of the major northern tribes; and their background often reflects Assyrian military intervention against the northern kingdom.

Clearly, these psalms date largely from before the fall of the northern kingdom in 722 B.C.E. The traditions they preserve date from even earlier. The Levite/prophet Hosea, who advocated Sinai theology in the northern kingdom a century before Deuteronomy, inherited his emphasis on the Sinai covenant partly in the form of these liturgical traditions.

The E strand of the Pentateuch is harder to situate than the Psalms of Asaph, but I believe that this source provides evidence of the Sinai covenant from at least a century before Hosea.[19] Exodus 19:5 (E) invites the Israelites to enter into a covenant with God as a subject people, requires

---

17. Hans-Joachim Kraus comments that "it is remarkable that L. Perlitt in his rejection of the covenant festival cult did not refer to Psalms 50 and 81 at all." Kraus views the hypothesis of a covenant renewal festival as the best way to explain the origins of Ps 50's subject matter—"a festival that reached back to the most ancient (Shechemite) traditions, one that originated in Northern Israel" (Kraus, *Psalms 1–59: A Continental Commentary* [trans. H. Oswald; Minneapolis: Fortress, 1993], 491).

18. See John Day, "Pre-Deuteronomic Allusions to the Covenant in Hosea and Psalm LXXVIII," *VT* 36 (1986): 1–12.

19. For one listing of references to the covenant in the E source, see Jenks, "Elohist," 480. On the dating of the E source to the ninth century, or even earlier, see further Jenks, "Elohist," 479; idem, *The Elohist and North Israelite Traditions* (SBLMS 22; Missoula, Mont.: Scholars Press, 1977), 1, 101–6; Fretheim, "Elohist," 260.

their reciprocation and obedience in light of God's election of them.[20] Exodus 24:9–15a and 32:15–20 are two other treatments of the covenant within E. Here, on tablets of stone, Yahweh gives Moses commandments equivalent to stipulations in ancient Near Eastern vassal covenants.

Some scholars argue that the authentic texts of the E strand do not show God making a real covenant with the people. Rather, the strand's key covenant text in Exod 24:9–15a involves only an intimate meeting of God with the people and their sharing of a sacred meal together.[21] The evidence of related biblical texts contradicts this position, however. The meal of Exod 24:11 is a characteristic feature of covenant-making and not simply a token of fellowship with God. Elsewhere in the Bible a special meal concludes a covenant between two parties. See especially Gen 26:28–31; 31:44–54; Deut 27:6–7 (cf. Ps 50:5); Josh 9:14–15; 2 Sam 3:12–21; and Obad 7. In each of these cases, the meal enacts and expresses the covenant relationship.

Ancient Near Eastern texts corroborate the biblical evidence.[22] One piece of evidence occurs in correspondence between the Egyptian pharaoh and one of his vassals in Palestine. The correspondence, from a period before the time of the Israelite settlement, mentions the covenant meal. In this Amarna letter (EA 162:22–25), the pharaoh chastises his subject, Aziru, for making a local pact without regard for the interests of the pharaoh. Aziru made the covenant with a man at odds with the pharaoh, and he ensured the covenant by eating and drinking with him.

From several hundred years earlier, a tablet from the north Mesopotamian city-state of Mari also bears witness to the covenant meal. The text (ARM 8:13) records a special business deal (an acquisition of developed land), the complexity of which required its parties to be in a covenant relationship. After the respective parties make their business exchange, the text specifies that they eat and drink together and anoint

---

20. Martin Noth assigned this text in Exodus to a Deuteronomic source. For discussion, see Anthony F. Campbell and Mark A. O'Brien, *Sources of the Pentateuch: Texts, Introductions, Annotations* (Minneapolis: Fortress, 1993), 187–88. As Levenson argues, however, the passage is probably much earlier (*Sinai and Zion*, 25). Scholars assigning this text to the E source include: Walter Beyerlin, *Origins and History of the Oldest Sinaitic Traditions* (Oxford: Blackwell, 1965), 11; Dennis J. McCarthy, *Treaty and Covenant* (AnBib 21A; Rome: Pontifical Biblical Institute, 1968), 270–73; Richard Elliott Friedman, *Who Wrote the Bible?* (New York: Harper & Row, 1987), 251.

21. McCarthy, *Treaty and Covenant*, 254; Campbell and O'Brien, *Sources of the Pentateuch*, 188 n. 59.

22. For a fine, brief overview, see Mendenhall and Herion, "Covenant," 1194, section G.1., "The Covenant Banquet."

themselves with oil. This meal surely had legal significance, because it concludes a specific business contract made in the presence of witnesses.

Incidentally, the Mari contract uses a special Akkadian term to speak of the business exchange: The text uses the Akkadian term *n-ḫ-l* ("allot") to describe the transaction as a permanent allotment of goods. This language vividly recalls how God receives Israel as a נחלה ("inheritance," "permanent allotment"). Both the covenant with Israel and the one at Mari share a common Semitic verbal root that designates a transfer for perpetuity of something highly desired.

More generally, recent extrabiblical and archaeological evidence supports the possible antiquity of the Sinai covenant between God and Israel. This evidence does not witness to Sinai theology itself, but it does show that Sinai theology could have known about and used the idea of a covenant between a people and a deity from as early as the second millennium B.C.E. Deities, as well as people, served as treaty partners in early Israel's cultural context.

One bit of proof comes in a twelfth-century text known as the "Marduk prophecy." In it, the god Marduk states that he has a special covenant relationship with a human prince. Marduk declares, "I alone, all you gods, have a covenant with him."[23]

This idea that a god could be a party to a covenant with humans also appears in a Hurrian text (*KTU* 1.128.14–15) at Ugarit, an ancient commercial center on the northern coast of Syria. The tablet comes from a few hundred years before the time of the "Marduk prophecy." The Ugaritic evidence refers to the Canaanite high god El by the title "El of the covenant."

It is doubtful that this Ugaritic title of El means only that El is a witness to a covenant. In the ancient Near East, multiple deities, rather than individual gods, witness to treaties. Rather, the title means that El is a covenant partner, as some parallel biblical evidence confirms. The biblical story of apostasy at the time of Abimelech mentions the same deity, "El/Baal of the covenant" (Judg 9:46/Judg 8:33; 9:4), and, as similar Hebrew terminology in Gen 14:13 (בעלי ברית) shows, this title designates him specifically as a "treaty-partner of a covenant."[24]

---

23. See S. D. Sperling, "An Arslan Tash Incantation: Interpretations and Implications," *HUCA* 53 (1982): 10; Theodore J. Lewis, "The Identity and Function of El/Baal Berith," *JBL* 115 (1996): 406.

24. See Lewis, "El/Baal Berith," 401–23, especially p. 408. Lewis references the work of F. M. Cross, E. Lipiński, and P. C. Craigie on *KTU* 1.128.14–15. See Frank M. Cross, *Canaanite Myth and Hebrew Epic* (Cambridge: Harvard University Press, 1973), 39; E. Lipiński, "Recherches Ugaritiques; El-Berit (RS 24.278, 14–15)," *Syria* 50 (1973): 50–51; and Peter C. Craigie, "El Brt.El Dn (RS 24.278, 14–15)," *UF* 5 (1973): 278–79.

A final piece of evidence comes from ancient Syria, from roughly the same time as the previous two texts (c. 1180). Text finds from the ancient Syrian city of Emar (Emar 373) describe a special covenant festival for a god. In the rituals of the festival, the people bring images of Dagon and other gods outside of the city to a shrine of upright stones where there is an offering and a feast. These activities redevote Emar to its divine lord, Dagon.[25]

The rite at Emar operated on a seven-year cycle. The Emar tablets refer to it as the *zukru* festival, probably based on the Semitic verbal root (*z-k-r*) for "remembering." The festival's name would then refer to "remembering," or rearticulating, covenant allegiance to the god Dagon. Semitic idiom at Emar used the root *z-k-r* with reference to swearing an oath. Thus, the ceremonies seem to have involved an address to Dagon, in which the people swore covenant fidelity to the god.

Emar's culture was not purely urban, revolving around a king and his palace. It included a mixture of urban and village ways of life. The fact that the *zukru* festival took place outside of the city walls of Emar suggests that it derived from the older, village- and elder-based substratum of the culture. I shall argue in subsequent chapters that traditions of the Sinai covenant in Israel had these very sorts of preurban, prestate roots.

The Land as Israel's Inheritance

In Sinai theology, the land of Palestine is of special concern to God, and it plays a key role in the relationship between God and God's people. According to our sources, the people of Israel are God's special "inheritance" (Deut 4:20; 32:9; Jer 10:16), but the land of Canaan is also God's "inheritance" (Deut 32:8–9; Jer 2:7; Ps 79:1, an Asaph psalm).

Because God's people and land share a joint relationship to God from the start, God's bringing of land and people into one, intimate interrelationship with each other and God's self is almost inevitable. God binds the people, the land, and God's self together by giving the land to the people as *their* "inheritance" (נחלה, Deut 4:21; 32:8; Josh 13:6; Jer 17:4).

Ancient Near Easterners thought of their various gods as possessing their own lands, claiming the devotion of the people whom they found in those lands. Sinai theology is unique, however. It understands that

---

25. I depend here on the investigations of Daniel E. Fleming. See his "More Help from Syria: Introducing Emar to Biblical Study," *BA* 58 (1995): 139–47; idem, *The Installation of Baal's High Priestess at Emar: A Window on Ancient Syrian Religion* (HSS 42; Atlanta: Scholars Press, 1992).

Yahweh chose a people for a special possession from outside of the land, and only brought them into the land subsequent to their election.

The land of Canaan is clearly God's own property in Sinai theology (e.g., Hos 9:3, 15; Josh 22:25; Jer 16:18); Josh 22:19 calls Canaan "the land that Yahweh possesses." Our sources of Sinai theology describe this land as a very special place. These sources interconnect and overlap to give a picture of the land characteristic of the Sinai stream of tradition. God's allotted land is secluded hill country, holy, wooded, and fruitful.[26]

Exodus 15:17 (E/D material) and Ps 78:54 (an Asaphite psalm) describe the land as God's mountainous highland—God's sanctuary, holy territory.[27] Joshua 17:18 adds that this hill country is woody or forested, and Jer 17:3 describes it as rustic. Deuteronomy 33:28 describes the land as both secluded and fruitful. Micah 7:14 echoes these two qualities but again reminds us that the territory is woodland. The wording of the passage in Micah is also close to that in Jer 50:19, which describes the land as a pasture for sheep in the highlands.

The tablets from Ugarit describing the mythological exploits of the gods show that the motifs and language Sinai theology used to describe Yahweh's territory were present in the surrounding culture as early as the fourteenth century B.C.E. Here again, the ancient Near Eastern evidence shows that Sinai theology was not necessarily a late, evolutionary development.

The Ugaritic tablets of the Late Bronze age are perfectly familiar with the idea of a deity possessing an allotted territory (arṣ nḥlt; CTA 1.III.1; 3.F.16; 4.VIII.14; 5.II.16).[28] Amazingly, the Ugaritic texts about Baal's establishment of a kingdom (CTA 3–4) even describe this god as possessing an inherited mountain. The wording, "my allotted mountain" (ǵr. nḥlty; CTA 3.C.27; 3.D.64), in the tablets parallels the language of Exod 15:17.[29]

God does not choose the Israelites to live as God's special people in a vacuum but in this special territory of Yahweh. Indeed, our Sinai texts

---

26. Stephen L. Cook, "Micah's Deuteronomistic Redaction and the Deuteronomists' Identity," in *Those Elusive Deuteronomists: The Phenomenon of Pan-Deuteronomism* (ed. L. Schearing and S. McKenzie; JSOTSup 268; Sheffield: Sheffield Academic Press, 1999), 225–26.

27. See Umberto Cassuto, *A Commentary on the Book of Exodus* (trans. I. Abrahams; Jerusalem: Magnes, 1967), 177; Nasuti, *Psalms of Asaph*, 90.

28. CTA 1.III = KTU 1.1.III; CTA 3 = KTU 1.3; CTA 4.VIII = KTU 1.4.VIII; CTA 5.II = KTU 1.5.II.

29. CTA 3 = KTU 1.3. On the mythic patterns in the Song of the Sea in Exod 15, see Thomas B. Dozeman, "The Song of the Sea and Salvation History," in *On the Way to Nineveh: Studies in Honor of George M. Landes* (ed. S. L. Cook and S. C. Winter; ASOR Books 4; Atlanta: Scholars Press, 1999), 101–4.

describe the land as promised to Israel's ancestors long before the time of the exodus. The following texts all agree on this explicitly: Gen 15:16 (E); Exod 13:5 (E); 32:13 (E); Deut 6:10, 23; 7:13; 10:11; Mic 7:20.

In addition, when Jacob purchases a piece of land at Shechem in Gen 33:19–20 (E), he implicitly expresses his faith that God has promised to give the whole land of Canaan to his progeny. Owning this small strip of ground was a token that the remainder of the land would follow. Likewise, the burial of Joseph's body in this plot (Josh 24:32) is a reminder of Joseph's faith in God's promise of the land.

After the exodus, God fulfills these promises by bringing the people into the land and apportioning it to them. God cannot give them the land outright, since it is God's own "inheritance." God has permanent ("inalienable") tenure over it. God can, and does, give the land to God's vassal people as a sort of fiefdom, however. God remains lord over the territory. The people hold the land "in fee" as subjects and servants of their liege lord, Yahweh.

The implications of this are significant. In Sinai theology, covenant fealty to Yahweh involves more than the obedience of true vassals many past studies of the covenant have implied. Yahweh is not merely Israel's foreign lord (suzerain), but also the overlord or "landlord" of the specific territory occupied by Israel.

Our sources of Sinai theology use their own special images and language to describe Yahweh's placement of Israel in the land. Exodus 15:17 (E/D) and Jer 2:21; 11:17 describe God planting Israel, like a seed or vine, in God's fertile highland. Jeremiah 2:21 reads, "I planted you as a choice vine, as a completely faithful seed."

Psalm 80:8–11, 15, an Asaph psalm, adds further details about Israel's transplantation: God first removed Israel, the vine, from Egypt; then God had to drive other nations from Canaan before planting it.

Without using the specific language of transplanting a vine, Deut 4:37–38 summarizes the same ideas. "Because he loved your fathers, he personally brought you out of Egypt, by his great power, driving out before you nations greater and mightier than yourselves, to bring you in, giving you their land for an inheritance, as it is still today."

Other Sinai texts pick up the same imagery from the tradition stream and apply it to Israel's future. Texts such as Hos 2:22–23 and Jer 31:27–28 use the familiar metaphors of gardening to describe Israel's restoration in the land after a time of punishment by God.

Sinai theology has concerns with the occupation of the land by Israel as a whole, and with how the subdivisions within Israel share in it. Once Israel occupies the land, according to our Sinai texts, they are to apportion and tenure it among their subdivisions—divide the land up between themselves, based on categories of genealogy or lineage.

The largest Israelite lineage segment is the tribe. Each tribe receives its own specific "inheritance" (e.g., Deut 29:8; Josh 11:23). Tribes contained smaller lineage segments known as kin groups or "clans," consisting of extended families. Land was distributed first to the tribes, then to the kin groups (e.g., Josh 13:23; 15:20; Judg 21:24), followed by the extended families (e.g., Josh 14:13–14; 17:3–4; 19:49–50; Judg 2:6).

The texts portray a process of lot casting to decide which land went to which lineage groups (Josh 14:2; 15:1; 17:5; 18:1–10; 19:51). The land lottery took place in sacral locations, such as at Gilgal and Shiloh at the doorway of the "tent of meeting." God controlled the lot casting and thus determined the allocation of the land.

Various theologies within the Bible know about the division of the promised land among the Israelites, but in Sinai theology, several characteristic motifs and idioms distinguish the special emphasis on land allotment. One such idiom describes Israel's apportionment of inherited land by combining the term "inheritance" (נחלה) with the term "line"/ "measure" (חבל).

Psalm 78:55, a psalm of Asaph, makes use of this combination of terms: "He [Yahweh] drove out nations before them; allotted them [their] *inheritance by line,* and settled the tribes of Israel in their tents." This particular terminology appears elsewhere only in Deut 32:9; Josh 17:14; 19:9; and Ps 105:11 [=1 Chr 16:18]. (The final text is a sort of "deutero-Asaphite" psalm, because Chronicles presents the Asaphites as speaking it.)[30]

The idiom refers to the distribution of land by means of the sacred lottery. Israel surveyed the land and divided it into plots before distributing it by divine lot. Measuring lines would specify the exact boundaries of the plots of land before their occupation. Eventually the term "line" became synonymous with one's inherited plot of land, assigned by lot from among surveyed plots.

A second sample idiom of Sinai tradition expresses the idea that entry into the promised land brings the nation "rest" (נוח; Exod 33:14 [E]; Deut 3:20; Josh 1:13, 15; 22:4). "Rest" refers to conditions where Israel can become sedentary and enjoy Yahweh's protection. Deuteronomy 12:9–10 and 25:19 combine the idea of the land as an "inheritance" with the idea that it is also a "place of rest" (מנוחה), or at least a place were God will eventually "give rest" to the people.[31]

---

30. For discussion of the idiom as a characteristic marker of Sinai tradition, see Nasuti, *Psalms of Asaph,* 91.

31. Gerhard von Rad, "The Promised Land and Yahweh's Land in the Hexateuch," in *The Problem of the Hexateuch and Other Essays* (trans. E. W. T. Dicken; Edinburgh: Oliver &

A third sample feature characteristic of Sinai theology is the motif that each of the nations of the earth has its own separate "inheritance" for a territory. This motif stretches from Deut 32:8 through Jer 12:14–15 and on to Mal 1:3.

Sinai theology holds that the land allotted to Israel's tribes, kin groups, and families is permanently theirs (cf. Josh 14:9). Deuteronomy 19:14 sums up the principle: "You must not move your neighbor's boundary marker, set up by former generations, on the property that will be allotted to you in the land that Yahweh your God is giving you to possess." Hosea 5:10 and Deut 27:17 express the same tenet. One must not steal even a part of a neighboring family's plot by moving a boundary marker. We will see later that one major reason for Sinai theology's antipathy toward kings and monarchical systems is that they often run roughshod over this covenant stipulation (see 1 Sam 8:14; 1 Kgs 21:2–4).

The Sinai covenant's system of permanently allotted land lent a strong material reality to the interpersonal and communal relationships fostered by the covenant. Land tenure provided a concrete basis for membership in the covenant community, for mutuality among covenant neighbors, who were co-vassals under Yahweh, and for the care of the helpless and the poor. The system created a social structure of interlocked land-owning families that cared for and nurtured primary groups and created peace and friendship among secondary groups within society.

Landowners were able to redeem kinfolk sold into slavery, or to buy forfeited land to keep it in the local kin group. They might even marry a widowed sister-in-law and father a son on behalf of her deceased husband. This practice provided for the impoverished woman and kept the dead brother's family line alive. In these, and numerous other ways, land tenure gave actual social and economic structure to covenantal community.

A variety of biblical and ancient Near Eastern sources makes clear that the land-oriented norms of the Sinai covenant addressed real, historical problems in the ancient world. The reality of infringements against land tenure is clear in Job 24:2; Prov 22:28; and the Instruction of Amenemope 7:11–19. The Amenemope text, which comes from Egypt at around 1100 B.C.E., reads, "Do not relocate the surveyor's stone to steal a field, nor move the surveyor's line to take a farm."

Recently surfaced archaeological evidence demonstrates what a live issue land tenure was in eighth- and seventh-century Israel. A new,

Boyd, 1966), 92; Daniel I. Block, *The Gods of the Nations: Studies in Ancient Near Eastern National Theology* (2d ed.; Evangelical Theological Society Studies; Grand Rapids: Baker, 2000), 97.

THE BASIC FEATURES OF BIBLICAL YAHWISM

inscribed potshard, called the "widow's plea" ostracon, dates from this era and actually uses the Hebrew term "inheritance" (נחלה).[32] This is the first time the word appears in a Hebrew inscription outside of the Bible. (The Semitic root appears earlier, of course, such as in the instances at Mari and Ugarit that I noted above.)

The shard is a letter of petition from a widow to a royal official. She notes that part of her family's inherited land has stayed within their lineage by passing on to the widow's brother-in-law, and she claims no personal right to the land. She does request, however, out of consideration for her needs, that the official allow her to use and enjoy some of her husband's remaining inherited land. The inscription confirms the importance of the disposition of family land in ancient Israel's social life, and gives us one case of the actual observance of the Sinai rule that estates should not pass out of a family's hands.

GOD AS SOLE LANDLORD

The life of the early Israelites revolved around subsistence farming. No question was more crucial to them than what deity had ultimate control over the land's fertility. Today, we often live so removed from the land that it is difficult to imagine the preoccupation of ancient peoples with this area of life.

The unequivocal answer of Sinai theology to the question of the land's ultimate source of fertility was unique in Israel's polytheistic environment. In Canaanite polytheism, various gods specialized in different areas of life. People turned to different gods in different situations. In contrast, Sinai texts urge Israel to pledge allegiance to one divine suzerain and landlord (Deut 6:4; Jer 3:19–20).

According to Sinai theology, Yahweh transplanted Israel into God's very own land as an *historical* act and sustained them on the land through continuing *fertility* acts. Yahweh is the God of history, covenant, and fertility—all three. In fact, Yahweh is in charge of *all* aspects of Israel's life.

Our source texts of Sinai theology make clear that Yahweh alone is responsible for fertility (Jer 14:22). Yahweh brings Israel into God's own land and personally looks after its ecology (cf. Deut 33:13–17, 28; Jer 5:24; 31:12).

God's eyes are always on the land. The seasonal rains that allow the land's productivity are proof of the special care that God takes in the

---

32. Pierre Bordreuil, F. Israel, and D. Pardee, "King's Command and Widow's Plea: Two New Hebrew Ostraca of the Biblical Period," *Near Eastern Archaeology* 61 (1998): 2–13.

land. Deuteronomy 11:11–12 reads, "The land into which you are about to cross to possess it, a land of hills and valleys, drinks water from the rain of heaven, a land for which the LORD your God cares; the eyes of the LORD your God are always on it, from the beginning even to the end of the year."

God takes personal pride in the fertility that results from this care. Yahweh speaks of God's own allotted land as a "plentiful land" full of "fruit" and "bounty" (Jer 2:7; cf. Deut 8:7–8). This bounty—including grain, wine, oil, and livestock—is all due to God (Hos 2:8; Deut 11:14–15).

Thus, Yahweh is the one to whom Israel should turn to meet their agricultural needs. God desires to feed Israel with "the finest of the wheat" and to satisfy them with "honey from the rock" (Ps 81:16, an Asaphite psalm; cf. Deut 32:13). Deuteronomy 28:8–12 promises that God will bless Israel with this sort of agricultural bounty—if the people keep the Sinai covenant.

Yahweh is the real owner of the land and calls upon Israel to recognize that right of ownership. Thus, the Israelites have the privilege and the duty to thank and recognize God both for the "feudal" grant of their land and for providing for its bounty. Since God had granted them their territory, they should be preoccupied with loyal devotion to God, including liturgical and sacrificial service.

The land is Yahweh's possession, and its harvests ultimately belong to God. Our source texts require the people to make gifts and offerings to Yahweh from these harvests as an expression of this basic religious belief. The bringing of gifts and offerings to God has a rich variety of meanings in our texts, but on a basic level, they are the peoples' tribute to their divine landlord.[33]

A characteristic of Sinai theology is its picture of God as one with whom people can deal in a *quid pro quo* fashion, by rendering tribute for land "held in fee" (i.e., under the "feudal" condition of homage and service). Thus, Deut 26 describes the people's annual presentation of the land's firstfruits to God as a major occasion for recognizing God's ownership and grant of the land. A basic assumption behind Hos 2 is that sacrifices recognize the sovereignty of the true owner of Israel's land, Yahweh (see 2:8, 13).

Malachi 1:7–8 is even more explicit. Malachi asks the priests to compare their religious sacrifices to tribute offered to their civil official, who in this case was an appointee of their Persian overlord.

---

33. Levenson, *Sinai and Zion*, 71, 209; Victor H. Matthews and Don C. Benjamin, *Social World of Ancient Israel, 1250–587 BCE* (Peabody, Mass.: Hendrickson, 1993), 191; Block, *Gods of the Nations*, 75, 90, 93.

Since Yahweh is the sole landlord of Palestine, liturgical and sacrificial worship of other gods is out of the question. Psalm 81:9–10, a psalm of Asaph, reads: "Let there be no strange god among you; nor shall you worship any foreign God. I, the LORD, am your God, who brought you up from the land of Egypt." Deuteronomy 5:6–7 states, "I am the LORD your God, who brought you out of the land of Egypt, out of the house of slavery. You shall have no other gods before me." Compare Exod 20:2–3; 20:23 (both E).[34] Our texts warn that if Israel turns to the gods of Canaan in worship, Yahweh may withhold the land's fertility to demonstrate God's sole control of it (Hos 2:9–12; Jer 3:2–3; Deut 11:13–17; 1 Kgs 8:35–36; 17:1).

Our sources of Sinai theology use characteristic language and idioms to prohibit Israel's worship of other gods besides Yahweh. Within the Hebrew Bible, 63 verses use the phrase "other gods," usually to speak against Israel turning from Yahweh to worship them. With only one possible exception, all of these verses are within Sinai texts (e.g., Exod 23:13 [E]; Hos 3:1; Deut 5:7; 6:14; Josh 24:16; 1 Sam 8:8 [B source]; 2 Kgs 17:35; Jer 7:6).

In addition, the Hebrew Bible uses two fixed phrases to talk about a "foreign god," and both of them are characteristic of our Sinai texts. "Foreign gods" are gods other than Yahweh, and Sinai theology deems them as nonnative to Israel. One term for "foreign god" (אל נכר) appears only in Ps 81:9 (a psalm of Asaph); Deut 32:12; and Mal 2:11. The other, אלהי (ה)נכר, appears almost exclusively in Sinai texts: Gen 35:2, 4 (E); Deut 31:16; Josh 24:20, 23; Judg 10:16; 1 Sam 7:3 (B source); and Jer 5:19.

Our sources also use characteristic language about defeating the Canaanites and removing the material items of their polytheistic religion from the land. Sinai theology views ongoing contact with the Canaanites as an unacceptable risk for Israel. "[The Canaanites] shall not live in your land, or they will make you sin against me; for if you worship their gods, it will surely be a snare to you" (Exod 23:33 [E]; cf. Exod 23:24 [E]; Deut 7:1–6; 12:2–3).[35] To remove this threat, God and Israel must "dispossess" (ירש, in the Hebrew Hiphil stem) the Canaanites from inhabiting Palestine (e.g., Num 21:32 [E]; Deut 7:17; 9:3; 11:23; Josh 13:12; 15:14).

---

34. On the emphatic condemnation of foreign gods in the E strand, see, e.g., Gen 35:1–4; Exod 20:23; and 23:24. For discussion, see Jenks, "Elohist," 481; Fretheim, "Elohist," 262.

35. See George Buchanan Gray, *A Critical and Exegetical Commentary on Numbers* (ICC 4; New York: T&T Clark, 1903), 449–50; Jacob Milgrom, *Numbers: The Traditional Hebrew Text with the New JPS Translation* (JPSTC; Philadelphia: The Jewish Publication Society, 1990), 284; Brevard S. Childs, *The Book of Exodus: A Critical Theological Commentary* (OTL; Philadelphia: Westminster, 1974), 608, 613.

The stress that Sinai theology lays on Yahweh alone as Israel's God amounts to a rejection of polytheism. Historically, Sinai theology struggled hard with the surrounding polytheism to maintain its minority viewpoint. Prophets such as Hosea and Jeremiah saw themselves in a conflict with their countryfolk, and strongly defended their Sinai traditions against both the Canaanite religion and the Israelite "syncretistic" religion around them.[36]

In a war, sometimes both sides use the same weapons. Hosea was not above co-opting Canaanite fertility imagery to win some battles. Other of our source texts lay bare the same struggle when they co-opt mythic images and poetry from polytheism to argue against it (e.g., Ps 82:6–7; Deut 32:8–9).

Related to the stress on liturgical ("cultic") allegiance to Yahweh alone is the strong injunction in our sources against making sculpted images for use in worship (Deut 5:8; Exod 20:4). Psalm 78:58–62, a psalm of Asaph, equates worship of Canaanite gods with the making of graven images (78:58). The psalm continues with a picture of how both cultic infidelity and graven images provoke God's wrath against God's inherited people (78:62).

The widespread use of cultic images as "icons" in Canaanite religion ties in with the belief that gods are beings, or forces, close to nature. They are even immanent in natural phenomenon and worship objects. Sinai theology holds a completely different view. Our sources depict Yahweh as quite separate from nature and as controlling its fertility from afar. God is numinous, unattached to natural phenomenon, and incomparable to earthly beings (Hos 11:9; Ps 50:21, an Asaphite psalm; cf. Exod 3:14 [E]; Num 23:19 [E]; Deut 4:15–24; Mic 7:18).

Archaeological evidence suggests that this view of God may not be a late development out of Canaanite religion, as many scholars argue today. One emerging new argument turns on the connection between "standing stones" in the Bible and those lying in the deserts south of Israel. Within Sinai theology, the E strand recalls that Israel's ancestors, such as Jacob, used standing stones as part of life and worship (e.g., Gen 28:18; 31:43–45).

For years now, archaeologists, such as Uzi Avner, have been identifying and documenting numerous such stones in the Negev and Sinai

---

36. "Syncretism" is the blending of two different streams of religion, in this case Yahwism and Canaanite religion. The term can sound pejorative, and this would be in keeping with how the Sinai texts disparage polytheism. Historians of religion often avoid the term in order to remain objective and neutral about the merits of the different religions of history. Since I admit that I am advocating Sinai theology and its antiquity, I retain the term.

deserts.[37] Whereas artisans worked and shaped most standing stones produced in urban, Canaanite contexts, these desert stone pillars constitute an alternative to divine images. They are worship objects, whose purpose is to allude to a god in an *abstract* manner. The stones involve no sculpture or anthropomorphic artistry.

The standing stones throughout the Negev trace to a different heritage than Canaanite worship, perhaps to the Midianite and Kenite cultures. Thus, the stones in the E strand represent a rejection of icons (i.e., "aniconism") in Sinai theology *with origins outside of Canaan*, dating back thousands of years before Israel's settlement.[38]

The implications for our study are significant. Sinai theology both abhors graven images and contains recollections that the ancestors used standing stones instead. These tendencies of Sinai theology are not a product of Iron-Age Canaanite culture but appear to have an independent heritage. This Hebrew cultural heritage is distinctly nonurban and dates to a distant past. The cuneiform tablets from Emar provide a parallel. I noted above that standing stones were an important part of Emar's *zukru* rituals. The location of the stones outside of the city of Emar seems to connect the *zukru* rites of covenant ratification back with a preroyal, prestate heritage.

Rather than oppose Hebrew culture and heritage, the Sinai covenant made use of the Hebrews' authentic cultural substratum where it could. Early Sinai texts of the Bible welcome the aniconism of the ritual "standing stones" of the desert. At the same time, Sinai texts prefer to narrow down the preferred number of standing stones to one (e.g., Josh 24:25–27).

As the battle between Sinai tradition and Canaanite polytheism became more acute, our sources of Sinai theology eventually disclaimed any approval of the liturgical use of standing stones (Exod 23:24; Deut 7:5; 16:22; Mic 5:13; 2 Kgs 23:14). In a reaction against the Canaanite use of sculpted and unsculpted stones, the Sinai stream of tradition made an inner shift between two types of *aniconism* (the rejection of icons). It shifted away from the idea that stone pillars might legitimately represent God (*material aniconism*) and moved instead to a stricter view. Either

---

37. See, e.g., Uzzi Avner, "Ancient Cult Sites in the Negev and Sinai Deserts," *TA* 11–12 (1984–85): 115–31; idem, "*Masseboth* Sites in the Negev and Sinai and Their Significance," in *Second International Congress on Biblical Archaeology in Jerusalem* (Jerusalem: Israel Exploration Society, 1990), 166–81.

38. For a fascinating discussion, see Tryggve N. D. Mettinger, *No Graven Image? Israelite Aniconism in Its Ancient Near Eastern Context* (ConBOT 42; Stockholm: Almqvist & Wiksell International, 1995).

nothing, or at most only an empty space, such as that above the ark of the covenant, could properly allude to God (*empty space aniconism*). Psalm 80:1, a psalm of Asaph, is a good example of empty space aniconism within Sinai tradition. It speaks of God enthroned above the ark's cherubim figures. (Our sources of Sinai theology do not lay stress on the ark of the covenant, but, in addition to Ps 80:1, they do mention or allude to it in Ps 78:61; Deut 10:8; 1 Sam 3:3 [B source]; and 1 Kgs 3:15.)

Conditional Tenancy

The Sinai covenant was a two-way, or bilateral, relationship. God's rescue of the people from Egypt was not due to any obedience or merit on the people's part but was a free act of divine favor. The Sinai covenant is about grace not legalism. At the same time, however, it is not about cheap grace. Once God rescues them and offers them a relationship, the people must choose to appropriate and respond to God's love and grow in discipleship. Our sources of Sinai theology are clear that the choice is a real one that the people must enter into freely. Israel has the initial free choice of entering the covenant, and each new generation must choose whether to renew the covenant or not (Exod 19:3b–8 [E]; 24:3, 7 [E]; Deut 26:17–19; Josh 24:15; Ps 50 [an Asaphite psalm]). The sources are also clear that these choices had consequences.[39]

To be a party to the Sinai covenant was to swear an oath of fidelity to God. In the ancient world, such oaths involved curses as guarantees. The Sinai covenant is no exception, and it includes divine sanctions as its guarantee. Fully developed presentations of the Sinai covenant, such as Deuteronomy, elaborate the guarantee in terms of lists of specific blessings and curses that conclude the treaty (Deut 28:1–14, 15–68). As in related ancient Near Eastern treaties, these blessings and curses follow directly the presence or absence of obedience to the covenant. Because the blessings of the covenant depend on obedience to its stipulations, the Sinai covenant is a *conditional* one. God may even revoke it completely, if the people utterly forsake God.

Many of our Sinai texts illustrate the application of covenant sanctions. In Ps 78:62, an Asaphite psalm, when the people make sculpted images God fills with wrath at the "inheritance" and delivers the people

---

39. Fretheim writes that for the E source, "The promises of God are not unconditional; they must be seen within the framework of the Sinai covenant (Exod 19:5; 23:21–22; 32:33)" ("Elohist," 262). Von Rad notes that from the Sinai perspective, even the promise of the land is not independent of obedience (*Studies in Deuteronomy*, 72).

"to the sword." Foreign nations also ravage God's "transplanted" people due to God's anger in Ps 80:12, 16, another psalm of Asaph, while 1 Kgs 8:35–36 anticipates that the people's sin may cause God to shut up the heavens and withhold rain from the people's inherited land. Micah 6:14–15 and Hos 4:10 prophesy that violating the covenant will bring experiences of futility, such as eating but not being satisfied. Such futility curses form a common motif in ancient Near Eastern treaties (cf. Deut 28:38–40).

Sinai theology holds that the people can even violate the covenant to such an extent that they defile the land. Deuteronomy 21:23; 24:4; Jer 2:7; and 16:18 all speak about the possibility that Israel could defile its inherited land. Such defilement can even make the land unlivable for God—make it unsuitable for association with God's name (Pss 78:60; 74:11 [Asaphite psalms]; Jer 7:12).

The ultimate consequence of defiling the land is that God will stop protecting it and allow the people's removal from the land. When the Canaanites had previously defiled the land, God expelled them. If Israel follows suit, their fate could well be the same: eviction (cf. Num 33:56, an apparently Deuteronomic text). God would have to clear out God's garden highland before attempting any new planting.

Our Sinai texts are clear that Israel's expulsion from Canaan is a viable possibility. Among other places, see Pss 74:7; 79:5, 7 (both psalms of Asaph); Hos 9:3, 15; Deut 4:26–28; 8:20; 28:64; Josh 23:13; and 2 Kgs 17:7. Jeremiah 17:3–4 provides one good example of Yahweh's threat to dispossess Israel because of covenant treason. "Your wealth and all your treasures I will give for spoil as the price of your sin throughout all your territory. By your own act you shall lose the inheritance that I gave you, and I will make you serve your enemies in a land that you do not know."

Several extrabiblical sources prove that the idea of a covenant oath between a people and a deity may have stretched far back into the beginnings of Israel as a people. Additional ancient Near Eastern evidence affirms the antiquity of the idea that a deity could suspend relations with a land and its people because of their rebellion.

One piece of evidence comes from the eighth century B.C.E. Erra Epic.[40] This poem describes the god Marduk as turning away from his city, angry with its people, thus leaving it to Erra's destructive wrath.

---

40. Luigi Cagni, *The Poem of Erra* (Sources from the Ancient Near East 1/3; Malibu, Calif.: Undena, 1973); Benjamin R. Foster, *From Distant Days: Myths, Tales, and Poetry of Ancient Mesopotamia* (Bethesda, Md.: CDL, 1995), 132–63. For discussion, see Block, *Gods of the Nations*, 125–26.

The ninth-century inscription of the Moabite King Mesha provides another example of this sort of thing.[41] The stele represents the perspective of the Moabites. It states that the Moabite god Chemosh allowed Israel to oppress Moab for many days because of the god's anger with the land.

Again, a Sumerian/Akkadian text, K 4874, describes how the gods abandon a land because of the regular evil and crimes of its inhabitants.[42] As a result, evil demons fill the land, its luck changes, and it diminishes. The text is a copy of a composition from the late twelfth century B.C.E.

TEMPERED RULE OVER THE INHERITANCE

Noticeably absent from our sources of Sinai theology is a monarch to rule over Israel. Except in late additions to our Sinai texts, we see no discussion of significant political functions of a king, no covenant with the Davidic dynasty or unconditional promises about Jerusalem and the royal line, and no hope for a royal, Davidic messiah. Israel's sacral conceptions about a special anointed one of Yahweh come from other biblical theologies, which stand in tension with Sinai theology.

There is little room for a human monarch in Sinai thinking, since all Israelites are co-vassals under Yahweh's divine rule as their liege lord.[43] It would almost violate the Sinai covenant if a group of Yahweh's vassals swore allegiance to an additional, local lord. Recall how upset the pharaoh was in the Amarna letter cited above when his vassal, Aziru, furthered his own interests by making a local pact with a third party. For Israel to desire a king would be to reject Yahweh's rule.

When the people reject Samuel's leadership and cry out to have a king as the other nations round about them do, Yahweh responds, "They have not rejected you, but they have rejected me from being king over them" (1 Sam 8:7, B source; cf. 1 Sam 10:19; 12:12, also B).

Besides implicitly rejecting God's role as sole landlord, setting up a monarchy also jeopardized the covenant networks of fellowship and support of Sinai theology. These networks depended strongly on families' ongoing possession of inherited lands, but the taxation policies of ancient kings often threatened land tenure. Kings tended to extract

---

41. *ANET*, 320–21; J. C. L. Gibson, *Hebrew and Moabite Inscriptions* (vol. 1 of *Textbook of Syrian Semitic Inscriptions*; Oxford: Clarendon, 1973), 71–83.
42. W. G. Lambert, "Enmeduranki and Related Matters," *JCS* 21 (1967): 128–31; Foster, *From Distant Days*, 197–201; Block, *Gods of the Nations*, 124.
43. Levenson, *Sinai and Zion*, 70–75.

wealth from society's periphery often impoverishing their client subjects and eventually taking away their land. Furthermore, kings tended to consolidate their political power by refashioning land boundaries. This broke up older bases of power competing with the monarchy.

In contrast to the rule of a monarch, Sinai theology favors a decentralized administration of the Israelite people. An E passage in Num 11:16–30 provides a good illustration. In the text, Yahweh has Moses distribute his administrative and judicial authority among 70 elders of Israel. This frees Moses from administrative duties and allows Israel's elders to handle most political and legal matters at the local, village level.

Moses singles out individuals who already have the role of lineage head in Israel's tribal culture. He appointments them to a "Mosaic" office within the Sinai covenant both affirming their local leadership of Israel's kin groups and giving them new, sacral recognition. The Sinai covenant intended to regularize and regulate Israel's decentralized political system, but it let Israel remain as a tribe without a central human ruler. Later texts within Sinai theology affirm this ideal of a decentralized polity (e.g., Deut 16:18–20; 17:2–7).

Sinai theology's tenet of decentralized rule was idealistic, but it was also impractical for many historical circumstances. Our sources recognize and make different allowances for some of these circumstances. In an emergency, such as a military threat, Israel's elders might assemble and appoint a chief or a military commander to deal with the crisis (e.g., Judg 11:6). Normally, a chief of this type would exercise power for only a limited period. Sinai theology seems to have had no conflict with the exercise of this type of intermittent, contingent human leadership.

A conflict with the Sinai covenant only arose when there was pressure for a chief to assume permanent rule. The judge Gideon, one of early Israel's temporary leaders, gives the correct response for Sinai theology to such pressure. The Israelites call upon him to create a royal dynasty after his victory over the Midianites. In Judg 8:23, however, Gideon replies, "I will not rule over you, nor shall my son rule over you; the LORD shall rule over you."

With time, according to our texts, old Israel's system of temporary leadership in the time of the judges seemed increasingly impractical to the people. As in the example of Gideon, they increasingly asked their tribal leaders for a human monarch. According to our Sinai texts, God eventually gave in to these requests and allowed the people a monarchy as a concession.

Having a human king will certainly not spell Israel's salvation (Mic 4:9; Hos 13:10). Sinai theology comes to permit a human king, but only against its better judgment. At one point, God furiously reminds Israel, "I gave you a king in my anger" (Hos 13:11; cf. 8:4). At the same time as it allows a king, however, Sinai theology attempts to temper monarchic rule through covenantal limitations and caveats.

Our source texts are fond of portraying Israel as sheep (Pss 74:1; 78:52; 79:13 [all Asaphite psalms]; Mic 7:14), and they allow that the owner of the flock (God) may contract with individual herders (leaders or monarchs) to care for the animals (e.g., Ps 77:20 [an Asaphite psalm]; Hos 12:13). Some Sinai texts thus allow for a monarchy because individual Israelites might serve as contracted herders over God's inherited flock (Ps 78:71–72, a psalm of Asaph). God may designate such a leader, and have a prophet anoint him (e.g., 1 Kgs 19:16). A sacral process of lot casting could subsequently confirm the choice (1 Sam 10:19–21, B source). Thus, just as the Israelites received land by lot as an "inheritance," so also in installing a leader, they receive an "inheritance" in him (1 Kgs 12:16).

If individual Israelites ever become permanent leaders of the people, however, their rule is to be severely tempered. The E strand at Exod 18:13–27 allows for a monarchy and a centralized judicial system, for example, but only under strict provisos. The success of the new centralized system depends entirely on its adherence to the instructions presented in vv. 19–23.[44]

Elsewhere, in the story of Balaam, the E strand charges Israel's prophetic leaders to hold the monarchy in check as a potentially dangerous institution. The figure of Balaam provides Israel with a model of how an inspired prophet must resist a king's command if it challenges divine authority (Num 22:38 [E]).[45]

At a later time than E, the book of Deuteronomy continues to support these Sinai tenets of a limited and tempered monarchy, especially in the firm rules concerning kings in Deut 17:14–20. Albrecht Alt devoted several pages of attention to this *law of the king* in his classic study of Deuteronomy's provenance.[46] He gleans the distinct impression from the passage that its authors thought Israel would be none the worse if it had never found its way to establishing a monarchy. Indeed, the only conceivable motive for introducing kingship in Israel that 17:14 can envision is a desire to be like other nations (cf. 1 Sam 8:5). The passage does not promote kingship but comes to grips with it as an extant reality that it can neither negate completely nor affirm without significant reservations.

According to Alt, the Deuteronomic law exercises what must have been its only feasible option for an inherently flawed institution. It takes

---

44. For a full discussion, see Stephen L. Cook, "The Tradition of Mosaic Judges: Past Approaches and New Directions," in Cook and Winter, *On the Way to Nineveh*, 295–96.

45. Jenks, "Elohist," 480; cf. Fretheim, "Elohist," 260.

46. Alt, "Heimat des Deuteronomiums," 250–75.

precautions against the threats that kingship poses by applying a covenantal regulation so stringent that it severely tempers the monarchy's role in societal life. Alt describes the price of the passage's restrictions as being the institution's loss of possibility for developing its role and, finally, almost any justification for its very existence.[47] For Deuteronomy, the king's main function appears to be copying the covenant and studying it on a daily basis (17:19).

Deuteronomy 17 gives Israel's kings no guarantees of a dynasty but makes hereditary kingship conditional. Verses 19–20 allow the king's descendents to stay in power only so long as they strictly observe the covenant and keep themselves from exalting their hearts above their countryfolk. In strong contrast to the Zion theology that flourished in royal circles in Jerusalem, this text in Deuteronomy envisions a situation more like the one in the northern kingdom, where rulers of varying ancestries successively held monarchical power.[48]

Recalling the problems that Solomon's wives caused him, Deut 17 limits the king's harem (17:17a; cf. 1 Kgs 11:1–8). Taking foreign wives sealed international treaties—allegiances in conflict with the Sinai covenant. Wives could also demand to worship their own gods, creating a contagion that could affect the king himself.

Deuteronomy's prohibition against building up royal wealth (17:17b) intends to protect the populace, their land tenure, and their land-vested networks of covenant fellowship. As noted above, unless checked, kings could extract so much wealth from client subjects that they drove their people off their inherited plots of land.

Verse 16's prohibition of "multiplying horses" is a restriction on the monarchy's ability to form a standing chariot force and a standing army. This verse is a clue that Sinai theology's ideal of tempered human rule has social and historical roots in prestate, premonarchic Israel, when there was no permanent, full-time army.

---

47. Ibid., 264. Contrast recent arguments that Deuteronomy aims to strengthen the centralized authority of the monarchy (e.g., Naomi Steinberg, "The Deuteronomic Law Code and the Politics of State Centralization," in *The Bible and the Politics of Exegesis: Essays in Honor of Norman K. Gottwald on His Sixty-Fifth Birthday* [ed. D. Jobling, P. L. Day, and G. T. Sheppard; Cleveland: Pilgrim, 1991], 161–70). For discussion of positive scholarly assessments of the Deuteronomistic view of the institution of kingship, see Gerald E. Gerbrandt, *Kingship according to the Deuteronomistic History* (SBLDS 87; Atlanta: Scholars Press, 1986), 18–38.

48. Von Rad writes, "It is quite impossible to construe Deuteronomy along [the lines of a royal theology]." He notes "the extremely insignificant position that the king occupies, nay more, the complete absence of the tradition of the Davidic covenant" (*Studies in Deuteronomy*, 62; cf. Levenson, *Sinai and Zion*, 189–90).

Even during contemporary, monarchic times, Deuteronomy wants Israel to rely on its old method of mustering troops from tribes and clans in times of crisis. Written at a time when royal, standing armies were a regular part of life, Deuteronomy's ideal looks like "repristination," like it is stuck in the outmoded traditional ways of its own past roots.[49]

This is one more clue that bodes well for the investigation in the following chapters. Ancient Near Eastern parallels showing the antiquity of Sinai notions and the presence in Sinai texts of vestigial elements—such as the ideal of a tribal muster—signal that Sinai traditions have deep roots in Israel's life and history. In the chapters ahead, these sorts of clues will help us trace biblical Yahwism back in time to its social origins. The Sinai traditions of some of the eighth-century prophets we examine betray even stronger clues than what we see here about their roots in early Israel's way of life.

---

49. Cf. von Rad, *Studies in Deuteronomy*, 62.

3

THE FLOWERING OF BIBLICAL YAHWISM

THE SINAI THEOLOGY DISCUSSED IN THE PRECEDING CHAPTER WAS A minority tradition of peripheral groups for much of Israel's history. Archaeology has demonstrated the polytheism of Israelite majority culture, and the Hebrew Bible itself represents the Israelites as in constant conflict with Sinai religion. The biblical writers state that the stream of preexilic religion that they are advocating is a dissenting, though venerable, viewpoint. It did not move to the center of society until the reforms of a few kings late in monarchical history.

Sinai theology did not permanently capture official, central power even with these reforms. Once the reforming kings died, other, more syncretistic, forms of Israelite religion again pushed Sinai theology to society's periphery. Sinai theology became the official religion of Israel with the triumph of the Hebrew Bible as Israel's written Scripture and with the rise of early Judaism.

JEHOIADA'S COUP

A palace coup d'etat in 836 B.C.E. helped push Sinai theology to the center of Judean society, when Jehoiada, a temple priest in Jerusalem, organized a coalition to overthrow Judah's Baal-worshiping monarch, Queen Athaliah (2 Kgs 11). Queen in Judah, Athaliah was also the daughter of northern devotees of Baal—King Ahab and Queen Jezebel.

Jehoiada's coup was successful in its political aim of killing Queen Athaliah and raising the young Davidic prince, Joash, to the throne. It also successfully accomplished some significant religious reforms.

Second Kings 11:17 describes a renewal of the covenant between the people and Yahweh in the clear language of Sinai theology (cf. Deut 4:20; 7:6; 14:2; Jer 7:23; 11:4). The language is noteworthy. This is the first time that the books of Kings report an unambiguous act of Sinai covenant-making during the period of the monarchy. In 11:18, the people's purge of the cult of Baal immediately following the covenant ceremony puts into action the Sinai ideal of Yahweh as Israel's sole landlord by destroying the temple of Baal, and killing Mattan, the priest of Baal.

Although it is difficult to independently confirm the historicity of Jehoiada's reform, there seems little reason to doubt that an initial flowering of Sinai religion took place at this time. As the child of infamous Baal worshipers, Queen Athaliah could well have advocated the Baal cult in Judah.[1] Indeed, the incidental mention of the Baal priest's name, Mattan, adds the ring of historical authenticity to the story.

Although some scholars suggest that later editors added religious coloring about reform of worship to a story that is essentially about political intrigue, this seems unlikely. The account has a literary unity about it, and Israel at that time did not know of our modern separation of religion and politics. It was the Yahwistic priest Jehoiada who oversaw the overthrow of Athaliah and her Baal priest. A political confrontation between two priests must have, *ipso facto*, involved a conflict between Baal and Yahweh.

Accidental facts in this narrative about Sinai reforms provide clues for identifying which circles within Israelite society harbored Sinai traditions. In describing Jehoiada's reform, the narrative lets slip that Jehoiada's pro-Sinai coalition included a group known as the "people of the land" (2 Kgs 11:18, 20). The text does not specifically identify the "people of the land," but I can tentatively describe them by critically weighing scholarly studies and proposals about this group.[2]

The "people of the land" cannot be the entire rural population of Judah. For one thing, common people and peasants are not politically active in advanced agrarian societies like ancient Judah. What is more, agrarian societies do not have a middle class like modern societies. Since the group is politically active here and it comes from the "land," by

---

1. Richard H. Lowery argues for the historicity of Athaliah's Baal temple as a sort of embassy, symbolizing Judah's alliance with the northern kingdom. See his treatment of the reign of Athaliah in *The Reforming Kings: Cults and Society in First Temple Judah* (JSOTSup 120; Sheffield: JSOT Press, 1991), 105–9.

2. Several scholarly studies have examined the "people of the land" and their elders. See, e.g., Ernst Würthwein, *Der 'amm ha'arez im Alten Testament* (BWANT 17; Stuttgart: Kohlhammer, 1936); Ernest W. Nicholson, "The Meaning of the Expression 'am ha'arez in the Old Testament," *JSS* 10 (1965): 59–66; Christopher R. Seitz, *Theology in Conflict: Reactions to the Exile in the Book of Jeremiah* (BZAW 176; Berlin: de Gruyter, 1989), 42–71; Joseph P. Healey, "Am ha'arez," *ABD* 1:168–69; Norman K. Gottwald, *The Politics of Ancient Israel* (Library of Ancient Israel; Louisville: Westminster, 2001), 231, 313 n. 110.

process of elimination it must consist of successful, even wealthy, landowners.

As Patricia Dutcher-Walls concludes in her book on Athaliah and Joash, "The people 'of the land' who were most likely to have the where-withal to participate in the making of kings are the landed aristocracy."[3] Thus, the people of the land appear in our narrative as a bloc of rural squires with definite political, social, and religious interests.

Although the people of the land were not poor, neither were they a Hebrew House of Commons. Rather, they appear to have operated on the periphery of the royal state. To exercise any effective clout, they must have allied with other, more central Judean subgroups. Their attempt, in our text, to form a coalition with official power-holders agrees with a general pattern in agrarian monarchies. Dutcher-Walls observes that in such societies, "The self-interests of subgroups can lead them to join forces with others in coalitions or factions that seek some sort of privilege or control of land or an office, especially the throne."[4]

In our narrative, the people of the land travel to Jerusalem from Judah's villages to ally with other societal segments in a contest over monarchic succession (i.e., Dutcher-Walls's final sphere of interest—the throne). A set of theological traditions and motivations drove the group in pursuing this political action. The rural self-interests of the group represented a theological agenda. Fifty years ago, Gerhard von Rad correctly identified this agenda as Sinai theology.[5]

The role and theological orientation of the people of the land in the narrative of Athaliah's downfall is significant, since they will repeatedly turn up in our investigation as supporters of Sinai traditions (e.g., 2 Kgs 21:24; cf. 23:1–3). Christopher R. Seitz anticipates the direction I am pursuing: "It would seem that one might reckon with the early dtr [i.e., Deuteronomistic/Sinai] traditions being nurtured and maintained by the 'people of the land.' Within this larger circle, and in the due course of time, scribal families emerged who gave not only the traditions of Deuteronomy specific literary shape, but also much of the present Book of Jeremiah."[6]

---

3. Patricia Dutcher-Walls, *Narrative Art, Political Rhetoric: The Case of Athaliah and Joash* (JSOTSup 209; Sheffield: Sheffield Academic Press, 1996), 150.

4. Dutcher-Walls, *Athaliah and Joash*, 152, cf. p. 155. In addition to the study of Dutcher-Walls, see Gottwald, *Politics of Ancient Israel*, 228.

5. The insight that the "people of the land" were significant bearers of Sinai traditions in ancient Israel originated with Gerhard von Rad. For von Rad's treatment of 2 Kgs 11, see his *Studies in Deuteronomy* (trans. D. Stalker; SBT 9; Chicago: Regnery, 1953), 63–65. Cf. also J. Alberto Soggin, "Der Judäische ʿam-haʾareṣ und das Königtum in Juda: Ein Beitrag zum Studium der Deuteronomistischen Geschichtsschreibung," *VT* 13 (1963): 187–95.

6. Seitz, *Theology in Conflict*, 69–70 n. 149.

The influence on the state politics of Jerusalem that our rural squires wield in the episode of 2 Kgs 11 is striking. They help install in power the monarch of their choice and orchestrate a public renewal of the Sinai covenant between the king, people, and God. They even institute a polit-ical covenant with the king, which presumably tempered his administrative powers, and secured his promise to pursue fair social and economic policies (11:17).

These actions are completely in line with an orientation toward Sinai theology.[7] They would clash, however, with the presuppositions of the power politics of the time. As Norman Gottwald notes, a political pact between the king and representatives of the rural populace was far from the norm in the state of Judah. It reflects the social world of earlier, tribal times. Gottwald writes,

> It is quite possible to recognize that covenantal/conciliar thinking, both religious and secular, probably stemming from tribal times, was current in Israelite and Judahite circles without being able to make much of an impact on the state.... It is, in fact, questionable whether any of the Syro-Palestinian tributary states, dependent as they were on exploiting the surpluses of their overwhelmingly agrarian and pastoral producers, could have prospered, or survived, had they adhered to policies of social and economic justice.[8]

Gottwald's observation is highly suggestive. Could the people of the land represent the remnants in Judean state society of a premonarchic, tribal power base? The specific idioms and customs they used to express their Sinai traditions suggest the answer may be *yes*.

Frank M. Cross recently noted the old, traditional terminology in the description of covenant renewal in 2 Kgs 11:17.[9] According to the verse, the purpose of the covenant at the time of Joash's coronation is that Israel should become the "kindred of Yahweh." This terminology is clear kin-ship language hailing from early Israel's tribal organization (see, e.g., Judg 5:11; 1 Sam 2:24).

Cross, like Gottwald, also finds an uneasy tension between the institu-tion of covenant and that of monarchy in biblical texts such as 2 Kgs 11.

---

7. Seitz characterizes the theology of kingship of the people of the land as follows: "If one wanted to find a succinct statement of their concept of kingship, it is best sought in the kind of sober declaration found at Deut 17:14–20. They accepted kingship in at most a kind of *plene esse* sense, and this in contrast to certain other positions on the matter (2 Sam 7:14–17; Ps 2)" (*Theology in Conflict*, 67).

8. Gottwald, *Politics of Ancient Israel*, 210.

9. Frank Moore Cross, "Kinship and Covenant in Ancient Israel," in *From Epic to Canon: History and Literature in Ancient Israel* (Baltimore: Johns Hopkins University Press, 1998), 12 n. 32.

The notion that covenant could limit kingship cannot derive from Israel's monarchic period. It must have "survived" from the prestate era of Israel:

> States, designed to centralize power, and to impose hierarchical rule, do not generate rules based on kinship. They do not legislate egalitarian laws, nor devise segmentary genealogies. On the contrary, the *survival* of the league and covenantal institutions in Israel placed limits on the evolution of kingship and the arbitrary powers ordinarily exercised by the monarchical city state.[10]

Beyond this tribal language of kinship, 11:14 refers to a custom for installing the king that bears notice. The verse mentions that Joash's inauguration ceremony involved taking a stand by a symbolic pillar. The reference is intriguing in light of what we observed in the preceding chapter about the significance of symbolic, standing stones in Israel's prestate, preurban heritage. Is the pillar a part of an ancient Israelite custom that predates the monarchy? This must remain merely a provocative question, until we explore the custom as it appears in earlier biblical texts.

KING HEZEKIAH'S REFORM AND HIS PATRONAGE OF SINAI THEOLOGY

King Hezekiah, who came to the throne in the late eighth century, launched the second of Judah's three major religious reforms. This reform was the first of its scale in Judah's history. According to 2 Kgs 18:4, Hezekiah removed the "high places" (rural shrines), where syncretistic and polytheistic religion was practiced, and he destroyed the land's images of other gods, such as Asherah. Second Chonicles 29 adds that he renewed the covenant with Yahweh (29:10) and cleansed the Jerusalem temple (29:16).

Historically, more than one stream of tradition may have helped instigate Hezekiah's reform. (Along with Sinai tradition, either the P source or the H source within the Pentateuch may have been a significant impetus.)[11] Nevertheless, the editors of 2 Kings, who are oriented toward

---

10. Cross, "Kinship and Covenant," 17 (italics added).

11. Menahem Haran, *Temples and Temple-Service in Ancient Israel: An Inquiry into the Character of Cult Phenomena and the Historical Setting of the Priestly School* (Oxford: Clarendon, 1978), 138–40; Richard Elliott Friedman, *Who Wrote the Bible?* (New York: Harper & Row, 1987), 210–11; Israel Knohl, *The Sanctuary of Silence: The Priestly Torah and the Holiness School* (Minneapolis: Fortress, 1995), 208–9.

Deuteronomy, present Hezekiah's reform as a victory for Sinai theology (2 Kgs 18:3, 5–6).

Among other things, the Deuteronomistic editors demonstrate their esteem for Hezekiah by the amount of space that they give his story (2 Kgs 18–20). The book of Jeremiah, another Sinai source, also supports the king. According to Jer 26:18–19, Hezekiah responded positively to Micah's prophetic message of judgment against Jerusalem.

THE HISTORICITY OF HEZEKIAH'S REFORM

The political situation of Hezekiah's time makes it easy to believe the biblical reports that he carried out a religious reform that pushed Sinai theology towards the center of Judean society.

Hezekiah came to power as Assyria was destroying the northern kingdom in the 720s B.C.E. The fall of the north in 722 would have given great credibility to the prophetic warnings of figures such as Micah, who challenged Hezekiah. Early in Micah's career, before the north's fall to Assyria, the prophet compared the northern kingdom's idols and syncretistic worship with an infection that was spreading south to Judah (Mic 1:6–7, 9).

With Samaria's fall, Hezekiah must have realized that idolatrous practices could literally bring about Judah's demise. The warnings against cultic apostasy in Micah's early prophecy disappear altogether in the main oracles of his book. (Micah 5:10–15 is a secondary expansion of the book from after the prophet's time.) Micah continues to denounce serious social abuses, but his silence about cultic infidelity suggests that from early on Hezekiah responded completely to this area of concern.

Archaeological evidence confirms this conclusion. Yohanan Aharoni connects Hezekiah's reform with two decommissioned altars at two southern archaeological sites, the regional center of Beer-sheba and the fortress of Arad. Although scholars disagree in interpreting the evidence at both sites, Aharoni appears correct, at a minimum, to date the dismantling of the altar at Beer-sheba to Hezekiah's times.[12] Judeans at Beer-sheba

---

12. Siegfried H. Horn, "The Divided Monarchy: The Kingdoms of Judah and Israel," in *Ancient Israel: A Short History from Abraham to the Roman Destruction of the Temple* (ed. H. Shanks; Englewood Cliffs, N.J.: Prentice-Hall, 1988), 132; Baruch Halpern, "Jerusalem and the Lineages in the Seventh Century BCE: Kinship and the Rise of Individual Moral Liability," in *Law and Ideology in Monarchic Israel* (ed. B. Halpern and D. W. Hobson; JSOTSup 124; Sheffield: Sheffield Academic Press, 1991), 25, 26, 67; Ze'ev Herzog, *Archaeology of the City: Urban Planning in Ancient Israel and Its Social Implications* (Tel Aviv: Yass Archaeology Press, Institute of Archaeology, Tel Aviv University, 1997), 247, 249; Israel Finkelstein and Neil Asher Silberman, *The Bible Unearthed: Archaeology's New Vision of Ancient Israel and the Origin*

took apart their huge altar and used some of its stone blocks for landfill and others to build a stable or storehouse. This is hard evidence for the historicity of the reform and its national scope.

The state-sponsored religious practice at Hezekiah's royal garrisons may have been an exception to his program of centralizing worship. (For example, Assyrian victory reliefs show that he left incense altars in place at his fortified citadel, Lachish.) Hezekiah did suppress worship at popular, rural shrines, nonetheless, as the Deuteronomistic tradition requires (2 Kgs 18:3–4; cf. Deut 12:1–14). Centralization had clear religious effect, disrupting syncretistic practices at the "high places" and enforcing belief in the oneness of Yahweh, Judah's sole divine landlord.

Did Hezekiah have ulterior motives beyond avoiding God's wrath at apostate worship? As Gottwald notes, monarchic leaders often take advantage of outside pressures for repentance and reform, co-opting them to strengthen their own political position. He writes, "As pressures for reform arose from outside the monarchic establishment, astute leaders within state circles would promulgate reform measures to serve state interests."[13]

Scholars have suggested that Hezekiah's centralization of worship might have had the political benefit of focusing the people's loyalties on his royal capital, Jerusalem. This would certainly have been to Hezekiah's advantage at a time when Assyrian military forces would soon put such loyalties to the test.[14]

Baruch Halpern has gone beyond previous scholars to see sophisticated political motivations behind Hezekiah's reform. In his view, the reform was likely an adjunct policy to Hezekiah's defense strategy against the Assyrians. This strategy would concede the countryside to the enemy and withdraw the populace to citadels for fortress warfare. What better way was there to prepare the rural populace for this strategy than to "desacralize" the countryside and centralize worship in the state capital?

Halpern argues Hezekiah's reforms were the ideal justification for "prising the peasantry into the forts, severing the old ancestral and customary ties, and securing the relation of the individual or the family to the central authority, instead of to the land."[15] If Halpern is right, Hezekiah certainly twisted one facet of Sinai theology to his own political ends.

---

of Its Sacred Texts (New York: Free Press, 2001), 250; Oded Borowski, Daily Life in Biblical Times (SBLABS 5; Atlanta: Society of Biblical Literature, 2003), 55, 103.

13. Gottwald, Politics of Ancient Israel, 293–94 n. 85.

14. See, e.g., H. H. Rowley, "Hezekiah's Reform and Rebellion," BJRL 44 (1962): 395–431; Lowery, Reforming Kings, 146, 157–61, 167–68, 212–13; Oded Borowski, "Hezekiah's Reforms and the Revolt against Assyria," BA 58 (1995): 148–55; Gottwald, Politics of Ancient Israel, 226–27.

15. Halpern, "Jerusalem and the Lineages," 27.

If this was Hezekiah's strategy before Assyria attacked, he seems to have rethought it after facing Assyria's fury. At least one biblical source, Jer 26:18–19, suggests that Hezekiah eventually yielded to Micah's full critique of his monarchy. He even took to heart Micah's complaint that abandoning the countryside entailed severe social injustices.

The scene in Jer 26 takes place a century after Hezekiah's reform. The text is really about Jeremiah and King Jehoiakim, not Micah and King Hezekiah. Nevertheless, it contains a fascinating sociological clue about the Sinai oriented reform party of Hezekiah's time.

A Reappearance of the "People of the Land"

The text of Jer 26 tells of the trial of Jeremiah in the temple precincts. His warnings that God is about to destroy Jerusalem and the temple land him on trial for his life. As the story unfolds, the state officials spare the prophet's life (26:16). Nevertheless, there is still a danger that the mob will lynch him. It is at this point that a circle of supporters of Jeremiah in the crowd recalls Micah's earlier prophecy against Jerusalem.

Years before, Micah, like Jeremiah, had warned that because of its leaders' social abuses, Judah would lose its privilege of living in God's land. The circle in the crowd even remembers Micah's exact words: "Zion will be plowed as a field, and Jerusalem will become ruins, and the mountain of the house as the high places of a forest" (Mic 3:12). Hezekiah had responded positively to these warnings and repented (Jer 26:19; cf. 2 Kgs 19:1; 2 Chr 32:26). Recollecting these facts saves Jeremiah's life.

Who is the group that has carried these traditions of Micah's Sinai theology for a century, to recall them at Jeremiah's trial? They are none other than the "elders of the land" (Jer 26:17), the same circle that supported the priest Jehoiada in his early Sinai-oriented reform of Judah.[16] They had probably stood behind Micah throughout his career as well, and had supported him in his early prophecy that sparked the cultic reforms of Hezekiah.

Other biblical texts contain additional clues for identifying the specific circles that made up the reform party of Hezekiah's time. They suggest that Micah and his supporters among the "people of the land"

---

16. See Klaus Koch, *The Growth of the Biblical Tradition: The Form-Critical Method* (trans. S. M. Cupitt; London: Black, 1969), 212, cf. 84 n. 21; Harry P. Nasuti, *Tradition History and the Psalms of Asaph* (SBLDS 88; Atlanta: Scholars Press, 1988), 94; and my more elaborate discussion in chapter 7 below.

were merely one part of a larger coalition. In various ways, the coalition's members helped to push Sinai theology to society's center.[17]

TRANSPLANTED NORTHERNERS IN HEZEKIAH'S COURT

At about the time that Micah was influencing Hezekiah's official policy, northern refugees were settling in Jerusalem. Many of the refugees came from the northern capital of Samaria, after Assyria destroyed it in 722. Some of these escapees brought with them northern versions of Sinai theology, such as the Psalms of Asaph and Hosea's prophecies.[18] They would have introduced these traditions within Hezekiah's orbit of influence. How else can we explain the presence of the Asaphite psalms within the Psalter, which was the "hymnbook" of the Jerusalem temple? How else can we explain the way that editors have modified the northern book of Hosea to show its relevance beyond its initial audience, "Ephraim"?

Psalms 50 and 78 provide good examples of how Judean editors added southern elements to the Psalms of Asaph. The structure of Ps 50 mirrors Israel's recitation of the blessings and curses of the covenant at the northern shrine of Shechem (see the commentaries on Deut 27). Furthermore, the northern prophet Hosea was familiar with the psalm. In Hos 5:14 he borrows the words of 50:22. Such evidence points to the psalm's origins in the northern kingdom. In the present form of the psalm, however, God shines forth in beauty "out of Zion" in Judah (50:2). Judean editors have clearly modified the psalm at this point.[19] Working within Jerusalem's temple, they must have partially adapted the psalm for use in Judean worship.

Originally, Ps 78 probably intended to cultivate repentance and hope in northern Israel in the face of eighth-century Assyrian military aggression. Hosea, prophesying under the same circumstances, shared these

---

17. For an excellent start at reconstructing the pro-Sinai coalition of Jeremiah's time, see Patricia Dutcher-Walls, "The Social Location of the Deuteronomists: A Sociological Study of Factional Politics in Late Pre-Exilic Judah," *JSOT* 52 (1991): 77–94.

18. See, e.g., Ernest W. Nicholson, *Deuteronomy and Tradition* (Oxford: Basil Blackwell, 1967), 83–106, especially p. 94.

19. For arguments, see Michael D. Goulder, *The Psalms of Asaph and the Pentateuch: Studies in the Psalter*, III (JSOTSup 233; Sheffield: Sheffield Academic Press, 1996), 39–40, 42–43. Cf. also the comments of Hans-Joachim Kraus, who sees the psalm's traditions rooted in an old covenant festival "that reached back to the most ancient (Shechemite) traditions, one that originated in Northern Israel" (*Psalms 1–59* [trans. H. Oswald; Minneapolis: Augsburg, 1988], 491, cf. p. 497).

aims. The language of 78:17 appears in the wording of Hos 13:2, and 78:29–31 has influenced Hos 13:6–7.

The psalm no longer has its original purpose and shape. In its present, modified form, God has fully rejected the northern tribes of Israel ("Joseph" and "Ephraim," 78:67). Israel's hopes lie only with God's new choices of "Judah" and "Zion" (78:68).

Clearly, northern Israelites would not have used 78:67–69 in their prayers to God for deliverance from the Assyrians. Rather, these verses reflect a new use that Ps 78 found in the rites of worship at Mount Zion in Jerusalem. As Michael Goulder notes, 78:9, 67–69 are secondary additions ("glosses") that reflect Jerusalem's appropriation of the Asaph psalms in Hezekiah's time.[20]

In concluding his study of the Psalms of Asaph, Harry Nasuti comments on the long history of their use. He notes that we owe a debt of gratitude to the southern king, Hezekiah, for our possession of these psalms as Scripture. Nasuti writes,

> One thinks in particular of the reform periods of Hezekiah and Josiah as times in which these [Asaphite psalms and their Sinai,] Ephraimite elements could most plausibly have gained access to the Jerusalem cult.... Such a setting [as part of Hezekiah's reforms] is also suggested by the combination of Ephraimite and more properly Southern elements ... in ... the language of the psalms.[21]

Like the Psalms of Asaph, the book of Hosea and its Sinai theology also comes down to us by way of monarchic Judah. Certain overt references to Judah and King David in the book offer particularly strong evidence of this. Though not every mention of Judah in Hosea is editorial, some of the references do appear to be secondary additions to the book (especially Hos 1:7; 3:5; 6:11a; 12:2).[22] They are not directly relevant to Hosea's immediate task, which was to warn his northern audience of God's imminent judgment. Subsequent handlers of Hosea's prophecies

---

20. Goulder, *Psalms of Asaph*, 112. For convincing arguments that 78:67–69 stems from Jerusalem-based editors, see his discussion on p. 126. Nasuti makes the more general comment that Ps 78 constitutes a southern appropriation of quintessentially northern traditions (*Psalms of Asaph*, 156). I shall discuss this psalm further in chapter 5 below.

21. Nasuti, *Psalms of Asaph*, 194.

22. Brevard S. Childs, *Introduction to the Old Testament as Scripture* (Philadelphia: Fortress, 1979), 379, 381; Hans Walter Wolff, *Hosea* (trans. G. Stansell; Hermeneia; Philadelphia: Fortress, 1974), 9 n. h, 20–21, 57 n. g, 63, 106 n. n, 123; James Luther Mays, *Hosea: A Commentary* (OTL; Philadelphia: Westminster, 1969), 29, 60, 102, 162; G. I. Davies, *Hosea* (NCBC; Grand Rapids: Eerdmans, 1992), 47, 104–5, 177, 272. Also note how the New English Bible emends Hos 1:7, and note the New American Bible's translation of Hos 12:2.

must have added them to the book to help impress the pertinence of Hosea's words on its readers in the southern kingdom.

We may assume that some southerners did find Hosea's prophetic words relevant to their own situation. King Hezekiah himself likely took Hosea's words to heart. I mentioned above that his early reform project was in line with the theology of Yahweh's exclusive worship. Along with Micah, Hosea blamed the north's military defeat and disaster on Canaanite fertility worship. In reaction, Hezekiah's reform removed Canaanite elements from Judah (2 Kgs 18:4, 22). He thus hoped to safeguard the south's welfare.

Hezekiah, who took the words of prophets seriously, certainly responded positively to an early phase of Micah's preaching. In all likelihood, he probably also lent state sponsorship to Hosea's disciples, who had brought the words of their prophetic leader to Judah (cf. 2 Kgs 19:2–7, 20–34; 20:1–19). He may even have supported them in producing a southern edition of Hosea's writings.[23]

Hezekiah's patronage may thus be a decisive factor behind our possession today of the book of Hosea. As Joseph Blenkinsopp states, many of the allusions to Judah in Hosea

> may be from the disciples of Hosea who went south after the fall of Samaria. It is even possible that they came to the attention of Hezekiah, who was inclined to listen to prophets … and whose reforms aimed at preventing Judah from suffering the same fate as its northern neighbor. This, at any rate, would help to explain the connections between Hosea and the development of the Deuteronomic reform movement in the Kingdom of Judah.[24]

THE PLACE OF LEVITES IN THE PRO-SINAI COALITION OF HEZEKIAH'S TIME

We know from 1 Chr 6:39–43 and 9:14–15 that the authors of the Psalms of Asaph were Levites. Descendents of Jacob's son, Levi, they

---

23. As Prov 25:1 witnesses, Hezekiah is associated with scribal and literary activity. Halpern states, "the codification and preservation of eighth-century 'classical prophecy' was a Hezekian programme" ("Jerusalem and the Lineages," 27, cf. p. 80). See also idem, "Brisker Pipes Than Poetry: The Development of Israelite Monotheism," in *Judaic Perspectives on Ancient Israel* (ed. J. Neusner, B. Levine, and E. Frerichs; Philadelphia: Fortress, 1987), 96.

24. Joseph Blenkinsopp, *A History of Prophecy in Israel* (Philadelphia: Westminster, 1983), 101, cf. p. 131 n. 61. Cf. Robert R. Wilson, *Prophecy and Society in Ancient Israel* (Philadelphia: Fortress, 1980), 227 n. 136; Jon D. Levenson, *Sinai and Zion: An Entry into the Jewish Bible* (San Francisco: Harper & Row, 1987), 193–94.

were one of several major priestly lineages within Israel. There is every reason to believe that the Levitical authors of these psalms were also the ones who carried them south to Hezekiah's Jerusalem.

Since the late nineteenth century, scholars such as Bernhard Duhm and Hans Walter Wolff have identified the Hosea circle, like the Asaphites, as Levites (or close associates of Levites).[25] Several scholars have followed up on these leads. I shall confirm their suggestions in subsequent chapters.

If the authors of Hosea, as well as of the Asaphite psalms, are really Levites, then clearly refugee Levitical groups teamed up with groups of Judean "elders of the land" to advocate Sinai theology in Hezekiah's Jerusalem. This conclusion ties in well with Gerhard von Rad's arguments that Levites from the Judean countryside spoke for the preexilic reform movements we have been tracing in the reigns of Joash and Hezekiah.[26]

Our investigation now draws us to a fascinating fact: in his reform program, Hezekiah went out of his way to incorporate outsider Levites, from both the northern kingdom and the Judean countryside, within central, Jerusalem temple circles.[27]

As part of his celebrations after he cleanses the Jerusalem temple, the king orders the Levites to sing Asaph psalms (2 Chr 29:30). Then, 2 Chr 29:34 reports that Hezekiah considered the Levites to be more conscientious than his own Jerusalemite priests. For this reason, he gives them specifically priestly tasks at the central temple. Later, at 2 Chr 30:22, Hezekiah speaks encouragingly to all the Levites, who "showed good insight in the things of the LORD."

---

25. Bernhard Duhm, *Die Theologie der Propheten als Grundlage für die innere Entwicklungsgeschichte der israelitischen Religion* (Bonn: Marcus, 1875), 130–31; Hans Walter Wolff, "Hoseas Gestige Heimat," in *Gesammelte Studien zum Alten Testament* (Munich: Kaiser, 1964 [1956]), 243–50; idem, *Hosea* (trans. G. Stansell; Hermeneia; Philadelphia: Fortress, 1974), xxii–xxiii, 79–81, 121–22, 144. See my discussion in ch. 8 below.

26. Von Rad, *Studies in Deuteronomy*, 66.

27. These textual implications support a key suggestion that Nasuti makes. He remarks, "What the Asaphite psalms clearly show is that at some point in the pre-exilic period the Ephraimites [i.e., the Asaphite Levites] did achieve at least something of a presence in the central cult [of Jerusalem]" (Nasuti, *Psalms of Asaph*, 194, cf. pp. 125, 148, 157, 175–78). For additional, specific comments on how Hezekiah seems to have welcomed previously disenfranchised, Mushite Levites into the priesthood of the Jerusalem temple, see Timothy Polk, "The Levites in the Davidic-Solomonic Empire," *Studia Biblica et Theologica* 9 (1979): 11 n. 27. For this theory, both Nasuti and Polk are relying on unpublished research by S. Dean McBride Jr. and Robert R. Wilson. Martin J. Buss anticipated Nasuti's attribution of the Psalms of Asaph to Levitical circles. Buss saw the traditions of some Asaphite psalms as belonging to a circle of Levites who moved to Judah after the fall of Samaria. See Martin Buss, "The Psalms of Asaph and Korah," *JBL* 82 (1963): 382–92.

The Levites were one of Israel's original tribes, and their history extends far back into Israel's prestate, village heritage. Their advocacy of the Sinai covenant may trace a considerable distance along this history.

In his recent article on "Kinship and Covenant," Frank M. Cross summarizes how priestly lineages, such as the Levites, played an essential role in uniting the twelve tribes of premonarchic Israel as a covenant people. Cross states, "Priestly families, linked by genealogy to create a priestly 'tribe,' were set aside to conduct rituals and sacrifices and to preserve religious lore.... Religious unity is undergirded by the institution of the pilgrimage feasts, where Israel's epic is sung, and covenant ceremonies or covenant renewal ceremonies reconstitute the league anew."[28]

KING JOSIAH'S REFORM AND THE APPEARANCE OF DEUTERONOMY

Judah experienced its third and final major, Sinai-oriented religious reform under the monarchy of King Josiah (639–609 B.C.E.). According to 2 Kgs 22:1—23:30, the discovery of a "book of the law" during repairs to the temple shook up the centers of power and motivated the reform. (A parallel account in 2 Chr 34–35 suggests the reform began even earlier than the book's discovery.)

The law book must have contained covenant curses as well as covenant stipulations for Josiah to have reacted with the fear and mourning seen in 2 Kgs 22:11. The words of the book completely unnerve Josiah. He realizes that "great is the wrath of the LORD that is kindled against us, because our ancestors did not obey the words of this book" (22:13).

After hearing the words of the law book, Josiah renewed the Sinai covenant, purged the temple and the land of foreign gods and their worship objects, did away with idolatrous priests, and centralized worship of Yahweh in Jerusalem. The scale of the reform was unprecedented. The text pictures the entire community binding themselves to the Sinai covenant and then making sweeping, radical changes in worship along the lines of Sinai theology. These changes affected not only Jerusalem and Judah but also stretched to Bethel and the former northern kingdom. Since the time of Wellhausen, nearly every modern biblical scholar has seen a major new departure in Israelite religion here.

---

28. Cross, "Kinship and Covenant," 12.

Josiah's cultic reform matches almost identically the requirements of the specific form of Sinai theology native to the book of Deuteronomy. More than a dozen cross-references link the details of his reform to Deuteronomy's specific language and injunctions. For this reason, since the work of W. M. L. De Wette in the early nineteenth century, scholars have identified the law book recovered in the temple during Josiah's reign as an early form of Deuteronomy.[29]

De Wette, intoxicated with Enlightenment rationalism, argued that the book was a "pious fraud," created out of whole cloth at Josiah's time. This is surely not the case. In the book of Deuteronomy, we see crystallized in a written, scriptural form the antique traditions of Sinai theology that had begun to flower already in the reforms of Jehoiada and Hezekiah.

Exactly when the "book of the law" had crystallized in writing, and whether its discovery was truly accidental, we do not know. It is clear, however, that its traditions are the same ones that Micah promoted in Hezekiah's time and that refugees from the north brought to Jerusalem after 722 in the form of the book of Hosea and the Psalms of Asaph. In subsequent chapters, I shall trace these traditions back in time.

Josiah's reign saw not only the appearance of Deuteronomy in written form but also, in time, an entire "Deuteronomistic History" of Israel (Deuteronomy through 2 Kings).[30] King Hezekiah had already sponsored scribal writing projects in the eighth century. By the time of King Josiah, social conditions were ripe for an official written overview of Israel's history from the perspective of the Sinai reform movement.

Popular literacy and state sponsored literature were becoming a societal norm at Josiah's time. As Israel Finkelstein and Neil A. Silberman write, "Judah had become a highly centralized state in which literacy was spreading from the capital and the main towns to the countryside. It was a process that had apparently started in the eighth century, but reached a culmination only in the time of Josiah.... The [Josianic edition of the] Bible offers a profoundly optimistic history.... Josiah would purge Israel from the abominations of its neighbors."[31]

---

29. For one good overview of this history of interpretation, see S. Dean McBride Jr., "Deuteronomium," *TRE* 8:536–38.

30. Frank M. Cross, *Canaanite Myth and Hebrew Epic* (Cambridge: Harvard University Press, 1973), 274–88; Richard D. Nelson, *The Double Redaction of the Deuteronomistic History* (JSOTSup 18; Sheffield: JSOT Press, 1981); Baruch Halpern and David Vanderhooft, "The Editions of Kings in the 7th-6th Centuries B.C.E.," *HUCA* 62 (1991): 179–244; William Schniedewind, "The Problem with Kings: Recent Study of the Deuteronomistic History," *RelSRev* 22/1 (1996): 22–27.

31. Finkelstein and Silberman, *The Bible Unearthed*, 284–85.

Several lines of reasoning converge to support the argument that Sinai theology flowered in an official, seventh-century work of history writing at Josiah's time. The Deuteronomistic History as we have it in the Bible today is a modification and expansion of a "Josianic" edition that described the story of Israel culminating in Josiah's reign.

First Kings 13:1–32 forms an initial piece of strong evidence. An editor from Josiah's time has sandwiched this text in between 1 Kgs 12:33 and 13:33–34. These passages describe the northern kingdom's first monarch, Jeroboam I, establishing nontraditional worship at Bethel and other northern sites. The editor's addition is rich with clues for the biblical sleuth.

The episode recounts the story of a man of God who travels to Bethel to prophesy against the shrine. The man's prophecy specifically mentions Josiah by name, and it announces that, in the far future, Josiah will destroy the altar at Bethel (1 Kgs 13:2; cf. 2 Kgs 23:15–16). This text, presenting the beginnings of Israel's monarchical history, clearly points ahead 300 years to Josiah's reign as the culmination of that history.

A second piece of evidence is that Huldah's prophecy about Josiah is not fulfilled. According to 2 Kgs 22:13–20, upon hearing his new law book Josiah looked for a prophet to receive God's advice. The king was keen to learn how to avert divine judgment. He also wanted someone to intercede with God on Judah's behalf.

The pro-Sinai coalition advising Josiah seems to have selected a prophetess named Huldah for the job. As part of her prophecy, Huldah assures Josiah that he has had the proper reaction to the law book and that "You shall be gathered to your grave in peace" (2 Kgs 22:20). These words were part of an edition of the History from before Josiah's death. In the present edition, Josiah meets an untimely and violent death (2 Kgs 23:29).

Finally, a third piece of evidence stems from the strange silence of the History about the prophet Jeremiah. Jeremiah, just a youngster during Josiah's reign, must have had his major impact only after a "Josianic" edition of the History was already in existence. If its authors had written the core of the History after Josiah's time, their failure to notice Jeremiah, Sinai theology's most famous prophet, would be inexplicable.

Some of Jeremiah's key supporters were the children and grandchildren of the pro-Deuteronomy reformers of Josiah's time.[32] For example, one supporter who helps protect Jeremiah's life at his trial at the temple is

---

32. Wilson, Prophecy and Society, 233–35, 241–48; Friedman, Who Wrote the Bible, 125–27; Nasuti, Psalms of Asaph, 94; Dutcher-Walls, "Social Location of the Deuteronomists."

Ahikam, the son of Shaphan (Jer 26:24). Shaphan, Ahikam's father, played a major role in Josiah's reform and first read the Deuteronomic law book to the king (2 Kgs 22:10).

Mainstream archaeologists agree on the historicity of several main elements of King Josiah's reform of Israel's worship in the seventh century. The king carried out an official program against worship images and made efforts to centralize worship in Jerusalem. Unfortunately, much of the scientific evidence for Josiah's reform still lies buried. Archaeologists have not yet located the Israelite shrine at Bethel, for example, so they cannot confirm the biblical report that Josiah decommissioned it. And although they have excavated a shrine at the southern Israelite citadel at Arad, they disagree about whether it bears evidence of Josiah's activities.[33] This uncertainty about Bethel and Arad is frustrating. Nevertheless, we do have some less ambiguous evidence of Josiah's reform.

By the late seventh century, in the wake of Josiah's reign, sacred images and symbols disappeared from the official seals used by Judean state officials. According to Finkelstein and Silberman, this "may possibly reflect the influence of Josiah's reform in insisting that the imageless YHWH was the only legitimate focus of veneration."[34]

The Lachish letters, a collection of correspondence between Judean military officials from the early sixth century, show that an exclusive veneration of Yahweh continued within some official circles after Josiah's time. The letters all begin with a greeting that mentions Yahweh. Moreover, the names of the people mentioned in the letters contain forms of the divine name Yahweh, rather than the names of Baal or other foreign deities.[35]

Archaeologists have also unearthed further evidence of Josiah's reform at 'En Hatzeva, a site in the Negev region from the seventh and sixth centuries. They found cult vessels in a shattered condition at the locale, about 20 miles southwest of the Dead Sea. Those who destroyed these cult objects threw them into a pit and crushed them with large hewn stones taken from a nearby shrine. Josiah's reform may well have been responsible for the leveling of the shrine and the destruction of its idols.[36]

---

33. The excavator of the temple at Arad, Yohanan Aharoni, associated its permanent decommissioning with Josiah's reform. More recent studies have questioned this dating, however. See, e.g., Horn, "Divided Monarchy," 138–39; Finkelstein and Silberman, *The Bible Unearthed*, 288. Halpern allows that Josiah may have at least decommissioned some elements of worship at Arad ("Jerusalem and the Lineages," 66 n. 1).

34. Finkelstein and Silberman, *The Bible Unearthed*, 288.

35. David Diringer, "Early Hebrew Inscriptions," in *Lachish III: The Iron Age* (ed. O. Tufnell et al.; London: Oxford University Press, 1953), 331–39; Horn, "Divided Monarchy," 139–41.

36. Rudolf Cohen and Yigal Yisrael, "Smashing the Idols: Piecing Together an Edomite Shrine in Judah," *BAR* 22/4 (1996): 40–51, 65.

As we saw with the other pro-Sinai reforms, incidental details in the account of Josiah's reform help point us towards its social roots. According to 2 Kgs 21:24, the "people of the land" again figure significantly in encouraging the reform. It is actually the people of the land who made Josiah king at the tender age of eight. They raised him to the throne in the turbulent period after the death of his father, King Amon.

Josiah's Sinai-oriented reform took place only after a decade of his minority under the tutelage of the people of the land. Their formative influence was probably a significant factor in the king's receptivity to the words of the law book that his courtiers discovered in his eighteenth year. Gerhard von Rad concludes that the book of Deuteronomy directly represents the interests of this circle of rural, landed gentry.[37]

As in Hezekiah's reform, outsider Levites, from both the former northern kingdom and the Judean countryside, may have also been a party within the pro-Sinai coalition of Josiah's court. The prophetess Huldah, for example, who prophesied for Josiah after he heard the law book read, seems to have been closely associated with outsider circles of Levites. She lived in the Mishneh, or "Second," Quarter of Jerusalem (2 Kgs 22:14), a section of the city that accommodated the refugees from the north who moved to Jerusalem after 722. Thus, she likely lived among the Levite associates of Hosea and the Asaphite Levites who carried northern versions of Sinai theology south to Jerusalem. Moreover, Huldah's husband, Shallum (2 Kgs 22:14), was probably a Levitical relative of Jeremiah, from the Levites of Anathoth (Jeremiah's hometown in the land of Benjamin; Jer 32:7; 1:1).[38]

We might have guessed that outsider Levites would have strongly backed Josiah's implementation of the newly found law book, since Deuteronomy and the Levites have distinct interconnections. The connections are sufficiently strong, in fact, that in the first half of the twentieth

---

37. Von Rad, *Studies in Deuteronomy*, 64–66. In a related argument, Enno Janssen suggested in 1956 that the author of the Deuteronomistic History was one of the people of the land (*Juda in der Exilszeit: Ein Beitrag zur Frage der Entstehung des Judentums* [FRLANT 69; Göttingen: Vandenhoeck & Ruprecht, 1956], 49–54). Cf. now Seitz, *Theology in Conflict*, 69–71. Even more recently, J. David Pleins has asserted that Deuteronomy is the literary product of Judah's landed gentry (e.g., see his *Social Visions of the Hebrew Bible: A Theological Introduction* [Louisville: Westminster John Knox, 2001], 60).

38. On the mushrooming of Jerusalem due to a wave of refugees from the northern kingdom after the fall of Samaria, see Magen Broshi, "The Expansion of Jerusalem in the Reigns of Hezekiah and Manasseh," *IEJ* 24 (1974): 21–26. On Huldah's connections with the Levites, see Wilson, *Prophecy and Society*, 222–23. Wilson also identifies other individuals involved with Josiah's law book as Levites, including Hilkiah, the priest who "found" the book, and Shaphan, the scribe who read the book to the king.

century, Aage Bentzen and Gerhard von Rad concluded that circles of country Levites actually penned Deuteronomy. Several subsequent scholars have agreed.[39]

The following passages of the book call for special charity for the Levites: Deut 12:12, 18, 19; 16:11, 14; 26:11. Further, Deuteronomy, unlike some other literature of the Bible, recognizes the Levites' full status as priests. The terms "Levites" and "priests" appear synonymous in the following texts: Deut 17:9, 18; 21:5; 24:8; 27:9; 31:9. Deuteronomy 18:6–8 even allows all Levites the right to serve as priests at the central sanctuary. As Richard Elliott Friedman summarizes:

---

39. Aage Bentzen, *Die Josianische Reform und ihre Voraussetzungen* (Copenhagen: Haase, 1926); von Rad, *Studies in Deuteronomy*, 66–69. For one good discussion of the relation of the Levites to Deuteronomy, see Aelred Cody, *A History of Old Testament Priesthood* (AnBib 35; Rome: Pontifical Biblical Institute, 1969), 128, 132–34. In addition to von Rad and Bentzen, many scholars, such as W. W. G. Baudissin, F. Horst, S. Dean McBride Jr., Robert R. Wilson, and R. E. Friedman have argued for a Levitical origin of Deuteronomy. Other scholars hotly debate the thesis. For a brief, suggestive response to the major alternative hypothesis of Moshe Weinfeld, see Seitz, *Theology in Conflict*, 69 n. 149. I agree with Seitz that the development of scribalism among the "people of the land" was a key factor in Deuteronomy's composition along with the work of the Levites. The question of whether outsider Levites would have supported Deuteronomy's focus on cult centralization has been the Achilles' heel of the Levite hypothesis. At least some outsider Levites ministered at the smaller shrines of the countryside. Would not Levite backers of Deuteronomic cult centralization have been working against the interests of their kinfolk at these rural shrines? Scholars have proposed several cogent scenarios under which the centralization program of Deuteronomy might have been considered in the interests of rural Levites. Von Rad argued that the focus on centralization was a late development within the Sinai stream of tradition. By the time that the stream flowered in the form of Deuteronomy, the Levites were more interested in preserving Sinai traditions than in performing priestly rites. Bentzen made the opposite argument, that the rural Levites were more than interested in priestly ministry in writing Deuteronomy. In fact, they were interested in upgrading their ministry by ascending to posts at the Jerusalem temple. They supposed that shutting down the high places would allow them to integrate themselves at the central shrine (see Bentzen, *Die Josianische Reform*, 68–72). Notably, Baruch Halpern has defended the idea that rural Levites could feasibly have pushed cult centralization as an economic program ("The Centralization Formula in Deuteronomy," *VT* 31 [1981]: 20–38). Halpern's work from as early as 1974 has influenced R. E. Friedman's understanding of Deuteronomy. Friedman argues that Deuteronomy's authors were not just any Levites, but the former priests of Shiloh. The Shiloh Levites had already enjoyed the experience of relatively centralized worship in the days of Samuel. In those days, Shiloh was a regional center of worship. Now at the time of the writing of Deuteronomy, they were hoping to revive the Shiloh experience. (See Friedman, *Who Wrote the Bible*, 122.) A final possibility might build on the theory of McBride and Wilson that already by the time of Hezekiah's reform, outsider Levites were being incorporated into the priestly ranks of the Jerusalem temple. The example of such newly integrated Levites would have heartened the rural Levites still outside the temple system, and led them to suppose that supporting centralized worship at Jerusalem would not be a self-destructive act.

[Deuteronomy] opens with the religious-centralization laws, which prohibit the people from doing their own sacrificing. It repeatedly requires the people to care for the Levite. It includes laws of religious tithes and offerings. It requires that the king write his copy of the law in front of the Levites. It declares the Levites to be the rightful priestly tribe. It regularly deals with this group's concerns. Most investigators, therefore, have related Deuteronomy's law code, in one way or another, to Levites.[40]

Josiah's reform program in support of Sinai theology did not survive his death. In Jer 3:10, God looks back on Josiah's reform and comments, "Judah did not return to me with all her heart, but rather in deception." Judah's religious and political situation underwent a radical devolution from this point on. The country spiraled towards destruction in the era of social abuse and political turmoil under Josiah's successors. It finally met with Babylonian destruction and exile in 586 B.C.E.

The failure of the people to remain faithful to the Sinai covenant, however, was a major factor in Sinai theology's capture of a dominating place within biblical religion. The fact that the Babylonian exile followed upon the people's consistent neglect of the Sinai covenant and its stipulations vindicated Sinai theology's central claim. It had always held that Israel's safe dwelling in God's land was conditional upon the people's covenantal fidelity.

The people in exile, searching for explanations for their political and religious crisis, saw that Sinai theology had proved correct. The Sinai covenant had warned that the covenant curse of dispossession of the land would follow covenant infidelity, and this seemed to be exactly what had happened with the Assyrian destruction of the northern kingdom in 722 and with the Babylonian's eviction of the people from the land in 586.

SINAI THEOLOGY AND THE FINAL SHAPE OF THE BIBLE

Because of its manifest ability to make sense of why the Babylonian exile had happened, Sinai theology gained increasing popularity and support during the exilic period. Representatives of other biblical streams of tradition cooperated with the advocates of Sinai theology in planning the restoration of Judah after the exile. In fact, they allowed Sinai theology a dominant voice in the final shape of the Hebrew Bible. Thus, the Deuteronomistic History provides the central biblical account of Israel's

40. Friedman, *Who Wrote the Bible,* 120. Cf. Wilson, *Prophecy and Society,* 18 n. 36, 234–35, 298–99.

monarchic period. (Of course, the books of Chronicles came in later as an alternative account of the history.)

The Deuteronomistic History, even in its final edition, holds up Josiah, the figure who brought Sinai theology to the center of Israel's life, as its great hero. Josiah, the great advocate of the Sinai covenant, is the unsurpassed king in the History, just as Moses, who first mediated the Sinai covenant to Israel, is the unsurpassed prophet in the Pentateuch. "Before him there was no king like him, who turned to the LORD with all his heart, with all his soul, and with all his might, according to all the Law of Moses; nor did any like him arise after him" (2 Kgs 23:25; cf. Deut 6:5).

After 586, the Deuteronomists reedited their History to respond to the crisis of the exile. The covenant infidelity of Manasseh, one of Josiah's royal predecessors, helped explain why the exile occurred despite Josiah's sweeping reform. Manasseh had defiled God's land even more than the Canaanites had before Israel arrived (2 Kgs 21:11). During Manasseh's reign, God had determined to "wipe Jerusalem as one wipes a dish" (2 Kgs 21:13) and to "cast off the remnant of my inheritance, and give them into the hand of their enemies" (2 Kgs 21:14).

Not only the Deuteronomistic History's final shape but also that of the Pentateuch puts the emphasis on Sinai theology. The final editors of the Pentateuch gave Sinai theology pride of place by setting Deuteronomy, the apotheosis of the Sinai covenant, as the Torah's capstone. By looking closely, one can see the evidence of their editorial work.[41]

The Pentateuch's closing words now round off the Torah with a final focus on Moses, the ultimate mediator of the Sinai covenant. Moses' epitaph in Deut 34:10–12 makes Moses the Bible's preeminent prophet: "Never since has there arisen a prophet in Israel like Moses, whom Yahweh knew face to face."

There are clear signs of editorial activity favoring Sinai theology elsewhere in the Bible. Several scholars have uncovered signs of Deuteronomistic editing and shaping of the prophetic books. Editors gave prophetic books special headings, new layers, and other additions in the process of collating a distinctively Deuteronomistic collection of

---

41. Deut 32:48–52 picks up and repeats in the form of a paraphrase the announcement of Moses' impending death in Num 27:12–14. This is a special editorial devise known as *epanalepsis*. The editors must have inserted Deuteronomy at the end of the Pentateuch, giving it an emphatic, final position (except for the P account of Moses' death in Deut 34:7–9). Then, because, with Deuteronomy's insertion, Moses now remains alive for over 30 chapters after his impending death has been announced in Numbers, the editors had to repeat Num 27:12–14 before the account of Moses' death near the end of Deuteronomy to compensate for the awkward literary parenthesis that their editing created.

prophetic writings. The resulting, early Deuteronomistic prophetic collection probably included Hosea and Micah, along with First Isaiah, Jeremiah, Amos, and Zephaniah. Later editors added other books and incorporated this prophetic collection into the emerging biblical canon of Scripture.

The closing words of our canonical collection of prophetic writings give Mosaic-Sinai theology the final emphasis. The biblical prophets end with this concluding word from God: "Remember the teaching of my servant Moses, the statutes and ordinances that I commanded him at Horeb for all Israel" (Mal 4:4).

The language and theological perspective of Sinai texts, especially Deuteronomy, now pervades and shapes much of the Hebrew Bible. It is not the only voice in the Bible. Other traditions—associated with wisdom, and surrounding David, Solomon, and Zion—parallel Sinai traditions within the Bible. These other traditions continue to offer alternative, sometimes opposing, points of view. Still, the canon has arguably given preeminence to Sinai theology. With some justification, this book can equate Sinai theology with "biblical Yahwism."

4

SINAI THEOLOGY IN THE EIGHTH CENTURY B.C.E.

HOSEA AND MICAH

THE BIBLICAL RELIGION THAT FLOWERED WITH HEZEKIAH, WITH JOSIAH, and with the production of the Hebrew Bible traces back at least to specific Israelite groups and networks of the eighth century B.C.E. These groups and networks on the periphery of Israelite society guarded the traditions of biblical Yahwism until they captured a central place in society. Their members were not powerful officials, but they did occupy some fascinating social niches.

In this chapter, I uncover these groups and networks in the writings of eighth-century prophets, especially Hosea and Micah. Study of their prophetic oracles puts our investigation on a rationally sound and historically firm footing. The prophetic books of Hosea and Micah preserve many of the actual words of these two prophets and provide us with major written witnesses to biblical Yahwism from a definite, fixed point in history.

Hosea is the first of the minor prophetical books known collectively as the Book of the Twelve. The prophet Hosea's career occupied a few decades beginning after the mid-eighth century B.C.E. He and his supporters lived and worked in the northern kingdom (Israel) during a time of apostasy in worship and of political turmoil. His career preceded the Assyrian Empire's conquest of the kingdom culminating in 722 B.C.E. Hosea proclaimed to the people that their coming destruction by Assyria was a direct result of their abandonment of Yahweh in their worship and political life.

The message of Hosea has two parts in the present form of his book. Chapters 1–3 present the story of Hosea's troubled marriage as an illustration of God's troubled relationship with Israel. Chapters 4–14, a series of prophetic messages to Israel, proclaim that God is disciplining the people because of their apostasy and false worship. These chapters emphasize woe and doom, but they also contain powerful words about God's love and care for God's people.

While Hosea was prophesying in the north, a similar prophetic figure, Micah of Moresheth, was at work, along with his supporters, in the southern kingdom (Judah). Micah, although sixth in the Book of the Twelve, was a near contemporary of Hosea. Some of Micah's early oracles assume that the northern kingdom has not yet fallen. His later oracles presuppose a new situation and a new Assyrian crisis some decades hence, around 701 B.C.E. These latter oracles thus date from a time after Hosea fell silent with the destruction of Samaria, the north's capital, in 722.

While Hosea denounced apostasy in worship, Micah's concern falls more on the social injustices of his time, particularly those that occurred in rural Judah. Micah traveled from the countryside to Judah's capital, Jerusalem, where he castigated the elites of the nation for oppressing and abandoning the land rights of the Judean country people. He prophesied that God would not allow this oppression to continue, but would surely punish Judah with destruction.

I aim to show in this chapter that Hosea and Micah proclaimed the same Yahwism that now characterizes the Hebrew Bible. They advocated the biblical Yahwism that later flowered at Israel's center with Hezekiah's and Josiah's reforms. I intend to overturn the current trend that considers this "biblical" Yahwism a late invention of the Deuteronomists, of the exile, or even of postexilic times.

The effort at this detective work is worthwhile. It shows that biblical Yahwism is a stream of tradition that generations of the faithful handed down over time. Biblical religion is neither the evolutionary culmination of a history of religious development nor the innovative, ideological creation of late Israelite writers. Julius Wellhausen, Lothar Perlitt, and their modern exponents are fundamentally mistaken.

The investigation in this chapter differs from previous study. It traces a broad stream of Sinai theology, not the narrow phenomenon of Deuteronomism. It sees this theological stream as a flow of traditions within both northern and southern channels.

Looking for southern channels of Sinai theology will seem brazen to some. Biblical scholarship in the twentieth century generally went in another direction. It tended to identify our major, Sinai-focused source texts, such as E and Hosea, with a northern geography.

The consensus that Sinai traditions are northern appears in most of those modern scholars who have tried to lead the biblical studies field

away from the idea that Deuteronomy evolved its unique covenant theology as a sudden breakthrough or innovation. Adam C. Welch,
Gerhard von Rad, Albrecht Alt, Ernest W. Nicholson, and Terence E.
Fretheim all traced the sources of Deuteronomy back to circles within
the northern kingdom.[1] Some of the work of these scholars will be helpful in this chapter, as we trace Sinai theology back through the northern
prophet, Hosea. It will not be nearly as helpful, however, in retracing the
southern currents of Sinai theology.

Fortunately, some researchers have bucked the scholarly trend of
seeing Sinai theology as something primarily northern. Jon Levenson is
one such scholar, and part of my argument in this chapter extends Levenson's insights. Levenson reminds us that all northern literature, such as
that of Hosea, comes to us through the southern kingdom, Judah. After
the north fell to Assyria, only Judah remained to preserve Israel's traditions. This is significant, since we usually connect only the very different,
royal traditions of Zion with Judah.

Both Sinai and Zion traditions must have coexisted in the southern
kingdom between 722 B.C.E., when the north fell, and 586 B.C.E., when the
Babylonians destroyed Jerusalem. Levenson thinks this was true even
earlier. He sees no reason to consider the presence of Sinai theology in the
south a "late and radical change."[2] The south may have harbored Sinai
traditions all along.

One of Levenson's keen insights is that a social-scientific approach to
the traditions of Sinai and Zion is better than a geographical one. There is
no reason that different groups holding different theologies cannot live
together in one geographical locale. Surely, this was the case in the southern kingdom of Judah even before the north fell. Levenson's conclusion is
correct: "Despite the royal cultus, or better, alongside the royal cultus, the
material that the scholarly consensus sees as northern existed in Judah."[3]

Levenson has anticipated my present project in his comments about
the southern prophet Micah, suggesting that Micah may be a particularly good example of a southern proponent of Sinai theology active
before Deuteronomy. Aided by Walter Beyerlin's 1959 study of the

---

1. See the discussion and bibliography in the following works: Jon D. Levenson, *Sinai and Zion: An Entry into the Jewish Bible* (San Franciscio: HarperCollins, 1985), 189; E. W. Nicholson, *Deuteronomy and Tradition* (Oxford: Basil Blackwell, 1967), 58 n. 1; Alan W. Jenks, *The Elohist and North Israelite Traditions* (SBLMS 22; Missoula, Mont.: Scholars Press, 1977); Terence Fretheim, "Elohist," *IDBSup*, 261.

2. Levenson, *Sinai and Zion*, 194.

3. Ibid.

Micah traditions, Levenson finds in Micah a definite example of the existence of a Moses/Sinai orientation in a figure from Judah.[4]

Other scholars have also seen Sinai theology in various parts of Micah. Since they have assumed that all Sinai theology must be northern, however, they have often concluded incorrectly that editors added this material after Micah's time. In other words, they have mistakenly supposed that late editors transplanted originally northern material into the book of Micah, a southern prophet.

In 1926, Cambridge scholar F. C. Burkitt presented the view that Mic 6 and 7 are northern prophecy. Again in 1962, Otto Eissfeldt interpreted Mic 7:7–20 as a psalm stemming from north Israel. Jan Dus strengthened and further specified Eissfeldt's thesis in 1965. Then, two years later in 1967, B. Reicke similarly identified all of Mic 7 as a north-Israelite liturgy. Finally, in 1971, Adam S. van der Woude, working at first without knowledge of these previous studies, reargued the position that Mic 6–7, which he distinguished as a "Second Micah," most probably forms a north-Israelite writing.[5]

In my view, scholars are mistaken in assigning a northern provenance to these texts near the end of Micah. They have rightly discerned the presence of Sinai theology in parts of Micah's book. Based on presuppositions about the theology's geography, however, they have been too quick to trace these parts of Micah to north Israel.

In view of the current uncertainty and skepticism about the antiquity of biblical monotheism and covenant thinking, a new look at the eighth-century prophets is in order. Specific passages from Micah and Hosea witnessing to Sinai theology in its eighth-century form are particularly of interest. Looking at these two biblical books will provide evidence of Sinai theology in both the northern kingdom and in Judah.

For convenience, I group my discussion of these passages under the five rubrics I used in chapter 2. These rubrics allow for a useful presentation of the main tenets of Sinai belief. Unlike the approach in

4. Levenson, *Sinai and Zion*, 195–200; Walter Beyerlin, *Die Kulttraditionen Israels in der Verkündigung des Propheten Micah* (FRLANT 62; Göttingen: Vandenhoeck & Ruprecht, 1959). I also made strong use of Beyerlin's work in my biblical interpretations of Micah below.

5. F. C. Burkitt, "Micah 6 and 7 a Northern Prophecy," *JBL* 45 (1926): 159–61; Otto Eissfeldt, "Ein Psalm aus Nord-Israel: Micha 7, 7–20," *ZDMG* 112 (1962): 259–68; Jan Dus, "Weiteres zum nordisraelitischen Psalm Micha 7, 7–20," *ZDMG* 115 (1965): 14–22; B. Reicke, "Liturgical Traditions in Micah 7," *HTR* 60 (1967): 349–67; Adam S. van der Woude, "Deutero-Micha: Ein Prophet aus Nord-Israel?" *NedTT* 25 (1971): 365–78. Also see A. van Hoonacker, *Les douze petits prophètes* (EBib; Paris: Gabalda, 1908); Otto Eissfeldt, *Der Gott Karmel* (SPAW; Berlin: Akademie Verlag, 1953), 7–8; John T. Willis, "A Reapplied Prophetic Hope Oracle," in *Studies on Prophecy* (ed. G. W. Anderson et al.; VTSup 26; Leiden: Brill, 1974), 64–76.

chapter 2, here we move ahead full steam at interpreting biblical passages as whole units. I shall also now take account of the passages' religious and historical contexts.

ISRAEL AS GOD'S ELECTED VASSALS

The Witness of Hosea

The best place to start tracing Sinai theology in Hosea and Micah is with Hosea's two overt references to the Sinai covenant. Hosea's first explicit mention of "covenant" (ברית) is in Hos 6:7–10, a passage that presents a direct speech of God about Israel.

> [7] But at Adam they transgressed the covenant;
> there they dealt faithlessly with me.
> [8] Gilead is a city of evildoers,
> tracked with blood.
> [9] As robbers lie in wait for someone,
> so the priests are banded together;
> they murder on the road to Shechem,
> they commit a monstrous crime.
> [10] In the house of Israel I have seen a horrible thing;
> Ephraim's whoredom is there, Israel is defiled.

The text is a catalog of treachery, in which God characterizes the sin of the land by referring to transgressions at several specific places (Adam, Gilead, and the outskirts of Shechem). Hosea may have given the prophecy around 733 B.C.E., so that its list of crimes explains the devastating blows that Assyria was inflicting on the country at that time. Verse 7 begins the list of transgressions by charging the people with a breach of "covenant." The charge introduces the theme that will categorize the rest of the passage.

Hosea is clearly holding Israel responsible to a committed relationship with God. This relationship includes their (unmet) obligation to keep specific rules that God has stipulated. The second half of 6:7 makes clear that the people's breach of covenant means that they have "dealt treacherously against me [God]." Furthermore, the Hebrew expression in 6:7 for "transgressing (or 'crossing over') the covenant" (עבר ברית) always refers to breaking covenant with Yahweh.[6]

---

6. John Day, "Pre-Deuteronomic Allusions to the Covenant in Hosea and Psalm LXXVIII," *VT* 36 (1986): 4.

All of the specific sins in Hos 6:7–10, along with their geographical links, are hard to identify and pin down historically. This is unfortunate, since insight into the specifics of 6:7, especially its reference to "Adam," might further illuminate Hosea's understanding of the covenant. Although there are very few bits of evidence to go on, there is one intriguing clue for interpreting 6:7 in Ps 78, an Asaphite psalm.

The Hebrew text of Ps 78:60 may read as follows: "He [God] abandoned his dwelling at Shiloh, the tent where he dwelt at Adam." If this translation is correct, the verse uses "Adam" as a kind of poetic, parallel term for Shiloh. ("Adam" is the name of a place here, not a reference to the first human. It is located about 15 miles east of Shiloh.) According to the psalm, God abandoned Shiloh during the settlement period due to the sins of Israel. Verse 58 of the psalm names the cause as unfaithful worship at "high places" and the use of "graven images."

If Hosea speaks of "Adam" in the tradition of Ps 78, he is referring to God's ancient judgment on Shiloh for breach of the covenant.[7] At a later period, Jeremiah will make a very similar reference to what happened at Shiloh (cf. Ps 78:60). Like Hosea, Jeremiah refers to Adam/Shiloh as a warning to Israel to be vigilant about covenant faithfulness (Jer 7:12, 14; 26:6, 9).

Hosea's second explicit mention of "covenant" (ברית) is in Hos 8:1–3. The text reads as follows:

[1] Set the trumpet to your lips!
  One like a vulture is over the house of the LORD,
because they have broken my covenant,
  and transgressed my law.
[2] Israel cries to me,
  "My God, we—Israel—know you!"
[3] Israel has spurned the good;
  the enemy shall pursue him.

These verses form a threat. They begin with a call to alarm. The prophet cries out, "Put the trumpet to your lips! [The enemy comes] like a vulture against the house of the LORD." The "house of the LORD" is the whole land, viewed as Yahweh's own manor (cf. Hos 9:15). The bird, no doubt, is the Assyrians. Like Hos 6:7–11a, just discussed, this passage

---

7. He seems to do so in a poetic wordplay using the words "Adam" and "cross over." Josh 3:16 names Adam as a place by the Jordan River. It played a key role when the Israelites first crossed over the Jordan and entered the promised land. Hosea may thus be saying that Israel "crossed over" the Jordan, where Adam is located, and soon afterward, they "crossed over" (i.e., transgressed) the covenant at Adam, that is, Shiloh.

may reflect the Assyrian incursion against the northern kingdom in 733 under the ruler Tiglath-pileser III.

God specifies the reason for the Assyrian incursion immediately at the end of 8:1. The people have transgressed "my covenant." This is the same Hebrew expression that we just saw in Hos 6:7, which also spoke of "transgressing (or 'crossing over') the covenant." Here again we have specific evidence that Hosea was an early, eighth-century, proponent of the Sinai covenant. In fact, Hosea's Hebrew expression עבר ברית will later become a specifically Deuteronomic idiom for violating the covenant (see Deut 17:2; Josh 23:16; Judg 2:20; 2 Kgs 18:12).[8] This fits perfectly the thesis that Hosea and his circle were forerunners of the Deuteronomists and their covenant theology.

Hosea's concept of the covenant was neither fuzzy nor undeveloped. The poetry of 8:1 sets the term "covenant" in parallelism with the term "torah" (תורה). The specific mention of torah ("instruction," "regulation") signals that the covenant involves stipulations given by God for obedience by the people. Hosea also uses the term torah elsewhere, in Hos 4:6 and 8:12. Hosea understands the covenant to involve specific, binding regulations on Israel.

Verse 3 reinforces the same idea. The verse's reference to the "good" suggests more than the covenant's good gift of abundant life. The same language appears in Mic 6:8 and 1 Sam 12:23 (B source), where it refers in particular to the covenant's "good" legal standards. Hosea understands the Sinai covenant includes obligation as well as grace.

Fascinatingly, Hosea comes very close to one of the Psalms of Asaph here. In Asaphite Ps 78:10, "covenant" and "torah" parallel one another just as in Hosea. In the psalm, to break one is to break the other. Hosea's use of language from Ps 78 is revealing. It suggests that his theology relies partly on the worship traditions that the psalm preserves. This is compelling evidence that Hosea's linking of "covenant" and "torah" is no late innovation. It derives from the earlier liturgy and psalmody of northern worship ceremonies.[9]

---

8. Moshe Weinfeld, *Deuteronomy and the Deuteronomic School* (Oxford: Clarendon, 1972), 364, 367.

9. Psalm 78 is difficult to date precisely, but it may well come from before 722 when the northern kingdom fell. After 722, southern liturgy preserved the psalm, probably altering it with additional verses at the time of King Hezekiah. In any case, the psalm seems clearly to preserve northern language and ideas of Sinai theology, and does not postdate the appearance of Deuteronomy in Josiah's time. Psalm 78:10 thus assures us that the idea of a Sinai covenant, with its accompanying notions of both promise and duty, was rooted in liturgical tradition by Hosea's time.

The presentation of Hosea's marriage in Hos 1–3 provides additional strong evidence that Hosea advocated the Sinai covenant. Scholars agree that Hosea's troubled marriage symbolizes and explains the nature and history of God's troubled relationship with Israel. Hosea's choice of a spouse who was sexually promiscuous, and the way that he gives doomful symbolic names to their children, provided Israel with a living, "theatrical" demonstration of how God saw them. In worshiping the fertility deities of Canaan, they had acted toward God like a promiscuous and unfaithful spouse, broken their "marriage" vows.

Hosea 1–3 does not overtly state that the prophet's marriage symbolizes a "covenant." However, he had no need to do so.[10] Marriage was a covenant in ancient times (cf. Ezek 16:8; Mal 2:14), involving a bilateral, mutually committed, and legally binding relationship. The understanding of covenant implicit in Hosea's marriage may not carry with it the full baggage of later biblical texts. In using marriage symbolism, however, Hosea shows the relationship between God and Israel includes at least the minimal features of what we call the Sinai covenant.[11]

Hosea's use of marital love to symbolize God's covenantal relationship with Israel may draw on some language in ancient vassal treaties from well before his own time. The parties to these treaties—human sovereigns and their subjects—spoke of their covenant relationship in terms of "love." As in Hosea, the vassal treaties use love language to emphasize the pure devotion and genuine obedience that should characterize covenant loyalty. One of the Amarna letters between the Egyptian pharaoh and his northern vassals (fourteenth century B.C.E.) refers to such treaty language. In the tablet (EA 114:68), the governor of Byblos, Rib-Adda, asks the pharaoh: "Who will love you, should I die?"[12]

The details of Hosea's naming of his third (probably illegitimate) child clinch the argument that his symbolic marriage is all about the Sinai

---

10. See, e.g., Frank M. Cross, "Kinship and Covenant in Ancient Israel," in *From Epic to Canon: History and Literature in Ancient Israel* (Baltimore: Johns Hopkins University Press, 1998), 13 and n. 36.

11. In their reuse of Hosea's symbolism, the writings of later prophets confirm this conclusion. Jeremiah and Ezekiel make explicit that the relationship pictured by Hosea's marriage is specifically a "covenant." Jeremiah 31:32 and Ezek 16:59–63 specifically interpret the symbolism of God's marriage with Israel, which derives from Hosea, as an analogy for the "covenant" (ברית).

12. Cf. William L. Moran, "The Ancient Near Eastern Background of the Love of God in Deuteronomy," *CBQ* 25 (1963): 79. To love the pharaoh is to serve him faithfully and exclusively. As the archaic Song of Deborah shows, Hosea would not have been the first within Israel to extend this political language of love as an analogy for Israel's proper relationship to God (Judg 5:31).

covenant and its undoing by the people. After the son is born, God commands Hosea in 1:9, "Name him 'Lo-ammi' [Not-my-people], for you are not my people, and I no longer belong to you." This specific type of language appears elsewhere in the Bible, but in an opposite, positive form. Usually, Yahweh promises Israel that "I will be your God, and you shall be my people" (e.g., Deut 29:12–13; Jer 7:23; 24:7). Since the late nineteenth century, scholars have called this formulaic expression the "covenant formula" (*Bundesformel*).[13] Since, in a verbal play, Hosea turns the formula on its head as an annulment of the covenant, the covenantal formula must predate the prophet. Hosea must have assumed that his audience was familiar with a formulaic expression about a bilateral, contingent covenant with God.

The Witness of Micah

While Hosea was symbolically enacting the Sinai covenant in the north, the prophet Micah was propounding it to the people of Judah in the south. Although Micah exercised his prophetic role in Jerusalem, his emphasis was not on the covenant traditions of Zion or God's promises to the Davidic line. In tension with the Jerusalem covenant of unconditional grant and promise (see 2 Sam 7), Micah instead staunchly advocated the bilateral and conditional covenant of Sinai.

Micah's advocacy of the Sinai covenant is clearest in Mic 6:1–8, a prophetic "lawsuit" (ריב) against Israel for breach of covenant.[14] The passage reads:

> [1] Hear what the LORD says:
>   Rise, plead your case before the mountains,
>   and let the hills hear your voice.
> [2] Hear, you mountains, the controversy of the LORD,
>   and you enduring foundations of the earth;
> for the LORD has a controversy with his people,
>   and he will contend with Israel.
> [3] "O my people, what have I done to you?
>   In what have I wearied you? Answer me!

---

13. The books of Jeremiah and Ezekiel both link the correlative formula "your God—my people" specifically with the term "covenant" (ברית). See Jer 11:3–4; 31:33; 32:38–40; Ezek 37:26–27.

14. The lawsuit pattern in Mic 6 is one of the pieces of evidence that leads A. S. van der Woude to connect the second part of Micah closely with Hosea and Jeremiah. See further van der Woude, "Deutero-Micha," 372.

[4] For I brought you up from the land of Egypt,
     and redeemed you from the house of slavery;
and I sent before you Moses,
     Aaron, and Miriam.
[5] O my people, remember now what King Balak of Moab devised,
     what Balaam son of Beor answered him,
and what happened from Shittim to Gilgal,
     that you may know the saving acts of the LORD."
[6] "With what shall I come before the LORD,
     and bow myself before God on high?
Shall I come before him with burnt offerings,
     with calves a year old?
[7] Will the LORD be pleased with thousands of rams,
     with ten thousands of rivers of oil?
Shall I give my firstborn for my transgression,
     the fruit of my body for the sin of my soul?"
[8] He has told you, O mortal, what is good;
     and what does the LORD require of you
but to do justice, and to love kindness,
     and to walk humbly with your God?

There is no doubt that a divine lawsuit is precisely what lies before us in this text. In 6:2 Micah proclaims that "Yahweh has a case against his people, and he will contend with Israel." In the course of the passage, the picture of 6:2 is confirmed as Yahweh presents arguments before witnesses. God is an injured party, that is, a plaintiff, upset about a preexisting agreement. The passage thus presupposes that Israel and God have bound themselves together in a legal agreement, a bilateral covenant. David Pleins rightly describes the covenant lawsuit as betraying covenant thinking in its simplest form.[15]

The suppositions of the passage are authentic to the historical prophet Micah. In 6:7, with its references to lavish offerings, the prophet

---

15. David Pleins, *Social Visions of the Hebrew Bible: A Theological Introduction* (Louisville: Westminster John Knox, 2001), 77. See also Graham I. Davies, *Hosea* (NCBC; Grand Rapids: Eerdmans, 1992), 272; Kenton L. Sparks, *Ethnicity and Identity in Ancient Israel: Prolegomena to the Study of Ethnic Sentiments and Their Expression in the Hebrew Bible* (Winona Lake, Ind.: Eisenbrauns, 1998), 147 nn. 63–64. The text pictures litigation against Yahweh's vassal people because of their dereliction, and this is true regardless of whether comparative study is able to pin the text's language to any one particular ancient treaty model. That a regularized depiction of Israel's covenant, such as that found in Deuteronomy, only developed with time is no argument against tracing earlier forms of Israel's covenant, which may appear less articulated. (In fact, however, components such as the involvement of cosmic witnesses in the Mican lawsuit [6:2] do parallel specific features of related ancient Near Eastern vassal-treaty forms.)

likely reminisces about the extravagant offerings of King Hezekiah depicted in 2 Chr 30:24.

The portrayal of the covenant between God and the Israelites in Mic 6:1–8 does more than merely agree with the general understandings of covenant in the Sinai stream of tradition. The passage uses actual motifs and idioms from the tradition stream to define the covenant's contours. Some of its language is so close to Deuteronomy that one has little choice but to consider this passage a precursor of Deuteronomy from the southern kingdom.[16]

Verse 4 begins a short, two-verse summary of the saving actions of God that first delivered Israel out of Egypt. The summary is highly reminiscent of the historical prologue of ancient vassal treaties. It begins by describing God's liberation of Israel "from Egypt land," from what is termed the "house of slavery." Only biblical texts within the Sinai stream of tradition use this language. The latter phrase, "house of slavery," occurs alone in Exod 13:3, 14 (both E). The double phrase, "from Egypt land" and "house of slavery," occurs in Exod 20:2 (E); Deut 5:6; 6:12; 8:14; 13:11; Josh 24:17; Judg 6:8; and Jer 34:13.

Further, Mic 6:4 is using rare diction in speaking of God's "ransom"/"redemption" of Israel out of the "house of slavery." This verbal combination occurs elsewhere in the Hebrew Bible only in Deut 7:8 and 13:5. This evidence particularly demonstrates that the Sinai theology of the book of Deuteronomy came from southern circles as well as from the north. As Leslie Allen states, "The second clause in verse 4 uses terminology closely associated with Deuteronomy.... If that book represents traditions treasured in the North and only made public in Judah in Josiah's reign, its use by Micah a century or so before constitutes a problem."[17]

Micah's short recitation of Israel's holy history ends as it began, using the language of the Sinai stream of tradition. Like other biblical texts about the Sinai covenant, 6:5 emphasizes "knowing" Yahweh. Hosea 4:1, for example, similarly complains about a lack of "knowledge" of God as

---

16. Some scholars rashly assign Mic 6:1–8 to a late editor from the era of Jeremiah or the exile, whom they say introduced its Deuteronomy-like features. See, e.g., James L. Mays, *Micah: A Commentary* (OTL; Philadelphia: Westminster, 1976), 130–31; Hans W. Wolff, *Micah: A Commentary* (trans. G. Stansell; CC; Minneapolis: Augsburg, 1990), 168, 170–72. This move is unnecessary, unless one presupposes either that Deuteronomy had no precursors at all, or that all of Deuteronomy's sources were northern.

17. Leslie C. Allen, *The Books of Joel, Obadiah, Jonah, and Micah* (NICOT; Grand Rapids: Eerdmans, 1976), 366 n. 18. Compare also the treatment of Walter Beyerlin, who argues that Micah's eighth-century language here was taken up by Deuteronomy (Beyerlin, *Kulttraditionen Israels*, 67–70).

part of a covenant lawsuit. Micah's phrase "the saving acts of Yahweh" (צדקות יהוה) is also significant. Outside of Micah, this phrase occurs only in Judg 5:11 and 1 Sam 12:7 (B source).

In 6:6–8, the final part of our lawsuit text, a courtroom dialogue ensues. A representative Israelite asks a series of questions and then receives a reply. The questions ask how to restore a proper relationship with God. The answer is noteworthy. It baldly states that the people of Israel have long known the requirements of the Sinai covenant: "He has declared to you, human, what is good" (6:8). Tradition recalls an identical declaration of Moses to Israel. Like Micah, Moses reminded Israel of its firm knowledge of covenant law since Sinai: "He declared to you his covenant" (Deut 4:13).[18]

The passage ends with a one-line summary of the covenant's requirements; its style and idiom betray its identity as a Sinai text (compare Hos 12:6; Deut 10:12; 1 Sam 12:24 [B source]). In particular, the combination of the terms "justice" (משפט) and "loyalty" (חסד) here, though not confined exclusively to the Sinai stream of tradition, is characteristic of that stream. The usage appears in Hos 2:19; 12:6; and Jer 9:24.

THE LAND AS ISRAEL'S INHERITANCE

THE WITNESS OF HOSEA

The book of Hosea makes clear in several places that the land of Canaan is Yahweh's possession. As we saw above, Hos 8:1 refers to this territory as "the house of Yahweh." Hosea quotes God using the same idiom in Hos 9:15, when God refers to the land as "my house." Removing any lingering doubts, Hos 9:3 unequivocally calls the territory "Yahweh's land."

The book of Hosea also makes clear that God has given the territory to the people of Israel. God remains the liege lord of the territory, but the Israelites hold the land as a fiefdom. Hosea 10:1 assumes Israel's possession of the fiefdom, calling it "his [Israel's] land." Similarly, Hos 5:7 refers to the Israelites' territory as their "portion" or "tract." The verse uses a Hebrew term (חלק) that summons up images of individual farmers working parcels of land to provide for their families (cf. Mic 2:4).

Beyond these individual focal verses, the whole book of Hosea revolves around the issue of land. Hosea's prophecies focus on agriculture

---

18. Beyerlin, *Kulttraditionen Israels*, 51.

and fertility. The people should be holding the land in gratitude, acknowledging Yahweh's lordship over it and cultivating its bounty in the interests of family and community. Instead, they have credited Baal, the Canaanite god of the rainstorm, with its fertility, and they do not recognize its covenantal significance.

The series of promises of reconciliation and covenant renewal in Hos 2:14–23 provide one good, detailed presentation of Hosea's theological tenet that the land is Israel's inheritance from God. The text reads, in part:

> [14] Therefore, I will now allure her,
>   and bring her into the wilderness,
>   and speak tenderly to her.
> [15] From there I will give her her vineyards,
>   and make the Valley of Achor a door of hope.
> There she shall respond as in the days of her youth,
>   as at the time when she came out of the land of Egypt.
>
> [21] On that day I will answer, says the LORD,
>   I will answer the heavens
>   and they shall answer the earth;
> [22] and the earth shall answer the grain, the wine, and the oil,
>   and they shall answer Jezreel;
> [23] and I will sow him for myself in the land.
> And I will have pity on Lo-ruhamah,
>   and I will say to Lo-ammi, "You are my people";
>   and he shall say, "You are my God."

Verses 14–15 conclude a larger passage that stretches from Hos 2:2 through 2:15. The verses sound a note of hope for the future. They probably come from the early period of Hosea's work, around 750 B.C.E.

Editors have attached three short messages of promise after this initial note of hope. These messages, in 2:16–17, 18–20, and 21–23, perhaps date to a point in Hosea's prophetic career two decades later, around 733. Among these messages, 2:21–23 is of most interest.

The hopeful tone of 2:14–15 should not mask the fact that this text is about apostate Israel's radical conversion. God leads all of Israel out of the land in a final, extreme attempt to convert the people. Once lured to the wilderness, Israel will finally see that the land lies open before them only through the grace of God. Their having to repeat their ancient settlement of God's land will demonstrate finally that the land is Yahweh's gift. As at the time of Joshua, the people will need to make their way into the heart of the land through the Valley of Achor (cf. Josh 7).

God's terse statement in 2:15 that "I will give her her vineyards from there [i.e., from the wilderness]," succinctly brings home these points.

Israel's arable land has always legally belonged to Yahweh. Israel possessed "her vineyards" only as God's gift. God can, and will, take them
away for a time because of Israel's unfaithfulness.

As noted, 2:21–23 add a short message of promise, which elaborates
on Israel's future conversion. The message describes God's act of resettling Israel in the land. The description uses a strong measure of fertility
language: Hosea declares Yahweh, not the Canaanite deities, sovereign
over land and fertility.

In 2:22 Hosea symbolically names the people "Jezreel." He likewise
symbolized the people with this name in Hos 1:4, but there "Jezreel" had
connotations of bloodshed and punishment (cf. 2 Kgs 10:11). Here, in its
literal Hebrew meaning, "God sows/plants," "Jezreel" has a clear conno-
tation of fertility and bounty (cf. Hos 1:11).

Verse 23 goes on to describe God's reestablishment of Israel in Palestine using the clear fertility image of God sowing the people, like seed, in
the land. The Psalms of Asaph preserve the very same imagery (see Ps
80:8–9, 15). In accenting the phrase "in the land," the prophet reiterates
Sinai theology's emphasis that Israelite farmers should have vested rights
to their arable land.

A look at another text, Hos 5:8—6:6, is helpful at this point. I am
especially interested in one verse, Hos 5:10.

[10] The princes of Judah have become
   like those who remove the landmark;
on them I will pour out
   my wrath like water.

In its context, this verse reveals Hosea's covenantal perspective on
sharing the land. The prophet decries Israel's abrogation of its vows to
apportion God's land fairly and share it in support of the livelihood of all.

The historical context of Hos 5:10 is Israel's war with Judah in the
730s—the Syro-Ephraimite war, in which the Israelites invaded each
other's kingdoms. Judah even annexed some of the northern kingdom's
territory as part of one counterattack.[19]

Hosea denounces Judah for this act. He obviously viewed it as a will-
ful disregard of the boundaries God established in distributing the
promised land among all Israel's tribes. Hosea's sympathy with God's
wrath reveals the breadth of his theology. Clearly, his theological concerns

---

19. The northern kingdom had provoked the war to get Judah to join them in a revolt
against the Assyrian Empire. Assyria entered the war on Judah's side, however, and the
north soon found itself counterattacked by Judah.

about Israel's use of God's land extend beyond issues of the land's fertility. In accord with the Sinai tradition stream, the way Israel shared its land among its members was also a key element of Hosea's theology.

In castigating Judah, Hosea uses an image of boundary stones dividing the fields of farmers. His imagery is the Sinai stream of tradition's specific way of speaking about the tenure rights of Israelite lineages to their inherited land. Deuteronomy 19:14 and 27:17 use the same, rare language. Deuteronomy holds that it is a sacred covenant duty to preserve the fixed landholdings that sacral allotment established for each of Israel's family lines. Hosea agrees. To offend against these land rights is to offend against Yahweh's covenant.

For this offense, among others, God announces in Hos 5:14 that God will tear Judah like a lion, and there will be none to deliver. Hosea takes the language of this threat straight from Ps 50:22. In this psalm of Asaph, God threatens Israel that "I will tear" (אטרף) and "there will be none to deliver" (אין מציל).

It is not remarkable that Hosea pronounced Hos 5:10, 14 against the southern kingdom, Judah. As a bearer of Sinai theology, Hosea was a messenger to all the tribes of Israel. He considered them one vassal people of God. What is unusual is that Hosea does not have more to say about maintaining the boundary lines God used to allot the promised land among the Israelite tribes and families in both north and south.

Forced to choose his battles, Hosea must have trained his prophetic focus on pronouncing Yahweh's ownership of a land that many others claimed for the Canaanite god, Baal. In doing so, he subordinated his concerns about Israelite farmers' rights to their allotted portions of this land. In a different situation in Judah, Micah was able to turn his undivided attention to the latter problem.

The Witness of Micah

Much of the burden of the book of Micah is to hold the ruling stratum of Jerusalem responsible for oppressing Judean country farmers and driving them off their land (Mic 2:2; 2:9; 3:3; 3:9–10). Briefly stated, Jerusalem's ruling nobles were mercilessly building up large landed estates, "latifundia," for themselves during Micah's time. Their gains were at the expense of Judah's country farmers. By harshly applying debt laws, they foreclosed on numerous farmers to accumulate vast plots of farmland to form estates. Militarization of the countryside in preparation for Assyrian invasion exacerbated the farmers' problems.

In Micah's Sinai theology, the land belonged to Yahweh, who had allotted it to Israelite lineage groups and families as a permanent, inalienable inheritance. He thus struggled against the land grabbing of his times, not only out of solidarity with his Judean countryfolk, but also because of his commitment to Sinai covenant tradition.

Albrecht Alt's classic, scholarly assessment of the social and economic scenario behind Micah is correct. The Jerusalem lords

> through a rigorous and excessive application of the law of obligations enslaved or drove away the impoverished, small farmer with his wife and children and formed estates out of the appropriated property, where according to the old sacral ordinance of Yahweh, the principle "one-man—one house—one inherited plot" should be and remain unconditionally valid.[20]

Micah's strong affirmation of Sinai tradition's view of the land comes sharply into focus in Mic 2:1–5, a prophetic oracle of woe.

> [1] Alas for those who devise wickedness
>   and evil deeds on their beds!
> When the morning dawns, they perform it,
>   because it is in their power.
> [2] They covet fields, and seize them;
>   houses, and take them away;
> they oppress householder and house,
>   people and their inheritance.
> [3] Therefore thus says the LORD:
> Now, I am devising against this family an evil
>   from which you cannot remove your necks;
> and you shall not walk haughtily,
>   for it will be an evil time.
> [4] On that day they shall take up a taunt song against you,
>   and wail with bitter lamentation,
> and say, "We are utterly ruined;
>   the LORD alters the inheritance of my people;
> how he removes it from me!
>   Among our captors he parcels out our fields."
> [5] Therefore you will have no one to cast the line by lot
>   in the assembly of the LORD.

Scholars agree that this text is authentic to Micah of Moresheth. Its message fully supports the prophet's basic complaint about the selfishness of Jerusalem's leaders. The oracle does not have details that fix its

---

20. Albrecht Alt, "Micha 2,1–5: ΓΗΣ ΑΝΑΔΑΣΜΟΣ in Juda," in *Kleine Schriften zur Geschichte des Volkes Israel* (ed. M. Noth; 3 vols.; Munich: Beck, 1959), 3:374.

date precisely, but it does seem to reflect a calm period and a thriving Jerusalem economy. Micah probably delivered it sometime in the late eighth century, when an Assyrian invasion of Judah was possible but still below the dawning horizon.

The oracle begins with a cry: "Alas for those devising wickedness, working out evil deeds on their beds!" (Mic 2:1). The picture is one of the Jerusalem land-grabbers lying awake at night, planning to seize new lands for their estates. Verse 2 makes this indictment unambiguous. "They covet fields, and seize them; houses, and take them away; they oppress householder and house, people and their inheritance."

Sentencing and punishment follow indictment. Thus, a lengthy announcement of imminent judgment takes up 2:3–5. By 2:4, the prophet's words even border on harassment.

However legal the land-grabbers' practices were under the Judean state law of Micah's time, the prophet condemned them as diametrically opposed to Sinai theological tradition. His forms of expression assure us of this. Consider, for example, the "coveting" (חמד) of neighbors' houses and fields, which Micah describes as going on in 2:2. This description has clear verbal ties with the Sinai prohibitions of coveting in Exod 20:17 and Deut 5:21.

The language of 2:3–4 further reflects Sinai traditions. Micah's quote of the future lament of the land-grabbers bears a close resemblance to a similar quote by Jeremiah, a known proponent of Sinai traditions and of the theology of Deuteronomy. Jeremiah 9:19, like Mic 2:4, combines the term "lamentation" (נהי) and the Hebrew root "devastate" (שדד). This usage of language does not occur elsewhere in the Bible.[21]

The language of Micah's final threat in 2:5 is a final direct link to Sinai tradition. The verse threatens the Jerusalem lords with exclusion from Yahweh's land. An epochal, new distribution of land is about to set affairs straight within Judah. The families of Judah will redivide the land of Israel in a just and even manner, and the land-grabbers will have no part in it. In describing the future ceremony of redistributing Judah's land, the verse uses colorful idioms and expressions. These idioms are worth a close look.

Micah combines the Hebrew term "cast" (שלך) and the term "lot" (גורל). This combination of terms is found elsewhere in the Hebrew Bible

---

21. The Jeremiah text uses the language to depict wailing at the time of the Babylonian invasion of 586 B.C.E.: "A sound of wailing is heard from Zion: 'How we are ruined!'" In Mic 2:4, Jerusalem's lamentation occurs earlier and for a more specific reason. The Jerusalem leaders, a subgroup within Judah, will lose their wrongfully amassed estates at the hands of the Assyrians.

only in Josh 18:8, 10. In this Sinai text about the original settlement of the land, Joshua "cast lots on behalf of" Israelites in several tribes in a process of sacral land allotment at Shiloh.

The use of the term "boundary line" (חבל) in conjunction with land allotment is also from Sinai tradition. Asaphite Ps 78:55 uses very similar language. The text reads, "He [God] drove out the nations before them [Israel]; allotted them [their] inheritance by line [חבל], and settled the tribes of Israel in their tents." With the possible exception of Amos 7:17, all other biblical passages that use this phraseology are associated with Sinai theology. Harry Nasuti is thus correct in arguing that this type of language is characteristic of the Sinai tradition stream.[22]

A second text from Micah, Mic 2:6–11, confirms our developing impressions about Micah's theology of land. The passage follows on the one we just examined, and presents a verbal controversy between Micah and some of his opponents. The controversy probably took place in the same period we have been discussing—early in Micah's prophetic career. In this text, in fact, Micah seems to be answering charges made against him precisely because he was delivering the type of woe oracle we have just looked at.

> [6] "Do not preach"—thus they preach—
>   "one should not preach of such things;
>   disgrace will not overtake us."
> [7] Should this be said, O house of Jacob?
>   Is the LORD's patience exhausted?
>   Are these his doings?
> Do not my words do good
>   to one who walks uprightly?
> [8] But you rise up against my people as an enemy;
>   you strip the robe from the peaceful,
> from those who pass by trustingly
>   with no thought of war.
> [9] The women of my people you drive out
>   from their pleasant houses;
>   from their young children you take away
>   my glory forever.
> [10] Arise and go;
>   for this is no place to rest,
> because of uncleanness that destroys
>   with a grievous destruction.

---

22. Harry P. Nasuti, *Tradition-History and the Psalms of Asaph* (SBLMS 88; Atlanta: Scholars Press, 1988), 91.

[11] If someone were to go about uttering empty falsehoods,
   saying, "I will preach to you of wine and strong drink,"
   such a one would be the preacher for this people!

The passage begins in its first two verses by quoting Micah's opponents, probably the elite circles that were doing the land grabbing. King
Hezekiah's army officers, who were militarizing the countryside at this
time, may be among those defending themselves here as well. The opponents try to silence Micah and his supporters. "All of you should stop
your ranting!" they announce. Their argument is that God is more committed to the people of Jerusalem than Micah supposes, and more patient
with their shortcomings (2:7).

The opponents probably base their defense—that God is patient—on
theological traditions in Israel alternative to those of Micah. Specifically,
their alternative tradition is probably the royal theology of Zion that was
popular in Jerusalem, especially among its leaders. The Zion theology
of Jerusalem's rulers and priests stressed God's permanent and long-
suffering loyalty to Jerusalem and to the royal line of David. Good
examples of the theme that God is very slow to anger appear in such
Zion-oriented texts as Pss 86:5, 15; 103:8; 145:8; and Joel 2:13.

Micah responds to his opponents in 2:8–9. According to Sinai theology, he reminds them, God's grace and promise are not cheap. Salvation
comes freely in the Sinai covenant, but, if accepted, it calls for a real
response. The Sinai covenant should provoke a sense of obligation and
responsibility from people. The behavior of the Jerusalem lords, however,
does not reflect such a sensibility. Despite the covenant's call to treat their
countryfolk as neighbors, the land-grabbers and military officers have
forced the country farmers to respond to them as a hostile "enemy" force.

Micah's specific accusations against his opponents strongly reflect
the legal stipulations of Sinai tradition. Verse 8 recalls the covenant stipulations protecting debtors in Exod 22:26–27 (E) and Deut 24:12–13.
Verse 9 charges the opponents with violating Sinai laws protecting
women and children, such as those of Exod 22:22 and Deut 27:19. The
Jerusalem lords are especially guilty of violating the principle of a
family's right to the ongoing tenure of their arable land, a principle clear,
for example, from Exod 20:17 (E) and Deut 25:5–10. Walter Beyerlin is
correct: Micah's meaning in 2:9 is that the land-grabbers are violating
Israelite progeny's fundamental Yahwistic right to the landed inheritance belonging to them.[23]

---

23. Beyerlin, *Kulttraditionen Israels*, 60.

Micah ends his dispute in 2:10–11 by announcing the fate of his opponents. Micah's opponents will experience eviction from the land, and the prophet depicts this punishment in a manner fully in line with Sinai perspectives and images. He states that the land-grabbers have forfeited the land as a "resting place" (מנוחה), reflecting the way in Sinai tradition that God gave Israel "rest" after their settlement of Canaan. As Mays states, here "מנוחה ['place of rest'] is understood in the specialized sense it has in the Deuteronomic vocabulary—as a term for the land as a gift of YHWH's salvation, a synonym for 'inheritance' (Deut 12:9; 1 Kgs 8:56)."[24] Micah's opponents have lost all rights to this Sinai-covenant blessing of "rest."

GOD AS SOLE LANDLORD

God is the liege lord of Israel's territory, according to Sinai theology, and sovereign over the land's recurring cycle of fertility. The land of Canaan with Yahweh's constant care alone supports Israel's life. Israel needed to acknowledge this care through offerings and sacrifices. As Victor Matthews and Don Benjamin summarize, "Yahweh was the only landlord in Israel; the land of Israel was to be used only as Yahweh prescribed, and only with a commitment to offer Yahweh sacrifices as a commission."[25]

Deuteronomy 26:1–11 encapsulates these truths. According to 26:10 Israel should respond to God's agricultural provision through proper worship, in particular through gifts of tribute each year from the initial fruits of the land's harvests. The text seems straightforward on the surface, but underlying its stress on acknowledging Yahweh in worship is the hint of an opposing threat. Unfortunately, the worship of alternative, Canaanite deities, who specialized in fertility, proved an almost irresistible temptation to Israel.

---

24. Mays, *Micah*, 71; cf. Gerhard von Rad, "The Promised Land and Yahweh's Land in the Hexateuch," in *The Problem of the Hexateuch and Other Essays* (trans. E. W. T. Dicken; Edinburgh: Oliver & Boyd, 1966), 92.

25. Victor H. Matthews and Don C. Benjamin, *The Social World of Ancient Israel, 1250–587 BCE* (Peabody, Mass.: Hendrickson, 1993), 188. The authors further note that it was the priests' duty to collect Yahweh's portion at harvest and to instruct the people in the correct use of Yahweh's land (188). The fact that Israel's sacrifices were mere tokens in comparison to Yahweh's agricultural blessings emphasized that the Sinai covenant was a suzerainty brand of treaty, that is, a relationship between unequals (191).

The Witness of Hosea

Hosea 2:8–13 perfectly illustrates the incredible seduction of Canaanite fertility religion. The text is part of a larger grouping of sayings about Hosea's unfaithful wife. As the reader will recall, the wife symbolizes Israel and its love affair with the fertility deities of Canaan. The unfaithfulness of the "wife," God argues, is more than sufficient grounds for trial and punishment. Verses 8–13 form a coherent subsection of this discourse. The pictures of prosperity (2:8) and ritual celebration (2:11, 13) within the passage suggest that it dates to an early point in Hosea's prophetic career. Perhaps it comes from around 750 B.C.E., when Assyria's military assaults still lay in the future.

> [8] She did not know
>> that it was I who gave her
>> the grain, the wine, and the oil,
> and who lavished upon her silver
>> and gold that they used for Baal.
> [9] Therefore I will take back
>> my grain in its time,
>> and my wine in its season;
> and I will take away my wool and my flax,
>> which were to cover her nakedness.
> [10] Now I will uncover her shame
>> in the sight of her lovers,
>> and no one shall rescue her out of my hand.
> [11] I will put an end to all her mirth,
>> her festivals, her new moons, her sabbaths,
>> and all her appointed festivals.
> [12] I will lay waste her vines and her fig trees,
>> of which she said,
> "These are my pay,
>> which my lovers have given me."
> I will make them a forest,
>> and the wild animals shall devour them.
> [13] I will punish her for the festival days of the Baals,
>> when she offered incense to them
> and decked herself with her ring and jewelry,
>> and went after her lovers,
>> and forgot me, says the LORD.

Verse 8's statement about Yahweh's provision of Israel's "grain, new wine, and olive oil" uses a string of vocabulary words that will later shape the language of Deuteronomy, the book that epitomizes the flowering of Sinai theology in Israel (Deut 7:13; 11:14; 12:17; 14:23; 18:4; 28:51).

Among the cross-references, Deut 18:4 commands Israel to "give [the Levites] the first fruits of your grain, your new wine, and your oil." This gift provides for the Levites' sustenance, and it allows Israel to acknowledge that God graciously provides God's people with their agricultural staples. H. W. Wolff takes the special language of 2:8 as "evidence for Hosea's close connection with those groups … to which Deuteronomy ultimately may be traced."[26]

According to Hosea, Israel is culpable for forgetting that Yahweh alone provides its staples—its "grain, new wine, and olive oil" (2:8). The fertility deities of Canaan had won Israel's affections. These gods, who generally represented the natural forces of the world, were more immanent in nature than Yahweh. They seemed in closer control of the land's forces of fertility. The tablets from Ugarit leave no doubt that the gods of Canaan claimed to provide the grain, wine, and oil that 2:8 cites (see KTU 1.16.III.12f.).

In response to Israel's forgetfulness about the true source of fertility, 2:9 threatens that Yahweh will "take back" all God's agricultural gifts. With a fourfold repetition of the possessive pronoun, God declares that God will withhold "my grain," "my new wine," "my wool," and "my flax." Indeed, first-person verbs occur near the beginning of each verse within 2:9–13, stressing Yahweh's sole control over the fertility of the land. This emphatic style aims to shake Israel into remembering the Sinai traditions that it has forgotten.

At the end of our passage, 2:13 contains at least three further examples of distinctive Sinai phraseology. First, the verse's statement that Israel "burned incense to Baal" (קטר לבעל) became a favorite expression in the Deuteronomistic editorial layer of Jeremiah (layer C; Jer 7:9; 11:13, 17; 32:29; cf. 2 Kgs 23:5). Second, the description of Israel's apostasy in worship as "going after [other gods]" ([אלהים אחרים] הלך אחרי) becomes a characteristic idiom in both Deuteronomy (Deut 4:3; 6:14; 8:19; 11:28; 13:2; 28:14) and Jeremiah (e.g., Jer 2:5; 7:9; 8:2; 9:13; 11:10). It also appears in Judg 2:12, 19; 1 Kgs 11:10; 18:18, 21; 21:26; and 2 Kgs 17:15.

Thirdly, 2:13's language about Israel's "forgetting God" (שכח) recurs later in Deut 6:12; 8:11, 14, 19; Jer 3:21; 13:25; 23:27; Judg 3:7; and 1 Sam 12:9 (B source). The liturgical traditions of the Psalms of Asaph were a source of the expression in Hosea (see Ps 50:22). Hosea, in turn, passed the expression on to the Deuteronomists. As Wolff states, Hosea's words here provide the Deuteronomists "their early theological antecedents."[27]

---

26. Hans W. Wolff, *Hosea: A Commentary on the Book of the Prophet Hosea* (trans. G. Stansell; Hermeneia; Philadelphia: Fortress, 1974), 37.

27. Wolff, *Hosea*, 40; cf. Weinfeld, *Deuteronomic School*, 367; Nasuti, *Psalms of Asaph*, 62.

Hosea 13:1–3, 4–8 is a second major text in Hosea witnessing to Hosea's belief that God is Israel's sole landlord. It reads:

¹ When Ephraim spoke, there was trembling;
    he was exalted in Israel;
    but he incurred guilt through Baal and died.
² And now they keep on sinning
    and make a cast image for themselves,
idols of silver made according to their understanding,
    all of them the work of artisans.
"Sacrifice to these," they say.
    People are kissing calves!
³ Therefore they shall be like the morning mist
    or like the dew that goes away early,
like chaff that swirls from the threshing floor
    or like smoke from a window.
⁴ Yet I have been the LORD your God
    ever since the land of Egypt;
you know no God but me,
    and besides me there is no savior.
⁵ It was I who fed you in the wilderness,
    in the land of drought.
⁶ When I fed them, they were satisfied;
    they were satisfied, and their heart was proud;
    therefore they forgot me.
⁷ So I will become like a lion to them,
    like a leopard I will lurk beside the way.
⁸ I will fall upon them like a bear robbed of her cubs,
    and will tear open the covering of their heart;
there I will devour them like a lion,
    as a wild animal would mangle them.

This section of Hosea presents two prophetic announcements of judgment against the northern kingdom, 13:1–3 and 4–8. The two announcements seem to come from the last five years or so of the northern kingdom's existence. Hosea's statement about Ephraim's death (13:1) probably looks back from the early 720s on devastations inflicted by Assyria in 733. God's extreme anger here, and particularly the ferocity with which God is determined to put an end to Israel (13:8), suggest a frustration that has been building over the course of Hosea's career. It will soon come to a head in the destruction of the northern kingdom in 722.

In Hos 13:1–3, the prophet begins by describing how Ephraim has fallen from being a respected and feared power. The people's power and success led them to abandon Yahweh and adopt the fertility religion of Canaan, with its Baal worship. This betrayal of Yahweh through failure of allegiance in worship broke a fundamental requirement of the Sinai covenant: exclusive worship of Yahweh as the landlord of Canaan.

Verses 1–2 indict Israel for this apostasy by naming its many ritual offenses. Israel is guilty not only of Baal worship in general but also of making molten images that the people worshiped as idols. The evocative language of 13:3 announces God's penalty. As in Asaphite Ps 83:12–13, those who try to wrest control of God's pastures from Yahweh end up as "chaff before the wind."

For Hosea, the prime example of Israel's resort to molten images, which were anathema to Sinai theology, was the bull image at the major northern shrine of Bethel. King Jeroboam I had erected this image two centuries before Hosea's time (cf. Hos 8:5–6; 10:5; 1 Kgs 12:26–33). Jeroboam and his cohorts may have presented the bull image of Bethel as simply a pedestal for the divine presence of Yahweh at the sanctuary. Nevertheless, many people worshiped it as an image of Baal—an "idol" (13:2).[28]

Before turning to 13:4–8, I should pause to note the distinctive Sinai idiom of Hos 13:1–3. Verse 2 echoes the language of Asaphite Ps 78. Hosea and the psalm agree that the people's main problem is their disregard of Yahweh despite God's provision (Ps 78:17–20). In both Hosea and the psalm, God (not Baal!) supplies wondrous provision, and yet the people unrelentingly "continue(d) to sin" (Hos 13:2; Ps 78:17).

Hosea goes on to emphasize that Israel's worship images are nothing more than the "work" of "artisans" (13:2b). Hosea's use of this particular vocabulary is striking. Deuteronomy 27:15 and Jer 10:3, 9 use the exact same phraseology. For very similar diction, see such Sinai texts as Mic 5:13; Deut 4:28; 2 Kgs 22:17; Jer 1:16; 25:6 (C layer).

These cross-references confirm that the distinctive Sinai idiom of Deuteronomy and Jeremiah had earlier antecedents. As I have been arguing, biblical Yahwism did not evolve out of nothing at the time of King Josiah's great reform. It traces back to Hosea and Micah, and, as I shall argue later, to even earlier times.

The second section of the passage makes up Hos 13:4–8. It begins in 13:4–6, which charges Israel with conduct very antithetical to their history with God. Although God specially elected Israel (13:4), cared for them in the wilderness (13:5), and gave them satiety in Canaan's arable land (13:6), Israel has responded with pride and infidelity to the covenant.

---

28. Verse 2 refers to kissing the calves, and 1 Kgs 19:18 explicitly links this ritual of kissing to the worship of Baal. Beyond a reference to the monumental images of Bethel and Dan, Hosea probably also thinks here of the many smaller molten images that Israelites of the time used in popular, family worship.

Hosea expresses the same complaint elsewhere in the book (e.g., Hos 4:7; 10:1). The marvelous care of God for Israel met only ingratitude. God's watchful care of the land's fertility should particularly have provoked the people's grateful response. Instead, their bounty focused the people completely on their harvests. James Mays correctly writes, "Israel's true love was the grain ... no matter whether they thought of themselves as Yahwists, their worship was a fertility cult."[29]

Asaphite Ps 78:29–31 closely mirrors the way that Hos 13:4–8 develops this theme. Like Hosea, the psalm describes how God provided for Israel after the exodus only to experience the people's ungrateful neglect. With their shared outrage that satiety from God's provision only alienates the people from God, both display a distinct motif of the Sinai stream of tradition (וישבעו, Hos 13:6; Ps 78:29). Eventually, Deuteronomy takes up this warning that satiety can make the people forget God. Like Hos 13:6, Deut 8:12–14 speaks of the "satisfaction" of the people leading to their "forgetting" God.

I observed above, in discussing Hos 2:13, that within Sinai tradition "forgetting" God (שכח; Hos 13:6; Deut 8:14) was characteristic phraseology for covenant infidelity. Here in Hos 13:4–6, as in 2:13, forgetting God means worshiping the local fertility deities of the land, mistaking the land's produce as gifts of these gods. Verse 4 confirms this. The covenant stipulation that Israel is violating involves knowing (i.e., covenanting with) other gods besides Yahweh.

The language of 13:4 draws on earlier texts within the Sinai stream of tradition, such as Exod 20:2 and Asaphite Ps 81:10. Each of these texts first pronounces God's identity as God of the exodus and of the Sinai covenant. They each then go on to assert that this identity gives God the right to set covenant policy for Israel's life in God's land. Fundamental to this policy is the people's obligation to worship Yahweh as the land's sole proprietor. Verse 4 takes its place alongside parallel Sinai texts in Exod 20:3; Ps 81:9; and Deut 5:7 that all command Israel to have "no other gods" besides their sole authentic landlord, Yahweh.

The Witness of Micah

The final editors of the book of Micah were the Deuteronomists, the school responsible for the flowering of Sinai theology. These Deuteronomistic editors added a few passages to the book of Micah, highlighting

---

29. James L. Mays, *Hosea: A Commentary* (OTL; Philadelphia: Westminster, 1969), 126.

their message about the exclusive worship owed to Yahweh. They wanted to be unmistakably clear that Yahweh is the sole overlord and landlord of Israel.

Micah 5:10–15 is one passage that Micah's editors added to the book. The passage looks forward expectantly to Israel's full purification from all foreign gods and worship items. It specifies that in the future God will cut off from Israel carved images, sacred pillars, and "Asherim." "You will no longer bow down to the work of your hands," the passage prophesies (Mic 5:13; cf. Hos 13:2, just examined).

This monotheistic ideal is not a late, foreign intrusion into Micah. We see it in earlier Micah passages as well, even in a passage dating from the very start of Micah's career. The passage that I have in mind is Mic 1:2–7.

> [2] Hear, you peoples, all of you;
>   listen, O earth, and all that is in it;
> and let the Lord GOD be a witness against you,
>   the Lord from his holy temple.
> [3] For lo, the LORD is coming out of his place,
>   and will come down and tread upon the high places of the earth.
> [4] Then the mountains will melt under him
>   and the valleys will burst open,
> like wax near the fire,
>   like waters poured down a steep place.
> [5] All this is for the transgression of Jacob
>   and for the sins of the house of Israel.
> What is the transgression of Jacob?
>   Is it not Samaria
> And what is the high place of Judah?
>   Is it not Jerusalem?
> [6] Therefore I will make Samaria a heap in the open country,
>   a place for planting vineyards.
> I will pour down her stones into the valley,
>   and uncover her foundations.
> [7] All her images shall be beaten to pieces,
>   all her wages shall be burned with fire,
>   and all her idols I will lay waste;
> for as the wages of a prostitute she gathered them,
>   and as the wages of a prostitute they shall again be used.

The destruction of Samaria, the capital of the north, is still pending in this passage (1:6). It comes from the same period—before 722 B.C.E., the date of the city's fall to the Assyrian army—when Hosea was active, early in Micah's career.

God makes an unusual physical appearance in this text (1:2–4, a theophany), an appearance for the specific purpose of punishing both the northern and southern capitals (1:5–7). God is clearly judging *cultic* apostasy in the land, not social and economic abuse. For starters, Micah indicts Jerusalem as a "high place," a shrine associated with aberrant worship (1:5).[30] He then goes on to prophesy that God's punishment of Samaria will destroy "idols" and "images," worship items anathema by Sinai standards (1:7).

This text in Micah appears strikingly akin to Hosea in its specific language about Israel's apostate worship. Take the language of 1:7, for example. According to the verse, when God destroys Samaria, "All her images shall be beaten to pieces, all her prostitute's pay shall be burned with fire, and all her idols I will lay waste; for as the pay of a prostitute she gathered them." The terms "image" (פסיל) and "idol" (עצב) in this quote are characteristic of Sinai tradition in general and of the prophecies of Hosea in particular.

Even more tellingly, as in Hos 2:12, presented above, and Hos 9:1, Micah metaphorically refers to the wealth of unfaithful Israel as "prostitute's pay" (אתנן). Micah and Hosea agree that Israel has misconstrued its wealth—its agricultural bounty and harvests—as the gift of fertility deities, such as Baal. The attraction of Israel to these deities, and the people's belief that the deities reward their devotion with bounty, amounts to wholesale "prostitution" as far as our prophets are concerned. What is worse, the people have funneled the wealth from the land's bounty—this "payment" for prostituting themselves to gods other than Yahweh—back into the production of images and into idolatrous worship.

Micah's distinctive, Sinai-oriented thought and language are so close to that of Hosea here that at least one scholar, Alfred Jepsen, has argued that Mic 1:6–7 is a misplaced utterance of Hosea.[31] Jepsen's thesis that Hosea authored a text in Micah is unacceptable, but scholars are generally agreed that Mic 1:7 certainly has the same ring as Hosea. Leslie Allen writes that Micah sounds "like a second Hosea" here; Wolff states that the verse's "diction is Hosean-Deuteronomistic"; and Mays writes that

---

30. Micah strongly resonates with Hos 10:8 here, which also parallels a term for transgression with the term "high place." It is in Sinai texts, such as those of Hosea and Micah, that preexilic references to high places have a clearly negative tone. Later on, within the Sinai stream of tradition, this antipathy will climax when 2 Kings attributes the destruction of Israel and Judah by their enemies largely to false worship on the high places (2 Kgs 17:9; 23:8, 13, 15, 19–20). See Nasuti, *Psalms of Asaph*, 92 n. 156; Wolff, *Micah*, 52.

31. Alfred Jepsen, "Kleine Beiträge zum Zwölfprophetenbuch," *ZAW* 56 (1938): 96–99.

the language of 1:7 reflects "Hosea's influence and that of the Deuteronomistic circles in which it was cherished."[32] This chorus of scholarly voices
strongly backs my contention that Micah is an eighth-century precursor
of Deuteronomy and the flowering of biblical Yahwism.

Other ties beyond its concern with idolatry link Mic 1:2–7 to the Sinai
stream of tradition. In 1:2 Micah uses the language of "witness" (עד) in
describing God's appearance and disruption of nature. This is characteristic language of Sinai tradition. Both Asaphite Ps 50:7 and Exod 19:21 (E)
associate God's theophany with God's "witnessing against" or "admon-
ishing" the people (עוד). In Mal 3:5, as well, God's epiphany is followed
by God's acting as a "witness."[33]

The blazing, earth-shaking divine appearance in 1:2–4 of our passage
strongly recalls God's theophany on Mt. Sinai. When Moses first
received the covenant, God's fiery appearance served as a witness of
God's character and as an admonishment to obedience (cf. Exod
20:18–19 [E]).

Additional features in our passage provide overwhelming evidence
that our passage is a Sinai text. Verse 3 describes Yahweh's abode as "his
place," just as Hos 5:15 does (cf. 1 Kgs 8:30). Verse 6 threatens that
Samaria will become a "heap of ruins" (עי), a term signaling Sinai tradition, as I shall discuss below in connection with Mic 3:12. Verse 7, finally,
prophesies the "smashing" (כתת) of Samaria's idols, an expression
occurring elsewhere only in Deut 9:21; 2 Kgs 18:4 and in a description of
Josiah's Deuteronomic reform in 2 Chr 34:7.

Despite the inclusion in Micah of the stress on worship of Yahweh
alone, I must admit that this Sinai tenet does not form a centerpiece of
Micah's message. Certainly, this stress is not present throughout Micah
the way that it is in Hosea. This fact requires an explanation.

I believe that we do not see more stress on cultic allegiance to
Yahweh in Micah because his early prophetic work in this area was
entirely successful. According to the available evidence, Micah had to
focus on the theme of faithfulness in worship only during the early part
of his career before King Hezekiah's accession.[34] It is tempting to link the
shift in Micah's message after Hezekiah began his reign directly with

32. Allen, *Micah*, 273; Wolff, *Micah*, 42, cf. pp. 18, 57; Mays, *Micah*, 47.

33. See Beyerlin, *Kulttraditionen Israels*, 37, 40; Mays, *Micah*, 40; Nasuti, *Psalms of Asaph*,
60; BDB, "עד," 729, 2.a.

34. As we have just seen, Mic 1:2–7 dates from before 722 B.C.E. After this prophecy,
Micah makes only sporadic, rather indirect, allusions to this theme (see Mic 1:13b; 2:10b; and
6:16a). These allusions mostly involve verses in which Micah uses vocabulary reminiscent of
complaints about wrongful worship elsewhere in the Bible.

Hezekiah's cultic reform (2 Kgs 18:1–6). Since this reform was in line with the hopes of Mic 1:2–7, I suggest that Micah's early advocacy of faithful worship positively influenced Hezekiah's promotion of Sinai standards of worship.

Although they likely approved of its cultic aspects, this does not mean that Micah's followers would have supported Hezekiah's entire political program. The group must have strongly objected to other, significant aspects of his policy, such as its aim of centralizing political and economic power in Jerusalem. Such centralization would have been at the expense of valued social structures and norms still intact in the Judean countryside.

This probable stance of the Micah group toward Hezekiah's policy would have meant that their castigations of Jerusalem's leaders for social oppression continued during his reign. This scenario explains the character of the book of Micah as we now have it. Indictments of economic and military injustice under Hezekiah's rule predominate over indictments for cultic wrongdoing.

CONDITIONAL TENANCY

In Sinai theology, the people cannot take the land for granted. Their tenancy is conditional. If the people forsake God, God may begin to sever the ties between God's land and the people (see, e.g., Deut 28:22–24). The land's fertility can diminish and plagues can strike. Enemy armies may attack, ravaging Israel's homeland and pillaging the bounty of the land. Ultimately, God, as the land's rightful proprietor, may even evict the people from the land (see, e.g., Deut 28:36–37, 41).

The Witness of Hosea

Extrabiblical, ancient Near Eastern treaties/covenants contain lists of curses that apply automatically to unfaithful vassals. One type of curse involves the frustration of various human efforts—especially efforts related to agriculture and related means of livelihood. Scholars commonly refer to such threats in ancient covenants as *futility curses*. Their standard form involves a description of an exertion of effort or labor paired with a promise that the exertion would prove fruitless. The presence of this type of curse in Hosea supports my argument that the prophet's theology stems from inherited covenantal traditions. It also witnesses to Hosea's belief that Israel's unfaithfulness to the covenant could disrupt their life on the land.

An initial pair of futility curses appears in Hos 4:10. The people shall eat, but they will not be satisfied, the prophet warns. They shall use indiscriminate sex to celebrate and promote fertility, but there will be no population growth. Both curses relate to the land's ability to sustain life. The people depended on the land to provide them nourishment and to foster fertility and reproduction.

The first of this verse's futility curses reappears in Mic 6:14, a text we shall examine shortly. The same type of warning also appears outside of the Bible in the Aramaic Sefire treaty, which dates from the eighth-century times of Hosea and Micah. (The Sefire treaty is our best extrabiblical source of the tradition of treaty curses among the West Semitic peoples.) The inscription urges, "Should seven nurses ... nurse a young boy, may he not be satiated; and should seven mares suckle a colt, may it not be sa[ted]" (*KAI* 222 A 21–24).

Another inscription, the Assyrian-Aramaic Hadad-yis'ī inscription, which dates from an earlier period (mid-ninth century), also attests to the futility idiom of Hos 4:10. The inscription, found on a statue at Tell Fakhariyah in Syria, lists the curse: "May a hundred women suckle an infant, but may it not be satisfied."

Additional futility curses appear in Hos 8:7; 9:12, 16. Hosea 8:7 proclaims that because of the people's idolatry, their best efforts at sowing grain will be frustrated. The stalks that grow will have no ears and will produce no meal. Were the crop to yield grain, foreigners would devour the flour.

I shall note below that Mic 6:15 prophesies the same frustration: "You will sow but you will not reap." Later, the curse list of Deuteronomy picks up the same language. Deuteronomy 28:38 reads, "You shall bring out much seed to the field but shall gather in little."

Hosea 9:12 and 16 zero in on a different type of frustration: futility in raising children. Even though the people will bear children and bring them up, they will end up bereft of them. Deuteronomy 28:41 may well draw on this part of Hosea: "You shall have sons and daughters but they shall not remain yours, for they shall go into captivity."

The mention of foreign captivity raises the specter of the ultimate covenantal curse: exile. Sinai theology threatens the people with diminished fertility and with related frustrations, but the climactic threat of conditional tenancy is the curse of expulsion from the land. This is God's final step in severing the ties between God's wayward people and God's land.

Hosea's relatively short book voices this threat of eviction and exile explicitly in at least seven places. Four-fifths of the land of Israel was lost to Assyria between 732 and 722 B.C.E. Hosea's Sinai traditions gave him a clear explanation of this to use with his audience.

Several texts in Hosea express the warning of eviction by naming specific countries as particular locales of exile. The Assyrian army was the major military threat in Hosea's time, so it is no wonder that the prophet points to Assyria as one possible destination for exiled Israel. He also uses the more symbolically rich threat of a return to Egyptian bondage.

Hosea prophesies captivity in both Egypt and Assyria at Hos 9:3 and 11:5 (LXX) (cf. also Hos 11:11). Egypt appears alone as a site to which Israelite refugees will flee (or be deported) in Hos 7:16; 8:13; and 9:6. The threat of a return to Egypt in these verses is highly symbolic. It is really a prophecy of the undoing of the covenant relationship. In a return to Egypt, Israel would revert to the life it had before God made Israel God's vassals at Sinai and guided them into God's land. Israel would live as if God never heard their cry for deliverance out of Egyptian bondage.

Hosea's threat of a return to Egypt is another point at which he anticipates the thought of Deuteronomy. Deuteronomy 28:68 makes returning to Egypt a consequence of Israel's disobedience, just as Hos 8:13; 9:3; and 11:5 do. The Deuteronomic verse presupposes a divine promise or a divine command—now lost to us—that Israel was not to endure Egyptian dependence and servitude again. Deuteronomy 17:16 cites the same divine pronouncement that banned any thought about a return to Egypt.[35]

The prophecy of Hos 7:16 that the Israelites will have to live under ridicule in the land of Egypt is of special interest. The verse has a clear connection with Ps 78:57, a psalm of Asaph. Hosea 7:16 and the psalm are unique in using the distinctive image of Israel as a "defective bow" (קשת רמיה). As a bow that is so warped that its arrows miss their target, Israel has failed the one who trusted in it.

It can be no coincidence that Hosea's circle and the Asaphite psalmists both use this unique image, which appears nowhere else in the Bible. We have identified another distinctive image from the Sinai stream of theological tradition. Sinaitic Yahwism was no late product of religious evolution, but a living body of historical tradition that minority groups in ancient Israel treasured and handed down over time.

---

35. For discussion, see Martin J. Buss, *The Prophetic Word of Hosea: A Morphological Study* (Berlin: Töpelmann, 1969), 97; Weinfeld, *Deuteronomic School*, 369. Significantly, Exod 13:17 (E) expresses the similar divine sentiment that the Israelites, despite their wayward proclivities, belong out of Egypt and in the promised land. It is a tremendous tragedy for Sinai theology that Israel is bent on a destructive path leading back to the place where the people do not belong.

One full passage in Hosea in particular, Hos 9:1–6, deserves close analysis, since it encapsulates Hosea's belief in Israel's conditional tenancy in God's land.

> [1] Do not rejoice, O Israel!
>   Do not exult as other nations do;
> for you have played the whore, departing from your God.
>   You have loved a prostitute's pay
>   on all threshing floors.
> [2] Threshing floor and wine vat shall not feed them,
>   and the new wine shall fail them.
> [3] They shall not remain in the land of the LORD;
>   but Ephraim shall return to Egypt,
>   and in Assyria they shall eat unclean food.
>
> [4] They shall not pour drink offerings of wine to the LORD,
>   and their sacrifices shall not please him.
> Such sacrifices shall be like mourners' bread;
>   all who eat of it shall be defiled;
> for their bread shall be for their hunger only;
>   it shall not come to the house of the LORD.
>
> [5] What will you do on the day of appointed festival,
>   and on the day of the festival of the LORD?
> [6] For even if they escape destruction,
>   Egypt shall gather them,
>   Memphis shall bury them.
> Nettles shall possess their precious things of silver;
>   thorns shall be in their tents.

Hosea made these pronouncements as part of a public, verbal dispute with an audience celebrating an annual harvest festival, probably the Feast of Booths (cf. Deut 16:13). Hosea did not oppose celebrating the Feast of Booths in principle. However, the way that Israel was celebrating the festival "like the peoples" (9:1)—that is, like the Canaanites, in a highly sexualized form—was diametrically opposed to his Sinai traditions. The date may lie in the early 720s.[36]

At least some of the festal rituals and celebrations were taking place outside of the host city at an agricultural threshing floor (9:1–2). The threshing floor, an important part of the harvest, was an appropriate location for festal events (cf. 2 Sam 24:18; 1 Kgs 22:10). It would have been

---

36. The people had come to rejoice at their harvest (9:1), so they must have been trying to put the Assyrian intervention of 734–732, and its devastations, behind them.

located in an open area, accessible to the pilgrims who had come from a distance to attend the festival and who camped in tents in the surrounding fields (9:6).

In 9:1 Hosea indicts the people for their false worship using highly loaded terms, such as "prostitute's pay." We have seen the term "prostitute's pay" (אֶתְנַן) above in two other Sinai texts, Hos 2:12 and Mic 1:7. The metaphor of prostitution in Hosea and Micah charges the people of Israel (the "adulterous wife," or "prostitute") with worshipping fertility deities ("lovers") in exchange for agricultural bounty—grain, wine, and olive oil (the "fee" of the prostitute).

With 9:2 Hosea begins to announce the covenant curses that Israel's false worship has evoked. He prophesies that the products of the threshing floor and the oil and wine presses, which he has just referred to as "prostitute's pay," will soon cease to sustain the people. The people may be enjoying a good harvest this year, but their abandonment of the covenant will soon put that to an end.

Hosea's language is reminiscent of the futility curses that we have seen elsewhere in his book. He seems to say that although Israel's future harvests will mature through the people's hard work, the people themselves will not enjoy the fruits of their labor. Instead, they will end up frustrated. In the theology of this passage, the people's enjoyment of good harvests is conditional on obedience to the Sinai covenant.

Verse 2 leaves the reader unsure as to exactly how the people will fail to enjoy their upcoming harvests. A natural disaster is one possibility. Verse 3 puts aside all speculation. God is beyond the stage of giving initial warnings. God is planning the ultimate judgment, to completely sever the ties between the people and the land. As Hosea states, "No more will they dwell in Yahweh's land." This bald threat is a blatant affirmation of the Sinai tenet of conditional tenancy.

The phrase "Yahweh's land" jumps out of this statement as a clear representation of Hosea's Sinai tradition stream. As in Hos 8:1; 9:8, 15 (cf. Jer 2:7; 16:18), the phrase expresses Sinai theology's view that the territory of Canaan is the peculiar property of its proprietor, Yahweh. Hosea uses the particular phrase here as a polemical jab at the cult of Baal. Yahweh, not Baal, is the owner of the land and controller of its fertility. This is precisely the belief that Hosea's audience had failed to demonstrate in their worship practices.

The next verses elaborate on the threat of exile in 9:3. Verse 4 drives home how as refugees and exiles the people will no longer be able to celebrate harvest festivals. The produce of God's own land will not be available for libations and for sacrifices in foreign countries. What is more, the people's forlorn state in exile will render what food is available to them there unfit for sacrifice. Deuteronomy 26:14 expresses a similar sentiment. Eating an offering during a period of mourning defiles it.

Verse 4 contains at least one technical term that is unique to the Sinai stream of tradition. The verse prophesies a coming time of exile when sacrifices will not "be pleasing" to God. The Hebrew terminology here for "pleasing" (ערב) God through sacrifices appears elsewhere in the Bible only in two other Sinai texts, Jer 6:20 and Mal 3:4.

The prophet's question in 9:5 is sarcastic and rhetorical. "What will you do on the appointed feast day, on the day of Yahweh's festival?" Nothing! There will be nothing possible to do. Dispossessed of God's land and relocated back in Egypt, the people will have no way to celebrate a harvest festival.

Verse 6 rounds off Hosea's treatment of the harvest festival and brings home the menace of conditional tenancy. Hosea makes a further reference to the curse of a return back to Egypt, this time mentioning the Egyptian city of Memphis with all its mortuary connotations. The refuges will die and make their graves in exile.

As for the precincts of their harvest festival back in Canaan, the grounds will lie abandoned. Weeds and thorns will cover up whatever signs of festive worship the exiles leave behind.

The Witness of Micah

Prominent as it was within Hosea's northern circle, the Sinai theme of conditional tenancy had equal urgency in the eighth century for some southern Israelite circles. Several passages within the book of Micah confirm the prominence of this theme for at least Micah's small, prophetic minority group in the south. Micah 6:9–16 is one such passage.

> 9 The voice of the LORD cries to the city
>   (it is sound wisdom to fear your name):
> Hear, O tribe and assembly of the city!
>   10 Can I forget the treasures of wickedness in the house of the wicked,
>   and the scant measure that is accursed?
> 11 Can I tolerate wicked scales
>   and a bag of dishonest weights?
> 12 Your wealthy are full of violence;
>   your inhabitants speak lies,
>   with tongues of deceit in their mouths.
> 13 Therefore I have begun to strike you down,
>   making you desolate because of your sins.
> 14 You shall eat, but not be satisfied,
>   and there shall be a gnawing hunger within you;

you shall put away, but not save,
>and what you save, I will hand over to the sword.
[15] You shall sow, but not reap;
>you shall tread olives, but not anoint yourselves with oil;
>you shall tread grapes, but not drink wine.
[16]For you have kept the statutes of Omri
>and all the works of the house of Ahab,
>and you have followed their counsels.
Therefore I will make you a desolation, and your inhabitants an object
>of hissing;
>so you shall bear the scorn of my people.

There is little reason to doubt the authenticity of the two-part judgment oracle in Mic 6:9–16, since its complaints about the lack of economic justice in Judah are the same found in Mic 2–3. Scholars generally accept the latter chapters as Micah's genuine words.

Micah probably delivered this oracle during King Hezekiah's reign, in the period before the major Assyrian invasion of Judah in 701 B.C.E. The prophet addresses all Israel ("O tribe," 6:9), so the passage has a wider audience than his earlier speeches. Broadening his audience beyond the elites of society probably relates to the growing threat to all of Judah of an imminent Assyrian invasion.

It is the content of its threats (6:13–15) that reveals the covenant thinking behind Mic 6:9–16. Strong linguistic parallels link these threats to Deut 28, which presents the treaty curses central to Sinai's conditional covenant. Of particular note is the presence here in Micah of the same futility curses that we have just seen in the oracles of the northern prophet, Hosea. Futility is a strong warning to the Israelite people that they have put their covenant with God at risk, and that the threat of eviction from God's land is looming over them.[37]

The start of 6:15 includes one brief curse: "You shall sow, but not reap." Deuteronomy 28:38 clearly echoes this poetic half-line: "You shall carry much seed into the field but shall gather little in" (also cf. Hos 8:7; Sefire, KAI 222 A 22–24). The second half-line of the verse is another futility curse echoed in Deut 28. The Hebrew clause "but not anoint yourself

---

37. In addition to its theme of conditional tenancy, Mic 6:9–16 betrays itself as a Sinai text by its particular diction. The language of 6:10–11, including the term "bag (for weights)" (כיס), resonates with that of the legal maxims of Deut 25:13–15. Again, the usage "I will give to the sword" (לחרב אתן), which God utters in 6:14, reverberates with Sinai language in Jeremiah (Jer 15:9). Or again, the combination of the terms "desolation" (שמה) and "hissing" (שרקה) in 6:16 occurs elsewhere almost exclusively in Jeremiah (Jer 19:8; 25:9, 18; 29:18; 51:37).

with the oil" is nearly identical both here in Micah and in Deut 28:40. Significantly, both texts use a rather unique Hebrew syntax, in which "oil" is an adverbial accusative of material. There is nothing quite similar elsewhere in the Hebrew Bible. Micah and Deuteronomy share a fixed idiom of Sinai tradition here.

The final futility curse in Mic 6:15 resonates with Deut 28:39. The Deuteronomic verse reads, "You shall plant vineyards and dress them, but you shall neither drink the wine nor gather the grapes." In Micah, the people get closer to enjoying the grapes than in Deuteronomy. However, the result is even more frustrating: "You shall tread grapes, but not drink wine."[38]

Micah's traditional futility language shows that his themes of social and economic justice do not represent any new ethical awareness within Israel's religious evolution. If this were the case, we would see Micah spouting out freshly coined, random threats. Instead, his idiomatic language presupposes that a covenantal agreement has long been in place. Delbert Hillers rightly assesses the implications of Micah's specific images of divine judgment. "Just these evils were coming because the Israelites had broken their covenant with God."[39]

Micah 3:9–12, a text from earlier in Micah's prophetic career, also witnesses to Micah's belief in his people's conditional tenancy in Canaan. This passage goes beyond threats of futility to warn directly of eviction from God's land.

> [9] Hear this, you rulers of the house of Jacob
>   and chiefs of the house of Israel,
> who abhor justice
>   and pervert all equity,
> [10] who build Zion with blood
>   and Jerusalem with wrong!
> [11] Its rulers give judgment for a bribe,
>   its priests teach for a price,
>   its prophets give oracles for money;
> yet they lean upon the LORD and say,
>   "Surely the LORD is with us!

---

38. The frustration of both wine and oil production in Mic 6:15 assures that the traditions behind this verse are related to, or identical with, those behind Deut 28:38–42. In both cases, mention of the frustration of these specific products follows the curse of a failed grain harvest.

39. Delbert R. Hillers, *A Commentary on the Book of the Prophet Micah* (Hermeneia; Philadelphia: Fortress, 1984), 82. Cf. Allen's statement: "There can be little doubt that Micah was aware of this covenantal setting of the futility curse and deliberately echoed it" (*Micah*, 379).

No harm shall come upon us."
[12] Therefore because of you
   Zion shall be plowed as a field;
Jerusalem shall become a heap of ruins,
   and the mountain of the house a wooded height.

Micah's audience must have been dumbfounded at the final verse of this passage. Micah prophesied the destruction of God's chosen city, Jerusalem, and the expulsion of its inhabitants. "Zion will be plowed as a field, Jerusalem will become a heap of ruins" (3:12).

It is hard to imagine a more direct statement of the Sinai theme of conditional tenancy of the land. We saw in Hos 9:6 that Hosea envisioned a northern worship site taken over by weeds and thorns. Here in Mic 3:12 Micah envisions a parallel future for Jerusalem and its temple. The south's central site of worship will become a "wooded height," overgrown with bushes and trees.

Threatening the sacred security of Zion would have unnerved Micah's audience. They supposed Zion inviolable, independent of any economic injustice and wrongdoing on their part. According to 3:11, Jerusalem's leaders "lean upon Yahweh and say, 'Surely Yahweh is with us! No harm shall come upon us.'" The statements are a parody of the confidence in Zion's invulnerability that appears in Pss 46; 48; 76; 84; and 87.

Although Micah is a southern prophet, he does not share the Jerusalemite royal theology found in these psalms and in some southern prophets, such as Isaiah. In Micah's prophecy, Sinai theology struggles against Zion beliefs. Micah counters his audience's false dependence on Zion's invulnerability with the conditionality of the Sinai covenant. What this implies for understanding the geographical extent of Sinai traditions is unmistakable. In ancient Israel, Sinai theology was not merely a northern stream of tradition but had significant advocates in Judah as well.

In 3:9–11 Micah names the reasons God is revoking the covenant and designates the officials of Jerusalem who are responsible. He does so using the language of Sinai tradition. The first poetic line of 3:11 is especially clear in assigning blame. The "priests" and "heads" are betraying the standards of covenant justice in Judah.[40] These are the very officials that Deuteronomy holds responsible as the ultimate arbiters of Yahweh's judicial will. For example, Deut 17:9 assigns final responsibility for juridical instruction to the "Levitical priests" (הכהנים הלוים) and to the "judges." The latter officials normally came from among Israel's village

---

40. Jerusalem's prophets, a third guilty party, also receive rebuke. Cf. Mic 3:5; Jer 6:13–14.

leaders, the "heads" of the people (ראשים, as here). The "rulers" (NRSV) of 3:11 are "heads"/"judges."

The charges that 3:11 levels against the designated officials of Judah are also from the Sinai stream of tradition. The complaint of the verse about judges taking a "bribe" (שחד) echoes other Sinai texts, such as Exod 23:8 (E) and Deut 16:18–19 (also cf. the language of 1 Sam 8:3 [B source]; Deut 10:17; 27:25). The covenant ethics of Sinai theology require that judges not distort justice by allowing bribes to blind them.

Micah's parallel indictment against the priests turns on their failure to teach the ethical stipulations of the covenant. The Hebrew verb "teach" (ירה) has a distinct sense here that is characteristic of the Sinai stream of tradition. Sinai texts in particular use this verb to speak of teaching authoritative torah (see, e.g., Exod 24:12 [E]). Deuteronomy links this language of "teaching torah" to the specific role and responsibilities of the Levitical priests (Deut 17:10, 11; 24:8; 33:10). Hosea maintains the exact same understanding (Hos 4:6).[41]

The peculiar idiom of 3:12 drives home the passage's identity as a Sinai text. The appearance of the term "heap of ruins" (עי) here in Micah (and paralleled in Jer 26:18–19) is a rare use of language in the Bible. Psalm 79:1, the beginning of a psalm of Asaph, is one of the few other places that use this distinctive term.

Psalm 79 comes from a relatively late period compared to most of the other Asaphite texts. It probably postdates Jeremiah's period and stems from exilic times. If so, the psalm laments the eventual fulfillment of Micah's and Jeremiah's predictions of Jerusalem's destruction.

At the time of the psalm, the nations have indeed invaded God's land ("your inheritance") and laid Jerusalem in "ruins."[42] The covenantal curse of eviction has happened as an historical reality. Besides the term "ruins," note that Ps 79:1 also uses the term "inheritance" (נחלה) to describe God's land as Micah does (see Mic 2:2, discussed above). Again, this type of reverberation of language supports Micah's tradition-historical placement within the Sinai stream of theological tradition.

A third and final example of the Sinai theme of "conditional tenancy" in Micah appears in Mic 4:9–10. The superscription of Micah (1:1) links Micah's activities with the reign of King Hezekiah, and some passages in the book may reflect the events of the crisis of 701 B.C.E. that Hezekiah had with Assyria. Micah 4:9–10 is one such passage. It is the first of a

---

41. See BDB, "ירה," 435, Hiph. 5.b; and cf. idem, "תורה," 436, 1.e; S. Wagner, "ירה III," TDOT 6:343–44.

42. See Nasuti, *Psalms of Asaph*, 94; and cf. Allen, *Micah*, 321; Mays, *Micah*, 92; Wolff, *Micah*, 109.

group of three oracles that each depict Jerusalem's plight under the siege of the Assyrian ruler, Sennacherib.

> [9] Now why do you cry aloud?
>> Is there no king in you?
> Has your counselor perished,
>> that pangs have seized you like a woman in labor?
> [10] Writhe and groan, O daughter Zion,
>> like a woman in labor;
> for now you shall go forth from the city
>> and camp in the open country;
>> you shall go to Babylon.
> There you shall be rescued,
>> there the LORD will redeem you
>> from the hands of your enemies.

The passage comes across as both coherent and authentic to Micah—except for the poetic line within 4:10 that refers to a rescue from "Babylon." This line, "And go to Babylon; there you will be rescued," is probably a secondary, interpretative insertion into the text from after Micah's time.[43]

Though its threat of Jerusalem's destruction did not occur in the Neo-Assyrian period, Mic 4:9–10 must have continued rich with meaning into the succeeding Neo-Babylonian times. It became clear after Micah's era that the Babylonians, not the Assyrians, had destroyed Jerusalem and exiled the people. The glossator who expanded 4:10 thus spelled out that it was actually from out of Babylon that God would redeem God's evicted people.

The passage paints a picture of Zion's radical judgment. In 4:10 Micah orders Zion to "writhe" and "groan" as the city falls to its besiegers. Driven from the city, the people have to camp in the "open country."

Like Mic 6:9–16, this passage argues against any false confidence in Zion's inviolability. Although the passage's final line holds out hope that God will deliver the people in the future, the venue of the future deliverance is *not* Zion. Yahweh will redeem the people from out in the open—"there" (4:10)—where they presumably will have recognized their

---

43. For discussion of the passage's reference to Babylon as a gloss, see Y. Kaufmann, *The Religion of Israel from Its Beginnings to the Babylonian Exile* (trans. M. Greenberg; Chicago: University of Chicago Press, 1960), 352; Hillers, *Micah*, 59. The insertion here is in line with the Deuteronomistic prediction in 2 Kgs 20:16–18 that Hezekiah's foolishness before Merodach-baladan's envoys would lead to Israel's Babylonian exile in 586 B.C.E.

full vulnerability to the Sinai covenant's curse of eviction from God's land. L. Allen aptly summarizes the thrust of the passage: "To huddle under promises concerning the holy city is useless.... [The Jerusalemites] can lay no claim to instant deliverance as the automatic right of God's covenant people."[44]

The passage does not give the reasons for the people's expulsion from the capital city. Using a sarcastic, "disputation" style, which also appears elsewhere in Micah, it does imply strongly, however, that the blame lies with Jerusalem's present rulers. Despite the positive effects of King Hezekiah's cultic reforms, Micah condemns the king's policy of militarization and political centralization as worthless. In spite of all of Hezekiah's economic and military preparations, the Assyrians still terrify the Jerusalemites, who behave as if they have no leader (cf. 2 Chr 32:18).

The passage uses the idiom of the Sinai stream of tradition to describe the pangs that the populace suffers from the failed policies of Jerusalem's royal leadership. It is in Jer 6:24 and 50:43 that one finds parallels to 4:9's combination of the Hebrew noun "pangs" (חיל) and the verbal root "seize" (חזק) (see also Jer 49:24).

A final remark about the theme of *promise* in this passage is in order, since we have now encountered the theme for the first time in Micah. (We have already seen Sinai texts of promise in Hos 2:14–15, 16–20.) It is unnecessary to agree with some scholars that references to redemption in Micah, such as that in 4:10 here, are inauthentic to the prophet from Moresheth. The labor and childbirth motif that so appropriately captures the mood of Sennacherib's siege in this passage naturally combines pain and promise. The motif provided the Micah group with conceptual elasticity—a logical construct binding notions of retribution and deliverance. The labor motif should thus caution scholars against pigeonholing Micah and his disciples too hastily as declaring Israel's judgment only and not its deliverance. (I will return to the problems raised by other, more elaborate promises of deliverance in Micah in the next chapter.)

TEMPERED RULE OVER THE INHERITANCE

Sinai theology's ideal form of administrative and judicial polity was a decentralized system, in which all Israelites were co-vassals under Yahweh's rule. A decentralized polity assured the people's recognition of Yahweh's sole suzerainty over them. It nurtured covenantal bonds

---

44. Allen, *Micah*, 333–34; cf. Mays, *Micah*, 105–6.

between people by allowing the heads of family lines to safeguard people's land and welfare at the local level. Once in power, a human ruler could extract goods and services from client subjects at levels high enough to disrupt or destroy local lines of communal solidarity.

When the Israelites eventually insisted on a king despite the warnings of Sinai theology, the bearers of Sinai traditions made clear that God would allow the turn of events only as a concession to the people. They also made strenuous efforts to offset, as far as possible, the undesirable effects of kingship. We see these efforts in various Sinai texts, which try to temper kingship and centralized administrative polity through covenantal reservations, caveats, and limitations. This tempering reached its climax in the so-called *law of the king*, in Deut 17:14–20.

The Witness of Hosea

Albrecht Alt, in his classic 1953 study of the provenance of Deuteronomy, traced Sinai theology's skepticism about kingship back to the eighth-century traditions of the prophet Hosea. Alt was wrong to limit the antimonarchic bent of Sinai theology to a northern geography, as our look at Micah's (southern) view of kingship in a moment will show. He was completely on target, however, in arguing that the view of kingship in Deuteronomy has clear roots in Hosea's traditions. The perspective of Hosea's prophecy and that of the *law of the king* in Deut 17:14–20 belong to the same theological stream of tradition.[45]

Alt has been far from the only researcher to link Deut 17:14–20 with Hosea. Several notable scholars of Deuteronomy's background have followed his example,[46] and the British scholar, Adam Welch, anticipated his argument three decades earlier, in 1924. Welch writes that, in terms of their attitudes toward kingship, "The connection between prophet [Hosea] and lawgiver [Deuteronomy] is unmistakable; and again it turns the eyes of the student of the Deuteronomic code to Ephraim [the northern kingdom] as the place where some of its peculiar legislation had its origin."[47]

---

45. Albrecht Alt, "Die Heimat des Deuteronomiums," in *Kleine Schriften zur Geschichte des Volkes Israel* (ed. M. Noth; 3 vols.; Munich: Beck, 1959), 2:263–68.

46. See, particularly, Gerhard von Rad, *Deuteronomy* (trans. D. Barton; OTL; Philadelphia: Westminster, 1966), 118–20.

47. Adam C. Welch, *The Code of Deuteronomy: A New Theory of Its Origin* (London: Clarke, 1924), 132.

Alt characterized Hosea's view of kingship as a radical No ("Nein") to the institution. The prophet believes that Israelite monarchs have no divine right to permanent, dynastic rule (e.g., Hos 8:4). Going even further, he prophesies that God must remove kingship with all its accouterments from Israel, at least for a time, to re-create the people's connection with God, lost long ago (Hos 13:11; 3:4).

Alt recognized that these strongly negative views about kingship in Hosea go beyond the skeptical, yet concessive, position of Deut 17. He aptly accounted for this difference, however, by noting that a prophet's shocking, absolute tone necessarily differs from the expectant, yet practical tone of a societal design, which tries to present itself to people as a feasible plan.[48]

Alt cited Hos 1:4–5; 3:4; 7:3–7; 8:4, 10; 10:3; and 13:11 as textual data supporting his interpretation of Hosea's position on kingship. Hosea's critique of the northern monarchy, both in practice and in principle, is generally transparent in these texts. The following additional texts, which are a bit more complex to interpret, contain further textual evidence for Hosea's skepticism about the institution of monarchy:

+ Hosea 1:11 (which avoids using the term "king" for Israel's eschatological leader, preferring instead the premonarchic term, "head" [ראש]).
+ Hosea 5:10 (which castigates the king's "officials" [שרים], a term for the officers of the king's centralized administrative system).
+ Hosea 9:15 (where the statement that "all their evil began at Gilgal" probably refers to the people's defection from Yahweh in proclaiming Saul their first king at this site [1 Sam 11:15]). (N.B. Scholars also often see an indictment of kingship in Hosea's somewhat obscure statements tracing Israel's sin back to "the days of Gibeah" [Hos 9:9; 10:9]. There is more than one way of interpreting Hosea's references to Gibeah, but he may be thinking in part of King Saul's use of the site as a headquarters of his monarchy [1 Sam 10:26; 11:4; 15:34–35].)
+ Hosea 10:7, 15 (which prophesy that the king of Israel will be "cut off").

I have only enough space here to closely examine two substantial passages in Hosea, each containing verses that Alt referenced. Exploration of

---

48. Alt, "Heimat des Deuteronomiums," 267.

Hos 8:1–7 and 13:9–11 should demonstrate, however, Hosea's use of Sinai traditions against kingship. Let us start with Hos 8:1–7:

[1] Set the trumpet to your lips!
    One like a vulture is over the house of the LORD,
because they have broken my covenant,
    and transgressed my law.
[2] Israel cries to me,
    "My God, we—Israel—know you!"
[3] Israel has spurned the good;
    the enemy shall pursue him.

[4] They made kings, but not through me;
    they set up princes, but without my knowledge.
With their silver and gold they made idols
    for their own destruction.
[5] Your calf is rejected, O Samaria.
    My anger burns against them.
How long will they be incapable of innocence?
    [6] For it is from Israel,
an artisan made it;
    it is not God.
The calf of Samaria
    shall be broken to pieces.
[7] For they sow the wind,
    and they shall reap the whirlwind.
The standing grain has no heads,
    it shall yield no meal;
if it were to yield,
    foreigners would devour it.

We have already examined 8:1–3, since it explicitly attests to Hosea's advocacy of the Sinai covenant. These verses introduce a larger section of Hosea with three parts: 8:4–7, 8–10, and 11–13. (An editor added 8:14 to round off the passage.) This section of Hosea dates to around 733 B.C.E.

The initial three verses of Hos 8 summarize generally the chapter's message of sin and judgment. Subsequent sections of the chapter go beyond this summary to give the specifics of Israel's betrayal.[49] Verses

---

49. Verses 4–7 specify no addressee. The section assumes the presence of 8:1–3, which supplies its context.

4–7 in particular help us clarify Hosea's Sinai-oriented viewpoint about human rule over Israel.[50]

Verses 4–7 fundamentally condemn Israel's monarchic government (8:4a) in practice and in principle. For Hosea, monarchy amounts to a rejection of God's suzerainty over the people, a prime example that Israel "has broken my covenant" (8:1). This becomes readily apparent when one interprets this passage in conjunction with related Sinai texts.

Verse 4 bears an especially striking family resemblance to 1 Sam 8 and 12, which are B-source/Sinai texts. According to these antimonarchic texts of Samuel, kingship arose in Israel due to the people's initiative, not that of God. Against Samuel and God's better judgment, and despite their warnings, three centuries before Hosea's time the people had demanded a monarchy. Hosea 8:4 virtually summarizes this Samuel B perspective: "They have set up kings, but not through me."

Hosea is likely also upset that Israel has elevated individuals to the throne without God's input.[51] The Samuel B texts hold divine direction to be an essential part of monarchic succession. God was unhappy in principle about kings, but retained the prerogative of selecting them in order to guide Israel's life (1 Sam 10:19–24; 12:1, 13). The *law of the king* in Deut 17:14–20 takes up this idea and legislates it. Verse 15 stipulates, "The king whom you appoint to rule you must be chosen by Yahweh your God."

The passage's perspective on kingship becomes clear not only through its echoes of other Sinai texts but also through the way it situates kingship within the category of idolatry. Hosea virtually equates kingship with idolatry in 8:4–7; 8:4 decries the two phenomena in one breath. Again, Hosea is very close to 1 Sam 8 (B source) here, since 1 Sam 8:7–8 reads in part, "They have rejected me from being king over them ... forsaking me and serving other gods."

The explanation for Hosea's intermingling of a critique of kings and a critique of idols—especially Israel's calf idols—lies in the perspectives of

---

50. There is not enough space here to study the rest of the chapter, 8:8–10 and 11–13. The former section switches to issues concerning foreign relations and politics; the latter section concentrates on the folly of sacrificial rites in the absence of obedience to the covenant. Note, however, that the LXX's rendering of 8:10 strongly reflects Hosea's general antimonarchic perspective. In the LXX, the second poetic line of the verse reads, "And they will cease in [or, 'for'] a while to anoint a king and officers." The NEB follows the LXX here, reading: "Then they will soon abandon this setting up of kings and princes." Compare also the NAB's translation. These versions may not represent Hosea's original text, but they do match Hosea's authentic judgment against the monarchic system in Israel.

51. This scenario fits the royal politics of Hosea's times. Political assassinations and a chaotic succession of dynasties were the order of the day, rather than any deliberate attentiveness to Yahweh's will.

Sinai theology. Sinai theology holds that human substitutes for God, even sculpted representations of the true God, are an affront to Yahweh's mysterious otherness and freedom. (On God's incomparability to created things in Sinai theology, see, e.g., Asaphite Ps 50:21; Exod 3:14 [E]; Num 23:19 [E]; Deut 4:15–24; Mic 7:18.) God's people cannot place God's numinous mystery at their disposal by tailor-making Yahweh "stand-ins." Yet, this is precisely what Hosea sees the people of his time trying to accomplish with their kings and calves. Kings and calves are known quantities. They are tangible and manageable. All the nations have them. They are available for petition, even when Yahweh is not (Hos 5:6!).[52]

Monarchy is a form of idolatry for Hosea that has spawned other idolatrous practices. King Jeroboam I instituted the worship of the northern kingdom's calf/bull image, which 8:5–6 highlights (1 Kgs 12:26–33). Bethel remained a monarchic shrine and a royal chapel of subsequent northern kings (Amos 7:13), who continued to sanction, encourage, and subsidize its bull cult. Hosea had more than one good reason for lumping together Israel's monarchy and the idolatrous calf/bull image of the northern cult.

The bull image of 8:5 and 6 was almost certainly located at Bethel.[53] Given this fact, it is noteworthy that Hosea refers to the image as "the calf of Samaria." This language intentionally blames the calf cult of Bethel on the monarchy in Israel's capital, Samaria. Robert Gnuse puts it this way: "To say, 'Your calf stinks, Samaria,' is to say, 'Your calf stinks, king.' The blame is put where it belongs."[54] The idolatrous calf is the king's creation!

It is this potential of human kingship for introducing foreign idols into Israel's worship that the *law of the king* will later caution against in Deut 17:15. If Israel must have a king, he is neither to be a foreigner nor to exercise any foreign influence upon Israel. Unlike Solomon with his many foreign marriages, and unlike Ahab with his marriage to Jezebel, Israel's ideal leader should never expose his subjects to the temptation of worshiping foreign gods (cf. Asaphite Ps 81:9; Jer 19:4). Deuteronomy is adamant. What happened in Hosea's time must never happen again.

---

52. For the traditions of Sinai theology, substituting creaturely stand-ins for God is a major transgression, which can only result in being "cut off" (למען כרת; see Jer 44:8 [C material]). This typical Sinai language of being "cut off" appears at the end of Hos 8:4.

53. Jeroboam I set up two major bull images for the northern cult, one there and one at Dan, but the Assyrians probably destroyed the latter image around the time of our passage (733 B.C.E.). Furthermore, Hos 10:5–7 makes clear that Samaria's primary bull image was located at Bethel. (The "Beth-aven" of the verse is Hosea's derogatory, pet name for Bethel.)

54 Robert K. Gnuse, "Calf, Cult, and King: The Unity of Hosea 8:1–13," *BZ* 26 (1982): 90 n. 21.

A second passage of Hosea, Hos 13:9–11, reinforces the Sinai traditions about kingship that we have been observing. In fact, kingship appears even more odious to God in this prophecy than in what we have seen thus far. A short exegesis quickly reveals this.

> [9] I will destroy you, O Israel,
>> because you are against me, against your helper.
> [10] Where now is your king, that he may save you?
>> Where in all your cities are your rulers,
> of whom you said,
>> "Give me a king and rulers"?
> [11] I gave you a king in my anger,
>> and I took him away in my wrath.

Hosea 13:9–11 is part of a larger grouping of prophetic speech in Hosea; yet, the verses stand out within their context because they focus on the monarchy. The way in which Hosea speaks directly to Israel in the second person singular ("you")—while he speaks of Israel in the third person ("he") in the surrounding verses—justifies considering 13:9–11 separately from its larger context.

The passage comes from a somewhat later time than Hos 8:1–7. Its rhetorical question, "Where now is your king?" (13:10), likely points to historical circumstances in which the northern kingdom's monarch has just been defeated or captured by the enemy. Exactly this circumstance arose in 724 B.C.E., just a few years before the northern kingdom's destruction. At that time, the Assyrian ruler, Shalmaneser V, imprisoned King Hoshea ben Elah for treason against the Assyrian Empire (2 Kgs 17:4).

The text begins in 13:9 by confronting Israel with its desperate, helpless condition. Israel has rejected its real "helper," God, its true suzerain and landlord. The people have instead embraced immediate, accessible "saviors," such as human rulers and idolatrous images, which are no help in time of crisis.

Notably, 13:9 shows strong associations with other biblical Sinai texts. The only other place in the Bible that refers to God directly as "your help" (עזרך) in the manner of Hos 13:9 is Deut 33:26, 29. An additional parallel is provided in 1 Sam 10:19 (B source), using somewhat different language. There, at Saul's proclamation as king, Samuel chastises the people for receiving a monarch at the price of rejecting "your God who delivers you."

Verse 10 of Hosea's text begins his direct attack on kingship, renewed from Hos 8:1–7. Hosea quotes God as ridiculing the false security that Israel's monarchy had given the northern kingdom for so long. The style and tone is very similar to Sinai passages in Deut 32:37–39; Jer 2:28; and Mic 4:9, the latter of which provides a particularly striking parallel. In what appears to be an uncanny southern version of Hosea's sarcastic, antimonarchic question, 4:9 of Micah's oracle derisively inquires: "Is there no king among you? Has your counselor perished?"

Verse 10 makes clear that not only the king but also the officers (שׂרים; NRSV "rulers"), through whom he controlled the state system, are the objects of God's scorn.[55] Kings alone are not the entire problem. They stand atop a whole centralized, monarchic polity that has overrun and disrupted the older, decentralized covenant networks that united and protected Israel as God's vassal people.

The rhetorical question of 13:10 expects no answer; it is obvious. Hosea 10:3 anticipated what Israel's confession would have to be at this point, when Assyrian destruction lay so close at hand. "Surely then they will say, 'We have no king, for we did not fear Yahweh. But even if we had a king, what could he do for us?'"

Verse 11 concludes this passage of Hosea with God's revelation of the true divine emotions surrounding the institution of monarchy in Israel. Like Hos 8:4, and the B source of Samuel, the verse traces kingship in Israel to the people's initiative. The people had to wrest kingship out of God. Notably, however, the verse goes farther than to merely echo established points. It states that God was not only reluctant to permit a monarchy in Israel but was also angry in allowing it.[56]

To summarize, this passage provides a sure witness that the Sinai position on kingship reaches at least back to Hosea, and that from at least this early, eighth-century period Sinai tradition linked kingship and divine wrath.

Verse 11 sounds the final note on kingship in Hosea's book, and it is perhaps the most strongly negative note on this theme among our Sinai texts. Despite this negative note, the Sinai stream of tradition as a whole never abandoned the hope that God could somehow redeem this problematic institution. We see this more positive side of the Sinai perspective on kingship in the book of Micah.

---

55. On the basis of the evidence at the end of the verse, and also in part based on the textual witness of the LXX, the verse's Hebrew text is best corrected so that it asks two parallel questions about the absence of king and state officers. A possible reading is, "Where now is your king, that he may save you? / And all your officers, that they may judge you? / Whom you requested, saying 'Give me a king and officers!'" //

56. Beyond its reference to God's angry granting of kingship at Saul's time, the verse may further associate divine anger with the entire history of kingship in Israel. The Hebrew verbs of the verse are in the imperfect, and its word "king" can have a collective sense. We can thus translate 13:11, "I gave you kings in my anger, and I take [them] away in my wrath."

The Witness of Micah

In discussing Hosea's views on kingship, I have alluded to Micah's similar views from about the same time. A close study of two passages in Micah, 5:1–6 and 2:12–13, will confirm the similarity. Since Micah, a southerner, held this theological viewpoint, it is safe to say that the perspective had southern as well as northern roots. Of course, the Sinai perspective on kingship takes on a special Judean coloring within Micah's circle.

Both Mic 5:1–6 and 2:12–13 are prophetic promise announcements, comforting Israel with the promise of future salvation. As such, they are less negative about issues of human leadership among God's people than much of what we have seen in Hosea. Indeed, they envision God blessing Israel with positive human leadership in future days. Like the *law of the king* in Deut 17:14–20, Micah holds out hope for a positive future experience of kingship if only it is tempered by the caveats of Sinai theology.[57] Even when using the genre of promise, however, Micah hints that he can be almost as negative about the institution of kingship as Hosea.

Micah 5:1–6, like 4:9–10, which I examined above, is one of a group of three oracles associated with the Assyrian siege of Jerusalem in 701 B.C.E. Each of the oracles starts with a description of Jerusalem's suffering under the Assyrian siege. Each moves to a promise of some type of divine deliverance from the crisis.

Some scholars date Mic 5:1–6 much later than the Assyrian period and argue it is inauthentic to Micah. There is little warrant for this move. Verses 5–6 name Assyria as the invading enemy, and 5:1 describes a siege that fits the Assyrian crisis of 701.[58] Furthermore, the passage's vocabulary and theology reflect the same Sinai traditions appearing elsewhere in Micah's book. The passage reads:

---

57. Micah and Deut 17 are not fully comparable, however. Whereas Deuteronomy proposes a societal plan for Israel in the present, Micah's vision of positive human leadership is eschatological—a vision for Israel's ideal future. In this sense, the Micah passages we are about to study are "messianic." I suggest this term cautiously. Being thoroughly oriented toward Sinai theology, Mic 5:1–6 and Mic 2:12–13 display a peculiar sort of messianism. These prophecies have little to do with the idea of a future descendant of David who will rule from atop Mount Zion. They are closer to the messianism of Hos 1:11. In this surprising verse in Hosea, the northern prophet looks ahead to an old-fashioned, village "leader" (ראשׁ) arising from among the people of Israel to lead them in an eschatological resettlement of God's land.

58. Verses 5b–6 may be an elaboration, from a later time, of an authentic Mican core oracle in 5:1–5a. (See Beyerlin, *Kulttraditionen Israels*, 79; Levenson, *Sinai and Zion*, 198 n. 15.) However, there is no need to date the entirety of Mic 5:1–6 later than Micah's period.

[1] Now you are walled around with a wall;
    siege is laid against us;
with a rod they strike the judge of Israel
    upon the cheek.
[2] But you, O Bethlehem of Ephrathah,
    who are one of the little clans of Judah,
from you shall come forth for me
    one who is to rule in Israel,
whose origin is from of old,
    from ancient days.
[3] Therefore he shall give them up until the time
    when she who is in labor has brought forth;
then the rest of his kindred shall return
    to the people of Israel.
[4] And he shall stand and feed his flock in the strength of the LORD,
    in the majesty of the name of the LORD his God.
And they shall live secure, for now he shall be great
    to the ends of the earth;
[5] and he shall be the one of peace.
    If the Assyrians come into our land
    and tread upon our soil,
we will raise against them seven shepherds
    and eight installed as rulers.
[6] They shall rule the land of Assyria with the sword,
    and the land of Nimrod with the drawn sword;
they shall rescue us from the Assyrians
    if they come into our land
    or tread within our border.

Like its sibling oracles, Mic 5:1–6 begins with Jerusalem under massive attack (5:1). The assault has chastised and humbled Israel's ruler, given him a devastating "slap in the face." The description correlates historically with Assyria's partial defeat of Hezekiah. The Assyrian ruler, Sennacherib, drove Hezekiah to despair (Jer 26:19; 2 Kgs 19:1), but left his capital and his kingship intact.

The Assyrian crisis proves to Micah that frail Hezekiah is not Israel's true deliverer; Micah's oracle states this at the start. The beginning of the oracle also contains a further, subtler critique of kingship, however. Verse 1 uses distinctive terms to describe Israel's king. Here Micah does not name Hezekiah but refers to him as "the judge" of Israel.

"Judge" (שֹׁפֵט) is a term that Sinai texts such as Deut 17:9 use to describe Israel's leaders (see also, e.g., Judg 2:16; Deut 16:18). Micah surely chose the term for weightier reasons than simply to form a Hebrew wordplay with the word שֵׁבֶט ("rod") in the same verse. He carefully selected the term "judge of Israel" in this verse to sharpen the contrast between Hezekiah, reformer though he was, and the ideal, Sinai type of ruler who relies on God's strength rather than on a fortified state. The latter, ideal and glorious "judge" appears in the verses that follow.

True to its generic pattern, with 5:2 the passage shifts to a promise of deliverance. In a highly poetic style, the verse addresses personified Bethlehem with glowing expectations. In coming days, Bethlehem will produce the true judge that Judah currently lacks. The coming ruler is no ordinary king but a messiah, who will rule "in the majesty of the name of the LORD his God," and who will be "great to the ends of the earth" (5:4). A close look at this figure's features and traits shows that they reflect Sinai ideals, not the Zion theology of Jerusalem's Davidic kings and state priests.

The most striking feature of 5:2 is that it turns its hopes for future leadership in Judah away from Jerusalem. In a classic study, A. Alt argued that Micah turned to Bethlehem in this passage because he had given up hope on any future for Jerusalem and its ruling dynasty.[59] What a shift from "normal" messianism!

The implications of this are profound. Only a radical break with the monarchic succession centered in Jerusalem could allow for such a turn toward Bethlehem. True, since David's father Jesse was an Ephrathite (1 Sam 17:12), Micah may not be giving up all hopes of the Davidic line continuing. The passage makes no promises about this, however. Micah barely leaves the door open for David's line, perhaps out of respect for, or hopes of dialog with, other, competing streams of tradition in Judah. James Mays thus aptly characterizes the radical implications of the passage's silence about David. "The oracle explicitly ignores the Davidic succession and revises the terms of Nathan's founding oracle."[60]

In abandoning Jerusalem, headquarters of Judah's monarchy, Micah sees a positive alternative in Bethlehem. With this move, Micah distances himself from Hezekiah's centralizing, militarizing state system in favor of the sort of decentralized, humble, and rural leadership of Israel that Sinai theology advocates (e.g., Asaphite Ps 78:70–72; Deut 16:18).[61] Verse 2 emphatically states that the anticipated messiah's city and clan are to be rural and peripheral. In fact, Ephrathah is so "little" that it barely deserves to be a Judean clan at all (cf. the NEB translation).

59. Alt, "Micha 2,1–5," 375–76.
60. Mays, Micah, 115; cf. Levenson, Sinai and Zion, 115.
61. On the parallel between Mic 5:4 and Ps 78:70–72, see Beyerlin, Kulttraditionen Israels, 84.

This antipathy toward a monarchic administration centered in a great capital is in full accord with what we find elsewhere in the book of Micah. In various texts, such as Mic 1:13; 3:10; and 5:10, Micah and his editors decry the Judean monarchy's program of military self-security, which focused on defending against Assyria. In this Micah reflects the Sinai stance on human monarchies that we saw in Hos 13:10 (cf. Hos 14:3; Deut 17:16).

The language of 5:2 about Ephrathah being a "little clan" recalls the motif in other Sinai texts of God's commissioning of leaders from insignificant family lines. For example, Judg 6:15, which describes the judge Gideon's undistinguished lineage, has very similar vocabulary to Mic 5:2. In response to his call, Gideon objects that his "clan" (אלף, as here in Micah) is the weakest in its tribe and that he is "the littlest" (הצעיר, again, as in this text) in his father's house. For the general *demurring* motif within other Sinai texts, see Exod 3:11 (E) and 1 Sam 18:18 (B source).

A notable feature of the messianic, Sinai leader in Hos 1:11 is that he stands at the head of all of Israel and Judah, gathered together as one people of God. This seems natural, since the notion that God's covenant vassals remain one people, despite all attempts of political states to divide them, is a strong general thrust of Sinai theology. (In addition to Hos 1:11, cf. Hos 3:5; 6:4; Deut 30:1–3.) Verse 3 of our Micah passage picks up this central Sinai tenet.

The return of the ideal ruler's kindred, which the verse describes, means the reversal of the Assyrian deportation of northern Israelites that occurred two decades before the oracle (in 722 B.C.E.). In other words, 5:3 is stating that Micah's messianic leader will preside over a re-formed, twelve-tribe confederacy of God's covenant people. The verse eagerly anticipates the realization of Sinai theology's ideal of a united "children of Israel."

I shall return to Mic 5:1–6 in a subsequent chapter. I believe that I have presented enough evidence for now to characterize the general contours of Micah's messianism. Micah clearly advocated a Sinai-oriented alternative to the Zion perspectives on monarchy held by many of his southern contemporaries. Mican messianism's break with Jerusalem and the dynastic ideal, its emphasis on decentralized, clan-based leadership, and its particular motifs and diction combine to associate Micah's stance on kingship with Sinai, rather than Zion theology.

A second, shorter, text of promise about kingship occurs in Mic 2:12–13. It is not a prophetic word of promise during a time of crisis, like Mic 5:1–6, but a pure divine oracle of assurance and hope. God's assurance of future blessing includes ideal leadership for God's covenant people.

¹² I will surely gather all of you, O Jacob,
  I will gather the survivors of Israel;
I will set them together
    like sheep in a fold,
like a flock in its pasture;
    it will resound with people.
¹³ The one who breaks out will go up before them;
    they will break through and pass the gate,
    going out by it.
Their king will pass on before them,
    the LORD at their head.

Scholars have struggled over whether this passage is authentic to Micah. Many have their doubts. The fact that it so clearly depicts God's salvation has led some to view the passage as the words of Micah's opponents in Jerusalem, elsewhere quoted as saying, "Surely Yahweh is with us! No harm shall come upon us" (Mic 3:11).

I disagree that Mic 2:12–13 represents the false, Zion-oriented hopes of Jerusalem's establishment. Contrary to the expectations of Jerusalem's nobles and false prophets, the text accepts the inevitability of contemporary punishment and looks for salvation only for a remnant that will remain alive beyond judgment. As Hillers aptly states, "This passage has been believed by some to be the words of the false prophets of Micah's time.... But Margolis already observed: 'It is not likely that the false prophets concerned themselves with the events following the downfall of the nation, which contingency they were most emphatic in denying.'"[62]

The motifs and language of the text express its theme of promise in terms authentic to Sinai tradition. The passage does not mention Jerusalem, Zion, or the Davidic dynasty. Rather, it presupposes a conditional covenant and a covenant curse of eviction from God's land. Further, the passage's image of God regathering the scattered remnant of Jacob as a "flock" has significant parallels in other Sinai texts (see Jer 23:3 and Asaphite Pss 78:52; 80:1). Micah's followers, who edited his book, may be presenting a promise that authentically traces back to Micah himself and his Sinai theology.

Verse 13 describes the leadership of God's covenant flock and thus engages our questions, in this section, about kingship. The language of the verse is tantalizingly ambiguous, making it unclear whether Israel's ideal, future leadership will be purely divine or will include a human

---

62. Hillers, *Micah*, 40.

element. The final poetic line of the verse speaks of both "king" and "Yahweh." The two words stand parallel as a poetic pair, suggesting two possible interpretations. The text may understand Israel's future king to be Yahweh, and only Yahweh. Alternatively, the poetry may understand the flock to organize itself around its own human bellwether, while Yahweh, God's self, emphatically heads the entire group.[63]

In either of 2:13's possible interpretations—and in the case that the verse is intentionally ambiguous—the verse attests that Micah's position on human leadership over Israel falls within the parameters of Sinai theology. God is Israel's true leader. Micah's Sinai viewpoint is further evident when he designates the place of leadership taken up by Yahweh (and perhaps also by the bellwether under Yahweh) as the "head" (ראש). "Head" is the term for leadership in Hos 1:11, and it is a favored term for leadership in Micah. In probing the background of Micah 3:9–12, in fact, we saw that Sinai texts in general link proper leadership in Israel with this term.

This brief discussion of Mic 2:12–13 concludes both my treatment of human rule within Hosea and Micah and this chapter's treatment of the five major tenets of Sinai theology as they occur in these two eighth-century prophets. The aim of examining as many biblical passages as I have in this chapter has been to furnish sufficient exegetical evidence to counter the very real doubts that many biblical scholars are currently expressing about the authentic antiquity and geographic breadth of biblical Yahwism.

Anyone's interpretation of an individual biblical passage is contestable, and my scholarly peers will no doubt contest many of the individual interpretations that I offer here. By offering thorough probes of almost twenty passages from two eighth-century prophets, however, I believe that I have assembled in this chapter an argument of sufficient *cumulative* weight to be difficult to assail in its overall conclusions. Biblical Yahwism, in the form of Sinai traditions, has demonstrable roots within peripheral circles active in both the northern and southern kingdoms at least as early as the eighth-century prophets, Hosea and Micah.

To present a fair overall picture of the book of Micah, I need to add a short follow-up chapter to this one. I want to be fully up front about the

---

63. This vision of tempered human rule, subordinate to God's divine leadership, corresponds better with Micah's position elsewhere in the book. Micah 5:4 speaks of Israel's messianic ruler as "shepherding" the people, but doing so solely in the strength and name of Yahweh. This is an approved scenario in Sinai theology. Human leaders are acceptable if they make themselves subservient to the terms of the Sinai covenant, and Mic 2:12, in either possible interpretation, makes clear that Yahweh is the people's true head.

presence in Micah of other promises to Jerusalem that I have not yet discussed. I need to acknowledge the presence of these Zion-oriented promises in Micah and to offer at least a preliminary explanation for their uneasy presence alongside Micah's Sinai traditions. After this brief excursus chapter, the book's remaining chapters turn to the challenge of tracing the Sinai theological stream of tradition back in time behind Hosea and Micah.

5

THE PLACE OF JERUSALEM IN SOUTHERN SINAI THEOLOGY: PROMISES TO JERUSALEM AND ZION IN MICAH

A UNIQUE OUTLOOK OF CONCERN FOR JERUSALEM IN MICAH, NOT present in Hosea, complicates the argument that Micah advocated Sinai theology. Unlike Hosea, Micah's prophecy has clear passions about Jerusalem. Micah seems preoccupied with the city, its temple, its leaders, and its theological traditions. Even the negative judgment that his prophecy focuses on Jerusalem highlights the city's central importance to God (Mic 1:5, 9, 12; 3:1, 10–12).

In addition, several passages in Micah give Jerusalem a positive, central role in God's ultimate, future salvation of Israel. In studying Mic 5:1–6 and 2:12–13 in the preceding chapter, I noted the ambiguity of Micah's prophetic language, which left open definite possibilities for some form of Davidic kingship in Israel's future. Examination of Mic 4:9–10 showed God promising to eventually redeem and rescue "Daughter Zion." Other passages in Micah, which I have not yet presented, focus God's promises for the future even more intensely on Zion (Mic 4:1–5; 4:6–7, 8; 4:11–13).

Why does Micah seem to contain elements of the theology of Zion? Such elements are associated strongly with Micah's opponents, namely, the Davidic monarchy and the priests of Jerusalem. All this preoccupation with Zion gives us pause. Is Micah a prophet of Sinai theology or not?

Although it is tempting to assume that elements of Zion theology in Micah are all later, secondary additions, jumping to this conclusion is too easy a way out of the problem.

We have already seen that some of Micah's own promise announcements have the authentic coloring of Sinai theology. This may be true of even stronger promises in Micah of Jerusalem's salvation. They may link integrally to Sinai tradition, and emerge as authentic to Micah.

Other oracles bearing clear Zion features are indeed probably late additions to the book of Micah. Accounting for them as "secondary" in this way, however, does not resolve the problem of their appearance in Micah. It merely postpones our questions. Micah's own disciples and followers preserved and edited his book. Whether it was the prophet himself, or some later followers, who introduced Zion passages into Micah, the same fundamental question remains: Why would adherents of Sinai theology include Zion traditions in their own book? Clearly, the Zion texts of Micah call for an explanation.

PROMISES IN MICAH BASED ON SINAI THEOLOGY

Of the various hopes for Jerusalem and David in Micah, it is easiest to comprehend the ones firmly based in Sinai theology. Promises based on Sinai traditions pose no problem for interpreting Micah as a Sinai-oriented prophet. Look again at Mic 4:9–10, paying particular attention to the theological background of its note of hope.

⁹ Now why do you cry aloud?
    Is there no king in you?
Has your counselor perished,
    that pangs have seized you like a woman in labor?
¹⁰ Writhe and groan, O daughter Zion,
    like a woman in labor;
for now you shall go forth from the city
    and camp in the open country;
    you shall go to Babylon.
There you shall be rescued,
    there the LORD will redeem you
    from the hands of your enemies.

Even a brief inspection shows that what we see here is perfectly compatible with Sinai theology. Verse 9 condemns Israel for trusting in a human king, Hezekiah, rather than in the Lord of the Sinai covenant. Such trust is futile, since human surrogates for God have no power to avert the agony of true, divine judgment.

Verse 10 does promise eventual salvation, but only for a remnant that has experienced the covenant curse of eviction from Yahweh's land. This message flies in the face of the false trust in Zion of Jerusalem's leaders, priests, and prophets. These state officials expected that mere residence in Jerusalem was sufficient to spare them from any such calamity (Mic 3:11).

They would certainly have judged blasphemous 4:10's claim that God's salvation would only come once they were "out of the city," dwelling "in the field."

Both 4:9 and 10 contain an image of the pains of childbirth, which further reinforces the passage's Sinai theology. New life will come for the people only after they have suffered the fall of Jerusalem to their enemies. God redeems Daughter Zion in this text only after Israel sees that it has broken the Sinai covenant. Redemption *postdates* Israel's experience of the covenant's ultimate curse. These notions of promise are Sinai notions.

As if the passage's internal Sinai features were not enough, the disciples and followers of Micah who preserved Mic 4:9–10 gave the passage a literary context that prompts the reader to interpret it from a Sinai perspective. They placed the text within a group of three passages with a common structure. Each passage begins with the word "now" followed by a vivid description of Jerusalem besieged by enemies. These descriptions of the contemporary suffering of Jerusalem, right "now," use striking quotes and rhetorical questions, forcing Judah to realize that Jerusalem is vulnerable to defeat. Without the support of its covenant suzerain, the city lies helpless, subject to the covenant's curses.

Once the passages make clear that Jerusalem is vulnerable to punishment, each announces that God can and will step in to resolve Jerusalem's crisis. By placing these three passages together, the editors force us to ponder the cycle that occurs in each of them. They encourage us to read each text as an illustration of the same sort of pattern that we see in the book of Judges. Judges repeatedly drives home the Sinai theme that faithlessness to the covenant inevitably and cyclically brings enemy oppression upon Israel, from which only repentance and God's intervention can save it.

Micah 5:1–6, which I examined in the preceding chapter, is another of the group of three passages in Micah that moves from a description of Assyrian siege to a promise of divine deliverance.

> [1] Now you are walled around with a wall;
>   siege is laid against us;
> with a rod they strike the judge of Israel
>   upon the cheek.
> [2] But you, O Bethlehem of Ephrathah,
>   who are one of the little clans of Judah,
> from you shall come forth for me
>   one who is to rule in Israel,
> whose origin is from of old,
>   from ancient days.
> [3] Therefore he shall give them up until the time
>   when she who is in labor has brought forth;

then the rest of his kindred shall return
    to the people of Israel.
[4] And he shall stand and feed his flock in the strength of the LORD,
    in the majesty of the name of the LORD his God.
And they shall live secure, for now he shall be great
    to the ends of the earth;
[5] and he shall be the one of peace.
    If the Assyrians come into our land
    and tread upon our soil,
we will raise against them seven shepherds
    and eight installed as rulers.
[6] They shall rule the land of Assyria with the sword,
    and the land of Nimrod with the drawn sword;
they shall rescue us from the Assyrians
    if they come into our land
    or tread within our border.

Despite its positive vision of monarchic rule, the text fits well with the authentic prophecy and theology of Micah, according to which Jerusalem and its oppressive lords are severely judged. Jerusalem's enemies deliver judgment directly to the king's face (5:1).

The passage envisions a future for kingship in Judah, but based elsewhere than in Jerusalem, the central capital. The text locates the future of kingship in lowly Bethlehem of the clan Ephrathah, insisting Jerusalem relinquish its pride of place (5:2). Jerusalem's Davidic family is granted a ray of hope for survival here—the messiah will come from David's ancestral home, Bethlehem—but the Davidides and their militarized, monarchic apparatus of state receive no justification or absolution.

The true, future judge of Judah, toward whom the passage directs its hopes, is not another tyrant. Rejecting the normal, worldly trappings of monarchy, the passage understands Judah's true ruler to be a peripheral figure, whose strength comes from his total reliance upon God. This model of decentralized, clan-based leadership is the antithesis of the model of leadership in the contemporary, royal theology of Jerusalem. Like Mic 4:9–10, Mic 5:1–6 is a promise text of Micah that in no way strains the argument that Micah's orientation was firmly toward Sinai.

Micah 5:1–6 appears clearly rooted in Sinai tradition, but differs markedly in character from the prophecies of Hosea in the north. Although the book of Hosea promises positive human leadership of God's people in the future at Hos 1:11, elsewhere it leaves us with the distinct impression that human leadership in Israel had best not take the form of monarchic rule. Setting up kings leads only to God's anger. Nowhere does Hosea support the idea of a royal family line with an ongoing, dynastic rule.

Micah 5:1–6, in contrast, leaves open this possibility. The passage does not specifically mention David, or his descendants. It does announce, however, that the future king of promise will come from Bethlehem, Ephrathah (5:2). According to 1 Sam 17:12, David's father Jesse was an Ephrathite. For Micah, God may yet continue God's traditional support of David's royal family.

The positions of Micah and of Hosea on kingship represent two points along a continuum of permissible perspectives within Sinai theology. As I noted in the previous chapter, Hosea's strongly negative conclusions about monarchic rule represent an extreme position. His hard-line standpoint would have been viable in the northern kingdom of Israel, where several different family lines had ruled and no firm commitment to one royal lineage existed. The case was otherwise in Micah's milieu in the south, where David's royal line enjoyed a remarkable permanence.

Micah 5:1–6 makes allowance for the possible truth of an essential facet of Zion theology: the eternal promises to David's family in Nathan's oracle of 2 Sam 7. With the announcement that David's ancestral home will be the birthplace of Israel's ideal ruler, Micah's group leaves open the possibility that the Davidic family may somehow continue on, past God's judgment of Jerusalem.

This passage about a messiah from Bethlehem is an initial piece of strong evidence that Micah's group advocated the covenant traditions of Sinai while plotting a middle way that did not exclude several distinctive Jerusalem traditions. Sinai and royal traditions come together and interact in Micah.

A convergence and interaction of these sets of traditions was not new in Judah. We see the same development as early as David's formation of a united Israel. David's political and religious measures to unite Israel's varying traditions included appointing two chief priests, Abiathar and Zadok. These head priests represented the Sinai and the Zion theologies, respectively.[1] By appointing both of them to high office, David set an example in Judah for respecting alternative religious traditions. Micah demonstrates this spirit of David in preserving a glimmer of respect for Jerusalem's royal traditions in his prophecies.

Walter Beyerlin offers a similar interpretation in his classic study of Sinai tradition in Micah. Beyerlin writes that the expectations for the

---

1. Thus, Jeremiah, the great prophet of Sinai theology, hails from among the descendants of Abiathar dwelling in Anathoth (Jer 1:1; 1 Kgs 2:26). Ezekiel, whose prophecies are full of Zion's symbols and of plans for Zion's glorious restoration, is a proponent of Zadok's priestly lineage (cf. Ezek 40:46; 43:19; 44:15; 48:11).

future in Hosea and Micah agree. Both want a new obedience to the Sinai covenant traditions of Israel's old tribal confederacy. He notes, nonetheless, that Micah combines his call for covenantal obedience with a measure of respect for Davidic traditions. Unlike Hosea, in Micah the traditions and worship ceremonies of Jerusalem influence and color both covenantal loyalties and eschatological hopes.[2]

Sinai texts elsewhere in the Bible, such as in Jer 23:5, demonstrate that circles bearing Sinai traditions within Israel could simultaneously embrace theological traditions of love for David. Most significantly, the editors of the Deuteronomistic History have included 2 Sam 7, and a special orientation on King David, in their history of Israel (Joshua through 2 Kings). Second Samuel 7 contains Nathan's oracle, which unconditionally promises David a royal dynasty that shall endure forever. It is a programmatic example of Zion theology. The Deuteronomistic editors viewed Davidic messianism as compatible with the Sinai stream of tradition.

David receives similar special affirmation in the books of Kings. This is true despite the fact that first and second Kings more consistently reflect the Sinai theology of the Deuteronomists than do the books of Samuel. The Deuteronomistic editors of Kings picture God sparing the southern kingdom because, as the idiom has it, God keeps lit a "lamp" for David in Jerusalem (1 Kgs 11:36; 15:4; 2 Kgs 8:19). The Deuteronomists see a high point of Judean history in the eventual, climactic arrival of King Josiah, the great Deuteronomic reformer. They affirm God's love for David as the reason God keeps the way "lit" for Josiah, David's great descendant, throughout the long years of Judah's checkered history.

If the editors of the Deuteronomistic History eventually forged a middle way between Sinai and Zion, might not Micah have tried something similar a century or more earlier? Might Micah's prophecy not only possess a local, Judean coloring but also reflect attempts by the prophet to win over his royal, Jerusalemite audience by affirming what truths he could within their traditions? Fascinatingly, the book of Psalms provides evidence about the way that Micah's group was probably able to make inroads into Jerusalem's official circles.

The Psalter—the "hymnbook" of Jerusalem—now preserves the Psalms of Asaph, with all their Sinai theology. I have already noted in chapter 3 that King Hezekiah's cultic reforms at the beginning of his reign

---

2. Walter Beyerlin, *Die Kulttraditionen Israels in der Verkündigung des Propheten Micah* (FRLANT 62; Göttingen: Vandenhoeck & Ruprecht, 1959), 75–77. Given Micah's critique of Jerusalem's priests and prophets (e.g., Mic 3:5, 11), Beyerlin is too optimistic in supposing that Jerusalem's worship preserved and advocated the Sinai covenant up through Micah's times. Micah's Sinai traditions must come from circles long alienated from the temple.

welcomed Asaphite psalms into the worship of Jerusalem. Second Chronicles 29:30 reports that Hezekiah and his officials ordered the Levites to sing praises with the words of Asaph. The words of Asaphite Ps 78 may well have been among their praises, and this psalm particularly illuminates our discussion.

Psalm 78 embodies Sinai theology by focusing on the teaching of God's saving deeds (78:5–7) and the observance of the covenant by walking in God's torah (78:5, 10). (This psalm is surely a precursor of later Deuteronomic texts, such as Deut 6 and 2 Kgs 17:7–23.) The worshiping community in Jerusalem added Ps 78 to its repertoire, eventually modifying it for temple use by adding verses near the end that highlight God's election of Judah and Mount Zion. The modifications to the psalm are clear evidence of its adoption in Jerusalem. Michael Goulder's judgment is on target: "An influence from the Asaph community ... was accepted in Jerusalem in Hezekiah's time, but with vv. 9, 67–69 as ... glosses."[3]

The stream of theology borne by the Asaph community, and by Micah's circle, won acceptance in Jerusalem's worship over time. Notably, however, this was due in part to its being adaptable to Jerusalem's tremendous love of David. Psalm 78:70–72 reflect the same openness of Sinai theology toward David that occurs in Mic 5:1–6. These verses—authentic to the original psalm—celebrate David as a humble, rural figure. David leads the covenant people here not as a monarch per se, but in the mode of a shepherd—Yahweh's contract herder. Although the imagery and idiom belong to the cautious traditions of Sinai theology, the psalm is unmistakably positive about David. It shows the sort of support of Davidic rule within Sinai theology that may have finally opened doors in Jerusalem to Micah's message. Micah's words may have found entrance into official temple circles by hanging on the coattails of the Asaphites' work.

Micah 4:11–13 is the third of the set of two-part passages in Micah dealing with the siege of Jerusalem.

[11] Now many nations
    are assembled against you,
saying, "Let her be profaned,
    and let our eyes gaze upon Zion."
[12] But they do not know
    the thoughts of the LORD;

---

3. Michael D. Goulder, *The Psalms of Asaph and the Pentateuch: Studies in the Psalter, III* (JSOTSup 233; Sheffield: Sheffield Academic Press, 1996), 112. Goulder gives convincing arguments that 78:67–69 is a Jerusalemite graft within the psalm on p. 126.

they do not understand his plan,
    that he has gathered them as sheaves to the threshing floor.
¹³ Arise and thresh,
    O daughter Zion,
for I will make your horn iron
    and your hoofs bronze;
you shall beat in pieces many peoples,
    and shall devote their gain to the LORD,
    their wealth to the Lord of the whole earth.

This text differs from its sibling passages in key respects. Whereas the other passages in its set focus on the actual Assyrian siege of Jerusalem in 701, in this passage that event is merely a portent of a still greater, eschatological crisis. God gives Daughter Zion a horn of iron and hoofs of bronze so that she may pulverize worldwide powers of injustice arrayed against Jerusalem. This enables Daughter Zion to win an ultimate, global victory for God's cause.

This passage must come from a circle of disciples later than Micah's time, oriented toward the end times and able to envision a rehabilitated Jerusalem. This admission still does not explain the passage's positive, pro-Zion stance. If Micah's later followers remained committed to Micah's Sinai theology, why in this text did they make Daughter Zion the locus of God's saving action?

Though Mic 4:11–13 dates from a later time than 5:1–6, I can proceed along similar lines in its interpretation. Although the Micah group has developed a radical, almost apocalyptic eschatology here, Micah's disciples continue to work within Sinai categories.

The attention that Mic 4:11–13 pays to the mystery of God's purposes is a prime indication of Sinai theology. In the Sinai perspective, God's thinking and planning are mysterious and even numinous. Not following familiar patterns, God's holy purposes are incomparable to human ways. Sinai texts such as Hos 11:9; Asaphite Ps 50:21; Num 23:19 [E]; and Mic 7:18 all agree on this point. Our passage picks up this Sinai theme in its statement that the besieging nations have seriously misjudged their position. The nations do not know Yahweh's thoughts or understand God's counsel.

Verse 12 expresses this perspective in a unique Sinai idiom. The pair of nouns here, "thought" (מחשבה) and "counsel" (עצה), is rare outside of Micah. It occurs elsewhere almost exclusively in Jeremiah (Jer 49:20, 30; 50:45).

The cross-references in Jeremiah strongly reverberate with Mic 4:12, contrasting God's plans with those of nations such as Babylon and Edom. (Jer 49:30 understands Nebuchadnezzar's plan as an instrument of God's judgment.) The connection between Micah and Jeremiah is so strong that

H. W. Wolff thinks a disciple of Jeremiah somehow authored Mic 4:11–13.[4] Wolff's suggestion is extreme, but it does support my argument that the authors of the Micah passage, like Jeremiah's disciples, were working within Sinai theology.

The text's central idea of a divine thwarting of human conspiracy fits well among the other Sinai themes of Micah. So too does the text's admission in 4:13 that God is the true victor in the defeat of the array of nations.

Sinai texts such as the books of Deuteronomy and Judges are well known for their view of Yahweh as the real Divine Warrior who defeats Israel's enemies. As here, God assures the victory of the covenant people in their battles. Our passage's conviction that the people should recognize that their victory belongs to Yahweh assures us again that we have a Sinai text before us. In 4:13 Israel devotes to God (חרם) the spoils of war. (Note that the verb חרם ["devote (as divine spoil)"] also stands out in calls to holy war in Jer 50:21, 26; and 51:3.)

What is puzzling in Mic 4:11–13 is that Mount Zion, in particular, has become the home and base of operations of the "Divine Warrior." Elsewhere in Sinai texts, the Divine Warrior storms forth directly from the desert mountain of Sinai (or at least in a manner suggestive of a home base at Sinai). In Deut 33:1–5 God comes from Sinai with lightning flashes, to advance with the covenant people. In Judg 5:4–5, God appears as the "One of Sinai." God marches forth from regions south of Israel as the clouds pelt down water. Here in Mic 4:11–13, by contrast, Mount Zion has become a surrogate Mount Sinai.

The interpreter need not puzzle long at this feature of Mic 4:11–13. That Micah's group should make this sort of connection between Zion and Sinai is not that peculiar. To be sure, Micah's followers could have seen no resemblance to Sinai in the contemporary Zion of Micah's day. There is reason to believe, nevertheless, that Micah and his later followers remembered a more faithful Jerusalem of the past—a Mount Zion that aimed for continuity with Mount Sinai.

Biblical scholars have long argued that after the tribes of Israel established themselves in the land of Canaan, the liturgical worship of their sanctuaries celebrated and renewed the founding events at the desert mountain of Sinai. In the northern kingdom, sanctuaries at places such as Bethel, Shiloh, and Shechem inherited Mount Sinai's legacy. (Asaphite Ps 78:60 mentions in particular God's choice of Shiloh as a divine dwelling place within Canaan.) In the southern kingdom, it was at the Jerusalem temple on Mount Zion where the covenant people continued

---

4. Hans W. Wolff, *Micah: A Commentary* (trans. G. Stansell; CC; Minneapolis: Augsburg, 1990), 137, 138. On the idiom here, see K. Seybold, "חשׁב," *TDOT* 5:239; Wolff, *Micah*, 141.

to celebrate the thunderous, mountain appearance (theophany) of Yahweh the warrior.

In the Sinai terminology of Deut 12:5, God eventually chose to associate God's "name" with Jerusalem (Jer 7:10, 11). As Jon Levenson writes, "Mount Zion fell heir to the legacy of Mount Sinai. Zion became the prime locus of theophany, the home of Yahweh, the seat of his government, from which he promulgated decrees and at which Israel renewed her partnership in covenant with him."[5] Such a Sinai-oriented past might have raised hopes within the Micah circle for the future reassociation of Zion with Sinai. Precisely such hopes appear in our passage.

The Psalms of Asaph, which sprang out of north Israelite worship, bear witness that sanctuaries in the land of Israel absorbed and renewed Mount Sinai, becoming symbols of God's abode. In its original form, before Jerusalem adopted it, Asaphite Ps 50 proclaimed God's stormy appearance within northern worship. God appeared at the psalm's northern shrine in a thunderstorm theophany, to settle accounts and renew the covenant life of the people. "Our God comes and does not keep silence, before him is a devouring fire, and a mighty tempest all around him. He calls to the heavens above and to the earth, that he may judge his people: 'Gather to me my faithful ones, who made a covenant with me'" (50:3–5).

God also appears as Sinai's Divine Warrior in Asaphite Ps 76. This theophany is especially illuminating of Mic 4:11–13, since its purpose closely fits the scenario of the Micah passage. From a home base at an Israelite shrine, God arises in anger to judge the enemies of God's people. "There he broke the flashing arrows, the shield, the sword, and the weapons of war" (76:3).

The original locus of the theophany may have been the northern shrine at Shechem. "Salem" of 76:2 could well originally have been the northern town, Salem, closely associated with Shechem.[6] In the present version of the psalm, of course, 76:2 has been modified to make the psalm suitable for use in Jerusalem. Jerusalemite editors have made "Salem" a poetic parallel term to "Zion," so that it seems a shortened name of Jerusalem.

Whereas most of the Asaphite psalms are northern, Micah was a southern prophet. When his prophecies transpose Mount Sinai to Canaan, they naturally tend to place it at Jerusalem. Micah 1:2–7 is a good example.

---

5. Jon D. Levenson, *Sinai and Zion: An Entry into the Jewish Bible* (San Francisco: Harper & Row, 1987), 187.

6. For discussion, see Goulder, *Psalms of Asaph*, 86–88.

Micah 1:2–7 is authentic to Micah and comes from an early point in his career, as I argued in the preceding chapter. God emerges to judge Israel here in the mode of a mysterious and terrible Sinai theophany. The apparition displays all the pyrotechnics that generally accompany the march of Sinai's Divine Warrior.

What is fascinating, though, is Micah's language in 1:2 about how God emanates from the "holy temple." This language almost certainly reflects a past interconnection between Sinai and Zion, a past era when Judah's premier "holy temple" of Jerusalem adopted and celebrated the Sinai theophany. At present God may be coming to judge Jerusalem and its sanctuary ("high place," 1:5), but in times past that sanctuary had absorbed and molded the Sinai experience so that Jerusalem's temple became the origin of God's tremendous appearances on earth.

Other texts in Micah, such as Mic 6:1–8, also recall a past ideal that a faithful Zion should aim to absorb Mount Sinai. God holds cosmic court on earth to judge the people in Mic 6. The trial arguments that ensue revolve around the sacrificial altar at Jerusalem's temple (6:6–8). Again, it sounds as if Zion has become the de facto locus within which God and Israel wrestle over the future of their Sinai-based relationship.

It may be, then, that Mic 4:11–13 looks ahead to an ideal, future time when Mount Zion would actually absorb the divine character of Mount Sinai. In the end time, according to this passage, Zion in truth becomes a surrogate Sinai. The disciples of Micah have become willing here to actively promote and build up this idea of "absorption," which had really only been an unconscious influence from past temple worship in the prophecy of the group's founder. If I am right about this, the Micah group is again showing a remarkable commitment to forge a middle way between Sinai and Zion. With this commitment, they are actively reaching out to competing groups bearing the traditions of Zion.

The Micah group must have attempted such a program of outreach, with varying success, over a long stretch of time. Their efforts received a significant boost when, as Jer 26:18–19 reports, King Hezekiah eventually responded to Micah's social critique. Apparently, Hezekiah eventually heeded Micah's warning that Zion could be "plowed as a field" and repented (cf. 2 Kgs 19:1; 2 Chr 32:26). If Hezekiah had allowed Asaphite psalms into Jerusalem's worship at the start of his reign, as I have suggested, these psalms and their Sinai theology had already set the stage for this act of repentance.

It is worth emphasizing that by incorporating Asaph psalms into its worship Zion actually made a large concrete step toward absorbing Sinai. Micah's ongoing circle would have kept pushing Zion in this direction. As new members of the temple community, the sons of Asaph would have been good allies in this endeavor. Over time, old northern Asaphite

psalms were edited, and new ones were created, with the aim of connecting Zion back to Sinai.[7]

ZION TEXTS WITHIN THE BOOK OF MICAH

Thus far, our look at passages in Micah favorable to Jerusalem has
concentrated on texts rooted in Sinai theological tradition. The book of
Micah, however, at places has also taken over and incorporated passages
from its major competing stream of tradition, the stream oriented toward
Zion. I turn to this problem now.

Micah's book provides significant clues that the Zion theology it contains did not originate with Micah's own circle. Furthermore, these clues
allow for theorizing about what the Micah group thought they were up to
in their handling of this alien theology. Our interpretation can build on
what I have already suggested about the group's efforts toward theological dialog with their opponents.

Micah 4:1–5 stands out as a clear example of Zion theology amid
Micah's Sinai oriented prophecies.

[1] In days to come
    the mountain of the LORD's house
shall be established as the highest of the mountains,
    and shall be raised up above the hills.
Peoples shall stream to it,
    [2] and many nations shall come and say:
"Come, let us go up to the mountain of the LORD,
    to the house of the God of Jacob;
that he may teach us his ways
    and that we may walk in his paths."
For out of Zion shall go forth instruction,
    and the word of the LORD from Jerusalem.

---

7. Jerusalemite editors modified the Sinai theophany of Ps 50 so that God now shines
forth "out of Zion" (50:2). They also grafted in the name "Zion" in Ps 76:2 to make clear that
Jerusalem has become God's unique "dwelling place." An additional clear sign of
Jerusalem's adaptation of the Asaphite psalms appears at Ps 78:67–69, as I mentioned above.
Finally, there is empathy with Zion in Asaphite Pss 74 and 79, though with a somewhat different backdrop. These Asaphite psalms may have been composed in the exilic period—a
good deal of time after the sons of Asaph had joined the Jerusalem community. They hold
up Jerusalem as the "dwelling place of [God's] name" (Ps 74:7), but from a perspective of
lamentation. They mourn the desecration of the divine abode on Zion, which the Babylonians had wrought in 586 B.C.E. (Jer 7:12–15 prophesies this eventuality using similar Sinai
language to that in Ps 74:7.)

[3] He shall judge between many peoples,
    and shall arbitrate between strong nations far away;
they shall beat their swords into plowshares,
    and their spears into pruning hooks;
nation shall not lift up sword against nation,
    neither shall they learn war any more;
[4] but they shall all sit under their own vines and under their own fig trees,
    and no one shall make them afraid;
    for the mouth of the LORD of hosts has spoken.
[5] For all the peoples walk,
    each in the name of its god,
but we will walk in the name of the LORD our God
    forever and ever.

Following on the heels of Micah's famous prophecy of Zion's destruction, the passage sounds a particularly jarring note of contrast with Micah's own prophecy. No sooner does Mic 3:12 announce that "Zion will be plowed as a field" than Mic 4:1–5 describes Jerusalem and the temple on Mount Zion as the center of the world, God's own dwelling place from whence God will reign on earth.

James Mays thus states that the passage "has no place in the mission of Micah ... and it is clearly a direct contradiction of 3:12." Adam S. van der Woude agrees and goes further, arguing that the passage represents the very message of Micah's opponents.[8]

While I do not believe that the passage represents the words of Micah's enemies, it does appear to be a secondary addition to Micah's book. It is original neither to the prophet Micah nor to the ongoing circle of his disciples. Micah and his followers simply would not have authored such a text, which embodies a centralized, hierarchical administration of power.

Evidence external to the book confirms the text's alien status within Micah. The very same passage as Mic 4:1–5 appears outside of Micah, in the book of the prophet Isaiah, in Isa 2:2–5. The passage has a more natural context in this alternative setting, since Isaiah's prophecies also advocate a form of Jerusalem's royal theology. This is not to say that Isa 2:2–5 must be the prophecy's original version. In fact, a shared piece of

---

8. James L. Mays, *Micah: A Commentary* (OTL; Philadelphia: Westminster, 1976), 95; Adam S. van der Woude, "Micah IV 1–5: An Instance of the Pseudo-Prophets Quoting Isaiah," in *Symbolae biblicae et Mesopotamicae Francisco Mario Theodoro de Liagre Böhl dedicatae* (ed. M. A. Beek, A. A. Kampman, C. Nijland, and J. Ryckmans; Leiden: Brill, 1973), 396–402.

liturgical material from Jerusalem temple worship likely stands behind both Mic 4:1–5 and Isa 2:2–5.[9]

Close study of Mic 4:1–5 and Isa 2:2–5 reveals that the editors of Micah have handled this liturgical source material in a unique way that illuminates our current line of investigation. Their idiosyncratic shaping of this material provides signal clues about what they were doing in adding Zion texts to the Micah corpus.

The parallel passages in Micah and Isaiah diverge in a variety of ways, but in no place more significantly than at Mic 4:4. Here the passage in Micah intentionally and strategically deviates from its counterpart in Isaiah. Micah's group has grafted an insertion into the passage at this point that places a critical *spin* on its pro-Zion vision. With this insertion, the editors have carved out a special place within the passage for their own theology. They have made sure that the passage's Zion-oriented goals of global harmony and world peace are not achieved at the expense of Sinai values.

The theological values that the editors have grafted into the passage in 4:4 are, in fact, the core theological tenets to which Micah of Moresheth devoted his prophetic career. The ideal future vision of 4:4 differs sharply from the aristocratic values dear to the heart of Micah's opponents, Jerusalem's rulers and priests. In contrast to royal, ruling-class ideology, 4:4's goal is that each Israelite family be able to enjoy the results of its own labor on the land. The verse sounds a powerful note of solidarity with those who live close to the land, especially with all whom the powerful have evicted from their land and exploited as day laborers.

The verse expresses values that the black, South African theologian Itumeleng J. Mosala has found easy to embrace. Mosala specifically points out how 4:4 deviates from the hopes that various Zion texts have for the ideal future. He writes that, in contrast to monarchic values, the vision of 4:4 is not symbolized "by the possession of luxury items such as oil, a garment of praise, buildings and cities." Rather the focus is on individual families' "repossession of land, the tools, the control of their labor for productive use, and their security."[10]

The emphasis in 4:4 on the localized peace and rest that each individual's plot of land provides comes straight out of Sinai theological tradition. Whereas in Zion theology, the Temple Mount forms a center of holiness that conveys stability and peace to its surrounding territory, in Sinai theology the whole of Israel is fully God's holy land. All

---

9. For discussion, see Mays, *Micah*, 94–95; Wolff, *Micah*, 115.

10. Itumeleng J. Mosala, *Biblical Hermeneutics and Black Theology in South Africa* (Grand Rapids: Eerdmans, 1989), 38, 152.

Canaan is God's special territory where all Israelites may enjoy tranquility and security.

Sinai texts convey this notion by highlighting the entire holy land as God's place of "rest" for God's people. In Exod 33:14 (E), God promises Moses to lead the people into the land to give them rest. The same terminology appears in Deut 25:19; Josh 21:44; and Jer 27:11. Deuteronomy 12:8–12 spells out some of what this "rest" in the land involves. For Israel, it spells "rest from all your enemies around you so that you live in security" (12:10).

This same vision of Israel dwelling undisturbed and secure from warfare appears in Mic 4:4. The Mican graft states that, with each Israelite family dwelling safely under its personal vine and fig tree, there will be "no one to make them afraid." (On the wording of 4:4 here, see Jer 30:10; 46:27.)

Deuteronomy 12:8–12 does more than clarify that the land as God's "resting place" means security from enemies. It also explains that the land only fully becomes a secure refuge when all Israelites actually possess it. Deuteronomy 12:9 and 12 describe the land as Israel's "inheritance" from God. The word "inheritance" (נחלה) in these verses is loaded language in Sinai theology. For Micah, it was a fighting word.

Saying that the land is an "inheritance" in Sinai theology makes clear its gift of rest passes to all Israel only as it is physically and fully apportioned among all families, when these families know that they are secure in their ongoing tenure on it (cf. Deut 3:18–20; Josh 1:12–15; 22:1–6).

Micah went head to head with the authorities in Jerusalem over this concrete aspect of Sinai theology. Micah 2:10 evicts the Jerusalem landgrabbers precisely from God's "place of rest," since they have hoarded the land and thus brought on themselves the ultimate covenant curse.

Against the monarchy's militarization of Judah as Jerusalem's buffer zone, and the land-grabbers' appropriation of Judean farmland to form huge, private estates, Micah stood up for the security of the individual Israelite farmer's possession of an inherited, family plot of land. He stood his ground firmly on the traditions of Sinai theology. As chapter 2 argued, Sinai theological traditions emphasize God's granting of the promised land to Israel as an "inheritance" (e.g., Deut 4:21, 38; 32:8), the apportionment of the land based on lineage categories (Josh 11:23; 13:7), and the principle of ongoing tenure of land within tribes, clans, and families (Deut 19:14; 1 Sam 8:14 [B source]; 1 Kgs 21:2–3).

Micah 4:4 inserts the Sinai theme of the land as an "inheritance" for all Israel's families into Zion's dreams for an ideal future. The graft comes at a critical point. By having 4:4 follow on the grand, cosmopolitan dream of world disarmament in Mic 4:3, the Mican editors point out that in

actual practice such a dream will require concrete economic and ideological change.

Judah's leaders cannot build Zion's dream on a foundation of local
oppression. If all are to give up swords and spears, everyone must possess, and remain content with, their own simple homestead—their own
vine and fig tree. That would mean radical changes in the tax structure
and profit system that drives military aggression—the sort of changes
that Micah himself promoted. Walter Brueggemann has put this well:

> [With verse 4 added, Mic 4] offers not only a grand dream, but a realistic
> hint of what is required.... The arms cannot be given up without aban-
> doning swollen appetites as well. There is here no desire to claim this
> oracle for Micah in the eighth century, but to observe that such an inter-
> pretation fits well with Micah's strictures against the surplus-value
> practice of the royal economy (cf. 2:1–5; 3:1–3).... [Verse 4] anticipates a
> modest life-style of not having more than one's own produce and there-
> fore a respect for the produce of others. It implies being ready to settle
> for one's own vines and figs without yearning for or coveting the vines
> and figs which others produce. The poet knows that the vines and fig
> trees of others will be safe only when the powerful are content with
> the grapes and figs they themselves produce.[11]

The proverbial expression about "vine and fig tree" in Mic 4:4 echoes
other Sinai texts and their descriptions of Canaan as the ideal land that
God calls Israel to inhabit in safety. Deuteronomy 8:8 describes the promised land as a land "of vines and fig trees." Hosea 2:12 laments that by
misunderstanding the identity of the land's true proprietor, Israel has
compelled God to destroy "her vines and fig trees," while Jer 5:17 and
8:13 consider one of Israel's greatest losses in its forfeiture of the covenant
to be the loss of "vines" and "fig trees." These cross-references all
strengthen my argument that 4:4 promotes Sinai theology.

The way that the graft in 4:4 resonates with authentic Micah
prophecy has specific implications for interpreting Mic 4:1–5. First, since
the editors used this graft to conform our passage to Micah's theology,
there is no reason to doubt that it was Micah's ongoing circle of disciples
who inserted Mic 4:1–5 into the book. It is unnecessary to take this passage as an accretion, added to the book by extraneous editors with no
connection to Micah. Micah's own disciples added this passage to the
book, perhaps already by the seventh or early sixth centuries B.C.E.

---

11. Walter Brueggemann, "'Vine and Fig Tree': A Case Study in Imagination and Criticism," *CBQ* 43 (1981): 193–94.

Second, their efforts at tempering Mic 4:1–5 through adding the graft imply that these disciples were at pains to promote conversation with the advocates of Zion theology. Group efforts at dialog with their opponents have progressed farther here than even what we saw in Mic 4:11–13. The latter passage sought to transform Mount Zion into a de facto Sinai. This passage celebrates Mount Zion in and of itself.

Their willingness to add Mic 4:1–5 to their collection of Micah's writings reflects changes in the Micah group, and particularly in its social location, toward the end of its history. In its late history, the group was probably absorbed into Hezekiah's or Josiah's royal establishment, just as the sons of Asaph had been slightly earlier. I want to elaborate on this suggestion briefly below.

A second example completes my treatment of the willingness of Micah's group to append Zion theology to their traditions. The example occurs in Mic 4:6–8. Like 4:1–5, the short passage sits very uneasily alongside Micah's condemnations of Jerusalem and its leaders. Micah's group must have added this foreign material to the book at a relatively late stage in their group history.

> ⁶ In that day, says the LORD,
>> I will assemble the lame
> and gather those who have been driven away,
>> and those whom I have afflicted.
> ⁷ The lame I will make the remnant,
>> and those who were cast off, a strong nation;
> and the LORD will reign over them in Mount Zion
>> now and forevermore.
> ⁸ And you, O tower of the flock,
>> hill of daughter Zion,
> to you it shall come,
>> the former dominion shall come,
>> the sovereignty of daughter Jerusalem.

Although Mic 4:6–8 has found its way into Micah, the evidence makes clear that it originated with competing, Zion oriented circles. The text is all about Jerusalem's identity as Mount Zion and its dominion as a ruling city.

Echoing divine promises in Isaiah to always preserve a holy remnant within Israel, 4:7 assures the reader that God will preserve a faithful group through all judgment, and then save and empower them as a mighty nation (cf. Isa 4:3; 10:20; 28:5). Explicitly emphasizing God's divine kingship, the verse promises God will reign over the remnant "in Mount Zion" (cf. Isa 24:23; 52:7; Ps 146:10).

Micah 4:8 goes on to address Jerusalem directly and assure the city it will again receive the regal status it previously enjoyed. Its Hebrew terminology refers to Jerusalem not only as the citadel of God's remnant people but also as a stately acropolis, which will regain its royal power. This hopeful picture of a centralized, royal realm is alien to the authentic writings of Micah's group.

Micah's followers who edited his book must have become remarkably open to Zion theology to incorporate this passage. Careful observation of how they used the passage to help give the book of Micah a unique internal structure, however, shows that they used Mic 4:6–8 to reinforce the book's genuine themes and messages, not contradict them. Micah's editors have not abandoned their original emphases. They have become willing to commingle these emphases with those of other Israelite groups.

By placing this passage where they have, right before Mic 4:9–10, Micah's editors have duplicated an earlier pattern in the book in which Mic 2:12–13 lies immediately before 3:1–4. The editors have created a parallelism between two sets of passages: On the one hand, 2:12–13 is followed up by 3:1–4. On the other hand, 4:6–8 is followed up by 4:9–10. With each set of juxtaposed passages, the editors have created a sequence that contrasts a future, ideal monarchic reign (2:13; 4:8) with Israel's contemporary misfortune of having inadequate and unjust leaders (3:1; 4:9). This editorial pattern reinforces Micah's original argument that human kingship threatens God's suzerainty, at least on this side of God's eschatological rule. The editors' reminders of how good things will be in the ideal future reinforce the critique of royal abuses inherent in Micah's authentic Sinai theology.

Micah's editors probably chose 4:6–8 to help them create this structural pattern within Micah because it shares key motifs with 2:12–13. Having the two sets of passages begin with similar motifs reinforces their parallelism. Although it knows nothing of the Sinai theology of kingship in Mic 2:12–13, our passage does use the motif of the "remnant" and the motif of God's people as "sheep." It also uses some identical Hebrew vocabulary, such as the verbs "assemble" and "gather."

Despite its Zion theology, Mic 4:6–8 may also have attracted Micah's editors because of its similarities to 5:2–5. Both of these passages are a rhetorical address to a Davidic city, which they personify as a center of a coming messianic reign. The similarities in genre, and the possibilities for reinforcing their authentic tradition, have made our passage too enticing for the editors to resist. The editors used these features of the passage to their best advantage by placing the text in a position to prepare the reader for the announcement of a coming messiah in Mic 5:2. The text announces a coming restoration of dominion in Israel and then forces the reader to wait until chapter 5 to learn more about the person through whom that restoration will occur.

But enough of this detailed exegetical work. It is time to summarize the findings of this chapter and to elaborate on some of what these findings suggest about the history of Micah's group.

SYNTHESIS

At base level, the interpretations of Micah's promise oracles and assurances to Jerusalem in this chapter support my basic thesis that Micah and his circle were proponents of Sinai theology. For the most part, the promise oracles of the book show every sign of being authentic to the Sinai theological stream of tradition. True, they are sometimes more positive about Jerusalem, the temple, and the family of David than what we find in Hosea's book. This is not much of a distraction, however, when one remembers that Micah's group had a far different milieu and background than Hosea's circle.

During Micah's time, many of the plain people of the land were experiencing the oppression of David's monarchic descendents. The mission of Micah's circle was to defend those commoners. Their alienation from contemporary royalty does not mean, though, that they had necessarily lost their love for David himself. David, after all, had started out as a simple, rustic shepherd. Not only had he come from rural roots, but he had also won over many people throughout the countryside through his charisma and bravery in battle.

People also remembered David for his determination, as king, to reach out to multiple constituencies. His rule was a negotiated one, since he based it on compacts forged with representatives of the people. So too, his reign had been conciliatory in tone, inclusive of multiple theological perspectives. One of David's two chief priests, Abiathar, represented the Sinai theological perspective in Jerusalem.

If Micah's constituency shared this sort of positive remembrance of David as shepherd and reconciler, they could easily have been open to a prophecy of a future king of promise who would be like the original David. Such an ideal shepherd-king would exercise a tempered, cautious human rule over the "flock" and "pasture land" of God—a rule in line with the traditions of Sinai theology.

Just as Micah's group operated amid strong feelings of loyalty to David, they also could not have completely avoided the emotional pull of the Jerusalem temple. Like the figure of David, the symbol of the temple would not have been one-sidedly negative for them. The members of the group were able to look back to a time when their ancestors experienced Sinai traditions celebrated in the temple. Furthermore, they probably hoped that in the future, after a period of judgment, the worship at Jerusalem would again follow the lines of Sinai traditions.

Although most of the book's hopes for Jerusalem stem from an authentic orientation toward Sinai, a few texts of Zion theology are also present. They claim "squatting rights" in this book. Micah 4:1–5 and 6–8, in particular, celebrate Zion. In Jerusalem they see God's holy mountain, which will someday tower in authority over all of Israel and even over the whole world.

These passages do not merely bear the special coloring that comes from operating within the gravitational pull of Jerusalem; they are actual Zion texts lying amid the authentic prophecies of Micah's circle. That is, they are *interpolations* over against the book's base orientation—as much "sore thumbs" as Hos 3:5, which upholds King David amid an overwhelmingly antimonarchical collection of prophecies.

Though the Zion texts within Micah are interpolations, Micah's own continuing school probably inserted them. Our brief examinations of the passages in question uncovered some factors that likely attracted Micah's editors to them and influenced how these editors put them to use. In the present structure and outline of the book, the interpolations reinforce some of the book's themes and accent some of the book's emphases.

It is insufficient, however, to account for the presence of these Zion traditions in Micah merely based on the good use to which the editors creatively put them in shaping the Micah collection. Their presence must also reflect changes that occurred in the Micah group toward the end of its history. In my view, the presence of actual Zion passages within the Micah collection signals that the Micah group eventually reached a stage of reconciliation and incorporation within royal and temple circles.

Compare what happened with the Asaphite psalmists. It seems obvious that it was due to incorporation within royal and temple circles that these psalmists began to incorporate features of Zion theology in editing and composing their psalms. By analogy, it is reasonable to argue that the Zion-oriented additions to Micah arose from a similar development. Such a development within the history of the Micah group was a significant event in the overall flowering of biblical Yahwism, a key moment in which biblical Yahwism moved to the center of Israelite society.

In chapter 3 I surveyed the history of biblical Yahwism's flowering, and described the reigns of King Hezekiah and King Josiah as pivotal periods in the history. It may have been during one or both of these reigns that Micah's circle moved towards society's center. Both Hezekiah and Josiah instituted cultic reforms that gave the Sinai covenant official standing. The witnesses of both the Psalms of Asaph and of Micah's prophecy stimulated the first of these reforms under Hezekiah.

It was only the Asaphite guild of singers, however, which gained inner access to the Jerusalem cult at the actual time of Hezekiah's cult reform. Despite the reform of the cult, Micah's circle was determined to maintain a peripheral stance over against Hezekiah's regime. From there, they were best able to criticize his economic and social policies.

Hezekiah seems to have repented even of social injustices later in his reign (Jer 26:19; 2 Chr 32:26). The overwhelming experience of the arrival of Sennacherib's army in 701 B.C.E. played a key role in his change of heart. Micah's circle may have moved into society's center after this royal conversion in 701.

The second reform period, under Josiah, is another plausible time when Micah's group may have taken up a central position in society. According to 2 Kgs 21:24 (cf. 2 Chr 33:25), it was representatives of the people of the land who raised Josiah to power after a palace coup killed King Amon. I argued in chapter 3 that these "people of the land" were strong supporters of Sinai theology. They must have influenced Josiah's formation in the decade of his reign before he reached an age of majority (cf. 2 Chr 34:3). Josiah ordered his major Sinai-oriented reform of the country when he reached his eighteenth birthday, and he summoned the elders of the land to initiate that reform with him. Together they held a public renewal of the Sinai covenant (2 Kgs 23:1).

The prophet Micah represented the people of the land, just as these elders did. The people of the land were Micah's own rural constituency, whose land rights he defended in Jerusalem. Micah's ongoing group, along with other representatives of the people of the land, could well have been part of a reform party that wanted to push Sinai theology to society's center at the time of King Josiah. They were a central component of Josiah's power base, profoundly influential in his reform program, recognized by him in public ritual.

Given these facts, there is no reason to doubt that after Josiah instituted his reform he gave Micah's group a permanent place within his court. It was from this social location that pro-Sinai court circles authored an early edition of the Deuteronomistic history during Josiah's reign. As noted in chapter 3, Josiah's pro-Sinai reign saw the production of a major edition of this biblical history of Israel.

The theory that Micah's group eventually formed part of the circle that scholars call the Deuteronomistic writers helps us envision how Zion theology found a place in their thinking.[12] Within the Deuteronomistic

12. For further evidence that the Deuteronomists included the ongoing Micah circle within their ranks, see Stephen L. Cook, "Micah's Deuteronomistic Redaction and the

history, 2 Sam 6 recognizes Jerusalem as God's chosen central shrine, where God causes God's name to dwell. Second Samuel 7 recognizes God's promises to the Davidic dynasty. Despite their commitment to Sinai theology, the Deuteronomists demonstrably found a way to work with their pro-Zion conversation partners within Jerusalem circles. They found a way to endorse some central texts of Zion theology by including them in their historical work.

Even at such a final stage of incorporation within King Hezekiah's or King Josiah's court, there is no evidence that Micah's editors ever abandoned or retreated from the core Sinai traditions at the heart of the Micah collection.[13] They never softened Micah's original Sinai-based polemic against Jerusalem and its leaders. Rather, they purposively edited Zion texts to make them better conform to the spirit of Sinai.

Perhaps the clearest example of this is that Micah's editors never altered Mic 3:12. They never accommodated this devastating critique of Zion to the new promonarchy and pro-Zion interpolations in the book. In the present form of the book, the verse stands without qualification as it always has: "On account of you, Zion will be plowed as a field, Jerusalem will become a heap of rubble, and the Temple Mount a forest ridge." The verse is now juxtaposed with the pro-Zion promise that follows it, but has not been harmonized with, or subordinated to, that following text.

Even at the end of their history, the Micah group archived and handed down their Sinai traditions in all their unadulterated power. These traditions remain alive and well within Micah's book. They stand ready to come into their own whenever occasion should warrant.

The traditions of the Sinai covenant in Micah stand ready to speak loudly to any occasion when God's people begin to trust in a cheap grace, which relies on God's blessing while all the while lacking any sense of reciprocal obligation to uphold God's requirements of justice. Micah's core theology stands as an undiluted witness that humans cannot oppress those around them and continue to remain within God's favor.

Deuteronomists' Identity," in *Those Elusive Deuteronomists: The Phenomenon of Pan-Deuteronomism* (ed. L. S. Schearing and S. L. McKenzie; JSOTSup 268; Sheffield: Sheffield Academic Press, 1999), 216–31.

13. In this, they followed the standards of their group founder. As Levenson has correctly observed, "There is no empirical basis upon which to assert that the Davidic theology blunted the impact of Micah's covenantal preaching" (*Sinai and Zion*, 199).

6

A SOCIAL-SCIENTIFIC MODEL FOR EXCAVATING THE ROOTS OF BIBLICAL YAHWISM

THE POINT HAS COME IN OUR SEARCH FOR THE ROOTS OF BIBLICAL Yahwism to probe behind the texts of Micah and Hosea for these texts' social origins. Our study thus far has already provided many hints about the general direction in which to proceed. The strong polemics and indictments of Micah and Hosea show that Sinai covenant theology was at odds with the majority culture of the eighth century. Before the reforms of Hezekiah and Josiah, at least, Sinai theology had to struggle against popular religion and its polytheistic beliefs and practices.

Further, there is no sense looking to Israel's monarchy or to official religion for the social background of Sinai theology. Its central tenets are diametrically opposed to the way that dynastic kingship and royal cult developed in Israel's history. In particular, Sinai theology opposed the way that the officials and priests of Jerusalem depended on the theological traditions of promise to Zion.

At the time of Micah and Hosea, and probably for a long time prior, biblical Yahwism was a minority religious perspective, peripheral to the central power structures of the northern and southern Israelite states.

In contrast to the values and assumptions of the Israelite states of their time, Micah and Hosea bear witness to alternative presuppositions and beliefs. They describe their hopes for the future using simple, agricultural ideals rather than in terms of the luxury items of economies that produce surpluses beyond the needs of local farmers. Their ideal future leader has the qualities of a rural shepherd, not the splendid trappings of a state official.

As for the present, the concerns of Micah and Hosea are traditional and conservative in nature. They consider their fellow Israelites to be one people, bound together by family ties—not the monarchical subjects of two separate states. They want to preserve the rights of Israelite families to their ancestral farmlands in the face of land grabbing by the newly wealthy, and taxation by an increasingly demanding monarchy. They want to head off threats to the fertility of those farmlands posed by the false fertility worship of the monarchy, with its royal chapels and appointed priests.

Our investigation has already revealed that the Sinai theological stream of tradition originates in an alternative societal system in Israel, different from the eighth-century, state-based society contemporary with our prophets. Micah and Hosea's traditions instead reflect an earlier, bygone stage of Israel's development as a society.

In the remainder of this book I test these suggestions and elaborate on their potential for making possible a more critical and precise understanding of the social roots of biblical Yahwism than that of much contemporary scholarship. I start by constructing a social-scientific model in this chapter that accounts for the conflict between societal systems that our study of Hosea and Micah has brought into focus. Then, in chapters 7 and 8, I return to the books of Hosea and Micah and test the model on their evidence about our prophets' early predecessors.

My model draws on results that revolutionary social-scientific investigations of the Bible have been discovering over the past twenty-five years. Some of these investigations clarify how two different societal systems overlapped within Israel during the eighth-century times of Micah and Hosea. These two superimposed social systems were in tension, and they must have often clashed.

The older of the two systems traces back to Israel's traditional, genealogical organization from at least the early Iron Age. The second system arose with the development of the Israelite monarchy in the tenth century (Iron Age IC), and it came into increasing conflict with the earlier system. The older system was never fully supplanted, and Micah and Hosea were nurtured within its remnants.

The model that I construct in this chapter finds particular strength and interest in drawing on descriptions that anthropologists and ethnographers have provided of overlapping social systems. Social scientists have observed such overlapping systems in various places around the world. Their cross-cultural studies clarify and illustrate the social scenario in which agrarian ideals confront the ideals of an emerging centralized state.

Cross-cultural comparisons also help us look behind the development of such a conflict to envision the agrarian, village based societies that may later be pressed toward societal centralization. They provide examples of the nature and workings of traditional, tribal societies that organize themselves around family ties and kinship.

I shall exercise appropriate methodological caution in using cross-cultural comparisons from anthropology and in applying a social-scientific model in interpreting biblical texts. In bringing in social-scientific studies, I shall draw on a broad enough range of sufficiently recent studies to avoid either oversimplifying theories from outside of biblical studies or accepting them uncritically.

In using a model to clarify the social world behind Micah and Hosea, I intend to allow for flexibility and variability among actual, concrete cases. It is counterproductive to force biblical texts to conform to rigid ideal types.

Finally, I understand models are hypotheses that the scholar must test against the evidence of biblical texts through generally accepted methods of biblical exegesis. Social-scientific models suggest a range of possibilities for understanding biblical texts, and they suggest new questions that may not occur to biblical scholars. It is only an exegesis of the biblical texts, however, that can either confirm or disconfirm whether a given model is applicable and helpful in a particular case, such as that of Micah or Hosea.

THE GENERAL BIBLICAL PICTURE

By the eighth-century times of Micah and Hosea, new, increasingly powerful monarchic systems of socioeconomic organization in both the northern and southern kingdoms were competing with Israel's older, tribal and village structures. They were competing and winning, although the old way of life continued with a measure of vitality well into monarchic times and beyond. Archaeology buttresses this biblical picture.[1]

---

1. Without question, societal centralization in Judah and Israel was an extended process, during which tribal systems and lifestyles persisted. I demonstrate in the present chapter, in fact, that tribal culture had an amazing longevity, surviving as a social substratum for centuries beyond the rise of the early Israelite kings. This fact in no way negates the historical reality of centralized monarchy in ninth- and eighth-century Israel, however.

We know that the northern kingdom was recognized as a great regional state as early as the mid-ninth century. In an artifact known as the Monolith Inscription, the Assyrian king Shalmaneser III mentions that the great chariot force of King Ahab of the northern kingdom participated in the battle of Qarqar in 853 B.C.E. There is a clear convergence of archaeology and the biblical narrative here.

The language of the Mesha stele (the Moabite Stone), another extrabiblical inscription, provides complimentary evidence supporting the general biblical picture. The rhetoric of the stone's inscription reflects the aspirations of the Moabite king, Mesha, to emulate how neighboring Israelite kings modeled royal legitimacy. If ninth-century Moab tried to model itself on a state system of polity in Israel, this presupposes a well-developed Israelite system of monarchy at the time. Far from an unexceptional case of ninth-century political consolidation in the Levant, the northern kingdom must have been an exemplar of state polity for other local societies to follow. (Ryan Byrne has summarized some of this evidence in a conference paper, "The Moabite Stone and State" [presented in the Social Sciences and the Interpretation of the Hebrew Scriptures Section at the annual meeting of the Society of Biblical Literature, Denver, Colo., 19 November 2001]. On state formation in Transjordanian Moab, also see Bruce E. Routledge, "Learning to Love the King: Urbanism and the State in Iron Age Moab," in *Urbanism in Antiquity: From Mesopotamia to Crete* [ed. Walter E. Aufrecht, Neil A. Mirau, and Steven W. Gauley; JSOTSup 244; Sheffield: Sheffield Academic Press, 1997], 130–44; idem, "The Politics of Mesha: Segmented Identities and State Formation in Iron Age Moab," *JESHO* 43 [2000]: 221–56.)

The evidence for an early centralized state in the south, in Judah, and particularly for a tenth-century united monarchy, is more controverted. Israel Finkelstein, for example, has argued that Judah crystallized as a real state power only around 700 B.C.E. See Israel Finkelstein, "State Formation in Israel and Judah: A Contrast in Context, a Contrast in Trajectory," *Near Eastern Archaeology* 62 (1999): 35–52; Israel Finkelstein and Neil Asher Silberman, *The Bible Unearthed: Archaeology's New Vision of Ancient Israel and the Origin of Its Sacred Texts* (New York: Free Press, 2000).

I disagree with this skeptical assessment of Judah's monarchic heritage. First, as Finkelstein admits, extrabiblical inscriptions confirm both the existence of a Davidic dynasty and the historical reliability of the biblical lists of David's royal descendants. These inscriptions are part of a whole body of evidence for monarchic centralization in Judah long before 700 B.C.E. Let us review some of this evidence, starting with the eighth century and then moving back in time.

By the eighth century, we find Micah and Isaiah complaining to royal officials about land grabbing and militarization in the countryside under monarchic, state-based rule. Archaeological evidence, such as elaborate new tombs in Jerusalem for nobility and officials, confirms the biblical picture of Judah as a developed monarchic state at this time (see chapter 7, below).

Micah's prophetic complaints to Judean officials (e.g., Mic 3:1–4) are especially significant because of their presuppositions. Micah assumes a tradition of covenantal tempering of state judicial practice. He echoes earlier, ninth-century texts in the E strand (such as Exod 18:13–27), which put significant strictures in place in response to the dangers of a powerful, centralized judiciary. The cautions and caveats in the E-strand about a centralized judiciary must predate Micah, since the E writers were still optimistic that royal judges could respect covenantal norms. Such optimism was no longer possible at Micah's time. (For a full discussion of this evidence in E and in Micah, see Stephen L. Cook, "The Tradition of Mosaic Judges: Past Approaches and New Directions," in *On the Way to Nineveh: Studies in Honor of George M. Landes* [ed. S. L. Cook and S. Winter; ASOR Books 4; Atlanta: Scholars Press, 1999], 294–98.)

There is even harder evidence for societal centralization in Judah in ninth- and tenth-century times. It is quite misleading for Finkelstein and Silberman to characterize Judah of this period as a society of dispersed villages amid rural farms. Tell en-Nasbeh, an old rural settlement, was transformed into a fortified administrative city of Judah in the ninth century. Tell Beit Mirsim experienced a similar incorporation into Judah's military and commercial administrative system during during the ninth and eighth centuries. See Ze'ev Herzog, *Archaeology of the City: Urban Planning in Ancient Israel and Its Social Implications* (Tel Aviv: Yass Archaeology Press, Institute of Archaeology, Tel Aviv University, 1997), 237–39, 242–44, 249.

The Bible describes Kings David and Solomon as the founders of monarchy in Israel. If we are to believe the biblical narratives about these early kings, the beginnings of new, state-based systems of political administration, economics, and judicial coordination in Israel trace back to their reigns.

David captured a non-Israelite city, Jerusalem, and established it as a new monarchic capital. Independent of the traditional territories of Israel's tribes, Jerusalem was the ideal center for a new political system (2 Sam 5:6–9). According to texts such as 2 Sam 8:15–18 and 20:23–26, David also began to institute a new, complex bureaucracy to administer the new monarchic state. The king further created a new military unit of body-guards and mercenary troops, who owed their loyalty to his royal person rather than to the people of Israel as a whole (2 Sam 8:18; 20:23).

As he took these measures to form Israel into a state, however, David also wisely sought to maintain the support of his traditional, tribal con-stituencies. The free, landowning people of Israel still controlled the ratification of rulers (cf. 2 Sam 2:4; 3:12, 17, 21; 5:1–3). For the near future, at least, Israelite monarchs would have to maintain a consensus of support

---

King Rehoboam of Judah was besieged by Pharaoh Shishak according to 1 Kgs 14:25–28, and archaeology corroborates the text's recollection of Egyptian conflict with an historical Judean state. Shishak's incursion against Solomon's son and successor left behind destruction layers at several sites in Palestine—including a destruction layer at Gezer, a city fortified by Solomon in buttressing his kingdom (1 Kgs 9:15–17). Two extrabiblical artifacts, a triumphal relief of Shishak (the Egyptian Sheshonk) at Karnak and a fragment of a stele at Megiddo, assure us that these destruction layers connect to the pharaoh's campaign into Palestine in 926 B.C.E. Monumental city walls and gates at Gezer from King Solomon's period further document the rise of the monarchy in the tenth century. They attest to Solomon's royal fortification efforts before Shishak's raid. See William G. Dever, *What Did the Biblical Writers Know and When Did They Know It? What Archaeology Can Tell Us about the Reality of Ancient Israel* (Grand Rapids: Eerdmans, 2001), 131–38.

Other evidence of a tenth-century state, administered from Jerusalem, comes from recent archaeological campaigns at the Judean city of Beth-shemesh. These excavations show that Beth-shemesh was a fortified administrative center of the united monarchy (cf. 1 Kgs 4:9), not an obscure, undefended village. Among the finds from the site is a game board inscribed with the name of its owner in tenth-century Hebrew script. Tenth-century Judean society was becoming at least partially literate as well as centralized. See Dever, *Biblical Writers,* 143–44; Shlomo Bunimovitz and Zvi Lederman, "Beth-Shemesh: Culture Conflict on Judah's Frontier," *BAR* 23/1 (1997): 42–49, 75–77.

A new appearance of burnished pottery vessels also reveals a new social order emerg-ing in Israelite society already in the tenth century B.C.E. This new ceramics helped mark public food consumption as a male domain, and food preparation and storage as a female domain. Such a change in perceptions of gender relations and social space is consistent with an emerging new societal centralization and state formation. For discussion, see Avraham Faust, "Burnished Pottery and Gender Hierarchy in Iron Age Israelite Society," *Journal of Mediterranean Archaeology* 15/1 (2002): 53–73.

among old Israel's leaders. These leaders included the elders of the populace, the commanders of the popular militia, and the heads of the various
priestly families.

To maintain the support of these traditional power brokers, David
wisely appointed not one, but two chief priests in Jerusalem—Zadok and
Abiathar—each representing a major genealogical line of priests (the
Aaronides and the Levites, respectively). David judged correctly that
Israel's older societal system would not simply bow out of the picture as
a new state system developed.

According to the biblical account, King Solomon, David's son and
successor, greatly furthered the development of a monarchic societal
system in Israel. First Kings 4:7–19, 27–28 report that Solomon reorgan-
ized the Israelite kingdom into new administrative districts, designed to
support the needs of the new centralized monarchy. Each one took a turn
supplying the monthly provisions of the royal palace in Jerusalem.

Solomon created these new divisions at the expense of Israel's older,
tribal organization. The new divisions of the land cut across and broke up
Israel's older tribal territories. Solomon's taxation of the new districts
extracted a great deal of their agricultural production, straining the economic bases that supported tribal Israel's traditional communal life.

The eroding effect on village Israel was exacerbated as Solomon com-
pleted David's work establishing the capital, Jerusalem, as Israel's central
(though not yet exclusive) place of sacrificial worship. Solomon's temple-
based system of worship and pilgrimage extracted additional support
from Israel's villages. This strained even farther the villagers' traditional
resources for supporting themselves as a community. After Solomon's
united monarchy split up after his death, the first northern king would
similarly centralize sacral power in his new kingdom.

Significantly, Solomon's monarchy did not merely extract material
goods from the country's populace. Texts such as 2 Sam 20:24; 1 Kgs
5:13–18; 11:28 depict forced labor as an element in David's, and especially
Solomon's, great public building projects. Some scholars are suspicious of
the accuracy of these texts, and it is hard to believe that the state could
have used the *corvée* for extended periods without destroying its agricultural tax base. The crown probably did extract some of the population's
forced labor for reasonable stretches of time, however.[2]

---

2. D. Snell, "Taxes and Taxation," *ABD* 6:339; John S. Holladay Jr., "Chapter 22. The
Kingdoms of Israel and Judah: Political and Economic Centralization in the Iron IIA-B (ca.
1000–750 B.C.E.)," in *The Archaeology of Society in the Holy Land* (ed. T. E. Levy; New York:
Facts on File, 1995), 382.

With Solomon, the monarchy also considered itself less dependent on the support of some traditional segments of society. The chief Levitical priest Abiathar lost favor with Solomon, since he deprived Solomon of crucial political support in his contest for succession. Solomon did not feel safe in killing Abiathar outright, but he did expel the priest from Jerusalem (1 Kgs 2:26). The king thereby disenfranchised the Levitical priesthood of much of their authority in Israelite society.

According to every indication, the centralizing programs of David and Solomon continued and intensified in both the southern and northern kingdoms throughout the monarchic period in Israel. The monarchy's practice of imposing forced labor on the populace continued well past Solomon's time. King Asa, at least, built the cities of Geba and Mizpah using forced labor according to 1 Kgs 15:22.

Israel's monarchs also created a professional, standing army in Israel (1 Sam 8:11–12). In the older, militia system, tribes and family groups mustered temporary troops to support the whole people in times of crisis. Under the new, monarchic system, Israel's populace was responsible for sustaining a permanent military apparatus at home and out on campaigns. In return for this support, they often found themselves at the mercy of the military's political, economic, and judicial will. As J. David Pleins writes:

> The populace would have to supply goods for the sustenance of the soldiers and military officials. In addition, the peasants would be called on to serve as forced laborers in the construction of military fortifications. The tendency would be for a military elite to develop, and this elite would acquire economic clout in the form of land given by the ruler as payment to military personnel for services rendered to the state (1 Sam 8:14–15).[3]

The economics of Israel's new societal system, however, had the most devastating impact on the people's older, village-based way of life. With the rise of state-based economics in Israel, the new phenomena of crown property and large, privately owned estates (latifundia) emerged in Israel. Royal officials and elite urban dwellers were able to accumulate vast land holdings at the expense of village Israel's extended families and kin networks, at least according to the indictments of the eighth-century prophets.

An expanding economy and a new centralized judiciary, favoring the rich and powerful (cf. Isa 1:21–23; 5:23; 10:1–2; 32:7), allowed the wealthy elite of society to drive small country farmers into debt, foreclosure, and

---

3. J. David Pleins, *Social Visions of the Hebrew Bible: A Theological Introduction* (Louisville: Westminster John Knox, 2001), 255; cf. Holladay, "Kingdoms," 382.

eventual permanent loss of their ancestral land. The elite confiscated the forfeited land and added it to their growing estates. The previous owners might then have to serve as day laborers or slaves on their ancestral lands.

Israel's new economic system, and the new practice of land grabbing, overlapped and competed with the rural populace's traditional norm of permanent land tenure. Both systems and sets of assumptions coexisted throughout the monarchic period. Several biblical texts express the fear, however, that the newer system was quickly outpacing and rendering obsolete the older norms and the communal ideals linked to them.

By the eighth century, the prophet Isaiah could aim his famous dirge against Israel's wealthy new land-grabbers, whose exploitative actions were threatening the collapse of Israel's traditional system of permanent land assignment among its lineages. "Woe to those who add house to house and join field to field, Until there is no more room, So that you have to live alone in the midst of the land!" (Isa 5:8).

Job 24:2–8 paints an even more detailed picture of the exploitation of old Israel's farmers by the new land-grabbers of the monarchic period:

> [2] The wicked remove landmarks;
>   they seize flocks and pasture them.
> [3] They drive away the donkey of the orphan;
>   they take the widow's ox for a pledge.
> [4] They thrust the needy off the road;
>   the poor of the earth all hide themselves.
> [5] Like wild asses in the desert
>   they go out to their toil,
> scavenging in the wasteland
>   food for their young.
> [6] They reap in a field not their own
>   and they glean in the vineyard of the wicked.
> [7] They lie all night naked, without clothing,
>   and have no covering in the cold.
> [8] They are wet with the rain of the mountains,
>   and cling to the rock for want of shelter.

Archaeology confirms that the growth of wealthy estates and the exploitation of the weak occurred in monarchic Israel, as the biblical texts report.[4] The degradation of traditional society, though real, never seems

---

4. See Holladay, "Kingdoms," 391–92; Marvin L. Chaney, "Whose Sour Grapes? The Addressees of Isaiah 5:1–7 in the Light of Political Economy," in *The Social World of the Hebrew Bible: Twenty-Five Years of the Social Sciences in the Academy* (ed. R. A. Simkins and S. L. Cook) *Semeia* 87 (1999): 105–22. Tell Beit Mirsim seems to have been one early Judean center for state-controlled oil production. See Herzog, *Archaeology of the City,* 242–44.

to have reached as devastating proportions as prophets such as Isaiah feared (or hyperbolized), however. Many Israelite kinship structures survived intact throughout the monarchy, and were extant at the time of the writing of 1–2 Chronicles.

At ʿIzbet Ṣarṭah in the foothills, one house is much larger, and has many more grain pits, than neighboring homes. At another site, pre-Omride Samaria, an individual estate has been unearthed that specialized in producing olive oil and wine. Emerging wealth distinctions are apparent at these early-monarchic, agriculturalist locales. The estates herald a more serious, coming threat of economic degradation of the countryside.

Archaeological surveys and excavations reveal increasing specialization of agriculture and land consolidation in eighth-century Judah and Israel. Among the evidence are many new olive and grape processing installations in the hill country. Sometimes, towers such as the one mentioned in Isa 5:2 were present near these installations, likely used to store wine in bulk for fermentation. In this era, the elite of society were putting both virgin and expropriated land to new use focused on the conspicuous consumption and export of wine and oil.

New archaeological studies are upending previous scholarly doubts about increasing socioeconomic stratification in monarchic times.[5] The eighth century saw a widening economic gap between the elite (officials and wealthy persons) and the poor. In the cities, for example, the former enjoyed grand public buildings and beautiful homes while the latter crowded into shabby neighborhoods.

OVERLAPPING SOCIETAL SYSTEMS IN SOCIAL-SCIENTIFIC PERSPECTIVE

Exegetical, historical, and archaeological evidence combine to confirm that two overlapping societal systems coexisted and competed in Israel at the time of Micah and Hosea. As Baruch Halpern states, "Israel was a traditional society, based in local kinship ties, on which a national administration was superimposed. This superstructure occasionally entered into conflict with the clans."[6]

---

5. For an example of such doubts, see Holladay, "Kingdoms," 392–93. Avraham Faust now successful disputes this view. See, e.g., his "Socioeconomic Stratification in an Israelite City: Hazor VI as a Test Case," *Levant* 31 (1999): 179–90. For evidence from Tell el-Farʿah (north), see Herzog, *Archaeology of the City,* 232.

6. Baruch Halpern, "Jerusalem and the Lineages in the Seventh Century BCE: Kinship and the Rise of Individual Moral Liability," in *Law and Ideology in Monarchic Israel* (ed.

The book of Deuteronomy, which first appeared in writing a half-century after Micah's and Hosea's time, is an excellent starting point for reviewing some sample exegetical evidence.[7] Deuteronomy's authors had grave misgivings about societal centralization. They admit to the development, nevertheless, and attempt to adjust to it.

Deuteronomy explicitly comes to terms with societal centralization in its treatment of the place of kings in society in Deut 17:14–20. In looking at this text closely earlier, it became clear that its authors accepted kingship as an extant, though flawed, reality. Accepting this reality, they focused on taking precautions against the threats that the institution posed.

Other texts in Deuteronomy come to terms with a monarch and with a monarchic administration with state officials. Deuteronomy 1:15–17, reflecting the development in Israel of a state-appointed and state-directed judiciary, is one such text. Though written in the light of later societal developments, the narrative is set at the time of Moses and the exodus. The authors of Deuteronomy picture Moses as allowing for a new, state-based judiciary (which actually only developed long after his time) and as tempering it with caveats. Moses tells the people:

> I took the leaders of your tribes, wise and reputable individuals, and installed them as leaders over you, commanders of thousands, commanders of hundreds, commanders of fifties, commanders of tens, and officials, throughout your tribes. I charged your judges at that time: "Give the members of your community a fair hearing, and judge rightly between one person and another, whether citizen or resident alien. You must not be partial in judging: hear out the small and the great alike; you shall not be intimidated by anyone, for the judgment is God's. Any case that is too hard for you, bring to me, and I will hear it."

B. Halpern and D. W. Hobson; JSOTSup 124; Sheffield: Sheffield Academic Press, 1991), 16. Cf. T. N. D. Mettinger, *Solomonic State Officials: A Study of the Civil Government Officials of the Israelite Monarchy* (ConBOT 5; Lund: Gleerup, 1971); B. Halpern, *The Constitution of the Monarchy in Israel* (HSM 25; Chico, Calif.: Scholars Press, 1981); H. Tadmor, "Traditional Institutions and the Monarchy: Social and Political Tensions in the Time of David and Solomon," in *Studies in the Period of David and Solomon and Other Essays* (ed. T. Ishida; Tokyo: Yamakawa-Shuppansha, 1982).

7. Deuteronomy clearly combines two different understandings about the organization of Israel's society. For a good discussion, see J. A. Dearman, *Property Rights in the Eighth-Century Prophets: The Conflict and Its Background* (SBLDS 106; Atlanta: Scholars Press, 1988), 85–99. The compilers of Deuteronomy faced the reality that Israelite society had outgrown the institutions of the past. Judah had undergone a process of centralization and had developed as a monarchy. Although Deuteronomy makes use of much preexisting material associated with the Sinai theological stream of tradition, the book crystallized in writing only late in the monarchic period. It surfaced at the time of King Josiah, around 640 B.C.E.

Clearly, the text reflects developments in Israel's monarchic period, when a centralized, hierarchical judiciary overlaid a much less stratified judicial system. The newer system drew on the resources of the older one by co-opting the leaders of Israel's tribes. At the same time, the text expresses a clear concern that the new monarchic judicial system be faithful to a divine ideal of justice.

By the time of the Babylonian destruction of Jerusalem in 586 B.C.E. and the exile of the people, the Deuteronomists are able to account for Judah's ultimate catastrophe as a result, in part, of the failure of the monarchic judiciary to actually live up to this divine standard.

Although the book of Deuteronomy comes to terms with a monarchic society, it also preserves clear understandings about how administrative and judicial practices worked in the traditional, village society of Israel. Its authors assume that Israel's older administrative customs could continue, at least at the local level, even though Israel was now a centralized, monarchic state.

For example, the command concerning a remission of debts every seven years in Deut 15:1–2 upholds old Israel's social norm of protecting each extended family's inherited land. So too, Deuteronomy assumes that the local functions of Israel's elders could continue, even though their duties and powers were now curtailed. It charges the elders with handling disputes and rebellions within their towns' family units (e.g., Deut 21:18–21; 25:5–10). They must also settle disputes between separate family lines within their clans (e.g., Deut 22:13–21).

Other biblical evidence that Israel of the Iron II period had overlapping societal systems comes from the book of Proverbs. State officials and scribes collected many of the biblical proverbs from Israel's traditional culture. Such a process of collection and archiving may well have been necessary in monarchic times (cf. Prov 25:1), to preserve traditional proverbs as older ways of life were increasingly threatened.

The traditional, folk proverbs in the biblical collection reflect the culture and values of old Israel's consanguineous, agrarian populace. Some proverbs uphold kinship solidarity, a central value in traditional societies. Proverbs 17:17 states, "A friend loves at all times, and kinsfolk are born to share adversity," while 18:19 reads, "An offended kinsman is worse than having to capture a fortified city."

Kin-based community does not exist apart from specific homeland territories, where kinfolk dwell in safety. Family lines and kin groups should retain their homelands across the generations. According to the proverbial maxims, one expects to inherit a home and land from one's ancestors (Prov 19:14).

Further, according to several proverbs one finds communal protection, economic support, and ideal marriage partners within the particular territory of one's kinfolk. Proverbs 27:8 states, "Like a bird that strays from its nest is one who strays from home."[8]

Continued life on ancestral land requires a strong work ethic, according to other biblical proverbs. For example, Prov 24:30–34 stresses diligence in working one's inherited, arable land. The text observes:

> I passed by the field of one who was lazy, by the vineyard of a stupid person; and see, it was all overgrown with thorns; the ground was covered with nettles, and its stone wall was broken down. Then I saw and considered it; I looked and received instruction. A little sleep, a little slumber, a little folding of the hands to rest, and poverty will come upon you like a robber, and want, like an armed warrior.

The book of Proverbs attests not only to Israel's traditional way of life but also to the new state system that overlaid it. Various biblical proverbs upheld the values of old Israel's agrarian, kinship-based culture in the face of threats that the monarchy posed to it.[9]

Proverbs 29:4 is concerned that a monarchic system could ruin Israel's traditional society. "By justice a king gives stability to the land, but one who makes heavy extractions ruins it." Similarly, Prov 13:23 reads, "The field of the poor may yield much food, but it is swept away through injustice." Proverbs 30:14 protests against the land-grabbers and royal tax collectors of a new society that threatened to kill off an older one: "There are those whose teeth are swords, whose teeth are knives, to devour the poor from off the earth, the needy from among mortals."

Proverbs 14:31; 22:16, 22; and 28:3 oppose the oppression of free citizens by power holders. Proverbs 17:15; 18:5; and 24:23 protest against the corruption of the judiciary under the Israelite monarchy.

Extrabiblical data buttresses the picture provided by this exegesis. Archaeologists have unearthed evidence confirming that overlapping societal systems coexisted in monarchy-period Israel. I already mentioned one piece of evidence, the "widow's plea ostracon," in chapter 2.[10]

---

8. The Plateau Tonga of Zambia have a proverb that mirrors one facet of this traditional territorial consciousness. Like the Israelites, the Plateau Tonga favor choosing one's wife from within the boundaries of one's region. Thus, their proverb states, "The bride does not go across a stream." See Friedemann W. Golka, *The Leopard's Spots: Biblical and African Wisdom in Proverbs* (Edinburgh: T&T Clark, 1993), 93.

9. Compare H. W. Wolff's argument that Micah's polemic against Jerusalem's royal officials reflects the proverb wisdom of Israel. See Wolff, "Micah the Moreshite—The Prophet and His Background," in *Israelite Wisdom: Theological and Literary Essays in Honor of Samuel Terrien* (ed. J. G. Gammie, et al.; Missoula, Mont.: Scholars Press for Union Theological Seminary, New York, 1978), 84 nn. 26–28.

10. See Pierre Bordreuil, F. Israel, and D. Pardee, "King's Command and Widow's Plea: Two New Hebrew Ostraca of the Biblical Period," *Near Eastern Archaeology* 61/1 (1998): 2–13.

The inscription on this potsherd (ostracon) attests to two intertwined societal systems within eighth- and seventh-century monarchic Israel. On the one hand, the ostracon is a letter of petition to a Judean royal official, presupposing a society where officials within a state administrative system wielded judicial authority.

On the other hand, the ostracon presupposes the persistence of traditional social norms. It assumes the ideal found in many traditional, tribal societies that ancestral lands should remain within family lines through the generations. The writer of the letter, a childless Israelite widow, states that the brother of her deceased husband has inherited her husband's wheat field. In order not to fall destitute, she requests the use and benefits of some other parts of her late husband's property until her own death.

Archaeological evidence also confirms the biblical picture that whole kin groups continued to control specific territories well into monarchic times. (*Kin group* is the anthropological term for a network of related families, all tracing decent through the same male line. Kin groups are often popularly called clans.)

Whereas the "widow's plea ostracon" provides material evidence of the persistence in Israel's state period of the traditional social norm of family-plus-land, the Samaria ostraca attest to the persistence through at least the eighth century of the traditional social norm of kin groups possessing ancestral territory.[11] In traditional, tribal Israel, genealogical descent determined not only individual families' relationships to plots of land but also the territorial identity and the social structure of much larger constituent segments of the population.

The Samaria ostraca—records on potsherds of how various districts around Samaria furnished the capital with oil and wine—provide evidence of a state-based socioeconomic system, recording how officials at a central capital, Samaria, received commodities from large country estates they controlled as absentee owners.

At the same time, these records document the continued existence in monarchic Israel of kin groups possessing rights to specific territories. The records refer to seven districts whose names correspond to traditional kin-group names of the tribe of Manasseh: Shemida, Abiezer,

---

11. Y. Aharoni, *The Land of the Bible: A Historical Geography* (trans. A. F. Rainey; 2d ed.; London: Burns & Oates, 1979), 315–27; Dearman, *Property Rights,* 117–23; Christopher J. H. Wright, *God's People in God's Land: Family, Land, and Property in the Old Testament* (Grand Rapids: Eerdmans, 1990), 51–52; S. Bendor, *The Social Structure of Ancient Israel: The Institution of the Family (Beit ʾab) From the Settlement to the End of the Monarchy* (Jerusalem: Simor, 1996), 219 n. 43; Philip J. King and Lawrence E. Stager, *Life in Biblical Israel* (Library of Ancient Israel; Louisville: Westminster John Knox, 2001), 312–14.

Helek, Asriel, Shechem, Hoglah, and Noah (see Num 26:30–33; Josh 17:2–3; 1 Chr 7:14–19).

As Christopher Wright states, the ostraca are "very valuable evidence that the ancient 'kin group' divisions had retained their identity and integrity into the late Monarchy. This fact is the more impressive if it is correct that the ostraca should be connected with the royal estates in the vicinity of Samaria, since it would show that they were able to preserve their identity even under the expansion of the royal domain."[12]

Recent archaeological analyses of rural villages during the period of the Israelite kingdoms (Iron Age II), such as those of Avraham Faust, buttress the above findings.[13] Village household dwellings of this period were often twice the size of their counterparts at urban and royal sites. They also had more than twice the number of internal divisions. Built to house a whole group of related nuclear families, the rural homes witness to the ongoing presence of the extended household in the countryside—the fundamental social unit of a traditional, kinship-based society.

In many rural sites, the houses are similar to each other, revealing that Israelite village society lacked marked social and economic gaps during monarchic times. Monarchic cities, by contrast, contain divergent house types, both small, flimsy dwellings and magnificent, spacious residences. At sites such as eighth-century Hazor, royal officials and a new, wealthy stratum of society lived in a different manner from the rest of the population.[14]

Faust has also examined the nature of food-processing installations in rural and urban contexts during monarchic times. The hallmark of rural villages was large communal installations, present in scant numbers in each settlement. Traditional lineage-sized units (clan sections) of kinship-based society likely managed these facilities. Monarchic-era cities, by contrast, possessed smaller processing units spread about individual houses. They were likely under the control of independent, nuclear families, not clan units.

The lineages of Israel's and Judah's rural sectors also controlled large, communal storage facilities. These village facilities had little in common with the grander, royal storehouses built by the state in the cities. Rather,

---

12. Wright, *God's Land*, 52.

13. Among several recent studies by Avraham Faust, see especially his "The Rural Community in Ancient Israel during Iron Age II," *BASOR* 317 (2000): 17–39; idem, "Differences in Family Structure between Cities and Villages in Iron Age II," *TA* 26/2 (1999): 233–52. See also Oded Borowski, *Daily Life in Biblical Times* (SBLABS 5; Atlanta: Society of Biblical Literature, 2003), 110, 112.

14. Faust, "Socioeconomic Stratification"; Herzog, *Archaeology of the City*, 232.

they witness to a local, village- and lineage-based management of society separate from an alternative, state-based management.

Lineages, composed of genealogically linked extended families, maintained local economic authority during the monarchic period in at least some areas of the countryside. This was true despite state attempts, since early monarchic times, to weaken the lineage basis of old Israel's communal life.

Let us turn now to examine the evidence about society in the times before this dual system of managing life in Israel and Judah developed.

A synthesis of the archaeological evidence, combined with a bit of Bible sleuthing, helps us begin to unearth Israel's traditional, kinship society, beneath the monarchic Israelite state. The task is not easy, particularly the archaeological component. One has to work hard to understand the actual social relations of a people whose remaining archaeological artifacts consist mostly of the foundations of homesteads, the outlines of settlements, cisterns for collecting water, and pottery.

The textual evidence of the Bible is only slightly less impenetrable than such archaeological remains. Most of the texts of the Bible come from the period of the Israelite monarchy or later. Even those biblical traditions from premonarchic Israel do not provide direct, objective information about the society of old Israel.

Archaeologists continue to investigate the remains of premonarchic, village-period Israelite society. They concur in focusing on the new settlements in the Canaan highlands in the period known as Iron Age I (i.e., beginning around 1200 B.C.E.). Their consensus is that the occupants of these new settlements were the earliest Israelites.

According to the archaeological evidence, the highland pioneers practiced both herding and farming. Some devoted themselves to moving herds between pastures, but all of them were tied to permanent farming settlements. As Carol Meyers summarizes, "While there was an important pastoral component to the family economy, the Israelites were farmers. They were what we today might call smallholders: 'rural cultivators practicing intensive, permanent, diversified agriculture on relatively small farms.'"[15]

---

15. Carol Meyers, "The Family in Early Israel," in *Families in Ancient Israel* (The Family, Religion, and Culture; Louisville: Westminster John Knox, 1997), 3. Meyers is citing Robert McC. Netting, *Smallholders, Householders: Farm Families and the Ecology of Intensive, Sustainable Agriculture* (Stanford, Calif.: Stanford University Press, 1993), 2. See also Paula McNutt, *Reconstructing the Society of Ancient Israel* (Library of Ancient Israel; Louisville: Westminster John Knox, 1999), 71; Victor H. Matthews and Don C. Benjamin, *Social World of Ancient Israel 1250–587 B.C.E.* (Peabody, Mass.: Hendrickson, 1993), 53. For good ethnographic illustrations of the connection of transhumancy to farming, see Ernest Gellner, *Saints of the Atlas*

Scholars continue to debate the origins of the highland settlers. What was their ethnicity, and did they infiltrate Canaan from outside or withdraw to the highland settlements from within Canaan itself?

One contemporary reconstruction that has won over many scholars posits that the early Israelites lacked any independent ethnic identity at all. According to this reconstruction, the Israelites were originally Canaanites, who withdrew from the Canaanite city-states and settled in the central highlands of the region. They banded together as a separate people around a common set of religious ideas. (Mendenhall's widely known view was that the covenant played the crucial role in creating Israel as a people.)[16]

Alternatively, a common set of egalitarian values and a shared political cause (liberation from the hierarchical city-states) led the highland people to unite through a fictitious "tribalization." (This is Gottwald's celebrated social-revolution hypothesis, according to which a religious revolution united disparate rebels.)[17] These reconstructions are, however, untenable.

In my view, regardless of where the early Israelites came from, only authentic, preexisting kinship bonds can account for their unity as the people "Israel"—a unity to which the archaeological material culture,[18] the Merenptah Stela, and the biblical evidence attest (see below). As

---

(London: Weidenfeld & Nicholson, 1969), 31–32; Godfrey Lienhardt, "The Western Dinka," in *Tribes without Rulers: Studies in African Segmentary Systems* (ed. J. Middleton and D. Tait; London: Routledge & Kegan Paul, 1958), 98.

16. George E. Mendenhall, *The Tenth Generation: The Origins of the Biblical Tradition* (Baltimore: Johns Hopkins University Press, 1973), 21. See the discussion in R. R. Wilson, *Sociological Approaches to the Old Testament* (Philadelphia: Fortress, 1984), 34.

17. Norman K. Gottwald, *The Tribes of Yahweh: A Sociology of the Religion of Liberated Israel 1250–1050 B.C.E.* (MaryKnoll, N.Y.: Orbis, 1979), 233, 290, 324–25, 328. Gottwald's classic volume is full of insights on tribal Israel. I am disagreeing here primarily with his original thesis that Israel's premonarchic tribal structure was a "pseudogenealogy." Gottwald wrote in *Tribes of Yahweh* that at all levels beyond the extended family in old Israel, kinship links were "fictitiously projected" (*Tribes of Yahweh*, 334). In more recent work, Gottwald views the model of Israel as a retribalizing society as only one of several constructs that illuminates prestate Israel's social structure (Gottwald, *The Politics of Ancient Israel* [Library of Ancient Israel; Louisville: Westminster John Knox, 2001], 170–71, 300 n. 31).

18. The hill country sites that appeared in Iron I share an assemblage of artifactual remains (e.g., "four-room houses," hillside terracing, household cisterns, stone-lined silos), suggesting the sites share an archaeological culture associated with an ethnic group. For a recent summary discussion, see Dever, *Biblical Writers*, 108–24. The consistent absence of pig bones in the hill-country sites perhaps best marks their occupants' shared ethnicity, and helpfully distinguishes the earliest Israelites from Canaanites. (See Finkelstein and Silberman, *Bible Unearthed*, 119–20; Dever, *Biblical Writers*, 113; Brian Hesse and Paula Wapnish, "Can Pig Remains Be Used for Ethnic Diagnosis in the Ancient Near East?" in *The Archaeology of Israel: Constructing the Past, Interpreting the Present* [ed. Neil A. Silberman and David B.

Gottwald himself points out, there is no biblical evidence that Israel ever called itself, or thought of itself, as "a people formed by covenant" (עם ברית) or "covenanters" (בני ברית).[19] This language does not appear in our sources.

Moreover, the covenant, in itself, cannot account for early Israel's societal bonding. Although a vocal minority within Israel strongly advocated the Sinai covenant, it was not pervasive in Israelite culture and society until the reforms of King Hezekiah and King Josiah.

Further, it is hard to imagine the actual viability of a pure covenant society. Could a society with only God as an external suzerain, and with no natural social structure or polity, sustain itself for long?

I have been arguing since chapter 2 that covenant is best distinguished from culture (and elements that make up culture, such as kinship). Covenant may overlay, regularize, and reinforce elements of culture, but it does not create culture. Biblical texts have distinct terms for Israel as a cultural system ("the tribes of Israel"; שבטי ישראל) and Israel in "covenant assembly" (קהל/קהלה).[20]

In Israel's case, covenantal norms set boundaries to distinguish Israel from its neighbors, reformed customary practices, and emphasized protection of the vulnerable. The covenant had its greatest impact in connecting Israel's culture with Yahweh's purposes in redeeming and liberating the Hebrews and settling them on God's land.

By the same token, I seriously doubt that a common value system centered on egalitarianism could have united the highlanders as one people. This value system did not even exist in old Israel.

Maintaining strictly horizontal relationships was not an early Israelite priority. Male landholders, especially male elders, had permanent special status in society (as we observed in Deuteronomy). Levites also received special deference. Further, Israel's elders and Levites continually faced the task of negotiating a balance of power between unequal societal segments. Some families and clans had more members or more influence than others did (cf. Judg 6:15; 1 Sam 9:21; 18:18).

Small; JSOTSup 237; Sheffield: Sheffield Academic Press, 1997], 238–70.) Most recently, a survey of stylistic homogeneity and settlement patterns has revealed the distinctive ethnic identity of the Iron I highlands. See Robert D. Miller II, "Identifying Earliest Israel," *BASOR* 333 (2004): 55–68. As Israelite culture entered the monarchic period, a distinctive Israelite ethnicity remains clearest in the archaeology of rural villages. See Avraham Faust, "Ethnic Complexity in Northern Israel during Iron Age II," *PEQ* 132 (2000): 2–27.

19. Gottwald, *Tribes of Yahweh*, 239.

20. Thus, Deut 33:4 refers to Israel in covenant assembly, while 33:5 refers to Israel as a tribal society. The term "assembly" (קהל/קהלה) has premonarchic roots, as Gottwald correctly notes (*Tribes of Yahweh*, 243). I shall argue in the next chapter that Mic 2:5 *repristinates* the term.

160   THE SOCIAL ROOTS OF BIBLICAL YAHWISM

At times, individuals and groups in early Israelite society rose to prestigious positions of societal leadership. The old social structure allowed for this, as ancient terms such as "field commander" (קָצִין) and "clan head" (רֹאשׁ) attest (e.g., see Judg 11:5–11). The stories in the books of Judges and Samuel depict the rise of such leaders, who were often members of prominent families or charismatic personalities.

Cross-cultural evidence buttresses the biblical data, demonstrating that many noncentralized societies have *inegalitarian* lineages. Priestly descent lines along with lay *dominant clans* often wield special authority in noncentralized societies. Over time, particular lines of descent tend to earn special deference.[21]

The evidence of the biblical texts and the social sciences thus cannot sustain the thesis that the families of early Israel banded together primarily through a voluntary covenantal or ideological association.

Rather, the evidence supports the view that the Israelites cohered together based on genealogical relationships. The highland pioneers of Iron Age IA and B were precisely the type of farmers and transhumant herders that typically organize their society along the lines of kinship. Indeed, they are the type of people that preserve the sort of wisdom sayings about family and kinship collected in the biblical book of Proverbs. In noncentralized, stateless societies, it is often kinship relationships that regulate the control of property, the practice and leadership of worship, and relationships of political power.

The configuration of the early Israelites' houses and villages supports this hypothesis. Individual houses in the highland sites often cluster in compounds that share a common courtyard. Such compounds probably formed the living quarters of extended families, the basic kinship unit in a lineage-based society.[22]

Perhaps a dozen such clusters typically make up an entire village. These networks of clusters appear to be associated with the next highest

---

21. Ernest Gellner forcefully makes the point that noncentralized societies are not ideological democracies or examples of egalitarian liberalism. The Berber tribes of Morocco, for example, give holy lineages special reverence and they make ownership of property a condition of full membership in society. See Gellner, *Saints of the Atlas*, 28–30.

22. Lawrence E. Stager, "The Archaeology of the Family in Ancient Israel," *BASOR* 260 (1985): 22; Halpern, "Jerusalem and the Lineages," 50; Meyers, "The Family in Early Israel," 13; McNutt, *Society of Ancient Israel*, 66. Carolyn S. Leeb has recently helped fill in this picture through a cross-cultural comparison with traditional Haitian practice, in which the Haitian extended family occupies a collection of dwelling units clustered around a shared courtyard ("Hebrew *Bêt ʾAb* and Haitian *Lakou*: A Comparison" [paper presented in the Social Sciences and the Interpretation of the Hebrew Scriptures Section at the annual meeting of the Society of Biblical Literature, Toronto, 23 November 2002]).

level of kinship organization in lineage societies, the kin group or clan. The kin group could also extend to include a larger regional group, living in more than one village.

At least in describing village society during the later, Iron Age II period, we may have to speak of an additional societal unit between the level of the extended family and the whole clan. A given Iron II village, if rather large, could encompass up to three or four of these intermediate units, which may be termed lineages or clan sections. Among other evidence, large or crowded chamber tombs, too big for individual family lines, witness to this supra-extended-family social unit.[23]

The evidence of an ancient biblical song, the "Song of Deborah," reveals that traditional Israel's kinship ties and responsibilities extended all the way to the intertribal level. The song, found in Judg 5, is very old Hebrew poetry, which preserves many accurate details about premonarchic Israelite society.[24]

The Song of Deborah recounts one of the many battles between the Israelite tribes and the Canaanites. Such battles must have become increasingly common as Israel established itself in Palestine during the "settlement" and "judges" periods. The song attests that the early Israelites and the Canaanites conceived of themselves as socially distinct, antagonistic entities.

This observation alone supports the central thesis of this book. As Kenton Sparks writes, "The entity called Canaan stands in opposition to the people of Yahweh, and it makes precious little sense constantly to emphasize that Israelite and Canaanite religion are of one cloth when even our earliest biblical sources stress the distinctions between them."[25]

The song depicts Israel as an ethnically bonded people, the "people of Yahweh" (עַם־יהוה, Judg 5:11, 13). They consist of segments, the largest of which are tribes (מטה; such as the tribe of Benjamin [5:14] or the tribe of Reuben [5:16]). This tribal organization facilitated the muster of troops in time of conflict, according to the song.

---

23. A. Malamat, "Ummātum in Old Babylonian Texts and its Ugaritic and Biblical Counterparts," UF 11 (1979): 535; Halpern, "Jerusalem and the Lineages," 52–53, 58; Faust, "Rural Community," 29–30; King and Stager, Life in Biblical Israel, 12–15. The matter of distinguishing clans and clan sections is complex, since the biblical texts use the same term (מִשְׁפָּחָה) for both.

24. There have been many scholarly studies of the Song of Deborah. See Kenton L. Sparks, Ethnicity and Identity in Ancient Israel: Prolegomena to the Study of Ethnic Sentiments and Their Expression in the Hebrew Bible (Winona Lake, Ind.: Eisenbrauns, 1998), 109–21; Baruch Halpern, "The Resourceful Israelite Historian: The Song of Deborah and Israelite Historiography," HTR 76 (1983): 379–401; B. Lindars, Judges 1–5 (Edinburgh: T&T Clark, 1975).

25. Sparks, Ethnicity and Identity, 119.

The tribes themselves break down into smaller kinship units. Judges 5:15–16 speaks of the "clans" (פְּלַגּוֹת; cf. 2 Chr 35:5) of Reuben. The clans are divisions of tribes based on kin relationships. Thus, 5:14 mentions the "kinfolk" (עֲמָמֶיךָ) of Benjamin.

The song presupposes kin loyalty among the Israelite tribes in responding to muster. It assumes that all the tribes should band together in mutual support in times of military conflict. In particular, 5:15–17 rebuke the tribes of Reuben, Gilead, Dan, and Asher for refusing to join Israel's battle against Sisera.

Extrabiblical evidence supports the general picture of Judg 5. The Merenptah Stela—a victory inscription of an Egyptian pharaoh discovered by Sir Flinders Petrie in Thebes in 1896—evidences the nature of Israel's existence in Canaan before the inscription's date of 1207 B.C.E. The name "Israel" ("El rules") in the stela is not Egyptian but is most likely Israel's own, West Semitic name for itself. Thus, the stela attests that the early Israelites shared a common sense of identity as a people. Moreover, the stela identifies "Israel" not as a city-state with fortified settlements but as a tribal/ethnic group occupying nonurban, village areas of Canaan.[26]

Egyptian-relief pictures that appear to correlate with the Merenptah Stela depict the Israelites for the first time in history and show they lack the fortified cities that the older inhabitants of Canaan occupied at this time.[27]

Now, before turning to some illuminating comparative evidence, a caveat is necessary about my argument thus far. I am not making blanket claims about the genetics of early Israel's highland pioneers. Lineage genealogies are foundational in structuring kinship-based societies, but they express a people's social and political *perceptions*, not their scientific genetic history. Cultural understandings of lineage bonds vary and develop over time, helping groups explain contemporary social realities or expand their membership.[28]

---

26. The evidence turns on the stela's hieroglyphic "determinatives." See, e.g., Sparks, *Ethnicity and Identity*, 105; Dever, *Biblical Writers*, 118–19; M. G. Hasel, "*Israel* in the Merenptah Stela," *BASOR* 296 (1994): 45–61; A. Rainey, "Reply to D. Edelman," *BAR* 18/2 (1992): 73–74.

27. Frank Yurco, "Merneptah's Palestine Campaign," *JSSEA* 8 (1978): 70; idem, "3,200-Year-Old Picture of Israelites Found in Egypt," *BAR* 16/5 (1990): 20–38.

28. A kinship-based society exists as an organized social entity only because its populace recognizes that a lineage principle is in place. This being said, it is also true that lineage genealogies primarily express *perceptions*, and they have a degree of fluidity that allows them to adjust to changing societal circumstances (e.g., societal growth by accretion). Neither capricious change nor pure invention are involved in this fluidity. Indeed, significant

Factual blood ties lie at the center of kinship-based societies, but do not necessarily extend to all members. The biblical texts allow for this picture. They admit, for example, that the Israelites were a "mixed company" even from the time of the exodus from Egypt (see Exod 12:38; Lev 24:10; Num 11:4).

Beyond the sort of cursory hints I have been describing, neither the Bible nor archaeology elaborate on the actual structure and inner workings of either state-system Israel or older, village-system Israel. To gain further understanding, it is quite helpful to examine social-scientific insights into these systems of society and how they may overlap.

In the remainder of this section I give some examples of superimposed political systems as they occur cross culturally. I also survey some insights that modern ethnographers have provided about the tribal roots behind such societies. My goal is to illustrate what Paula McNutt and others report: "Anthropologists have noted a tendency for tribal structure to remain intact even after a tribal territory has been incorporated into a state system."[29]

The Kingdom of the Zulu of South Africa, in the late 1700s and early 1800s, provides one actual example of a newer state organization of society coexisting with an older, tribal organization.[30] This kingdom was founded when a head of the Zulu tribe named Shaka conquered a number of other tribes and organized them into a nation. Shaka ruled as a tyrant over his new kingdom until 1828, when his brother, Dingane, assassinated him and took his place as king.

---

factors retard genealogical change in all traditional societies. When individuals or groups put forward such changes, the majority of the populace must come to accept them before they are established. See Robert R. Wilson, *Genealogy and History in the Biblical World* (Yale Near Eastern Researches 7; New Haven: Yale, 1977), 27–36, 157–58, 199–202; Saul M. Olyan, *Rites and Rank: Hierarchy in Biblical Representations of Cult* (Princeton: Princeton University Press, 2000), 73; King and Stager, *Life in Biblical Israel*, 39. Christopher P. Jones has recently described how appeals to (often semilegendary) kinship frequently functioned in ancient Greece and Rome as a tool of diplomacy between societies (*Kinship Diplomacy in the Ancient World* [Cambridge: Harvard University Press, 1999]).

29. McNutt, *Society of Ancient Israel*, 87; cf. pp. 164, 174. See also Itumeleng J. Mosala, *Biblical Hermeneutics and Black Theology in South Africa* (Grand Rapids: Eerdmans, 1989), 80–81; Wilson, *Sociological Approaches*, 46–47; Norman Yoffee, "The Decline and Rise of Mesopotamian Civilization: An Ethnoarchaeological Perspective on the Evolution of Social Complexity," *American Antiquity* 44 (1979): 5–35; Maurice Godelier, *Perspectives in Marxist Anthropology* (Cambridge: Cambridge University Press, 1977); Michael Moerman, "Being Lue: Uses and Abuses of Ethnic Identification," in *Essays on the Problem of Tribe* (ed. June Helm; Proceedings of the Annual Spring Meeting of the American Ethnological Society, 1967; Seattle, Wash.: University of Washington, 1968), 153–69.

30. See Max Gluckman, "The Kingdom of the Zulu of South Africa," in *African Political Systems* (ed. M. Fortes and E. E. Evans-Pritchard; London: Oxford, 1940), 25–55.

Shaka and Dingane, in turn, shifted political power in the society to a new monarchical system, away from the basis in kinship that it previously possessed. They established political boundaries within the nation and deprived several heads of traditional kin groups of their political power. Nevertheless, the older system continued to function intact, at least at the smaller, local level of society, where social groups remained relatively constant.

Members of the society still understood themselves to be part of the kinship-based groups that had previously formed the foundation of their societal life. They retained and continued to promote many of their traditional values. Where it could, the newer, monarchical organization of society incorporated, rather than destroyed, much of the older tribal organization.

Another example of a people with two superimposed political organizations occurs in the case of the Ngwato of Botswana (the former Bechuanaland Protectorate) in Africa. I. Schapera reports that although the Ngwato people are under the central leadership of a chief, traditional tribal structures of the society continue to operate.

Despite his central authority, the Ngwato chief's rule depends on the support of the traditional hereditary heads of wards (*motse*) within Ngwato society. The Ngwato have the saying "The chief is chief by grace of the tribe" ("Kgosi ke kgosi ka morafe").[31] When tribal disputes erupt or when the chief has a conflict with his relatives, representatives of the whole people often convene in tribal assembly at the chief's council place (*kgotla*). On occasion, the tribal assembly overrules the chief.[32]

Fascinating evidence for the stubborn persistence of kinship-based social structures often emerges when external, colonizing forces destroy a native state. Eric Wolf reports, for example, that the Spanish conquest of the New World in the sixteenth century destroyed extant, native state systems. This destruction, in turn, allowed older, prestate, native political features to resurface in the local culture.

These prestate societal features emerged particularly in new Native American communities that the Spaniards called "repúblicas de indios." These new communities formed as the Spanish conquerors created a system of large landed estates and settled the indigenous population nearby to labor upon them. Wolf stresses that the repúblicas were not pristine, prestate communities. Nevertheless, anthropologists have been

---

31. I. Schapera, "The Political Organization of the Ngwato of Bechuanaland Protectorate," in Fortes and Evans-Pritchard, *African Political Systems*, 79.

32. Ibid., 72.

very interested in what they reveal about early Native American history and societal organization.[33]

The reports of some ethnographers provide rich insights about the nature of the centralizing forces that begin to form a state out of a traditional people and lead to two overlapping organizations of society. Fascinatingly, it is sometimes worship innovations, or the appearance of new sacral functionaries, that bring about such a situation.

For example, foreign oracle agents were the instruments of centralization in the case of the Ibo people of Eastern Nigeria. From 1650 to 1850 C.E., these oracle agents, the Aro, spread out from their own area and brought their unique oracle system to the Ibo. The Aro formed colonies among the Ibo, which began to integrate society. The colonies provided oracular consultations that handled matters beyond the resources of the Ibo's traditional, local authorities. They also carried on extensive trade that helped to further interconnect the Ibo people.[34]

The Berber tribes living in the Moroccan mountains (siba-land) have sometimes experienced competing models of societal organization in their history. Although the Berber peoples have a purely tribal, noncentralized mode of life, they sometimes come under the influence of centralizing religious forces. The Berbers believe themselves to be Muslims, but the Muslim garb of their rituals is generally not a force with any centralizing effect among them. They normally reject any state form of government and are quite accustomed to living with the tensions between tribal and Muslim practices. On occasion, however, the concept of being a Muslim has created groups among the Berbers with a size and cohesion beyond what is possible in a traditional tribal polity.

In these cases, a religious leader will use the sacred power of Islam to unite and organize competing groups. During medieval times, Muslim religious reformers began to unite the Berbers. During subsequent centuries, a centralizing appeal came from persons possessing special Islamic holiness through descent from the Muslim Prophet. Despite these periodic moves toward state formation, the Berbers' traditional, tribal ways of life persisted and, indeed, persistently triumphed.[35]

33. Eric R. Wolf, *Europe and the People without History* (Berkeley and Los Angeles: University of California Press, 1982), 145.

34. Robert McC. Netting, "Sacred Power and Centralization: Aspects of Political Adaptation in Africa," in *Population Growth* (ed. B. J. Spooner; Cambridge: Massachusetts Institute of Technology, 1972), 230–31.

35. Ernest Gellner, *Saints of the Atlas,* 18–19, 46.

As these brief examples demonstrate, it is possible for a people, such as the Israelites of Hosea and Micah's time, to live with two active, over-lapping administrative and judicial societal organizations.

Rather than multiply cross-cultural instances of such superimposed systems, I would like now to push the focus back behind these stages of overlap, sketch the contours of prestate societies before any pressures towards state formation arise in them. Anthropologists have studied many nonstate societies, which feel no need for centralized rule. Having only dispersed and localized authority, they are tribes without rulers (*acephalous* peoples).

Throughout the twentieth century, ethnographers provided a great deal of insight into how stateless societies generally structure themselves along genealogical lines. In particular, they base themselves on the type of genealogy known as a *segmentary genealogy*.[36]

Such a genealogy expands and forms various *segments,* or branches, as families grow and descendants proliferate over the generations. (When descent passes through males, as in Israel, anthropologists call the system *patrilineal.*) These systems look like branchy, upside-down trees, with a particular ancestor (if known) at the top of each branched segment. Among the Bantu of Kavirondo in Kenya, for example, one Bantu tribal unit known as the Logoli believes that all of its clans descended from one remote tribal ancestor called Murogoli. All of the members of another Bantu tribe, the Vugusu, believe they have descended from an epony-mous ancestor known as Muvugusu.[37] In these societies, everyone descended from a given ancestor is a member of a particular segment of the genealogical tree.

Noncentralized societies that organize themselves based on the kinship relations that a segmentary genealogy schematizes are called segmented tribal societies or segmentary societies.

The Nuer tribes of the southern Sudan in Africa are a good example of a segmentary society. Only its lineage system provides a Nuer tribe with its unity. There is no centralized government. Furthermore, each kin group within a Nuer tribe is highly segmented, with each segment itself organized along genealogical lines. Such an organization fits the picture of early Israel in the Song of Deborah. The song presupposes that the Israelites have a unity as one people, but that they also lack centralization and belong to distinct, rather uncooperative groups.[38]

36. Wilson, *Genealogy and History,* 40–44, 158.
37. Günter Wagner, "The Political Organization of the Bantu of Kavirondo," in Fortes and Evans-Pritchard, *African Political Systems,* 200.
38. On the Nuer, see E. E. Evans-Pritchard, "The Nuer of the Southern Sudan," in Fortes and Evans-Pritchard, *African Political Systems,* 284; Eric O. Ayisi, *An Introduction to the Study*

The members of a tribal system of life accord allegiance and respect to those standing at the heads of the system's genealogical segments. As an individual gets older and the person's descendants increase, the individual builds more kinship bonds and holds membership in an increasing number of societal groups. Thus, a traditional society's elders have the best position to support societal unity and to mediate between societal groups. They are the ones who generally end up wielding political and economic influence.

Segmented systems that have grown large enough to form whole societies, however, have no living elders high enough up the genealogical scheme to command universal respect and obedience. No figure or group can maintain the order of the society from a central position. Therefore, the system must maintain its stability through noncentralized means.

The primary means of maintaining order in the system is a dynamic, balanced opposition between its segments. At every level of segmentation, from intertribal relations, to kin-group relations, to relations between extended families, a balance of power between groups organizes the life of a segmentary society.

Since kinship-based societies lack both centralized authority and any official means to enforce decisions, traditional kinfolk must negotiate all tensions and conflicts. The aim is to achieve a consensus among all interested parties. Persuasion, mediation, honor, and negotiation achieve such a consensus.

This system of maintaining order is most stable at its lowest, localized levels. Disputants experience greater pressure to resolve their conflicts when they are closely related and when their common ancestors may still be alive. Thus, traditional peoples make every effort to keep conflicts to the lowest possible level of their segmentary schema.

The genealogical ties of many traditional peoples are vested and grounded in their relations with land. Though it is hard for modern Westerners to imagine, in many traditional societies kin groups and family lines exist only in direct dependence on the plots of arable land to which they are permanently tied. Membership in genealogical descent

---

of African Culture (2d ed.; London: Heinemann, 1979), 59. On the argument that organization by segmented genealogy best explains the societal tensions and oppositions in Deborah's Song, see Sparks, Ethnicity and Identity, 117. The role of marriage norms within segmentary societies is fascinating, but beyond the scope of the present study. Traditional Israelite culture seems to have practiced endogamous marriage, preferring that a man marry a wife from within his own larger kin group (but outside of his local, extended family). Endogamous marriage is firmly attested among actual kin-based societies, Berber society being a good example. See Gellner, Saints of the Atlas, 38.

groups expresses itself primarily in rights to occupation and cultivation of land.[39]

Large kinship groups often control whole territories. Among a plethora of examples, one could cite the Bantu of Kavirondo in Kenya. The Bantu Kavirondo tribes—which, like the old Israelite highlanders, are herders as well as farmers—each occupy a continuous stretch of territory.[40] Or, one thinks of the Nuer in the southern Sudan, whose tribes all have territorial unity and exclusiveness.[41]

Within tribal territories, smaller family groups hold individual plots, fields, and vineyards. This land, which they pass down over the generations, provides families with both their residence and the basis for their livelihood. It is through possession of land that family lines sustain and perpetuate themselves. In any given generation, it is through their inherited, ancestral land that extended families enjoy cohesion, honor, and self-sufficiency.

Possession of land also enables families to reach out to support the needs of their wider network of kinfolk. The family that loses its land in a traditional, agricultural society is at the mercy of others. Without landowning kin networks to assist them in a time of crisis, the newly landless can often do no better than to sell themselves as slaves to survive.

Cross-culturally, family lines often practice the burial of family members on ancestral land. Even contemporary "westernized" Africans often feel a compulsion to continue this practice. They may now permanently reside in urban "houses," but they must be buried at "home," where their ancestors lie.

One international student from Africa, who has studied with me, writes, "Although within modern times people have acquired for themselves plots away from their ancestral land, or bought for themselves houses in the big cities.... Whatever they may have away in the city does not *count*. In case of death in these 'alien' places, the body has to be taken home to rest with the ancestors."[42]

In traditional cultures, a lineage may further cement its connection to its land through cyclical religious rituals. International students from Africa have discussed such rituals in my courses. One African student explained, "As the blood [shed during the various rites and initiations of family members] went into the soil, the ancestors shared

---

39. Fred Eggan, "Kinship: Introduction," *IESS* 8:392.

40. Wagner, "Bantu," 200.

41. Evans-Prichard, "Nuer," 278.

42. Dorcas Chanya Ndoro, "Biblical Inheritance: An African Interpretation—Today" (MTS thesis, Virginia Theological Seminary, Alexandria, Va., 1997), 16.

the spirit of the individual. It was not only the blood at circumcision that brought this unity. The burying of the umbilical cord at birth had the same significance. Because of this bond with the soil and the ancestors, there was a sense of belonging [both to the ancestral land and to one's people]."[43]

Because family lines are so closely tied to ancestral lands, many traditional societal systems lack our modern western notions of permanent sale and purchase of land. Traditional people often hold land in trust, rather than owning it. They may give their land as an inheritance or gift only to persons within the confines of a specific inheritance circle. If one falls into desperate financial straits and must sell some of one's land, members of one's larger kin group must take measures to keep the land within the care of the closest relative possible.

The African student whom I have been quoting explains the traditional system among her own people:

> Redemption of land in the African tradition is vital.... They had a system of "weka rehani," which in Swahili means "to lease" the land to an able relative, who would then meet the pressing need of the impoverished family. This land could be received back by paying back the money given or by giving unpaid service to the "redeemer." Never was land sold to a complete stranger, because strangers were, as the Wasagalla people would call them, *"wamaiza"* ["agents of the devil"].[44]

The centrality of land in traditional systems of organizing society is clear in the case of the Tallensi people of northern Ghana in West Africa. The possession of ancestral land holds Tale kinfolk together and creates continuity within lineages over the generations. An individual receives his farm as a precious patrimony from his forebears, and he holds it in trust for future generations. An individual parts with his home farm, called a *saman,* only under the direst of circumstances. To sell one's land is to betray one's descendants and, in some areas, to sin against the earth.[45]

43. Ibid. Carolyn Leeb reports similar practices within traditional Haitian society linking the extended family to their ancestral land ("Hebrew *Bêt ʾAb* and Haitian *Lakou*").

44. Ndoro, "Biblical Inheritance," 21.

45. M. Fortes, "The Political System of the Tallensi of the Northern Territories of the Gold Coast," in Fortes and Evans-Pritchard, *African Political Systems,* 249–50.

A MODEL FOR EXPLORING MICAH'S ROOTS: THE ELDERS IN MONARCHIC ISRAEL AND IN VILLAGE ISRAEL

By the time of Micah and Hosea in the eighth century, a centralized administrative and judicial system was challenging the traditional authority of Israel's elders. The shift within Israel from one system of administration and justice to another was a slow process, which remained incomplete, even up through the exile.

At first, Israel's new state-based administration and judiciary simply attempted to supplement the older village system, where elders held sway. It made overtures towards affirming the older system by drawing on the cooperation of the elders. Even when the newer system proved destructive of the traditional one, however, it never fully supplanted it. The two systems coexisted in Israel in dynamic tension.

The archaeology of Iron Age II Israel reveals bodies of elders, still making decisions for rural communities well into monarchic times.[46] Rural, monarchic-period settlements erected and maintained modest boundary walls as local initiatives, presupposing the existence of a local administrative body. The most likely body capable of administering the totality of a large village's extended families and lineages would be an assembly of that settlement's elders.

Who were the traditional elders of old Israelite society? The Bible does not directly define who Israel's elders were, but they must have been the senior male members of the various extended families in an Israelite village. They were the individual heads of the family households, which could each include three to four generations of a family.

The size of rural Israelite dwellings of Iron Age II shows that the people's elders eventually presided over twenty-five to forty total family members. Archaeology of the highland villages of the pioneering, "settlement" era suggests that this number may have been somewhat smaller in earlier times, perhaps fifteen or so family members.

I am particularly interested in the differing strategies that Israel's elders pursued as their older ways of life came under attack. A major source of biblical evidence about the rise of a centralized judicial system in Judah, and its effect on the people's elders, is 2 Chr 19:4–11. The text clearly depicts how Israel's monarchs overlaid Israel's older reliance on elders for administrative and judicial leadership with a new reliance on a state-based administration and judiciary.

---

46. Holladay, "Kingdoms," 389; Faust, "Rural Community," 26–28, 30–31; idem, "Ethnic Complexity," 14.

The portrait of judicial change in 2 Chr 19:4–11 does not aim to provide a neutral and objective historical account of the events it depicts. The Chronicler clearly wrote his history in a creative, programmatic style. Nevertheless, his text does attest to an actual systemic social change within Israel's history, and he provides a reasonable date in Israel's history for when this change took place.[47]

The text is set during the reign of the southern king, Jehoshaphat (ca. 873–849 B.C.E.). It reads as follows:

> Jehoshaphat resided at Jerusalem; then he went out again among the people, from Beer-sheba to the hill country of Ephraim, and brought them back to the LORD, the God of their ancestors. He appointed judges in the land in all the fortified cities of Judah, city by city, and said to the judges, "Consider what you are doing, for you judge not on behalf of human beings but on the LORD's behalf; he is with you in giving judgment. Now, let the fear of the LORD be upon you; take care what you do, for there is no perversion of justice with the LORD our God, or partiality, or taking of bribes."
>
> Moreover in Jerusalem Jehoshaphat appointed certain Levites and priests and heads of families of Israel, to give judgment for the LORD and to decide disputed cases. They had their seat at Jerusalem. He charged them: "This is how you shall act: in the fear of the LORD, in faithfulness, and with your whole heart; whenever a case comes to you from your kindred who live in their cities, concerning bloodshed, law or commandment, statutes or ordinances, then you shall instruct them, so that they may not incur guilt before the LORD and wrath may not come on you and your kindred. Do so, and you will not incur guilt. See, Amariah the chief priest is over you in all matters of the LORD; and Zebadiah son of Ishmael, the governor of the house of Judah, in all the king's matters; and the Levites will serve you as officers. Deal courageously, and may the LORD be with the good!"

The text pictures King Jehoshaphat establishing a new judicial system in the state of Judah in the ninth century, over one hundred years before the time of Hosea and Micah. Jehoshaphat extends judicial authority from a center in his capital, Jerusalem, to all the fortified cities of Judah. The administrators of this new judicial authority are royal appointees (19:5), who serve under a chain of command (19:11). Thus, the new judiciary is centralized and hierarchical. The king's aim was to create a unified and nationalized judicial system in Judah, organized from the top down.

---

47. For discussion, see Cook, "Mosaic Judges," 306 n. 1.

The narrative is not clear about the details of the older system that Jehoshaphat's new judiciary overlays, although it alludes to the older system in 19:8 in noting that the king drew on some of its resources in implementing his innovative system. Verse 8 states that Jehoshaphat invested some of old Israel's heads of extended families with new state-based judicial authority.

It was precisely such tribal lineage heads, along with the Levites, who wielded judicial power in village-period Israel. At least many biblical texts, including the following passages in Deuteronomy, assume such a picture: Deut 1:9–18; 17:9; 19:12; 21:1–9; 21:18–20; 22:13–19; and 25:7–9.

Jehoshaphat knew that his new state judiciary could not immediately replace Israel's traditional system run by the elders. Thus, he attempted to gain footholds for his new judicial system starting with the country's fortified cities where the state already had bases of control (2 Chr 19:5). At the lowest, immediate level of justice in Israel's villages, local elders of Israel's older societal system remained responsible for justice long after Jehoshaphat first initiated his legal innovations.

As he established a new state judicial system, Jehoshaphat also attempted to co-opt the resources of the older judicial system by appointing some of its judges to new state roles. In addition to the elders the king appointed as appeals judges in Jerusalem, some of the new royal appointees in the fortified cities were likely local elders whom Jehoshaphat pressed into new, official roles. This move to co-opt the leaders of an older, traditional system in service of establishing a new state system also appears in parallel cross-cultural evidence that I will present shortly.

Israel's new monarchic system easily won over many of old Israel's leading elders. With time, many powerful families and lineages established themselves in the royal court, both as judges and as other types of royal officials.[48] Others of the monarchy's new officials eventually wielded local authority at traditional assemblies in the gate complexes of towns, alongside traditional authority figures.

As J. A. Dearman notes, the new bilevel judicial and administrative system must have often created local conflicts of interest. "The traditional authority of the local assembly would now be overlaid and circumscribed by the authority of the appointed officials. In many cases the appointees would have been drawn from the local assembly, thus elevating a community leader above his peers. A local citizen taking a

48. See John Rogerson and Philip Davies, *The Old Testament World* (Englewood Cliffs, N.J.: Prentice-Hall, 1989), 59–62.

case to the gate could find his/her case adjudicated by people whose interests ran against his."[49]

Some officials under the monarchy used their new offices and new authority to pursue personal interests. They took full economic advantage of the new state system, its new wealth, and its new rules. These officials made a career of buying up land, creating expansive estates, and becoming land barons—latifundia lords.

Discussion above of key texts in Micah revealed the prophet's disdain for these land-grabbers, who lay awake at night refining their plans for seizing new lands (Mic 2:1). With crown authority now overshadowing their local judicial system, Micah's kinfolk had little protection against a constant threat of hostile takeover of their farmland. Their situation was further aggravated in that their locale (the Shephelah) was a strategic military zone. Local tensions with Judah's state system were exacerbated by the insolence of royal military commanders, with their ability to declare martial law.

Not all elders became land barons or royal commanders. Despite attractive new opportunities under monarchy, many elders chose to continue a traditional lifestyle as far as possible. They chose not to betray their kin groups, extended families, and ancestral traditions. Miraculously, Judah's and Israel's new state systems never succeeded in driving this second group of elders into poverty and oblivion.

A sufficient number of rural elders remained solvent throughout the monarchic period to keep village-system society in existence as a substratum. Some of these elders were well off. Second Kings 15:19–20 reports that as late as 740 B.C.E. there were over sixty-thousand rural gentry (גבורי החיל) in the northern kingdom who could contribute fifty shekels of silver toward a tribute payment to the king of Assyria.[50]

We saw above in chapter 3 that the rural gentry were a social force in Judah even as late as King Josiah's time (640–609 B.C.E.). It was the elders of the land who arranged for Josiah to become king after the death of his father, King Amon (2 Kgs 21:24; 2 Chr 33:25).

A good place to begin a cross-cultural look at elders in dual-system societies is the Kingdom of the Zulu of South Africa. As I noted in the preceding section, a newer state organization of society in Zululand coexisted with an older tribal one from the late 1700s. At that time, a figure

49. Dearman, *Property Rights,* 144. J. Pedersen makes a similar point: "The class of officials thus formed [by new royal appointment] must have mixed with the old aristocracy, to which no doubt they often belonged" (*Israel: Its Life and Culture* [2 vols.; London: Oxford, 1947], 2:76).

50. For discussion, see Bendor, *Social Structure,* 224–27, 269.

named Shaka subjugated a number of tribes and organized them into a centralized, monarchic state.

Despite their new political organization, the kingdom's people retained their kinship groupings, and they continued to hold respect for the lineage heads of their family lines. Many of these lineal heads continued to play their traditional judicial roles, at least at the local level, throughout the reigns of Shaka and Dingane, his successor. For example, the kinfolk of lineal heads would take inheritance cases to them for adjudication.[51]

The Ngwato of Botswana are another centralized people among whom elders still perform traditional roles. As I noted above, a chief rules over the Ngwato people, and he has a centralized administrative system at his service. At the same time, however, hereditary headmen retain leadership of local wards that number between two hundred and four hundred people. Along with other ward elders, who head the ward's various family groups, the local headman of a particular district deals with lawsuits and handles regional business. Despite the centralization of the society, headmen and elders still handle such lawsuits and administrative matters at a council place ("kgotla") within their own hamlet.[52]

Beyond their local functions, the headmen may also represent their constituencies before the chief. Kin heads even retain some ability to check the chief's power. On occasions when their constituencies have had serious grievances against their ruler, leading headmen have even publicly challenged his authority. Schapera writes, "If the chief flagrantly misruled the tribe, or in other ways incurred the hostility of the people, the leading headmen would withdraw their support and publicly attack him at tribal gatherings." "The people might even begin to plot against him, in the hope that ... one of his more popular relatives [would] take his place."[53]

A less exact anthropological parallel to the persistence of traditional elders in state-period Israel occurs in some historical cases of Western colonization of indigenous peoples. In many of these cases, Western, colonizing powers overlaid tribal administrations with colonial ones. An example of this type of overlap of societal systems occurred in the period of British colonial administration of the Anang people in southeastern Nigeria.[54]

---

51. Gluckman, "Kingdom of the Zulu," 28, 36.
52. Schapera, "Ngwato," 58.
53. Ibid., 80.
54. Golka, *Leopard's Spots*, 72–76; John C. Messenger Jr., "The Role of Proverbs in a Nigerian Judicial System," *Southwestern Journal of Anthropology* 15 (1959): 64–73.

During their administration, the British created a system of official courts for the whole Anang tribe. At the same time, nevertheless, the traditional courts of the Anang continued to function. They operated primarily at the village level and at the level of the extended family, handling offenses ranging from theft to adultery. In the indigenous courts, the older men of the village, and some older women, listened to litigants argue their cases before a local audience. After the contestants presented their evidence, the court reached a verdict based on consensus.

In one typical case, the parents of a pregnant daughter brought charges against a local boy. The girl's father used a traditional proverb to argue that the court should hold the boy responsible for usurping sexual privileges normally reserved for those who are married. His proverb, which won the case, was: "The *ekenuk* (= small rat) tried to eat as much as the *okono* (= large rat) and his stomach burst."[55]

The comparative, anthropological evidence reveals that as a segmentary people undergoes centralization and state formation, they often draw on traditional societal resources to ease the transition. In particular, they often co-opt the elders of the older system into new, official state roles.[56] This evidence corroborates the understanding of the history of administrative centralization in Israelite society that I have been developing.

Although kinship was no longer the official basis of political power in the Kingdom of the Zulu, for example, the new monarchic system drew on the resources of the older kin-based system in establishing itself. The new system continued to use kinship terms for political officers. The heads of some kin groups lost their political power in the new kingdom. In various other parts of Zululand, however, traditional kinfolk heads became chiefs who acted as the political representatives of their kin groups.[57]

---

55. Golka, *Leopard's Spots*, 75.

56. In some cases, an entire lineage group may acquire special administrative authority as a society reorganizes as a state. A study of the administrative seals of the Bronze Age Harappan civilization of the Indus Valley provides an illustration. As state power emerged in this society, the special emblem of a particular descent group (a unicorn) began to dominate the official seals of public administration across the excavated sites of the Harappan region. The Harappan "unicorn"-group apparently became most involved in the changing society's trade and rule over time, and eventually became the society's ruling elite. Other kinship groups must have concurrently lost much of their traditional political authority. See Shereen Ratnagar, "Ideology and the Nature of Political Consolidation and Expansion: An Archaeological Case," in *Ideology and the Formation of Early States* (ed. H. J. M. Claessen and J. G. Oosten; Studies in Human Society 2; Leiden: Brill, 1996), 170–86.

57. Gluckman, "Kingdom of the Zulu," 29, 37.

So too among the Ngwato of Botswana, centralization of the society
gave new hierarchical office to some of the culture's hereditary headmen.[58] When the great chief, Kgama III (ca. 1837–1923), moved to extend
his administrative control of the country, he placed resident governors in
the remote villages of the land. Often, he appointed one of his own relatives as the governor. Sometimes the chief chose a local headman for the
new position, however, especially if someone particularly prominent or
reliable was available.

As state systems develop in a society, and many of their colleagues
align themselves with new ways of life, a society's lineage heads will
eventually begin to see their authority dwindle and their roles replaced.[59]
As this process proceeds, elders often become increasingly unable to prevent radical sociocultural change. They may experience much of this
change as horrifying, since it is disruptive of traditional social patterns
that they treasure.

Anthropologists have observed typical disruptive changes that
accompany the centralization of many societies. These include an
increase in the power of officeholders, a loss of cohesion within traditional land-controlling groups, and the emergence of the idea that land is
"alienable" (that is, that control of land can permanently transfer out of
the hands of its traditional holders).[60] These typical changes create conditions ripe for land grabbing.

The social phenomenon of land grabbing when new systems and
new rules appear in a society is all too common cross-culturally. One can
find examples from around the world for comparison with what
occurred in monarchic Israel. In each case, an influx of new wealth, which
the elite invest in land, and the shrugging off of old rules weaken or even
collapse a traditional system of small farm holdings. In place of the old
system, vast estates grow up with the victimization and eviction of small
farmers. In many cases, the new land barons further exploit their victims
by putting them to work as day laborers or slaves on land that they previously owned.

A community's traditional leadership often divides over new conflicts about land. Some leaders support their traditional constituencies
and help their kinfolk rise up against new land barons. Conversely, other
leaders join sides with the new systems and rules, sometimes even
becoming land barons themselves. Eric Wolf describes such an internal

---

58. Schapera, "Ngwato," 61.
59. Jack Goody, "Kinship: Descent Groups," *IESS* 8:403.
60. Daniel P. Biebuyck, "Land Tenure, Introduction," *IESS* 8:566; Rogerson and Davies,
Old Testament World, 59.

differentiation in local community leadership that occurred in response to the land grabbing involved in the sixteenth-century Spanish conquest of the New World.[61]

As their conquest proceeded, the incoming Castilian Spaniards built up a system of landed estates, called *haciendas*. The owners of these estates put tremendous pressure on local native communities, since they needed their members as serf-tenants. The local populace resisted this pressure as best it could, lodging complaints in the "Indian courts" against estate owners trying to take over native lands. Sometimes a traditional leader within a local native community would unite his people against the encroachment of a *hacienda* owner. In other cases, local leaders would join the Spaniards.

The practice of destroying family farms to create vast agricultural estates has been common in contemporary Central America. In a first-hand report, Rigoberta Menchú, a native Quiché woman, offers us a popular account of land grabbing and exploitation of agrarian families in Guatemala.[62] Menchú has experienced the human cost of the creation of large Guatemalan plantations (*fincas*), focused on enriching elite owners through producing cash crops. She summarizes what it is like for a small elite to benefit from growing and exporting cotton and coffee on *fincas*:

> We spent four months in our little house in the *Altiplano* [the mountain-ous region in the northwest of Guatemala] and the rest of the year we had to go down to the coast, either in the *Boca Costa* where there's coffee picking and also weeding out the coffee plants, or further down the South coast where there's cotton.... A very few families owned the vast areas of land which produce these crops for sale abroad. These landowners are the lords of vast extensions of land.... Where we live in the mountains...the land isn't fertile, you can barely grow maize and beans.... But on the coast [the *fincas*] the land is rich and you can grow anything.[63]

Menchú describes how living as contracted laborers on *fincas* breaks down native community. She details the many forms of exploitation that her people endure under landowners and overseers. The elite *finca* owners conspire to cheat their workers out of every centavo possible:

61. Wolf, *People without History*, 146–47.

62. Rigoberta Menchú, *I, Rigoberta Menchú: An Indian Woman in Guatemala* (ed. E. Burgos-Debray; trans. A. Wright; London: Verso, 1984). I am indebted for this reference to Kitty Guy, a student in my "Hosea and Micah" course in 1996 at Virginia Theological Seminary.

63. Menchú, *I, Rigoberta Menchú*, 5.

There's an office in every *finca* where all the work you deliver is taken. It's weighed and noted down for their accounts. Towards the end, my brothers (who are not stupid) managed to figure out the ways in which they fiddled the amounts weighed. They have tricks to make it weigh less, when the real amount is much more.... It's part of a long process which starts the moment the agents contract the workers in their villages and load them into the lorries like animals. It's one long process of robbing them of their pay. They're charged for absolutely everything, even for the loading of the lorry. Then, in the *finca,* the overseers steal from the workers from the very first day. The *cantina* steals from them too.[64]

In the African continent, the colonial era provides many more examples of land grabbing. The practice was rampant under the new social dynamics that the colonizing Europeans introduced.[65] The Europeans displaced many Africans from the most fertile farmlands, pushing the natives to the less productive parts of the countryside. In place of a system of inherited plots, vast agricultural plantations arose. To add insult to injury, the colonizers put African natives to work tilling the new plantations. Hut taxes and head taxes allowed the colonizing authorities to extract a goodly amount from what little the natives were able to produce for their own sustenance under the new system.

The observations of ethnographers have much to teach us about the roles and functions of elders in society before any centralizing systems overlay their traditional modes of operation, before the advent of monarchic power and land-grabbing practices.

A look at the general practices and values of traditional elders can help us envision the destructive impact that societal centralization would have on their lives. A huge amount of comparative material is available for survey, but the scope of the present project limits me to a brief sketch. I shall highlight those features most relevant for comparison in the next chapter with the social background of Micah's prophecy.

We have already seen that in traditional society elders play key administrative roles. On a part-time, mostly local basis, they meet together as a group. Such meetings normally include only other elders of their own kin group.

Take the examples of the Logoli and the Bni Bataw. The elders of the Logoli people in western Kenya meet every morning around a campfire in

---

64. Ibid., 41–42.

65. Some international students have reported on this in term papers that they have written in my courses. I rely here on a paper entitled "Hosea and Micah," by Dorcas Chanya Ndoro and Mercy Nyagah, submitted in OT 108, Virginia Theological Seminary, Alexandria, Va., fall semester, 1996.

a pasture. They call their assembly an *oluhia*.[66] The Bni Bataw of Morroco have a "community council," in which male heads of households informally discuss their collective obligations.[67]

Within such councils, traditional elders perform administrative and judicial tasks through discussion and consensus building. They work out agricultural strategies, plan the movement of herds in search of pasture, facilitate the transfer of inheritances, help look out for the interests of the needy, and deal with legal disputes. In all their activities, the council of elders passes on the ancestral traditions of their kinfolk. In performing their roles, the elders constantly bring up and rehearse a tribe's maxims and traditional case law.

Clearly, many of the administrative and judicial functions of elders involve land. Kinfolk turn to the elders in times of land disputes, such as conflicts over irrigation rights. The elders also settle disputes over land between local inhabitants and outsiders. Among the Logoli people, for example, the interests of the entire patrilineal kin group are involved in each member's use and disposal of land. The elders of this people thus must take an active interest in regulating land tenure.[68]

In traditional societies cross-culturally, not all elders are equal. Individuals usually earn special authority through their ability to end fights or to convince combatants to enter arbitration before the assembly of elders. Others earn special recognition through prowess as warriors or through a reputation for giving great feasts.

Furthermore, in many noncentralized societies dominant, noble, or aristocratic descent lines develop. Internal ranking develops between senior and junior lines of descent from the same ancestor. External ranking results as particular lineages distinguish themselves by forming successful alliances, managing people well, and achieving agricultural superiority. Farm plots vary in fertility; vicissitudes of weather may aid the families of certain regions; personal health of family members may differ; and people make differing use of technology.[69]

As social rankings solidify, a gentry may establish itself. A populace will accord special deference to the elders from such a gentry. The special elders of leading lineages, often termed clan heads, can act as spokespersons before other, external kin groups within a tribe.

---

66. Wagner, "Bantu," 220.
67. See the discussion of Eickelman's observations in McNutt, *Society of Ancient Israel*, 80.
68. Wagner, "Bantu," 217.
69. Ayisi, *African Culture*, 40–41; Wolf, *People without History*, 94; McNutt, *Society of Ancient Israel*, 74, 83, 85, 91, 100.

Although there are no hereditary or formal offices in the case of the Logoli, some elders do rise above their colleagues to become clan heads.[70] The Vugusu people, who together with the Logoli form the Bantu Kavirondo, also have special, leading elders. They call such clan heads, *avagasa*, which means "men who talk gently and wisely." An individual rises to prominence as a leading elder through such avenues as wealth, eloquence, and reputation as a warrior.[71]

The position of clan head is more of an actual institution among the Tallensi people of northern Ghana. Although the Tallensi have no centralized state or tribal government, most heads of maximal lineages hold the special office of clan chief.[72]

One case of a lineage society in which whole clans exercise dominance occurs among the Nuer in southern Sudan. Tribespeople from other Nuer kin groups consider members of these clans gentry.[73]

In several traditional cultures elders from more than one kin group can act in interclan concert. Elders representing various clans communicate through messengers, or meet in person to plan collective action. The Logoli sometimes send a delegation of elders from several principal kin groups to a rainmaker in order to retain his services in time of drought. They probably feel more comfortable taking a collective approach, because the rainmakers of that region belong to a hostile people (the Nyole).[74]

The Berbers of the Atlas Mountains of Morocco have a tribal-wide assembly, in which representatives of clans can interact in concert. The assembly, known as the *jema'a*, convenes at various hierarchical levels of Berber society, ascending the segmentary levels of the genealogical system as occasion warrants.

The various subgroups of society participate in the assembly through representatives. Elders and other delegates attend on behalf of their respective segmentary groups. Some assembly meetings convene at high enough levels to embody very large segments of Berber society. At these higher levels, not all society's elders are able to attend. Select, leading clan heads must represent their colleagues.

The *jema'a* is not a centralized institution. It has no permanent officers, bureaucracy, secretarial staff, or records. It has no existence apart from the Berber's autonomous societal segments, of which it is an assembly.[75]

---

70. Wagner, "Bantu," 221.

71. Ibid., 232–36.

72. Fortes, "Tallensi," 255.

73. Evans-Pritchard, "Nuer," 284.

74. Wagner, "Bantu," 211, 224.

75. Gellner, *Saints of the Atlas*, 89–90; cf. King and Stager, *Life in Biblical Israel*, 60–61.

A MODEL FOR EXPLORING HOSEA'S ROOTS: THE LEVITES IN MONARCHIC ISRAEL AND IN VILLAGE ISRAEL

As new monarchic organizations of society arose in Judah and the northern kingdom in Iron Age IC and II, new state systems of liturgical and sacrificial practice appeared. This new, centralized worship began to override traditional worship systems. The systems of worship associated with old Israel's lineage-based society now found themselves in competition with centralized cults and their priests.

In Judah, King David eased this transition by taking pains to see that his new monarchy respected old Israel's traditional priesthoods and symbols of worship. David appointed as chief priests both Zadok and Abiathar, who represented respectively the traditional priestly lineages of the Aaronides and the Levites.

King Solomon later dismissed the priest Abiathar for political reasons, however, so that the Levitical line of priests ended up losing its representative in the capital of the Judean state. With Abiathar's dismissal, one traditional priestly lineage suffered a significant loss of its authority in Judean society.

The situation was more jarring in the northern kingdom, where, after the time of David and Solomon, the northerners refused to renew the united monarchy. The Bible reports the people's particular dissatisfaction with Solomon's son, King Rehoboam of Judah. The northerners eventually rejected Rehoboam and created a separate monarchic state under the rule of King Jeroboam I (ca. 922–901 B.C.E.).

King Jeroboam immediately faced the task of solidifying his new kingdom as an independent state. He correctly sensed that a sacral and ritual focusing of his kingdom's new centralized power would be a key means of ensuring his success. As anthropologist Robert McC. Netting states, sacral factors may be crucial in regrouping a people as a centralized body, particularly where the people's traditional organization is based on kinship. These factors include "religious belief," a "shared cosmology," and "unity made visible in ritual."[76]

Jeroboam established a new, northern state-based ritual and sacrificial system. The new system would have its own integrity, independent of the worship practice of Judah. Jeroboam established the shrines at Dan and Bethel as official *northern* alternatives to the Jerusalem temple. He instituted new holidays and new religious symbols at the shrines, to

---

76. Netting, "Sacred Power," 233. Also see Stephen L. Cook, "The Lineage Roots of Hosea's Yahwism," in Simkins and Cook, *Social World of the Hebrew Bible, Semeia* 87 (1999): 145–62.

distinguish them from Jerusalem's worship celebrations and symbols. A major text describing Jeroboam's reorganization of Israel's ritual system is 1 Kgs 12:25–33. The narrative reads as follows:

> Then Jeroboam built Shechem in the hill country of Ephraim, and resided there; he went out from there and built Penuel. Then Jeroboam said to himself, "Now the kingdom may well revert to the house of David. If this people continues to go up to offer sacrifices in the house of the LORD at Jerusalem, the heart of this people will turn again to their master, King Rehoboam of Judah; they will kill me and return to King Rehoboam of Judah." So the king took counsel, and made two calves of gold. He said to the people, "You have gone up to Jerusalem long enough. Here are your gods, O Israel, who brought you up out of the land of Egypt." He set one in Bethel, and the other he put in Dan. And this thing became a sin, for the people went to worship before the one at Bethel and before the other as far as Dan. He also made houses on high places, and appointed priests from among all the people, who were not Levites. Jeroboam appointed a festival on the fifteenth day of the eighth month like the festival that was in Judah, and he offered sacrifices on the altar; so he did in Bethel, sacrificing to the calves that he had made. And he placed in Bethel the priests of the high places that he had made. He went up to the altar that he had made in Bethel on the fifteenth day in the eighth month, in the month that he alone had devised; he appointed a festival for the people of Israel, and he went up to the altar to offer incense.

Like David before him, the northern king tried to ease the transition to centralized worship by including traditional cult sites and symbols in his ritual program. Dan and Bethel, for example, were ancient worship sites in Israel (cf. Gen 12:8; 35:1–16; Judg 18:30). The king's shrewd use of elements of tradition, however, should not obscure the fact that his reorganization program aimed primarily at sacral *centralization*.

Jeroboam molded a new centralizing cult to secure and promote his monarchic power and the development of his new centralized state. He was no romantic, wishing simply to revive Dan and Bethel. His aim was to elevate these sites as national shrines, associated with his new central authority. They were to become royal chapels, where the king himself had the right to preside, to control the ritual calendar, and to offer sacrifices (1 Kgs 12:32–33).

Bethel in particular became "the king's sanctuary," "a temple of the kingdom" (Amos 7:13). Our study in chapter 4 of Hosea's view of Bethel confirms this. Hosea considered the north's royal capital, Samaria, to be the controlling authority behind Bethel's bull worship (Hos 8:5–6; 10:5).

It was no accident that the traditional cult sites Jeroboam chose to elevate were located at the strategic northern and southern borders of his kingdom. Their location virtually defined the northern kingdom as an independent political entity, separate from Judah. Bethel was even located on the road up to Jerusalem in Judah. The choice of Bethel placed Jeroboam's alternative pilgrimage site directly "in the face" of all would-be pilgrims to Jerusalem.

Jeroboam's reorganization of the northern cult's personnel was perhaps his most radical cultic innovation. In old Israel, sacred power was organized along kinship lines. Membership in a family line of priests determined one's sacral authority, not appointment by a centralized authority. In particular, Levites were priests in the northern kingdom, as 1 Kgs 12:31 and other texts, such as Judg 18:30, show.

The latter text, Judg 18:30, states that "Jonathan son of Gershom, son of Moses, and his sons were priests to the tribe of the Danites until the time the land went into captivity." We know from Judg 17:7, 13 that this Jonathan, the ancestor of the priesthood at Dan, was a priest of the Levitical family line.

The Levites, of course, were a tribal organization in old Israel, Levi being one of the traditional tribes of Israel. Judges 18:30 further specifies that Jonathan was a member of that line of Levites that traced their descent from Moses, a great-grandson of Levi.[77] In other words, Jonathan was a *Mushite* Levite.[78]

According to 1 Kgs 12:31–32, Jeroboam departed from tradition by using his new royal authority to consecrate non-Levites as state priests. He "appointed priests from among all the people, who were not Levites," alienating the affections of the traditional Levites.

He seems to have gone farther than this, however. Second Chronicles reports that Jeroboam and his royal descendants actively prevented the Levites from serving as priests of Yahweh (2 Chron 11:13–17). It says flatly that Jeroboam drove out the Levitical priests. He appointed instead anyone who could provide a young bull and seven rams for his priestly consecration (2 Chron 13:9; cf. 1 Kgs 13:33).

Some scholars, such as F. M. Cross, dispute the historicity of Jeroboam's dismissal of the Levites.[79] These scholars argue that such a move

---

77. See Exod 6:16–20. Cf. Exod 2:1; 4:14, which confirm that Moses was a Levite. Psalm 99:6 actually calls Moses a priest.

78. As Roland de Vaux explains, "Mushite is generally interpreted as a *nomen gentilitium* derived from Moses" (*Ancient Israel: Its Life and Institutions* [New York: McGraw-Hill, 1961], 370).

79. Frank M. Cross dismisses the assertions of 1 Kings as "Deuteronomistic polemic" against Jeroboam. See F. M. Cross, *Canaanite Myth and Hebrew Epic* (Cambridge: Harvard University Press, 1973), 74, 199. Compare E. W. Nicholson, *Deuteronomy and Tradition* (Oxford: Basil Blackwell, 1967), 75.

would have been a political blunder, undercutting a key support base of the new monarchy. I disagree with this skeptical assessment.[80]

Biblical monarchs were quite capable of risky, political machinations. Not long before Jeroboam's acts, King Solomon risked alienating sectors of his populace by dismissing the Levite chief, Abiathar. Biblical monarchs are not alone in tolerating some disaffection to consolidate royal power. I shall present cross-cultural evidence below that new centralizing sacral power often arises in a culture at the expense of traditional lineage-based priesthoods.

The expulsions of Levitical cult personnel by Solomon and Jeroboam certainly alienated and disenfranchised this traditional priestly lineage. It by no means obliterated them, however.

Some Levites seem to have continued to function as priests at the shrine at Dan throughout the existence of the northern kingdom. In the southern kingdom, other Levites doubtless continued to serve at the Jerusalem temple, though as underlings. Still other Levites must have continued to serve at peripheral, rural shrines or found fellowship in base communities, sustaining themselves through nonpriestly activities.

The book of Deuteronomy argues that in the ideal Israelite society, Levites will mediate the covenant to the people (Deut 27:9–10, 14–15; 31:9–13). They will also perform key judicial functions (Deut 17:9). They will even be welcome to serve alongside other priests at the Jerusalem temple (Deut 18:6–7). The book thus clearly presupposes that the Levites are alive and well in the seventh century B.C.E. (cf. Deut 12:12, 19; 14:27, 29; 26:11–13), ready to return to their traditional roles in society.

Despite cultic centralization in the society, circles of Levites clearly perdured, preserving their own ritual traditions, passing them on to their descendants.

I argued in chapters 3 and 5 that among these traditions were the Psalms of Asaph. The Levites preserved these psalms until Jerusalem's liturgy took them over in Hezekiah's time. Thus, the traditions of a lineage-based ritual system persisted in monarchic Judah and Israel as a

---

80. Aelred Cody argues that the fact that the text is explicitly antagonistic toward Bethel (12:32) but that it does not complain about non-Levitical priests at Dan may be an argument for its historicity (*A History of Old Testament Priesthood* [Rome: Pontifical Biblical Institute, 1969], 111). Factual detail would not impinge in this way, if our text were a purely invented polemic. Further support for the historicity of much of 1 Kgs 12 comes from an exegesis of Exod 32:25–29. (Cf. H. W. Wolff, "Hoseas Geistige Heimat," in *Gesammelte Studien zum Alten Testament* [Munich: Kaiser, 1964], 244–45.) I shall argue in chapter 8 that this Exodus text reflects the hostility of the disenfranchised Levites toward the calf cult of Jeroboam I.

substratum until the cultic reforms of King Hezekiah and King Josiah. These two reformer kings seem to have elevated some of the Levites back into power.

Comparative evidence from the work of social scientists greatly illuminates the social dynamics that were involved in the history of the Levites in Israel. The evidence demonstrates that lineage-based and state-based ritual systems can coexist in a society. It also reveals in what specific ways the latter system may be destructive of the former.

Cross-cultural study shows how the rise of new, centralizing political power within a lineage-based society may disenfranchise traditional ritual functionaries (priests). The case of the Western Dinka in the southern Sudan is a good example. The Dinka people are accustomed to shifting their alignments between priests in accordance with changes in the prestige and reputation of these figures. A new descent group of priests may gain the advantage if it proves itself more effective in prayer, attracting followers, and creating harmony.

An extreme form of realignment behind a new priesthood occurs when powerful new sacral forces push Dinka society toward centralization. This may happen when a Dinka priest rises to power by claiming special inspiration from a sky spirit. Such a figure may be able to unify widely separated Dinka groups. Even hostile tribes and foreign groups may find themselves drawn in by the centralizing appeal of such a figure. G. Lienhardt reports one case of this actually happening in connection with a Dinka priest named Arianhdit.[81]

Traditional priests also found themselves supplanted when a new, centralizing cult sprang up among the Lugbara people living in northwestern Uganda and the adjoining area of Congo (Kinshasa).[82] The new cult, known as *Yakan,* spread through north and central Lugbara territory in 1895 C.E. and later around 1910 C.E. Adherents found the cult able to ward off epidemic sickness and to bring about a rule of peace and order. Because of its sacral powers, the cult unified the Lugbara tribes. Its wide expansion culminated in a military revolt against the Europeans in 1919. The popularity of the *Yakan* movement largely displaced the traditional ritual functionaries of Lugbara society for a time. Indeed, during this period many of these traditional functionaries voluntarily aligned themselves with the movement.

---

81. Lienhardt, "Western Dinka," 118, 131–32; idem, *Divinity and Experience: The Religion of the Dinka* (Oxford: Clarendon, 1961), 212–16.

82. John Middleton, "The Political System of the Lugbara of the Nile-Congo Divide," in Middleton and Tait, *Tribes without Rulers,* 224–25.

New state rulers may not wait for a populace to chose sides between kinship-based and state-based priesthoods. Monarchs are not above dismissing or destroying traditional cults and their leaders to consolidate their power.

The Zulu ruler Shaka, discussed above, exercised this kind of tyranny over some of the traditional ritual functionaries of his society after he came to power. After making himself king, Shaka took over and militarized the tribal ceremonies of his people from prestate times. Further, Shaka claimed for himself sole control of the weather, and he expelled all rainmakers from his kingdom.[83]

When the British imposed centralized rule upon the Kofyar people of Nigeria (a noncentralized, stateless people), they displaced the traditional Kofyar priest-chiefs. Among the Kofyar, the priest-chief (*Miskagam*) has prerogatives and functions that are mostly ritual and mystic in nature. In natural calamity, for example, the *Miskagam* priest performs a ritual sacrifice of a goat (the *ya fu yil* ritual). In recognition of their ritual importance, the Kofyar people donate special jars of beer (the *mwos miskagam*) to their priests at brewing time.

In imposing their rule, the British replaced the Kofyar priest-chiefs with their own administrative appointees. The priests' disenfranchisement did not spell their demise, however. They continued in their liturgical roles, and they continued to expect their traditional jar of donated beer. The older and newer officials existed side by side under British rule, although conflict between them was always a potential reality. In one village, conflict naturally flared up when one administrative appointee made claims to the priestly beer of the traditional *Miskagam*.[84]

When new centralizing power emerges from either inside or outside of their society, traditional priests do not vanish (unless state authorities physically expel them). Faced with new state authorities, priests must choose between differing strategic reactions. They may resist centralizing authority. They may cooperate with it, if possible. Or, they may pursue their own interests by secretly working with the new authorities while falsely assuring their own tribal constituencies of their continuing allegiance.

During one period, three different genealogical branches of priests among the Moroccan Atlas Berbers pursued each of these three alternatives.[85]

---

83. Gluckman, "Kingdom of the Zulu," 31.
84. Netting, "Sacred Power," 222–25.
85. Gellner, *Saints of the Atlas*, 150, 250.

In the early twentieth century, a French incursion into Morocco confronted the Atlas Berbers and their priests with new, state-centered power. In the face of the French incursion into their society, one priestly branch reacted with all-out resistance. A second branch engaged in open collaboration with the French. A third priestly branch played a double game. They attempted to maintain favor with both their tribal folk and the French. When the French achieved victory in Morocco in 1933, they advanced the leaders of the two cooperative priestly groups to new administrative posts. The French granted the hostile priests no such reward.

The new priestly officials of centralized, state cults may have no hereditary credentials for their office. Their appointment by an emerging centralized society may fly in the face of traditional norms of priestly lineage continuity.

The contrast in the organization of the priesthood between the tribes of Morocco and its towns gives us a clear example of this.[86] The Moroccan evidence illustrates what can happen to priesthood lineage norms when societies centralize.

Priests (*igurramen*) among the tribal people of the Atlas of Morocco are actual kin groups, just like the other tribal segments of their society. They are members of their priestly lodge (a *zawiya*) by birth. In fact, the Berber priests of the Atlas as a whole consider themselves a single holy lineage descended from the Muslim Prophet himself.

The value that they place on their line of descent comes across clearly in the detail of their personal, priestly genealogies. They preserve genealogies that are much more complete than the laypeople in their society do, with many more names along their line of descent. Gellner observes that "a typical successful saint [i.e., priest] will possess a genealogy which contains a long string of names of whom only a few have the role of defining existing corporate groups."[87]

In contrast, birth and lineage play a minor role in the priestly lodges in urban parts of Morocco, where centralized authority is the norm. Although the urban lodges may have a nucleus defined by kinship, heredity is not what determines membership. Ritual practices, rather than kinship, define their identity. They recruit their membership based not on birth but simply on identifying parties interested in joining their numbers.

The cross-cultural evidence suggests that a centralizing society's move away from a hereditary priesthood may be a radical change. The

---

86. Ibid., 8–9.
87. Ibid., 40.

ritual functionaries of many traditional cultures highly value their hereditary qualifications for priestly office.

The Akans of Ghana, Africa, have certain preeminent lineages that
always supply the people's ritual officials.[88] Likewise, priesthood is the
prerogative of one set of lineages in the culture of the Tallensi people of
northern Ghana. Their priests (*tendaanas*) must come from the *Talis*
genealogical branches. Either seniority or divination determines which
living heads of the *Talis* lines succeed to priestly office.[89]

So too, the Mossi people of Burkina Faso (formerly Upper Volta) in
West Africa limit their priestly office to a specific lineage, called the
Savadogo. This priestly lineage maintains dwellings amid the various
other lineages of each Mossi village.[90]

Genealogical descent also determines succession to various sacral
and priestly offices among the Bemba tribe of the northeastern plateau of
Zambia. The Bemba society maintains its original kinship structure intact.
Membership in all Bemba social groups depends on kinship, and priestly
offices are no exception.[91]

In southern Sudan, the priests of Dinka society, known as "masters
of the fishing-spear," come only from distinct priestly clans, the *bany*.
(These ritual functionaries take their name from the symbol of their
office, the sacred fishing spear.) The hereditary ties of spear-masters
with their kin groups are of utmost importance to them. They believe
that much of the strength of their relationship with their clan deities
comes from the genealogical continuity of their hereditary line through
successive generations.[92]

The rise of centralizing sacral power disrupts more than just the lineage norms of a society's hereditary priesthoods. New centralizing cult
features undercut preexisting ritual bonds that provide traditional tribal
groups with a sense of belonging to a larger whole.

The various genealogical segments of a stateless society may share
basic rites and ritual schedules on a tribal scale. Although they do not
lessen the normal spirit of autonomy and competition of segmentary systems, these collective ritual forms encourage tribal solidarity.[93]

---

88. Ayisi, *African Culture*, 50.
89. Fortes, "Tallensi," 255, 261.
90. Peter B. Hammond, "Economic Change and Mossi Acculturation," in *Continuity and Change in African Cultures* (ed. W. R. Bascom and M. J. Herskovits; Chicago: University of Chicago Press, 1959), 246.
91. Audrey I. Richards, "The Political System of the Bemba Tribe—North-Eastern Rhodesia," in Fortes and Evans-Pritchard, *African Political Systems*, 94–96.
92. Lienhardt, *Divinity and Experience*, 8, 216; idem, "Western Dinka," 104.
93. John Middleton and David Tait, "Introduction," in Middleton and Tait, *Tribes without Rulers*, 15.

Many examples of sacral interlocking within tribal societies are available for study. Ritual collaboration in a cycle of "Great Festivals," for example, is a force for societal cohesion among the Tallensi. Embracing all of the Tale settlements, the cycle is tribal-wide. Its ritual and ceremonial observances bring out a sense of common allegiance among the people. The observances help them to think of themselves as different from non-Talis outsiders. The Tallensi have no central government, as I have noted above, so besides their kinship networks these ritual ties are all that bind this kinfolk together as one people.[94]

Sacral collaboration and coordination is also a force for cohesion among the Logoli tribe in Kenya. On semiannual occasions, the people stop all garden work and send representatives to a special sacral cave on the slope of a wooded hill. There they sacrifice to an ancestral spirit (*Mung'oma*) and a tribal deity (*Asai*).

The Logoli's traditional priests play key roles in the sacrifices. While most of the people's representatives sing ceremonial songs at the bottom of the hill, several others join Logoli priests to perform sacrificial ceremonies inside the cave. These priests maintain and perpetuate tribal relationships and laws across the generations.[95]

The Logoli also perform circumcision rites on a tribal scale. The whole people do not assemble in one place for these rites, but they perform them at the same time every few years.

The Logoli have no central authority, such as a chief or a tribal council. Their cultic rites, along with their kinship bonds, create their unity as a people. G. Wagner concludes that the Logoli's tribal-scale cult and rites "create a feeling of unity which serves as a sanction for close cooperation in all matters affecting the tribal group."[96]

In addition to disrupting their roles in collective ritual practices, the rise of central sacral power may degrade traditional priests' roles as mediators in society.

Priestly mediation is another common force for societal solidarity among traditional peoples. Tribal priests, acting as supernatural intermediaries, represent their whole people before the gods. At other times, they intervene in conflicts between societal segments to help them avoid violence. The role of priests as social mediators is most effective when priestly lines are independent of other genealogical segments of society.

The priests of the Berber tribes in Morocco provide a good example. As hereditary priests with their own lineage, they are automatically

94. Fortes, "Tallensi," 245, 263.
95. Wagner, "Bantu," 210–11.
96. Ibid., 200.

"professional neutrals." They are genealogically unaffiliated with the competing, feud-addicted groups that surround them. When disagreements or rivalries over pasturelands heat up between tribal segments, these priests help maintain the precarious, genealogically based balance of their society.[97]

The effectiveness of priestly mediation increases when ritual functionaries do not limit their dwelling places to one territory of a people. Thus, priestly descent groups spread out among the segments of society in the case of several traditional peoples. (Berber priests have geographically discontinuous settlements, whereas lay tribal groups tend to occupy continuous territory.[98]) Dispersing themselves among a society's various kin groups, priestly lineages create a sort of interlocking social glue (an interpenetrating sodality).

The ritual functionaries of the Nuer of southern Sudan, the leopard-skin chiefs, often act as mediators between kin groups.[99] They have impartial status in lineage disputes, since they stand outside the system of lay lineages. When blood feuds look inevitable between societal segments, these priests step in. They typically arrange compensation payments, or perform ceremonies of reconciliation that end conflict.

The ritual functionaries of the Tallensi, the *tendaanas* described above, also have significant mediatory roles in society.[100] Their mediatory power is linked to their special relationship with the land, which the Tallensi people believe abhors bloodshed.

Because of the people's strong kinship ties, all of their disputes immediately become conflicts between genealogical groups: extended families, lineages, and kin groups. Fortunately, *tendaanas* live among these various societal segments, interlinking with each other through kinship and ritual ties. Their presence amid various conflictive parties is a powerfully positive force for solidarity. The *tendaanas* act as privileged intermediaries when lineage heads meet to try to resolve the disputes of their groups. They often succeed in helping the parties overcome their differences.

Similarly, the priest-chiefs of the Kofyar people of Nigeria often arbitrate between villages in conflict, willing to work out differences between warring factions on the battlefield. Upon resolution of the conflict, the priestly representatives of the disputants make a joint sacrifice to cement the reconciliation they have negotiated.[101]

---

97. Gellner, *Saints of the Atlas*, 33, 55, 64, 78.
98. Ibid., 69.
99. Ayisi, *African Culture*, 59–60; Middleton and Tait, "Introduction," 16.
100. Ayisi, *African Culture*, 60; Fortes, "Tallensi," 261, 268.
101. Netting, "Sacred Power," 224.

Like the Kofyar priests, the priestly masters of the fishing-spear among the Dinka are mediators and peacemakers within society. The spear-masters support not only their own kin group but also everyone in their community. Unlike the deities of other clans, their deities will help whole subtribes and tribes.[102]

In a typical peace-making liturgy, a master of the fishing-spear will stand between two feuding camps. He will divide the right leg of an ox into two parts and throw one part at each camp. This ritual embodies the separation between the two camps and, at the same time, signals the conclusion to their hostilities.[103]

One special kin group of spear-masters permeates almost all of the tribal segments among the Dinka of the West Bank of the Nile: the Pagong clan. The wide dispersal of this lineage is a strong resource for intertribal community among the Dinka tribes. The masters of the fishing-spear of Pagong have an especially strong reputation for making effective peace between tribal segments. Some Dinka recall times past when only this renowned lineage of priests was able to mediate between hostile, highly autonomous Dinka tribes. The Pagong clan of priests thus prevented large-scale wars at volatile times in Dinka history.[104]

The people's association with specific territories and farmlands is fundamental at all levels of many segmentary societies. A major part of the role of traditional elders centers on the care, use, and disposition of land. It should not be surprising that the role of many traditional priests likewise has much to do with land, its sacral dimensions, and its fertility.

Lineage-based priesthoods naturally oppose new, centrally administered fertility rituals that override their traditional, sacral management of the land.

Traditional priests often preside over agricultural and animal sacrifices, which in their very substance connect to the land. Plant and animal sacrifices are offerings to a deity from the produce of a society's farms and pastures. The symbolisms and the ritual processes behind sacrifice are complex, and vary from culture to culture. At one primary level, however, sacrifices are gifts that allow a people to acknowledge a deity's control over their land and its animal and agricultural produce.

Sacrifice involves both reciprocity and inequality. In granting the land fertility and bounty, the deity gives much more to the tribe than the sacrificers will ever give back. The inequality of the exchange is not necessarily offensive to the deity, however. It establishes the deity's

---

102. Lienhardt, *Divinity and Experience,* 145, 168, 211.
103. Ibid., 287–88.
104. Ibid., 216–17.

superiority, and reinforces the hierarchical relationship of the god and the members of the tribe.[105]

In this regard, sacrifices are comparable to *tribute* in the ancient world. In offering tribute, a vassal people acknowledge their indebtedness and subservient relationship to the liege lord.

It is not difficult to find examples of the link between sacrifice and arable land in traditional societies. Traditional Hawaiian farmers made regular offerings in recognition of their deities' role in fertility. Every time a farmer cooked an oven of food, he offered a potato or a *taro* to his deity. This was a simple ritual act, which the farmer performed himself. He simply placed his offering on an altar or put it on a tree.[106]

I noted above the prominent role of sacrifice in the tribal life of the Logoli in Kenya. Although sacrifices among the Logoli secure divine help on a variety of concerns, including epidemics and failed raids, promoting the land's fertility is often a central purpose. Their sacrifices often petition the ancestral spirit or the tribal deity for crops to ripen quickly or for a calamitous drought to end.[107]

The practice of *firstfruits* sacrifices in some traditional societies is a clear illustration of the link between sacrifice and land. In these sacrifices, a traditional people gather the earliest products of a harvest and offer them to a deity. The ritual is an acknowledgment of a deity's gift of a land's fruitfulness.

Valerio Valeri's study of ritual and society in ancient Hawaii provides a good example of this type of sacrificial acknowledgment of the gods' fructifying role.[108] The ancient Hawaiian farming family would always prepare a sacrificial celebration when crops reached maturity. They would consecrate the firstfruits (*kāmauli hou*) of the harvest and then cook them over the sacrificial fire. Each participant in the celebration would eat a share of the first oven of food.

Each New Year, the whole community would collectively offer an annual firstfruits sacrifice. The community would also make a collective sacrifice of firstfruits anytime that a famine ended. Similarly, traditional Hawaiian people offered the first part of their annual fish catch as a sacrifice to the gods. They understood the sacrifice as token recognition of the divine provision of all the fish that they would catch during the fishing season.

---

105. Valerio Valeri, *Kingship and Sacrifice: Ritual and Society in Ancient Hawaii* (trans. P. Wissing; Chicago: University of Chicago Press, 1985), 62–75.

106. Ibid., 43.

107. Wagner, "Bantu," 210.

108. Valeri, *Kingship and Sacrifice*, 43, 79.

The Akwapim and Akwamus people in the southeastern part of Ghana observe a firstfruits festival, called the *Odwira* festival. The festival is an affair of the whole people, uniting various lineages, kin groups, and tribes in celebration of the land's harvest. Preparing food and special meals for deceased ancestors is a central activity at the festival. It is only right to recognize the ancestors at harvest time, since the people's belief is that they are closely associated with the land. Devotion to ancestral spirits is also a way to reach the Supreme Being, one of whose main names is *Onyame*. Fertility and bountifulness are associated with this central byname of the deity.[109]

Similarly, the Mossi people conduct harvest ceremonies to close the economic year, with offerings representing all their farms. Young people accompany emissaries to the ceremonies, breaking off stalks of millet from various fields as they travel. They present these stalks from their journey as offerings upon arrival at the festival.[110]

With the aid of their priests, traditional farmers honor sacral responsibilities on the land at other key junctures, such as the opening of new fields. The Tallensi people refer to each priest (*tendaana*) as a "Custodian of the Earth." These priests break the soil and preside at sacrifices when a family opens a new farm or digs a new grave. They have a right to a portion of the sacrificial animals.[111]

The Mossi people also call their priests "Custodians of the Earth." In fact, many West African peoples have this ritual office. As with the Tallensi, an earth custodian among the Mossi must grant permission and receive an offering for the earth deity before a farmer clears any new plot of land. Farmers make their offerings at the shrine (*tenga*) of the earth custodian.[112]

IMPLICATIONS FOR INTERPRETING BIBLICAL TEXTS IN MICAH AND HOSEA

In the following two chapters, exegesis of Micah and Hosea will test the thesis that these prophets operated amid the same type of overlap and conflict of societal systems seen in the cross-cultural examples. They owed their allegiance to the older, kinship-based system within this conflict.

---

109. Ayisi, *African Culture*, 79, 83–85.
110. Hammond, "Mossi Acculturation," 250.
111. Ayisi, *African Culture*, 60.
112. Hammond, "Mossi Acculturation," 246–47.

Our probes into Micah and Hosea reveal agrarian, kinship-oriented features and ideals. The cross-cultural evidence of the present chapter creates a social-scientific model of the type of lineage-based, segmentary society of farmers and herders compatible with these observations.

The cross-cultural evidence suggests new, specific things to look for as we return to Micah and Hosea in search of their social roots. Specific clues could confirm the roots of their theology in genealogically organized segments of old Israel. A sample telltale clue would be a perspective evaluating monarchic officials by standards relevant mostly to traditional clan leaders. Or, it would prove telling to observe a stubborn advocacy of rural smallholders of land. Or, again, other signal clues would involve special emphases on values such as lineage continuity, kin unity, or ritual collaboration in society.

Armed with the social-scientific model of this chapter, I can now fully examine the social and historical roots of our eighth-century prophets and their forebears, and bring the ancient social roots of Sinai theology in Micah and Hosea into sharp focus.

7

THE SOCIAL ROOTS OF BIBLICAL YAHWISM I:
MICAH AND THE CLAN ELDERS OF JUDAH

THE BOOK OF MICAH IS A SMALL PART OF THE HEBREW BIBLE, BUT IT reveals a huge amount about the social roots of biblical Yahwism. Thus far, our biblical studies of the texts of Micah have shown that Micah carried the traditions of biblical Yahwism (Sinai theology) in the southern kingdom of Judah in the eighth century B.C.E. They have proved that the Sinai theological stream of tradition traces back before the reforms of Kings Hezekiah and Josiah to Micah's time, and that its geography extends beyond northern Israel to include Judah. Armed now with a social-scientific model for excavating behind Micah's times, let us see what more we can learn about the social background of Micah's traditions.

In this chapter I defend the thesis that Micah, his support group, and his forebears closely parallel the kin-group elders of noncentralized, non-state societies. Micah's Yahwism hails from a bygone, lineage-based era in Israel.

MICAH'S VILLAGE PROVENANCE

THE CLAN-BASED SOCIAL SETTING OF THE LANGUAGE OF MICAH

Our Bible studies of Micah show that the prophet came to Jerusalem from the Judean countryside to defend his country folk there. His major complaint was that the officials and wealthy elite of Jerusalem were violating the traditions of Sinai theology by grabbing his neighbors' farmland.

Micah's thinking and his language are from the countryside. They reflect the world of village Israel and its kin groups. A closer look at Micah's agrarian, kinship-based language is thus a good starting point for tracing the social roots of Micah's Yahwism. His distinctive, clan-based diction is clearest when the prophet expresses his message using the language of clan mourning ritual.

The language of the mourning ceremonies of Judah's rural lineages lies remarkably close to the surface at several points in Micah. H. W. Wolff especially has pointed out the unmistakable mourning language in Micah and its roots in Judah's agrarian clans. The very first chapter of Micah shows the prophet enacting a clan lament. He dramatically expresses an extremely vivid sorrow in the course of a prophetic vision of the devastation of his homeland.

The background of the passage is straightforward. The Assyrian army was on the move against the northern kingdom, and the Assyrians will not stop at reducing Samaria to rubble. Micah sees that they will move on to attack his homeland—Judah. Micah 1:8–9 reads:

> [8] For this I will lament and wail;
>   I will go barefoot and naked;
> I will make lamentation like the jackals,
>   and mourning like the ostriches.
> [9] For her wound [i.e., Samaria's infectious apostasy] is incurable.
>   It has come to Judah;
> it has reached to the gate of my people,
>   to Jerusalem.

Micah describes a miniature ceremony of mourning, beginning with language typical of funerals (1:8). A similar combination of funeral terms, including the Hebrew words for "lamentation" and "mourning," occurs in Amos 5:16–17.

The cross-reference in Amos illuminates the social setting of Micah's language. It associates this language with an agrarian setting. Amos pictures such wailing and sorrow as taking place not in a central temple or in the buildings of a state capital, but in the squares, streets, farms, and vineyards of rural towns. The bereaved are villagers, farmers, and professional mourners.

Funeral language continues to color Micah's wording in the succeeding verses of Mic 1. In 1:10–16 the prophet traces the destructive course of the Assyrian army as it heads toward Jerusalem. Using wordplays and the mourning language of Judah's clans, Micah bids his audience to grieve for all in Assyria's path.

In 1:10 Micah summons the community at Beth-leaphrah to roll in the dust as a physical expression of their mourning (cf. Josh 7:6; Job 16:15; Jer 6:26; 25:34). In 1:11 he pictures the lamentation of the town of Beth-ezel in much the same terms as his own enactment of grief in 1:8. He finally turns to Jerusalem, the goal of Assyria's invasion, in 1:15–16 (cf. 1:9, 12).

Jerusalem is to shave itself as bald as a vulture, an act of mourning for the dead (cf. Deut 14:1; Job 1:20; Isa 15:2; 22:12; Jer 16:6; Amos 8:10).

Other chapters of Micah also display clan language of mourning, or at least extreme sorrow. The words of sorrow and woe that the prophet utters over his opponents—grabbers of land—in Mic 2:1–5 purposely sound like an obituary. By holding their funeral in advance, so to speak, Micah is warning the land barons of the dire fate that most certainly awaits them.

The woe oracle begins in 2:1 with the Hebrew word "alas," "how terrible" (הוי)—an exclamation of sorrow made at funerals (cf. 1 Kgs 13:30; Jer 22:18; 34:5).[1] When 2:4 envisions the last words of the barons, they are also words of lamentation. The song that those who taunt them put in their mouths sounds like the cry of country farmers gathered to mourn an agricultural disaster.

The prophet alludes to yet another clan-based funeral practice in Mic 5:1–6. Recall that this text is Micah's prophetic announcement of the coming siege of Jerusalem and its messianic deliverance. The very first verse of the passage reflects the custom of self-mutilation at clan funerals (cf. Deut 14:1: Jer 16:6). The NRSV translation speaks of besieged Jerusalem as being "walled around with a wall," but Micah's Hebrew terminology (the Hithpolel of גדד ["cut," "muster," "wall"]) has a very different alternative nuance. The Hebrew may also mean to cut oneself in expression of mourning. Leslie Allen thus translates the first part of Mic 5:1 as follows: "Now you are gashing yourself, Lady under attack."[2]

According to this possible translation of Micah's Hebrew, when Jerusalem falls under Assyrian siege its inhabitants act like bereaved attendants at a funeral, frantic with despair. In Micah's prophetic forevision, the mourners expect that the funeral that they will soon be attending will unfortunately be their own.

Micah's clan-based language, though striking, is not sufficient to assure that the background of his message lies in the customs and stereotypical speech of the Judean countryside. After all, clan-based funeral language and an indictment of oppressions in rural areas also appear in urban, centralized prophets. The prophet Isaiah, an urban figure with

---

1. See H.-J. Zobel, "הוי," *TDOT* 3:361–62; Leslie C. Allen, *The Books of Joel, Obadiah, Jonah, and Micah* (NICOT; Grand Rapids: Eerdmans, 1976), 286; James L. Mays, *Micah: A Commentary* (OTL; Philadelphia: Westminster, 1976), 62; Hans Walter Wolff, *Micah: A Commentary* (trans. G. Stansell; CC; Minneapolis: Augsburg, 1990), 73.

2. Allen, *Books of Joel, Obadiah, Jonah, and Micah*, 339; cf. Wolff, *Micah*, 129. Four major modern commentaries on Micah favor translating the first occurrence of גדד as "gash" here. See Allen, *Books of Joel, Obadiah, Jonah, and Micah*, 341; Mays, *Micah*, 111, 114; Wolff, *Micah*, 131, 142; and Delbert R. Hillers, *Micah* (Hermeneia; Philadelphia: Fortress, 1984), 62.

links to Jerusalem's royal theology, delivered a woe oracle in Isa 5:8–10 with a style somewhat similar to that of Micah.

Fortunately, literary evidence in the book of Micah beyond the coloring of the prophet's language confirms his ties to Judah's rural kinship networks. To be sure, Micah carried out an urban mission in the city of Jerusalem, but not because he felt at home in the capital. The prophet felt obliged to visit Jerusalem, rather than remain among his countryfolk, to represent his *constituency* at of the taproot of their oppression.[3]

MICAH'S CLAN-BASED CONSTITUENCY

Prophets sometimes use traditional language in unconventional ways and in new settings. Close study of Micah, however, reveals that he uses traditional, agrarian language in a traditional mode at home in the rural kin group. Take the first chapter of Micah, for example. The prophet does not use clan-based mourning language here to judge or mock those of whom he speaks. He does not give mourning language a new social setting foreign to the rural clan.

Nothing in Mic 1:8–16 indicates that the people for whom the prophet laments are blameworthy and deserve the disaster that they will experience. Guilty Jerusalem is attracting the "incurable punishment" (1:9) from the north. Many innocent people lie in the path of the moving disaster. The prophet expresses frantic sorrow and consternation at the tragedy of "collateral damage" it will cause.

Micah identifies the innocent victims of the coming disaster by naming their specific geographical locales. A look at this geography quickly reveals that Micah focuses his deep concern on his own Judean country folk. The places he names are villages and towns in the Shephelah, his own homeland (Mic 1:1). Micah 1 thus already reveals the prophet's constituency. Micah's village language corresponds to the village homeland of his own people, whom he mourns.

Statements within 1:10–16 confirm that Jerusalem is the guilty target of the coming punishment, not Micah's villages. Judah's capital is responsible for national apostasy, militarization, and neglect of the rural populace. For example, 1:12 explicitly blames the suffering of Maroth on Jerusalem, while 1:13 indicts "Daughter Zion" and her fortress-satellite

---

3. The oppression's central, urban character strongly suggests that Jerusalem was its base of operations. For arguments to this effect, see J. Andrew Dearman, *Property Rights in the Eighth-Century Prophets: The Conflict and Its Background* (SBLDS 106; Atlanta: Scholars Press, 1988), 41, 44.

Lachish for the "sin" and "rebellion" that is attracting the coming disaster (cf. Mic 1:5; 5:10). Finally, 1:15–16 conclude Micah's lament with a picture of Jerusalem as ground zero. Her leaders are hiding at Adullam, just as David once did (1 Sam 22:1; 2 Sam 23:13).

Micah 1:8–9 makes it clear that the prophet identifies with the victims in the villages of 1:10–16. These verses show Micah's personal, emotional involvement by presenting the prophet's own outpouring of grief over the inhabitants of the Shephelah. The use of the word "howl" (the Hebrew root is ילל), a term of sheer passion, particularly betrays the prophet's communal solidarity with the victims that he describes.[4] This frenetic reaction signals authentic empathy and solidarity.

A final feature of Micah's lament in chapter 1 clinches my argument that the prophet understands the villagers of the Shephelah as his authentic constituency. Verse 9 specifies that the victims of the coming blow will include Judah in general and "my people" (עמי) in particular. Micah unmistakably uses the term "people" here to refer to the inhabitants of the Shephelah. His use of this language in reference to a Judean subgroup rather than to the whole people of Yahweh is remarkable. More remarkable still is the vivid possessive sense of Micah's language, which emphasizes his identification with the group.

In contrast to the term's general use in prophetic books such as Amos, Hosea, and Isaiah, Micah uses "my people" in its traditional sense of a local kin group (cf., e.g., Gen 23:11; 49:29; Judg 14:3; Ruth 1:16). For Micah, the term refers to lineage networks in his homeland, the Shephelah, whose interests he represents and whose members seem entrusted to his care.

The special usage "my people" occurs elsewhere in Micah outside of chapter 1. A double occurrence appears in the middle two verses of Micah's dispute with his Jerusalem opponents in Mic 2:6–11. The prophet argues with Jerusalem's officials in this speech, confronting them for violating the land-tenure norms of Sinai theology. As we saw in chapter 4, Micah draws the warrants of his argument directly from specific covenant stipulations. The E strand of the Pentateuch and Deuteronomy now preserve these fundamental Yahwistic legal traditions. In the midst of the argument, in 2:8–9, Micah twice refers to the rural victims of his opponents as "my people." The context demands that Micah must mean his own people here and not merely the people of Yahweh as a whole. In this type of "disputation" genre of the Bible, the speaker is always the

---

4. Mays, *Micah,* 54; A. Baumann, "ילל," *TDOT* 6:86.

prophet, not God. Micah is speaking about his clan here; Yahweh is not speaking about his whole people Israel.[5]

Micah uses the term "my people" to refer to his kinfolk in Mic 3:1–4 as well. Micah, not Yahweh, announces judgment, as the reference to Yahweh in the third person ("he," not "I") in 3:4 shows. Hence, "my people" in 3:3 refers to Micah's landholding kith and kin, for whose persecution he indicts the Jerusalem establishment in the oracle.[6]

THE NATURE OF THE PROPHET'S CONSTITUENCY

Micah's prophecies detail the nature of the people he represents, particularly in describing the people's endangered social networks. These kinship networks, which protected the ancestral lands of Judah's extended families, were threatened in the eighth century by the same forces we saw in the cross-cultural evidence.

Four passages of Micah are particularly instructive about the character of Micah's constituency. Micah 2:1–5, 6–11; 3:1–4; and 6:9–16 provide helpful details about the landholders of the Judean country, whose fields and houses have become fair game for Jerusalem's barons under Judah's new state polity. Each of the four passages indicts the elite of Jerusalem and evokes a genuine sympathy for those they are injuring. The detail with which these passages describe Jerusalem's victims is distinctive. (Contrast, for example, the lack of such detail in Isa 5:8.)

Micah 2:1–5 especially describes who exactly is being victimized. Verse 2 reads:

> They covet fields, and seize them;
> > houses, and take them away;
> they oppress householder and house,
> > people and their inheritance.

The verse identifies a representative victim as a "householder" (גבר; a "freeholder"), one who holds an "inheritance" (נחלה; an "ancestral

---

5. Mays, *Micah,* 71; Wolff, *Micah,* 82. The Hebrew text of Mic 2:8a is difficult. The emended reading of the NRSV is possible: "But you rise up against my people" (cf. the critical note of BHS). The MT as it stands may be intelligible, however, as stating the emerging opposition of Micah's constituency to their oppressors: "Recently my people have risen against an enemy." Micah's own verbal counterattack on behalf of his people shows that not all Judean villagers suffered oppression passively.

6. See Wolff, *Micah,* 82, 100; Allen, *Books of Joel, Obadiah, Jonah, and Micah,* 308. This special use of "my people" also occurs at Mic 3:5.

plot," "landed patrimony") and who defends an "extended household" (בית).[7]

Land grabbing by wealthy officials and militarization in preparation for invasion increasingly turned freeholders into victims in eighth-century Judah. The victimization, along with the state politics that supported it, was fully at odds with the tribal economic system of old Israel. As ethnographers have observed, kinship networks may continue to exist in a state-based society, but the rules and modes of production of the new system generally contradict and dominate them. Micah's constituency acutely felt the contradiction.

Delbert R. Hillers' summary is apt: "The economic and social ideal of ancient Israel was of a nation of free landholders—not debt-slaves, share-croppers, or hired workers—secure in possession, as a grant from Yahweh, of enough land to keep their families."[8]

It is further disclosed in Mic 6:9–16, our second passage, that those seizing the farmlands are not waiting passively for their victims to fall into bankruptcy. According to 6:10–11, the state leaders in Jerusalem with the authority and wealth to supply emergency credit and grain are increasing the economic pressure on their victims through swindling. Their fraud in selling grain and in receiving loan and rent payments must have greatly hastened the forfeitures of the farmlands they coveted.

The officials no doubt continued to cheat the country freeholders even after they eventually reduced them to day laborers on latifundia. The "wicked scales" and "dishonest weights" of Mic 6:11 sound strikingly similar to what Rigoberta Menchú describes as the fiddling that goes on in the *finca* offices of contemporary Guatemala. (See my discussion in the preceding chapter.) The contracted laborers on the *finca* sweat blood for every centavo they can earn, but the *finca* officers make the work they deliver appear to weigh much less than its real value.

Verse 12 of the passage adds that the Jerusalem leaders furthered their violent ends through corrupt law courts (cf. Mic 3:11). The perjury of Jerusalem's less wealthy residents aided and abetted them. The cross-cultural evidence of the last chapter revealed that traditional farmers often try to use court systems to prevent estate owners from taking over their lands. They stand little chance of prevailing, if the courts represent the interests of new centralized systems and officers.

---

7. See H. Kosmala, "גבר," *TDOT* 2:377.

8. Hillers, *Micah*, 33. Compare Norman K. Gottwald, *The Hebrew Bible: A Socio-Literary Introduction* (Philadelphia: Fortress, 1985), 324; I. J. Mosala, *Biblical Hermeneutics and Black Theology in South Africa* (Grand Rapids: Eerdmans, 1989), 80–81.

In the sixteenth century C.E., the native farming communities of New Spain took the new *hacienda* owners to court on many occasions. Unfortunately, their legal efforts were largely futile. They were restricted solely to special "Indian courts," which the Spaniards established.

Micah 2:6–11 makes clear how completely the new state polity of Judah overturned traditional norms. Despite the legal traditions of the Sinai covenant—which permitted lineages to forfeit land only temporarily—the *alienation* of land was now a real possibility. Verse 9 stands out. Since even the descendants of victims, their "children," are losing rights to family land, the core issue must be the *permanent* loss of the ancestral farmlands of kin groups and extended families. In fact, the verse states that Micah's "people" are losing their land "forever."

The social dimensions of Micah's dispute bring the antiquity of the Sinai legal traditions into sharp relief. As much as Micah may want Judah's state officers to play by the rules of Sinai theology, the rules no longer seem to fit their reality. They are operating under new social and economic norms that contradict and dominate the traditional societal system of old Israel.

Though he may overstate the situation, James Mays is on target: "The old family properties around the villages were being broken up and the clan system pressed out of existence."[9] Micah's Sinai norms fit old Israel's society well. At the same time, they look outdated in the new struggle between societal systems in Micah's contemporary world.

The wrenching emotional effect on Micah of his constituency's predicament of disinheritance is most clear in our fourth passage, Mic 3:1–4. Here, the prophet's anguish leads him away from concrete accusations and toward metaphorical descriptions. He arrives at a metaphor of economic cannibalism. All that is left of his previous literal complaints is his verb "tear away," which he had used previously in Mic 2:2. His new metaphorical language still focuses on how the new rulers of Israel (Mic 3:1) are "tearing away" (3:2) ancestral lands from the lineages. He now speaks of carcasses (3:2–3) to describe the result of this "tearing," however.

There is a clear mood of inhumanity in Micah's metaphorical images, and it highlights more than just Micah's anguish and humiliation at the vicious economic and legal "devouring" of his country neighbors. Micah is emphasizing that the destruction of village Israel's family-plus-land units will inevitably result in the collapse of traditional kinship-based solidarity in Israel.

---

9. Mays, *Micah*, 64; cf. Wolff, *Micah*, 74–75, 78.

Micah strongly defends the old social formula of kinfolk-plus-territory, which formed the material infrastructure undergirding the Sinai covenant's communal goals. The ultimate goal of Sinai theology was to nourish the people's full humanity within community. To squelch this goal by removing its material, physical infrastructure was to dehumanize Yahweh's people. It was to "flay their skin off them, break their bones in pieces, and chop them up like meat in a kettle" (3:3).

Let me sum up. Without question, texts from Mic 2, 3, and 6 identify Micah's constituency as the patrimony-holding, full participants in traditional Israel's kinship networks. They were Israel's traditional, landed freeholders before the state leaders of eighth-century Jerusalem built great country estates and fortified outposts at their expense.

As Gerhard von Rad notes, the technical term for such consanguineous farmers and herders of the Judean country was "the people of the land" (עם הארץ).[10]

The "people of the land," whom Micah represented in Jerusalem, were not land-poor proletariat or uneducated peasants. Micah never claims to speak on behalf of the "poor" and "needy." He is defending the freeholders of the countryside, many of them gentry—members of rural leading lineages.

As H. W. Wolff states, "He has in mind the *'man'* capable of military service (גבר), the *'citizen'* who possesses full legal rights and obligations (איש), whose rights and freedoms have been violated. To this status especially belongs landed property as 'hereditary possession' (נחלה) [Mic 2:2b]."[11] The figure of wealthy Boaz in the book of Ruth exemplifies the type of person that Micah represents in Jerusalem.

Micah can certainly be considered a fearless political activist, but the radical social changes of Mic 2:3–5, 10 are reducible to neither a political platform nor a blueprint for revolution. As Albrecht Alt noted long ago, "Micah, unlike the Greeks, did not make the revolution of the social and economic order that he recognized as necessary into the principal item of a reform-program that his fellow country people were supposed to carry out by themselves in a struggle..., a struggle carried out from within existing structures." Rather, Micah "saw a different assumption about all

---

10. Gerhard von Rad, *Studies in Deuteronomy* (trans. D. Stalker; SBT 9; Chicago: Regnery, 1953), 63. Compare Ernst Würthwein, *Der 'amm ha'arez im Alten Testament* (BWANT 17; Stuttgart: Kohlhammer, 1936), 17, and my treatment of this group in chapter 3.

11. Wolff, *Micah*, 78; cf. idem, "Micah the Moreshite—The Prophet and His Background," in *Israelite Wisdom: Theological and Literary Essays in Honor of Samuel Terrien* (ed. J. Gammie et al.; Missoula, Mont.: Scholars Press for Union Theological Seminary, New York, 1978), 81; Dearman, *Property Rights*, 53.

human roles in these matters in a violent intervention of Yahweh, which would destroy Jerusalem and thereby would remove all obstacles in advance to the restoration of the old sacral order in Judah."[12]

Alt's choice of the term "old sacral order" is a key insight. Micah's constituency has not evolved an innovative ethics. A new ideology is not their motivating force; a theological stream of tradition, specifically Sinai tradition, is. That was the burden of my arguments in chapter 4. Because their hopes are sacral and theological, they can look to divine intervention rather than to human revolution to achieve them. That does not mean that Micah sits on the sidelines. Against all human odds, he boldly confronts state authorities at great risk to himself.

The fundamental dilemma of the "people of the land" is that a rapid shift in societal systems has outpaced significant time-conditioned aspects of Sinai tradition, threatening to render it outdated. Despite dice loaded against them, they hope God will repristinate the traditional societal moorings of Sinai theology—in Alt's words, to revive an older sacral order. On the one hand, their reactionary goal of turning back the clock makes them appear unrealistic to our modern eyes. On the other hand, the fact that the book of Micah so closely associates Sinai theology with such a historically conditioned social agenda lays bare before us the roots of biblical Yahwism.

It must have been within groups of the "people of the land" that Sinai traditions remained alive, despite the strength of different ideals in Jerusalem. Traditional agrarian groups would readily treasure focal Sinai values. The norm of Mic 4:4 fits them to a tee: "They shall all sit under their own vines and under their own fig trees." James Mays is correct to conclude that Micah "was from the villages," from the countryside "where the old traditions of Yahweh and the tribal league continued to inform the faith of those who were loyal to Yahweh."[13]

Gerhard von Rad defended an even sharper conclusion. The "people of the land" were the authentic bearers of the traditions of the Sinai covenant, specifically the traditions that crystallized in the book of Deuteronomy. Though his approach to the problem of the roots of Deuteronomy was not through the book of Micah, von Rad anticipated my general thesis in the present chapter.

---

12. Albrecht Alt, "Micha 2,1–5: ΓΗΣ ΑΝΑΔΑΣΜΟΣ in Juda," in *Kleine Schriften zur Geschichte des Volkes Israel* (ed. M. Noth; 3 vols.; Munich: Beck, 1953), 3:380–81.

13. Mays, *Micah*, 17.

CLAN ELDERS AS TRADENTS OF SINAI TRADITIONS

Micah's burden for his countryfolk, which he expresses with passionate language, including his term "my people" (עמי), strongly suggests that the prophet's responsibility goes beyond altruism and is linked to a social role. Specifically, Micah's repeated reference to "my people" has suggested to scholars that he was one of old Israel's kin-group elders. As Wolff states, "Micah's active defense of those whom he calls 'my people' is not the concern of a solitary, small landowner or even that of an (exceptionally) righteous estate owner who has regard for the distress of the little people; rather, it is best understood as that of an elder."[14]

Evidence in various texts of Micah bolsters this hypothesis about Micah's role as a clan elder. His judgment oracle in Mic 3:5–8 provides particularly strong support. This passage has an unusual conclusion in 3:8, which supplies the sort of background information about Micah that is rare in this type of prophetic announcement.

Micah indicts his target audience, the false prophets of Jerusalem, and pronounces a divine threat against them. This much is normal. He then goes beyond the normal pattern of judgment oracles, however, and explains how he as a prophet differs from those he condemns.

> But as for me, I am filled with power,
> > with the spirit of the LORD,
> > and with justice and might.

In contrast to Jerusalem's mercenary prophets, "justice" (משפט) and "might" (גבורה) characterize Micah. In old Israel, people considered elders to be the special custodians of "justice." They were the ones who pronounced verdicts in the village gate. Elders also played other authoritative roles and commanded special respect in their lineages and kin groups. Micah probably understands his term "might" with reference to this traditional "clan influence" wielded by elders.

Judges 6:12 uses the same vocabulary in describing the judge Gideon, a member of the rural aristocracy. So, too, Ruth 2:1 uses these terms to describe Boaz's high social standing within the Ephrathite clan. Just as his clan standing aided Boaz in the legal process of Ruth 4:1–12, a leading

---

14. Wolff, *Micah*, 7; cf. pp. 59, 75. Israel's elders did not form a monolithic substratum. They were differentiated in authority and viewpoint. Various circles of elders perdured during the monarchic period. They retained some localized authority in the countryside, such as their judicial role in the town gates, and they remained concerned to influence the affairs of Israel as a whole.

position in his respective lineage system seems to have empowered Micah in pursuing justice in Jerusalem at a much later time.[15]

The way that Micah relies so heavily on his standing in a village-based, lineage system helps us understand the dynamics of his confrontations with Jerusalem's state officials. He does not challenge Jerusalem's ruling stratum and their support staff on their own terms. Rather, he demands respect based on the prerogatives of his role in a different, overlapping societal system.[16] His mandate derives from social concepts rooted in prestate Israel.

Like most lineage elders, Micah did not operate alone. His prophetic texts bear witness that a group of colleagues aided him in representing the people of the land in Jerusalem. These colleagues doubtless later helped preserve Micah's oracles. We have them to thank for our present, biblical book of Micah. The several textual supplements that the book now contains (see especially the examples in chapter 5 above) reveal this circle's existence and their concern with Micah's legacy.

The biblical evidence that Micah had a support group conforms to the general cross-cultural pattern, in which elders tend to work in a collaborative mode. Elders normally fulfill their local administrative roles by cooperating in council. When their collective interests warrant it, elders will also act in concert at higher levels of their genealogical system.

Consider the examples of the Logoli and the Ngwato peoples, whom I discussed in the preceding chapter. The elders of the Logoli people act in interclan concert in times of drought. Their principle kin groups each commit a leading elder to a delegation, which goes as a group to secure the services of a rainmaker. In the case of the Ngwato people, a group of leading headmen will sometimes conspire together to check the power of the tribal chief.

Remarkably, Jer 26 explicitly pictures a team, or delegation, of agrarian elders upholding Micah's words and treasuring his legacy. The scene is part of Jeremiah's prophetic career, long after Micah's death. The reader will recall the narrative context from my brief overview of this text in chapter 3. In the spirit of Micah, Jeremiah has gone to the Jerusalem temple and prophesied its destruction. The reaction to his message is

---

15. See Kosmala, "גָּבַר," *TDOT* 2:374; R. L. Hubbard Jr., *The Book of Ruth* (NICOT; Grand Rapids: Eerdmans, 1988), 133.

16. H. W. Wolff, "Wie verstand Micha von Moreschet sein prophetisches Amt?" in *Congress Volume: Göttingen, 1977* (ed. J. A. Emerton, W. L. Holladay, and A. Lemaire; VTSup 29; Leiden: Brill, 1978), 407; idem, *Micah*, 7, 105. Compare Mosala's discussion, drawing on South African evidence, of the tension between ruling class and the class of elders in a tributary system (*Biblical Hermeneutics*, 81).

decidedly unfavorable. Urging a death sentence, the state priests and
prophets of Jerusalem put Jeremiah on trial before a royal judiciary.

The court officers come out of the royal palace and assemble at the
temple to hear the case. They disappoint the temple staff, however, by
mercifully ruling in Jeremiah's favor. Their arguments do not satisfy the
mob that has gathered. Only the suggestion that the crowd should judge
Jeremiah's case in light of Micah's much earlier precedent is able to save
the prophet's life.

This well-timed suggestion does not come from the state judges, or
any official quarter. A peripheral group—"some of the elders of the land"
(אנשים מזקני הארץ)—brings it up from the sidelines.

The elders of the land recall the prophecy of Micah and offer up his
example. They quote Micah's exact words to the assembled mob. This
narrative in Jeremiah thus witnesses that at least one circle of country
elders, acting in concert, actively preserved Micah's prophecy as oral theological tradition for a century after his time.[17]

Amid a multiplicity of party tensions in Jer 26, the delegation of
elders works with other groups in support of Jeremiah and his theological cause. Only the coordinated efforts of several circles are able to
achieve the prophet's release. The text does not specify the exact level of
partnership between these circles, but their cooperation clearly cuts
across various lines of social standing.

The episode of Jeremiah's trial reveals that, at this time, even some
members of the royal court supported the peripheral prophet. In 26:16 the
royal judiciary rules in Jeremiah's favor. They respect his Sinai-oriented
message. According to 26:24 another monarchic insider, Ahikam the son
of Shaphan, also supports Jeremiah and his Sinai theology.[18]

Some years before Jeremiah's trial, a delegation of elders of the land
took a stand at an unstable time and played an instrumental role in
making Josiah king (2 Kgs 21:24). Moreover, they may well have helped
orchestrate his Sinai-oriented reform program by participating in his tutelage during his years of minority. Thus, it is not surprising that at the
time of Jeremiah's trial we find the elders of the land working in partnership with Ahikam son of Shaphan (Jer 26:24). Ahikam and his family
were highly involved in the Deuteronomic reform of Josiah's time.

17. Klaus Koch, *The Growth of the Biblical Tradition: The Form-Critical Method* (trans. S. M.
Cupitt; London: Black, 1969), 212, cf. 84 n. 21; von Rad, *Studies in Deuteronomy*, 60–69.

18. Despite the high standing of some of their number, however, Jeremiah's supporters
were clearly a minority faction within the post-Josiah royal court. Kings Jehoiakim and
Zedekiah, Josiah's successors, end up following political courses diametrically opposed to
Jeremiah's advice.

Ahikam's father, Shaphan, was the one who physically carried the newly discovered scroll of Deuteronomy to Josiah. He was the one who read the young king its Sinai covenant curses (2 Kgs 22:8–11). Ahikam himself was among those who helped Josiah respond positively to what Shaphan read (2 Kgs 22:12–20).[19]

More than likely, country elders worked with several such figures as Ahikam to advocate Sinai theology in Judah's late-monarchic royal court as part of a coalition of groups. Country gentry, royal servants, scribes, and others banded together at this period to lobby for Deuteronomic policies in Jerusalem.

In a well-argued study, P. Dutcher-Walls surveys the biblical evidence and cogently characterizes the sociology of the pro-Sinai faction of Jeremiah's time. Her social-scientific model allows a prominent place for the elders of the land among the faction's membership. Dutcher-Walls summarizes her findings as follows:

> The faction is associated with Josiah's enthronement and carries out his reform ... [and it] continues to pursue its interests in the closing years of the state, under kings less open to its influence.... The descendants of Shaphan figure prominently in the circle, although the influence of the Deuteronomistic world-view extends well beyond that family, cutting across and including various social roles.[20]

In sum, biblical evidence external to the book of Micah strongly suggests that some elders of the land preserved Micah's words and that they worked with other groups to push the Sinai theology he defended to the center of Judean society. Specifically, the elders of the land were part of a coalition of groups that supported those, such as Josiah and Jeremiah, who attempted to reform Judah along the lines of the book of Deuteronomy.

Internal literary evidence in the texts of Micah confirms the external evidence that elders handed down Micah's prophetic words. The texts reveal elders surrounding and supporting the prophet during his career. This evidence comes from the same texts in which Micah displays the role of elder himself by defending the clan folk entrusted to his care, those whom he calls "my people."

---

19. Robert R. Wilson, "1 & 2 Kings: Introduction and Annotations," in *The HarperCollins Study Bible: New Revised Standard Version with the Apocryphal/Deuterocanonical Books* (ed. W. A. Meeks; San Francisco: HarperSanFrancisco, 1993), 597; Richard E. Friedman, *Who Wrote the Bible?* (New York: Harper & Row, 1987), 99, 125; Harry P. Nasuti, *Tradition History and the Psalms of Asaph* (SBLDS 88: Atlanta: Scholars Press, 1988), 94.

20. Patricia Dutcher-Walls, "The Social Location of the Deuteronomists: A Sociological Study of Factional Politics in Late Pre-Exilic Judah," *JSOT* 52 (1991): 91–92.

Turn back to Micah's disputation with Jerusalem's leaders in Mic 2:6–11. A close look at the text shows that a number of people are involved. The prophet holds his dispute with the barons of Jerusalem before a third group. The passage begins in 2:6 as follows:

"Do not preach"—thus they preach—
  "one should not preach of such things;
  disgrace will not overtake us."

Note how Micah does not address his opponents directly, but refers to them indirectly in the third person ("thus they preach"). Micah is complaining about his Jerusalem opponents to a non-Jerusalem body that shares his sympathies. In light of the cross-cultural parallels, it is likely that such a body would have been a group of elders, associates of Micah from the Judean country.

This scenario is nearly the same as that of Ruth 4, in which Boaz confronts Ruth's nearer kinsman "before the elders of my people" (4:4). Whereas Boaz addresses his elder associates in a rural town gate, Micah probably addresses this group at Jerusalem. Although Wolff suggests the former, Boaz-like scenario,[21] Micah's address to his elder associates more likely took place during one of their delegation's visits to Jerusalem. The setting was probably similar to that of Jer 26.

The role of Micah's colleagues goes beyond simply providing sympathetic support to the prophet. The wording of Mic 2:6–11 shows that they joined Micah in actively defending the traditions of Sinai theology in Jerusalem. Although the English of the NRSV cannot convey it, the negative command of Micah's opponents in 2:6 is plural in form. The original Hebrew behind "Do not preach!" (אל־תטפו) literally says, "You *all* are not to preach!" The opponents are trying to order around a whole group in Micah's company.

Micah must not have been the only elder defending the country people by propounding Sinai traditions in Jerusalem. The voices of an entire elder delegation joined him. Wolff's statement must be correct: "If the 'powerful' people (cf. [Mic 2:]1bβ) seek to silence not only Micah but a number of others (v. 6a), then included with the prophet are probably his associates from among the circle of elders."[22]

Like Mic 2:6–11, the text of Mic 5:1–5a illuminates the role of group forces from the countryside in trying to advance Sinai norms in Jerusalem. I am most interested in 5:2–5a, since these verses have strong

---

21. Wolff, *Micah*, 75.
22. Ibid.; cf. Allen, *Books of Joel, Obadiah, Jonah, and Micah*, 295; Hillers, *Micah*, 36.

innerbiblical connections with the mode of operation of the elders of the
land in Jer 26 and in 2 Kgs 21:23–24. Like these texts, the passage pictures
an intervention of the clans of the countryside in the state politics of
Jerusalem at a time of crisis. The verses read as follows:

> 2 But you, O Bethlehem of Ephrathah,
>   who are one of the little clans of Judah,
> from you shall come forth for me
>   one who is to rule in Israel,
> whose origin is from of old,
>   from ancient days.
> 3 Therefore he shall give them up until the time
>   when she who is in labor has brought forth;
> then the rest of his kindred shall return
>   to the people of Israel.
> 4 And he shall stand and feed his flock in the strength of the LORD,
>   in the majesty of the name of the LORD his God.
> And they shall live secure, for now he shall be great
>   to the ends of the earth;
> 5 and he shall be the one of peace.

Recall from chapter 4 that this passage promises a coming true judge,
who will arise out of Bethlehem and replace Judah's contemporary failed
leadership. The traits of the promised leader reflect the ideals of Sinai theology. He rules in complete dependence on the strength and majesty of
Yahweh, his God. As Yahweh's "contract-herder," his concern is not military self-security but the feeding of God's "flock." Not merely the
citizens of the state of Judah, but the whole tribal "people of Israel" com-
pose this flock.

The social roots of these Sinai ideals seem clearer, now that we have
developed our social-scientific model for elucidating Micah. A clash
between polities characterizes Micah's social milieu, and his Sinai theology fits much better with the older of the two societal systems. By
Micah's time, the kings of Jerusalem and their statist model of monarchic
succession have proven incompatible with the Sinai covenant. Hence,
Micah wants to abandon Judah's newer state polity in favor of a return to
rural leadership and a noncentralized society.

Our social-scientific model suggests that a contest to control the succession of a people's leadership may lie just below the surface of a
dual-system society. Applying this model to Micah, we may infer that the
prophet hoped to heat up such a contest in his times. He may well have
believed his hopes to be realistic, since the same contest had boiled up
previously in Judah at the time of the succession of Joash, a Deuteronomistic reformer king.

Micah most likely hoped to raise his new leader from Bethlehem to the throne by evoking the same social forces that had enthroned Joash a century earlier. The account of the succession of Joash appears in 2 Kgs 11. Micah 5 shares the same social and political scenario that lies behind this text. Micah's messianic leader resembles King Joash even more than the better-known Sinai leader, King Josiah.[23] At least the installation of the two figures is parallel.

Micah 5 is in the language of condensed poetry, but we can use 2 Kgs 11 almost as a prose commentary for its poetic allusions—especially its allusions to social groups and their sacral rites. Cross-reference to 2 Kgs 11 highlights the elders of the land as the social force that installed Joash. It suggests that Micah was counting on these same elders to install his coming leader of promise.

As in Mic 5, 2 Kgs 11 pictures the development of a crisis in the monarchy of Jerusalem. In both passages, the respective monarchic crises reveal the coexistence of superimposed political systems. Because the newer of the two systems has broken down, Judah reverts to an older, underlying system to produce a new, ideal leader. The older resources and practices of the underlying system functioned as a societal substratum until Jerusalem's monarchic succession derailed.

In Mic 5, due to the crisis in the capital, the entire apparatus of leadership shifts from Jerusalem to Ephrathah, a clan in the countryside. Leadership does not quite physically transfer out of Jerusalem in the earlier 2 Kgs 11 episode. Leaders from the countryside and its older lineage-based systems intervene in the capital, where they enforce latent, prestate practice (see 11:14, 18 and the discussion below).

Parallels in the language of the two texts make clear that the practices of Sinai covenant making that emerge in 2 Kgs 11 are the same ones discernible behind Mic 5:2–5a. Perhaps most striking is the parallel, idiomatic use both passages make of the Hebrew verb "stand" (עמד). The idiom refers to how new leaders in Israel should "take a stand in covenant." Its social setting appears to be a sacral installation ceremony.[24]

A shared, Sinai-covenant ritual behind the two texts of Mic 5 and 2 Kgs 11 is assured. Their use of this idiom involving the word "stand" is rare. The idiom occurs overtly elsewhere in the Bible only in 2 Kgs 23:3, when Josiah renews the Sinai covenant.

---

23. I described the evidence for the occurrence of Sinai oriented reforms at the times of King Joash and King Josiah in chapter 3. See the discussion and bibliography cited there.

24. See BDB, "עמד," 764, Qal 7.b. As Allen suggests, the idiom probably has a setting in an anointing ceremony, in which a new leader was installed beside a pillar (*Books of Joel, Obadiah, Jonah, and Micah*, 346).

According to Mic 5:4, Judah's promised new ruler will take his "stand [in covenant]" before shepherding God's flock. Second Kings 11 fleshes out exactly what this involves. A coalition of groups ousts the usurper queen, Athaliah, and replaces her with Joash, their own choice of monarch. As the process unfolds, Queen Athaliah hears the noise of Joash's installation, comes to the temple precincts, looks, and to her horror, "there was the king *standing* by the pillar, according to the custom" (11:14).

Indirect allusions to "taking a stand in covenant" occur in other biblical texts (e.g., Judg 9:6; 16:25), suggesting the rite has deep roots in Israelite culture. The idiom of "taking a stand" seems to stem, in fact, from a ritual practice in old Israel in which leaders covenanted with the people at a standing-stone pillar. The "tent of assembly," used for covenant assemblies before the temple was built, probably had a standing stone nearby for this ritual.[25] Comparison of 2 Sam 20:8 with 2 Chr 1:3 suggests such a stone was a conspicuous landmark near the tent of assembly at Gibeon. Numbers 11:24 (E) pictures tribal leaders taking a stand in covenantal office at the same tent during Israel's earlier wilderness wanderings, probably at a stone pillar.

The manner in which the covenant rite of standing by a pillar echoes the ritual use of standing stones in ancient Near Eastern tribal ceremonies is intriguing. I noted in chapter 2 the ritual importance of standing stones at Emar and in the deserts south of Israel. This ancient Near Eastern evidence links Israel's ritual use of stone pillars to pre–Iron Age, nonurban culture. In light of this evidence, we must take seriously the memories of an archaic use of standing stones in biblical texts such as Gen 28:18 and 33:20 (emended) (both E). Such texts likely provide authentic testimony to the ritual use of standing stones in old, prestate Israel.[26]

Old Israel used standing stones to witness the making of treaties and covenants (e.g., Gen 31:43–46 [E]; Josh 24:26–27). The bearers of Sinai covenant traditions preserved and adapted the old custom for the installation of new leaders into covenantal office. In the monarchic period, a pillar at the temple in Jerusalem likely substituted for the older standing stone of the traditional rite.

Second Kings 11:17 elaborates on the institutional practices involved in the old Israelite custom of "standing by the pillar." The verse describes

---

25. Cf. Tryggve N. D. Mettinger, *No Graven Image? Israelite Aniconism in Its Ancient Near Eastern Context* (ConBOT 42; Stockholm: Almqvist & Wiksell, 1995), 186, fig. 7.30.

26. The fact that Deuteronomic and later Sinai-oriented writers disapproved of the ritual use of standing stones (Deut 12:3–4; 16:22) helps confirm that their ritual use in covenant ratification is archaic.

the making of as many as three different covenants when Joash takes up leadership of God's flock. As part of Joash's installation, the priest Jehoiada presides over covenants between Yahweh and the king, Yahweh and the people, and the king and the people.

Micah 5:4 may refer to the special covenant between the king and Yahweh in its reference to Yahweh as "his [that is, the future ruler's] God" (cf. 1 Sam 30:6). This would be an additional piece of evidence that Mic 5 and 2 Kgs 11 offer a shared picture of a specialized practice of Sinai covenant renewal associated with the installation of shepherd-leaders over Israel.

The Sinai covenant practices of leadership installation in our texts are the prerogative of the people of the land. Second Kings 11—fleshing out the compressed poetry of Mic 5—makes this clear. The overthrow of Queen Athaliah succeeded due largely to the presence in Jerusalem of representatives of the people of the land (2 Kgs 11:14, 18), the very group of country folk over whom Micah later had charge. Credit goes to von Rad for bringing this discovery and its relevance for tracing the roots of biblical Yahwism to light. Von Rad states:

> The accounts of what took place at the removal of Athaliah and the raising of Joash to the throne contain one or two particulars which are of value now for helping us to answer the question about the provenance of Deuteronomy. One at least of the forces which took a hand in affairs then was manifestly the עם הארץ ["people of the land"] ... that is, the section of the people which we have already mentioned above as the proper people liable for military service, who in the event of war made their appearance in the levy of the [older tribal] militia.... Their presence in the Temple while the dramatic events were enacted was certainly no accident.[27]

The representatives of the group to which von Rad refers must have been their elders, as in Jer 26:17. They function in 2 Kgs 11 as agents and proponents of village Israel's covenant practices. The prominence of these elders of the land in the covenant operations of 2 Kgs 11 strongly suggests we should envision them behind the same operations visible in Mic 5:1–5a. This conclusion further confirms the thesis I am defending of old Israel's elders as Micah's support group and bearers (*tradents*) of the Sinai theological stream of tradition.[28]

---

27. Von Rad, *Studies in Deuteronomy*, 63.

28. As I discussed in chapter 3, the elders of the land were active again in the monarchic succession of Josiah, the best-known Deuteronomistic reformer. According to 2 Kgs 21:19–26, the people of the land intervened after Josiah's father, Amon, was assassinated in a

The proposal set forth here, that representatives of the people of the land were bearers of the traditions of the book of Deuteronomy, was earlier proposed by von Rad in his monograph *Studies in Deuteronomy*. Von Rad arrived at this conclusion not at all through a study of the book of Micah, however. He came to it through an exegetical and historical study of the accounts in 2 Kings about reforming monarchs, such as the accounts of Kings Josiah and Joash.

This angle of approach deprived him of a key insight. In drawing his conclusions, von Rad did not have before him the model that Micah provides of a leading, kin-group elder, filled with "justice and might" (Mic 3:8), who also was outspoken about Sinai covenant traditions. Thus, he identified the spokespeople of the people of the land not as their kin-group elders, as now seems natural given our study of Micah, but as Levites living in the Judean country. Von Rad argued that such country Levites are the logical candidates for the Sinai-oriented authors of Deuteronomy.[29]

As is clear by now, in contrast to von Rad's view, country elders, the members and forebears of the Micah group, are logical candidates, as are the Levites, for the bearers and spokespeople of the Sinai tradition stream. This is not to say that von Rad was wrong about a significant involvement of the Levites in the bearing and flowering of Sinai tradition. Circles of elders and of Levites must have shared in this role.

In the case of the succession and Sinai-oriented reform of Joash, the people of the land found a powerful ally in the priest Jehoiada, whom 2 Kgs 12:2 pictures as one of Deuteronomy's ideal Levites. He provides Joash with the sort of instruction for which the Levites are responsible (e.g., Deut 33:10; Mic 3:11).[30] Based on this account of Jehoiada's actions, it seems likely that although Jehoiada held a post in Jerusalem he continued to operate in solidarity with his Levitical kinfolk in the Judean countryside.

---

palace coup. They killed the conspirators, derailing their program, whatever it was, and selected Josiah to be king. In von Rad's judgment, furthermore, "It is manifestly impossible to miss the connection between this elevation of Josiah to the throne by the עם הארץ ['people of the land'] and the whole policy, including the reform, which this king [Josiah] pursued" (*Studies in Deuteronomy*, 65).

29. Von Rad states that "The actual spokesmen of this movement were the country Levites, whom Deuteronomy presumes to be living here and there in the country towns. At any rate, the authors of Deuteronomy are to be sought amongst those Levites" (ibid., 66).

30. See the discussion of Mic 3:11 in chapter 4 above and BDB, "ירה," 435, Hiph. 5.b; S. Wagner, "ירה III," *TDOT* 6:343–44; Patricia Dutcher-Walls, *Narrative Art, Political Rhetoric: The Case of Athaliah and Joash* (JSOTSup 209; Sheffield: Sheffield Academic Press, 1996), 87–88.

THE PRESTATE SACRAL FORMS REPRISTINATED IN MICAH

ELDERS AND FACTIONAL CONFLICT

I described above how already in 1955 Albrecht Alt interpreted Micah's career as an attempt to revive an older sacral order in Judah. Our investigation has supported Alt's general argument. The sacral traditions of biblical Yahwism trace back through peripheral factions of the monarchic period to a traditional Yahwism at home in an older phase of Israel's society.

Though his overall picture of Micah's background is on target, I part company with Alt on several significant matters of detail. A brief critique of Alt's reconstruction of Micah's setting at this point may further clarify the actual social roots of the prophet's Sinai theology.

Central to Alt's reconstruction of Micah's background is a kind of dualism. Alt envisioned a simple, basic polarity between the land-grabbers of Jerusalem, on the one hand, and the country farmers they oppressed, on the other. He held that Jerusalem and Judah were fundamentally different entities, that only the strong personality of King David held the two territories together.[31] Furthermore, he argued that Canaanite overlords were the ideological ancestors of the nobles of Jerusalem.[32]

Alt was wrong about this. The major social tension that Micah confronted was not a clash between Canaanite and Israelite social ideologies.[33] The data of the book of Micah better fit the model of social tensions within a dual-system society, which I developed in the preceding chapter. Micah's society struggled with the superimposition of a state political, economic, and judicial system over an older, tribal administrative system. The basic evil that Micah faced was not Canaanite ideology but the loss of traditional, valued social forms that often accompanies centralization and state formation.

The leaders Micah confronted in Jerusalem were not Canaanites. The cross-cultural evidence shows that when new state systems arise in a

---

31. Alt states that Jerusalem consistently considered itself an actual state, although it was tied with the kingdom of Judah through a Davidic "personal union" ("Micha 2,1–5," 373; see also the references in Alt's n. 2 and cf. 378, 381). In Alt's view, this coupling of the Judean kingdom with the city-state of Jerusalem, which was a completely different entity, was the "basic evil" that Micah attacked (ibid., 376, cf. 378–79).

32. If the Jerusalem leaders got their way, according to Alt, a "Canaanite paradigm" would prevail. Judah would become merely a "very extensive hinterland" of the city-state of Jerusalem (ibid., 379).

33. See Zechariah Kallai, "Judah and Israel—A Study in Israelite Historiography," *IEJ* 28 (1978): 251–61; Hillers, *Micah*, 33; Dearman, *Property Rights*, 48.

society, they often draw on the leadership and resources of preceding systems. When Shaka centralized his society into the Kingdom of the Zulu, he gave new state power to some of the old lineage heads of the tribes that he subjugated. When the great Ngwato chief, Kgama III, established resident governors in the hinterland of his country, he sometimes appointed local headmen to these posts.

In conformity with this pattern, the new monarchic leaders of Judah and Israel kept some older kin-group leaders in power and even placed some of them in positions of new state authority. However much Jerusalem's new rulers and officers resembled Canaanite overlords in ideological terms, they were actually quite different.

In contrast to Alt's view, the Jerusalem land-grabbers of Micah's time were largely descendants of clan elders similar to the prophet himself. Thus, in attacking many of the nobles of Jerusalem, Micah confronts figures who in an earlier historical period would have been his colleagues.[34]

The language of Micah's prophecies shows that he was well aware of how the state system of Judah had co-opted groups of elders from within Israel's village, kinship networks. Look closely at how he addresses the officials of Jerusalem in texts such as Mic 3:1 and 3:9. He does not use the nomenclature of state-based leadership. The terms "king" (מלך) and "royal officers" (שׂרים) are noticeably absent. He uses prestate leadership terms instead—such as "lineage head" (ראשׁ) and "militia commander" (קצין).

Micah, a master of complex poetry and wordplay, is not struggling with a limited, rustic vocabulary. He stubbornly sticks to the terms and categories of Israel's older lineage system out of a theological conservatism. Aware that not too long ago, Jerusalem's new officers were actually old-style leading elders and kin-group heads, he tries to hold them responsible for the legal customs of the Sinai covenant based on their ancestry. Their social roots make them responsible for enforcing the covenant's stipulations. "Is it not for you to know customary justice?" he demands of them (Mic 3:1).

Micah's subtle, rhetorical way of arguing demonstrates the roots of Sinai theology in the prestate period. When, in Mic 3:1, the prophet indignantly assumes a link between "lineage heads" and "the justice" (of the Sinai covenant), he repristinates a social organization in which such

---

34. See Hillers, *Micah*, 33; Dearman, *Property Rights*, 144. Alt, in fact, did allow that members of well-to-do families in the land of Judah participated in the exploitations of the new, state economic system and the resultant destruction of the old Israelite order. He said that in doing so, however, they became colluders in "the society of the Jerusalem nobles" and could scarcely be viewed any longer as "authentic Judeans." See Alt, "Micha 2,1–5," 374 n. 2.

heads of lineages were responsible for sacral administration of the Sinai covenant in the kin group and village.[35] The Sinai theological stream of tradition traces back in time to Israel's existence as villages.

This brief critique of Alt highlights how complex Israelite society was, both at Micah's time and in earlier village times. Major fissures divided what we might expect to be homogeneous guilds. In the eighth century, different groups of elders had very different relationships to the traditions of Sinai theology.

Micah's delegation of elders and Jerusalem's band of co-opted elders have little left in common. We should not assume that their differences arose only in the wake of the centralization of Judean society. Differing viewpoints between lineage leaders may have always been the rule in Israel. I doubt that all elders of the land responsibly bore Sinai traditions in the prestate period. Consider how awry things got in the stories of the book of Judges. Even in the village era, it was probably up to minority factions, such as the Micah group, to keep biblical Yahwism alive.

Though they were major holders of power in an older Israel, Micah's forebears moved to the outskirts of new centralized systems with the rise of the Israelite kingdoms.[36] As their counterparts took on new roles in the Judean monarchy, the elders of the land found their own traditional roles restricted to local administrative functions (e.g., at the village gate). New ways of life and thinking in Israel reduced them to circles or sets, which kept alive their memories of old, village kerygma and sacral institutions. The book of Micah witnesses to the old institutions that such circles of elders preserved. I now want to explore what Micah can teach us about these old institutions associated with the Sinai covenant in Israel's village era.

The "Covenant Assembly" of the Elders

Study of Micah has thus far identified factions of clan elders as among those who transmitted Sinai theological traditions over the generations. It is now time to look more closely at the social institutions of these Yahwistic elders. Additional evidence in Micah helps to clarify the village institutions that originally harbored the elders and their Sinai

---

35. Cf. Rolf Knierim, "Exodus 18 und die Neuordnung der mosäischen Gerichtsbarkeit," ZAW 73 (1961): 158–59; Hillers, Micah, 42.

36. Recall from the discussion of chapter 2 that biblical Yahwism was a minority stream of tradition at least until the time of Hezekiah and Josiah, the reforming kings.

covenant traditions. Two text references in particular, Mic 2:5 and Mic 6:9, helpfully illuminate the institutional base of Micah's forebears.

We have had several occasions to interpret various aspects of Micah's woe oracle against the land-grabbers in 2:1–5. It is a deep mine of information. The text reads in part:

> [1] Alas for those who devise wickedness
>   and evil deeds on their beds!
> When the morning dawns, they perform it,
>   because it is in their power.
> [2] They covet fields, and seize them;
>   houses, and take them away;
> they oppress householder and house,
>   people and their inheritance. . . .
> [5] Therefore you will have no one to cast the line by lot
>   in the assembly of the LORD.

I argued in chapter 4 that the oracle upholds the thematic emphasis of Sinai theology on the care of God's land. God intends God's land to remain permanently apportioned among the clans, lineages, and families of Israel. Beyond its theme, the imagery and unique idiom of the passage stamp it as a Sinai text. The language of 2:5 about the sacral determination of each "boundary line" (חבל) in Israel is Sinai diction. Asaphite Ps 78:55 uses the same unique idiom.

The same verse associates these characteristic Sinai themes and idioms with an institution of old Israel. The verse roots the Sinai stream of tradition—especially its viewing Israel's land as an "inheritance" from Yahweh—in an institution of old, village-period Israel: the "assembly of Yahweh" (קהל יהוה).[37]

The verse is able to instruct us about an ancient Yahwistic institution, rather than merely a contemporary one, because of its frame of reference. The text foresees a time of coming judgment that will open the way for a full-scale revival of ancient sacral forms. Because the courtiers and officials of Jerusalem have misused Yahweh's land by confiscating it for their own estates, Micah threatens them with a devastating judgment. The judgment will permanently remove the officials' land from them, making it available for restoration to the covenant community. The extent of the coming judgment will be sufficiently massive to require the community to organize a full resettlement of God's land.

---

37. Micah 2:5 is a highly controverted verse, but I contend that its significance is clear. See chapter 6, n. 20 and Norman K. Gottwald, *The Tribes of Yahweh: A Sociology of the Religion of Liberated Israel, 1250–1050 B.C.E.* (Maryknoll, N.Y.: Orbis, 1979), 243.

Micah envisions a radical new beginning for Israel. He looks to a future in which the whole of the Judean countryside stands open, waiting for distribution among his kinfolk. Here, Alt was correct:

> If, then, the estates that have been fused to form latifundia are stripped of their holders, they should not remain without owners and revert to a depopulated state. Rather, it is incumbent on the old local population of the land, which was not pushed out by the judgment, to survey and to apportion among themselves the entire arable land, inclusive of the latifundia, which would be vacant at this stage, in such a way that the original order that was oriented toward small farmers comes into power again. The families that had fallen into bondage under the Jerusalem regime and had now won back their freedom would naturally have to be given preference above all in this, in order to bring about as balanced as possible a settlement.[38]

In Micah's view, this coming change in the ownership of land in Judah formed an ideal occasion for reinstating an older administrative institution—opposite to the one in place in Israel as a state. His Sinai theology could then flourish in its original, natural institutional structure—the "assembly of Yahweh" (קהל יהוה). According to Deut 33:4, Moses had entrusted the preservation and transmission of the torah to this very institution. The Sinai torah was to belong to the assembly.

This institutional structure is clearly sacral as well as political. Its primary function in this text is to administer the requirements of the Sinai covenant about God's land. The land has a divine landlord, Yahweh, so Micah must stipulate a sacral institution as the venue in which future land administration will take place.

As Alt states, "Since ... in the whole country it was an issue of land that ... stands under the overlordship [Obereigentum] of Yahweh, the whole [land reallotment] procedure, in order to be valid, had to be carried out in terms of traditional sacral forms, which indeed had perhaps already been left behind at a great distance, but certainly were not completely forgotten."[39]

The assembly of Yahweh embodied all the people of the covenant. One can define it as the comprehensive totality of the children of Israel working in sacral coordination. The assembly, however, was under the jurisdiction of the elders of the land. When the assembly

---

38. Alt, "Micha 2,1–5," 380. Compare how Mays aptly relates the redistribution of land heralded by Mic 2:5 to the pattern set by the account of the settlement of the land in the Deuteronomistic History (Micah, 66).

39. Alt, "Micha 2,1–5," 380.

met in premonarchic times, as in Judg 20:2, the kinship heads of the people presided. Even texts about the monarchic period, such as the one describing Jeremiah's trial at the temple, continue to speak of the elders presiding over the people's sacral assembly (קהל; Jer 26:17). In fact, Ps 107:32 specifically identifies the assembly of the people (קהל) as the "seat" of the elders, where they met in council.

The assembly of Yahweh in Mic 2:5 clearly conducts the business of the entire covenantal network of landholding families in Judah. It has the task of resettling every freeholder. It would be impractical for all of Judah's family heads to convene in one place, so the text must assume that lineage and clan leaders will represent the larger populace at the assembly.

Micah 2:1–5 demonstrates how central the need for holding ancestral land was to the original Sinai covenant. Membership in the sacral institution of the assembly of Yahweh requires landholdings. The covenant community does not exist apart from its occupation of the land that God gave Israel as an inheritance. To lose the gift of a sacral grant of land is to be extirpated from the inherited people of Yahweh, left outside the covenant.

The language of Mic 2 suggests how the assembly of Yahweh administered sacral grants of land in old Israel. I want to wait to discuss the specific workings of the assembly, however, until I have had a chance to review the second major reference to the assembly in Micah. It occurs in Mic 6:9–16, where the prophet quotes God addressing the people of Judah. The text reads in part:

> [9b] Hear, O tribe and assembly of the city!
> [10] Can I forget the treasures of wickedness in the house of the wicked,
>   and the scant measure that is accursed?
> [11] Can I tolerate wicked scales
>   and a bag of dishonest weights? ...
> [13] Therefore I have begun to strike you down,
>   making you desolate because of your sins. ...
> [15] You shall sow, but not reap;
>   you shall tread olives, but not anoint yourselves with oil;
>   you shall tread grapes, but not drink wine.

As I argued in chapter 4, this text may come from a somewhat later time than Mic 2:1–5. It has a broader audience. Nevertheless, the two passages have much in common. As in the earlier passage, the unique themes and idioms of Sinai tradition stamp Mic 6:9–16.

The futility curses in 6:14–15 are an especially obvious link to the covenant and to the conditions it placed on occupying God's land. Threatening these covenant curses, Micah calls the people to account based on their use of God's land. Like the earlier oracle, this passage roots the Sinai covenant and its curses in the assembly of Yahweh, the sacral institution administered by old Israel's elders.

Micah's rhetorical tactics allow us to probe to the social roots of the Sinai traditions. In this passage, the prophet continues his stubborn insistence on addressing the contemporary state leadership of Judah using the sacral idioms of old, tribal Israel. This language defines from the outset their responsibilities under the Sinai covenant.

Micah calls his audience to attention in 6:9b, using obvious kinship vocabulary. "Hear, O *tribe* (מטה)!" he calls. Micah's summons does not stop at lineage vocabulary, however. He immediately extends his address in an extremely telling manner. "Hear, O tribe and *assembly* (מועד) of the city!"[40] Like the term "tribe," Micah's term "assembly" stands out as foreign to his state-period context. It is certainly not at home in the political life of eighth-century Jerusalem. Going simply on the surrounding context in Mic 6, one might gather that it is some sort of locus where Israelites of the tribal era would value membership, and the futility curses of the Sinai covenant would be respected.

While not at home in the royal capital, the term "assembly" (מועד; a different Hebrew word from the one in Mic 2:5) does fit an earlier phase of Israel's history. It is highly reminiscent of the "tent of assembly" (אהל מועד) that plays a key role in Israel's wilderness experiences before entering Canaan.

The stories in the Pentateuch about these experiences date from the monarchic period in Israel, but often preserve traditions from earlier times. The tent of assembly they picture may reflect an actual covenant institution of village Israel, perhaps the same institution as the "assembly of Yahweh" (קהל יהוה; Mic 2:5). More particularly, perhaps it is the body charged with overseeing the assembly of Yahweh.

To follow up on this possibility, we shall have to proceed critically. The term "tent of assembly" appears with different meanings in the different literary strands of the Pentateuch—literary sources of varying date, historicity, and theology.

Since Micah bears the traditions of Sinai theology, it makes most sense to zero in on the evidence about the "tent of assembly" in the E-source and in the Deuteronomic texts of the Pentateuch. A careful reading of these sources reveals that, in contrast to other strands, they

---

40. I am following the NRSV in this translation. There are problems with the Hebrew text here, but this emended reading (based partially on the LXX) enjoys wide support among scholars and English translations of the Bible. Among other modern versions, Phillips, JB, NJB, TEV, NEB, and NAB all have a similar reading.

know of a special wilderness tent that seems highly relevant to what we know of Micah. They assume the existence of the Levites' tabernacle, but they are more concerned with another tent pitched outside the camp. They call the latter tent the "tent of assembly."[41]

Exodus 33:7; Num 11:16; 12:4; and Deut 31:14 (all Sinai texts) explicitly mention this tent. It lies outside Israel's encampment, not at its center. It is associated with oracles and tribal decision making, not priests and sacrifices. Moreover, it has nothing to do with housing the ark. Menahem Haran describes the tent as follows: "This tent has nothing in common with any temple ... it is nowhere associated with priests (or Levites), still less with sacrifices or permanent rituals, or indeed with any cult in the priestly sense of the word."[42] Rather, as in Micah's oracle, the tent is a locus for the transmission and application of the norms and penalties of the covenant.

In his research Haran has successfully established the thesis that "the tent of מועד ['assembly'] and the ark are two different institutions derived from different social and spiritual spheres of ancient Israelite life ... each of which evolved its own particular symbols and rites."[43] Haran does not go far enough, however, when he simply links the tent to the sphere of prophecy, as opposed to that of priesthood. The sphere of prophecy encompassed many social groups in ancient Israel. We can be more specific about the actual circle for which attachment to the tent of assembly meant empowerment for prophetic roles.

The evidence of Num 11:16–29 (E) in particular designates the tent of assembly as the bailiwick of Israelite clan elders, the forebears of the prophet Micah. In this passage, Moses becomes exhausted in administering the life of the whole people of Israel and has to delegate some authority to others. He selects representative elders from among the people and reinforces their traditional leadership role in tribal society with new sacral, covenantal authority.

Just as Micah's messianic tribal chief takes his "stand" (עמד) in covenant (Mic 5:4), Moses causes a group of seventy kin-group elders to

---

41. Menahem Haran gives a long list of scholars, including Wellhausen, Holzinger, Driver, Eissfeldt, and Pedersen, who have mistakenly viewed E's tent as cultic in essence and as housing the ark. See his *Temples and Temple Service in Ancient Israel: An Inquiry into Biblical Cult Phenomena and the Historical Setting of the Priestly School* (Winona Lake, Ind.: Eisenbrauns, 1985), 263 n. 5. E and D assume the existence of a cultic tent for the ark within the camp, according to Haran. He argues, however, that such a priestly tent must be distinguished from the tent outside the camp on which E and D focus (*Temples*, 263–69).

42. Ibid., 267.

43. Ibid., 271.

take a "stand" (עמד) in covenant (Num 11:24). Just as the "spirit [רוח] of Yahweh" empowers the leading elder Micah to enforce the covenant (Mic 3:8), Yahweh gives the seventy elders of the wilderness story a special gift of the "spirit" (רוח) that is upon Moses (Num 11:17, 25). Anticipating exactly what we find in Micah, the prophet's forebears in this wilderness story receive the sanction and regularization of having their traditional social roles incorporated within the structures of the Sinai covenant.

The institutional setting of the elders' new sacral empowerment in Num 11 is the tent of assembly. In 11:16 God tells Moses to gather the elders, "bring them to the tent of assembly, and have them take their place there with you." Then, according to 11:24–25, Moses "placed them all around the tent. Then the LORD came down in the cloud and spoke to him, and took some of the spirit that was on him and put it on the seventy elders; and when the spirit rested upon them, they prophesied."

On the basis of this evidence, I conclude that the "tent of assembly" (אהל מועד) in Sinai texts of the Bible symbolizes the chief administrative instrument within the assembly of Yahweh. This instrument consisted of Israelite society's traditional council of elders, who were placed under the regularization and empowerment of the Sinai covenant.

F. M. Cross has observed an ancient Near Eastern parallel to the biblical "tent of assembly" that supports this conclusion. In studying the ancient Egyptian "Tale of Wen-Amun" (ca. 1060 B.C.E.), Cross noted some striking similarities between the nomenclature and functions of the city "assembly" of Byblos and the "tent of assembly" in the Pentateuch.

At Byblos, the assembly convenes to consider a request for the extradition of Wen-Amun. It is clearly a political and judicial instrument within society. The biblical "tent of assembly" dates to the same era as the tale and may have performed functions similar to Byblos' assembly. Comparison of the two institutions suggests that the tent of assembly had an early function regulating village Israel's tribal confederacy. Cross states, "From such passages we gather that the Tent of Meeting, or properly the Tent of Assembly, originally referred to the amphictyonic or political aspect of the tent."[44]

The old covenantal assembly of elders was a lineage-based institution in old Israel. Micah 6:9 associates it with tribal Israel, and Num 11 sets it at the periphery of the wilderness camp, linked to the decentralized

---

44. Frank M. Cross, "The Priestly Tabernacle," *BARead* 1:223–24. For an English translation of the "Tale of Wen-Amun," see *ANET*, 25–29.

leadership of traditional kin-group heads. Thus, it is clearly a vestige by Micah's time.

Among the cross-cultural data, we observed a comparable tribal institution in the *jema'a* of the Moroccan Berbers. Although this Berber assembly can meet to coordinate the life of much of Berber society, it has no centralized power or leadership. It simply embodies the normal, segmentary organization of Berber society. The biblical assembly might differ from the *jema'a* only in being a specifically sacral institution.

SOCIAL FUNCTIONS OF THE COVENANT ASSEMBLY

The *covenant assembly*—that is, both the whole congregation (the "assembly of Yahweh," קהל יהוה; Mic 2:5) and its administrative instrument (the elders' assembly, מועד; Mic 6:9)—performed several social functions in old Israel. Evidence from Micah helps clarify these functions, by which the assembly enforced the norms and stipulations of the Sinai covenant. Examination of this evidence helps clarify the institutional roots of the Sinai theological stream of tradition and establish the early, prestate dating of these roots.

One of the assembly's original functions was allotting land among Israel's genealogical subdivisions through sacral lottery. Micah 2:5 threatens that in the future, when Israel reapportions its land, the land-grabbers of Jerusalem will have no one apportioning them "territory by lot" in the assembly of Yahweh. Conversely, Micah's countryfolk will be fully represented in the assembly's land lottery.

Micah's land lottery is reminiscent of the descriptions in Joshua and Judges of Israel's original division and settlement of the land after the exodus and wilderness wanderings. According to these texts, a sacral process of lot casting determined how Israel divided its new land among its lineage groups (Josh 14:2; 15:1; 17:5; 18:1–10; 19:51). The "tent of assembly" was the location of the sacred lottery. (The editor of Joshua may have understood the "tent of assembly" to have been the priestly tabernacle. However, since the heads of Israel's households participate with Joshua in carrying out the lottery, it seems reasonable to think that the actual social institution was the assembly of the elders.) Though the picture of Joshua personally casting lots on behalf of the Israelites at the tent is idealized, the early Israelite pioneers in the highlands of Canaan must have used similar means to apportion the land.

A bygone era must have used the land lottery of Mic 2:5, but this would not have been true of the prophet's own times. By then, very little land within Judah remained to be apportioned. What common land did remain in Judah, the monarchy likely claimed for itself.[45] External growth in territory was not a significant source of new, unclaimed land at Micah's time. And when Judah did conquer new territory during the monarchic period, the king would have assigned newly conquered land to chosen subjects.

For these reasons, any institution apportioning new land must have fallen dormant in monarchic times. In attempting to revive the sacral land lottery, Mic 2:5 aims to turn back the clock. Micah's Sinai kerygma is moored in an archaic function of a village-era institution.

The only alternative scenario would be to suppose that Mic 2:5 refers to a periodic reallocation of communally owned land in the monarchic period.[46] This idea does not fit the context of Mic 2:1–5 and is generally untenable. Micah 2:1–5 is not concerned with communally owned land but with individuals' rights to inalienable, immovable land.

In Micah's Sinai theology, the assignment of land among lineage segments in Israel was permanent and carefully protected. This theology coordinated well with Israel's traditional social customs, such as the practice of family burial on their lands.

From at least the start of the Iron Age, Israelite families buried their dead on family land to help cement their perpetual claim to their patrimonies (נחלה) and to allow them to conveniently maintain the burial plots of their kin. E. Bloch-Smith writes, "The majority [of Israelites] buried their dead in family cave and bench tombs located in proximity to the patrimony. Biblical references and inscriptions on a tomb at Khirbet Beit Lei testify to family burial.... Isaiah rebuked Shebna, an official of King Hezekiah, for having hewn an ostentatious individual tomb in Jerusalem, rather than being buried with his family (Isa 22:15–16)."[47]

The covenant assembly selected and covenanted with temporary tribal leaders as occasion warranted. Deuteronomy 31:14, in particular, situates the installation of Joshua as the leader of the conquest of Canaan at the "tent of assembly" (אהל מועד). When the Deuteronomistic History pictures King Joash and King Josiah, two of its ideal Sinai-brand rulers, "taking a stand in covenant" at a specially designated pillar at the temple, it portrays a monarchic-period revival of an earlier ritual at the covenant assembly (2 Kgs 11:14, 17; 23:3). We have a retro-ritual here.

---

45. Alt suggested that royal grants of such crown lands to the civil-service nobility of Jerusalem gave the land-grabbers their first footholds out in the Judean countryside ("Micha 2,1–5," 379; cf. Dearman, *Property Rights*, 115).

46. See Allen, *Books of Joel, Obadiah, Jonah, and Micah*, 291, and the bibliography cited in Hillers, *Micah*, 33; Dearman, *Property Rights*, 47.

47. E. Bloch-Smith, "Burials (Israelite)," *ABD* 1:787; cf. Hubbard, *Ruth*, 118–19.

Among the texts of Micah, Mic 5:1–5a is most likely to shed light on leadership selection within Israel's ancient covenant assembly. Here Micah details his model, "messianic" leader, describing the figure in ideal agrarian, kinship-based terms. One might anticipate that his treatment should recall the archaic institutional base of this old style of leadership.

Indeed, Mic 5:1–5a itself declares that the preferred, Sinai-style leadership characterizing Micah's theology originates in prestate customs. For example, 5:2 says that the promised leader's origin is "from aforetime" (מקדם), and his social and political roots are "in the olden days" (מימי עולם).

In Asaphite Ps 77:11, "aforetime" (קדם) refers to Israel's earliest history, as the reference to Moses and Aaron in the psalm's final verse shows (cf. Mic 6:4). The term "olden days" (ימי עולם) occurs in Deut 32:7 in the context of God's original election of Israel to be God's inherited people. Isaiah 63:9, 11 uses the same phrase in a comparable reference to the Mosaic period.

As James Mays states, Micah's oracle returns "to a period now viewed as an era behind the current order and so belonging to 'ancient days.'" It "recalls the procedure by which Yahweh selected directly an individual to lead Israel, a procedure that had been replaced by the election of the Davidic succession as bearer of Kingship."[48]

The social scenario behind the Micah passage is tribal Israel's call to arms. Its topos closely follows the procedure that premonarchic tribes used intermittently to organize for war under a "judge." Just as the judges sometimes demurred when first commissioned (see Judg 6:15; 1 Sam 9:21; 18:18), 5:2 demurs that the messianic leader will come from a group almost too "small" (צעיר) to be one of Judah's clans.

Just as early Israel's militia force assembled out of its clan structure, 5:2 uses the special Hebrew term for "clan" that recalls this muster. It calls the future leader's "clan" an אלף, which depicts the clan in its particular function as a source for old Israel's troops.[49] Von Rad is correct

---

48. Mays, *Micah*, 115–16; cf. Gottwald, *Tribes of Yahweh*, 277.
49. As von Rad notes, before Israel's hereditary kings instituted standing armies, "the old wars had been waged by the militias of the tribes raised from levies of the free citizens possessed of property" (*Studies in Deuteronomy*, 46). The term אלף apparently referred at first to that sized fighting unit that could be mustered from any given clan (cf. 1 Sam 8:12). With time, the size of such units was regularized, with the eventual result that the term was understood to designate 1,000 soldiers (see BDB, 48). Here in Micah, as Hillers notes, the term "refers to a basic and ancient feature of Israelite social organization, the 'thousands,' the troops raised from each tribal subdivision.... It recalls the premonarchic times of Moses, Joshua, and the judges" (*Micah*, 65–66; also see Allen, *Books of Joel, Obadiah, Jonah, and Micah*,

that "regardless of all the changes that had taken place [in society]," a pronouncement such as this essentially declared the "old patriarchal form of defense binding" for its own time.[50]

As the people began to organize for war, the old tribal confederacy might convene the covenant assembly of the elders to strategize. Judges 20 pictures such a convocation. In Judg 20:2, lineage representatives of "all the tribes of Israel" gather at the "assembly" (קהל עם האלהים; cf. Judg 21:5, 8). This assembly of Israel's elders has nothing to do with the ark. The tribal representatives assemble to Yahweh at Mizpah (20:1), while the ark is located three miles away at Bethel (20:18, 26–27).

The Hebrew term for the assembled elders in Judg 20:2 depicts them as "chiefs" or "commanders." The language suggests that as the elders gathered, the prominent warriors among them claimed official command of various militia regiments. Those elders renowned for valor essentially became "elders-at-arms" as they strategized at the covenant assembly.

I believe that Micah identifies his messianic leader as one of these valorous kinship heads. This coming leader will be installed in a setting just like that in Judg 20:2, in the same way that Joshua, Joash, and Josiah all were (see my arguments above). A key messianic text in Zech 10 confirms that the kinship-based "chiefs" of Judg 20:2 are indeed potential military saviors. Paralleling Mic 5:2–5, Zech 10:4 describes a coming military messiah using the selfsame term, "valorous chief" (פנה), found in Judg 20:2.

A sacral lottery, parallel to the assembly's land lottery, revealed God's choice of leadership before the convocation of elders. Biblical texts are not explicit about the details, but the way that Sinai texts, such as 1 Sam 10:19–21, picture using sacral lots to select Israel's early leaders supports this reconstruction. Lending further support are other biblical passages, such as 2 Sam 20:1 and 1 Kgs 12:16, which use the metaphor of land allotment to describe an Israelite leader. These texts refer to the Israelite chief as a kind of patrimony (נחלה), staked out by the members of the assembly of Yahweh.

Micah is again trying to turn back the clock to revive Israel's older levy system of tribal muster and contingency-based militia leadership. King Hezekiah's centralization and militarization of Judah in preparation for an invasion by the Assyrian army ran diametrically opposite to these older institutions. Hezekiah's royal policy essentially abandoned the

---

343 n. 24; Wolff, *Micah*, 144; Gottwald, *Tribes of Yahweh*, 270). That אלף is a (military-political) synonym of משפחה, the more general Hebrew term for "clan," is shown, e.g., by the parallel use of the two terms in 1 Sam 10:19–21. Other occurrences of the term אלף in its meaning of "clan" include Josh 22:14; Judg 6:15; and 1 Sam 23:23.

50. Von Rad, *Studies in Deuteronomy*, 46.

countryside of Judah and its militia. He based his defensive strategy instead on a centrally controlled army and a system of fortified cities, such as Lachish (Mic 1:13). These fortified cities formed defensive nodes, or military satellites, of Jerusalem.

Baruch Halpern calls Hezekiah's strategy a "hedgehog defense," presumably since hedgehogs (porcupines) roll themselves up into spiny "strongholds" when threatened. In Halpern's reconstruction, "Hezekiah's policies created a Judah in which the rural landowners and clans had been stripped of their power, in which court parties and the standing army were ascendant."[51]

In the face of this new militarization of Judah, Micah's advocacy of kinship-based leadership and troop recruitment is pure repristination. Von Rad observed the same retreat to past institutions in the book of Deuteronomy. He characterized the various attempts in Deuteronomy to revive the older, covenant-system of military defense as "consciously archaizing." "Deuteronomy desires—by 'utopian' anachronism—to impose the old order ... on the state of the later monarchical period."[52]

Decentralized Convocations of the Covenant Assembly

Judges 20, with similar texts, such as Josh 18:1; 24:1, presents an idealized and schematized picture of the whole convocation of archaic Israel assembling to act in concert. Judges 20:2, for example, would have us believe that 400,000 foot soldiers assembled at Mizpah, all of them of one mind. The actual social reality behind the archaic convocations of the covenant assembly must have been rather different, at least most of the time.

A. Alt reasoned that the "assembly" of Mic 2:5 might have brought together large unions of the people on rare occasions. More often, however, it would have come into play as a *dispersed* entity—in every local community.[53] Similarly, N. Gottwald has argued that the covenant assembly generally convened in the form of dispersed, localized gatherings. Rather than taking place at any single location, "multiple regional gatherings may be meant."[54]

---

51. Baruch Halpern, "Jerusalem and the Lineages in the Seventh Century BCE: Kinship and the Rise of Individual Moral Liability," in *Law and Ideology in Monarchic Israel* (ed. B. Halpern and D. W. Hobson; JSOTSup 124; Sheffield: Sheffield Academic Press, 1991), 59.

52. Von Rad, *Studies in Deuteronomy*, 64 n. 2.

53. Alt, "Micha 2,1–5," 380.

54. Gottwald, *Tribes of Yahweh*, 243.

The suggestions of Alt and Gottwald correlate with old Israel's non-centralized, tribal organization. The anthropological evidence of chapter 6 showed that traditional peoples convene in tribal assembly at various levels of their genealogical system. We saw this with particular clarity in the *jema'a* assembly of the Berber tribes of Morocco. There are hierarchies of assemblies of the Berber *jema'a*, which correspond to the graded strata of the Berber genealogical system. Assemblies normally convene locally, at lower levels, within the lineage and kin group. The Berbers consider the local meetings to be regional extensions of a tribes-wide institution. Gatherings of the *jema'a* higher up the system, at levels inclusive of multiple kin groups, are also possible. In the latter case, delegates represent their respective constituencies.

In many cultures, a plurality of meetings, at various local settings, constitutes a full convocation of an entire tribal people. The way many traditional societies collaborate to synchronize localized rituals provides evidence of this social principle. The Logoli people in Kenya perform circumcision rites every few years in local settings, for example, but they coordinate the rites so that they all perform them at the same time. In performing the coordinated rites, the people have "assembled," in a sense, as a sacral congregation.

At least one Sinai text, Asaphite Ps 74, seems to allude to the dispersed and localized nature of the biblical covenant assembly. In its present form, the psalm is an exilic-period lament. It describes how the Babylonians have destroyed the temple (74:4) and wrought havoc on the land in general. Verse 8 notes, fascinatingly, that among the havoc the enemy Babylonian troops have burned all the "assembly places of God" (מוֹעֲדֵי־אֵל) in the land.

The Hebrew terminology here recalls that of Mic 6:9 ("Hear, O ... *assembly* [מוֹעֵד, see *BHS* note]") and of the Sinai texts of the Pentateuch about the tent of assembly. Since the psalm belongs to the same stream of tradition as these texts, it may well have the covenant assembly of the elders in view.[55] If so, the psalm depicts the institution as a plurality of assemblies in the countryside.

It is remarkable that Ps 74 understands that there remained vestiges, at least, of the elders' assemblies in the Judean country at the time of the Babylonian invasions. When the original economic and political functions of the covenant assembly ceased in the state period, groups of elders

---

55. Cf. Anthony Gelston, "A Note on Psalm LXXIV 8," *VT* 34 (1984): 85; Marvin E. Tate, *Psalms 51–100* (WBC 20; Dallas: Word, 1990), 249–50.

must have kept alive both its remnants and memories of its kinship-based social functions.

It bears repeating that specifically the forebears of figures such as Micah—not all elders—are at issue in this regard. Groups of clan elders not co-opted into Israel's state system are likely candidates for at least one type of *tradent* of biblical Yahwism's sacral traditions and institutional memories.

8

THE SOCIAL ROOTS OF BIBLICAL YAHWISM II: HOSEA AND THE TRADITIONAL PRIESTS OF THE ISRAELITE TRIBES

HOSEA'S UNIQUE PROPHECIES, AS CHAPTER 4 PROVED, DEMONSTRATE THE vitality of the Sinai covenant in monarchic Israel. Hosea's group, along with Micah's, advocated covenantal Yahwism in Israel in the eighth century B.C.E.

Hosea's stream of theological tradition did not originate in his own times; its headwaters are centuries earlier. As with Micah, his traditions betray a premonarchic, prestate provenience.

The same social-scientific model that clarified Micah's social background applies equally here. The social roots of Hosea's theology extend deep into Israel's village-era, lineage-based society. Applying my model to Hosea, I aim to identify Hosea's forebears as lineage members of a traditional priesthood in old Israel.

HOSEA AS A TRADITIONAL PRIEST

THE LINEAGE-BASED LANGUAGE AND THOUGHT-FORMS OF HOSEA

As in Micah's case, our initial clues to the provenance of Hosea come from his thought-forms and language. Judging by his means of expression, Hosea saw his surroundings differently from his royal and priestly contemporaries. In his prophecies, Hosea beckons us away from a world of urban prosperity, bureaucratic proliferation, and international intrigue. We enter instead a social world where genealogical lineage, ancestral farmland, and fertility intertwine to form the fabric of everyday life.

In chapter 4, the references in Hos 5 to the southern kingdom of Judah attracted our attention (Hos 5:10, 12, 13, 14; cf. 6:4). These references to southern Israelites are not peculiar or out of place.[1] The passage's particular historical context was the Syro-Ephraimite war with Judah. A text about this extensive conflict between Israel and Judah might easily have occasion to mention the latter kingdom.

What is peculiar is that Hosea, a citizen of the Ephraimite (i.e., northern) state, repeatedly presents Judah as a poetic equivalent of Ephraim. Hosea overlooks state borders and stubbornly ignores that his addressees see themselves as two warring monarchies. Hosea holds Ephraim and Judah responsible to the same, unique set of norms.

Hosea 5:9 speaks not of two separate states but of one tribally structured entity, the "tribes of Israel" (שבטי ישראל). God's plans encompass this whole people. Verse 10 pictures the contemporary military conflict as an inner-Israel dispute over tribal boundary lines, not a foreign invasion. Traditional norms, not diplomatic agreements, prevent moving such boundaries. In sum, Hosea doggedly promotes a traditional unity among the whole Israelite people.[2]

Hosea's ideal of one, intertwined Israelite people matches Sinai theology. It would have grated, however, against the assumptions of contemporary monarchic authorities. Hosea's easy, natural manner about the topic makes it difficult to imagine him as a royal subject. A role in old Israel's lineage-based society fits him much better.

In particular, the cross-cultural evidence suggests Hosea had the traditional role of a ritual functionary—a priest. Among traditional peoples, such as the Berbers, the Nuer, the Tallensi, the Kofyar, and the Dinka, ritual functionaries promote kin-group and tribal solidarity. They are the primary traditional figures that play such a mediatory role. Otherwise, only a balanced opposition between genealogical segments holds non-centralized societies together.

Hosea presupposes not only the traditional unity of his audience but also their collective possession of a homeland. Their intimate interconnection with their land is nowhere clearer than in Hos 9:1–6. I examined this text in chapter 4, and it is worth a repeat look.

---

1. Stephen L. Cook, "The Lineage Roots of Hosea's Yahwism," in *The Social World of the Hebrew Bible: Twenty-Five Years of the Social Sciences in the Academy* (ed. R. A. Simkins and S. L. Cook) *Semeia* 87 (1999): 156; Hans Walter Wolff, "Hoseas Geistige Heimat," in *Gesammelte Studien zum Alten Testament* (Munich: Kaiser, 1964), 235; originally published in 1956; Else Kragelund Holt, *Prophesying the Past: The Use of Israel's History in the Book of Hosea* (JSOTSup 194; Sheffield: Sheffield Academic Press, 1995), 82 n. 117.

2. Cook, "Lineage Roots," 156; James L. Mays, *Hosea: A Commentary* (OTL; Philadelphia: Westminster, 1969), 89, 96–97; Wolff, "Heimat," 235.

The passage presupposes that the people of Israel occupy a specific territory, which is unequivocally "the LORD's land" (9:3a). Their occupation is now forfeit; Hosea threatens the people with eviction. His threat has real bite, since exile out of the land would be disruptive to the point of communal disorientation. As exiles, the people would become refugees in a foreign land, reduced to mourning and eating "unclean" (טמא) food (9:3b). Cut off from acceptable sacrifices and shrines, their communal rites of worship will cease (9:4–5). The prophet assumes the people's identity is grounded in their land.

Hosea is advocating Sinai theology and its emphasis on Israel's land as a special inheritance from their divine liege lord, Yahweh. At the same time, Hosea acts like a traditional priest. Like ritual functionaries among many traditional peoples, he knows a homeland is central to his kinfolk's group identity.[3]

Hosea assumes personal responsibility for managing his kinfolk's sacral connection to their homeland. Trying to wield authority, he publicly interrupts a national worship festival of the northern kingdom. Behind his vigorous arguments, he assumes that Israel identifies as a people with its own sacred territory.

The ethnographic evidence in chapter 6 revealed traditional priests as the figures who expect deference during festival worship. They preside over festival sacrifices, with which a people acknowledge a deity's control over their land and its agricultural bounty. Hosea urges the people to reform their sacrificial worship while they still can. Sacrifices will be impossible in exile, since in Egypt and Assyria there will be no homeland produce for the people to offer God.

A cross-cultural example illuminates the social assumptions behind Hosea's argument. In modern times, a group of Mossi colonists migrated from the Yatenga area of West Africa to work at an irrigation project among the Bambara people in what was then the French Sudan.[4] Among the Bambara, the Mossi settlers felt isolated from the supernatural forces

---

3. On the witness of Hos 9:1–3 to Israelite ethnicity and identity, see Kenton L. Sparks, *Ethnicity and Identity in Ancient Israel: Prolegomena to the Study of Ethnic Sentiments and Their Expression in the Hebrew Bible* (Winona Lake, Ind.: Eisenbrauns, 1998), 158–59. On the concept of "homeland" as a frequently important component of group identity, Sparks references the following studies: H. Isaacs, "Basic Group Identity," in *Ethnicity: Theory and Experience* (ed. N. Glazer and D. P. Moynihan; Cambridge: Harvard University Press, 1975), 29–52; F. W. Riggs, ed., *Ethnicity: Concepts and Terms Used in Ethnicity Research* (International Conceptual Encyclopedia for the Social Sciences 1; Honolulu: COCTA, 1985), 30–37.

4. Peter B. Hammond, "Economic Change and Mossi Acculturation," in *Continuity and Change in African Cultures* (ed. W. Bascom and M. Herskovits; Chicago: University of Chicago, 1959), 238–56.

controlling their home territory. Their sense of social isolation was so intense, in fact, that they ceased practicing their traditional religious obligations. The settlers did not reject their previous sacral ideas and practices but found themselves unable to bring them from their Yatenga homeland. They entrusted them instead to elders and priests (ritual functionaries, i.e., "earth custodians") remaining back home.

Other prophetic passages within Hosea emphasize the converse of Hos 9:1–6. Rather than discrediting the idea of sacrifices to Yahweh on foreign soil, they condemn worship of foreign deities on Yahweh's soil. Hosea symbolizes fertility worship as marital unfaithfulness. Metaphorical texts such as Hos 2 present Baal and related deities as false "lovers" of Israel, who have misled Israel into "prostitution," into thinking they—not Yahweh—control Canaan's fertility.

I have not yet mentioned Hosea's derogatory terms for Israelite worshipers of Baal, terms such as "children of prostitution" (2:4) and "foreign children" (5:7). The expression "foreign children" (בנים זרים; 5:7) especially is worth attention.

Elsewhere in Hosea, the term זרים in 5:7 refers to actual, ethnic foreigners (7:8–9; 8:7). By using the term here, Hosea confirms that Baal worship is foreign to the people and land of Israel. He is echoing Asaphite Ps 81:10: "There shall be no strange god among you; you shall not bow down to a foreign god." As Kenton Sparks states, "Hosea viewed Baal not only as a competitor of Yahweh but also as a foreign competitor."[5]

Hosea used categories of kinship and ethnicity for his people's sacral bonds with their land. Like many lineage-based priests, Hosea viewed his people as an ethnic body with a homeland. Like them, he conceived of his people's God as the native deity of their territory. The gods of other ethnic groups, by contrast, are foreigners.

A final set of presumptions further links Hosea to the thought-world of old Israel: his assumptions in interacting with political leaders. Adopting the radical skepticism of his Sinai traditions about kingship, Hosea confronts Israel's monarchs over theological issues. There is bound to be trouble when kinfolk and homeland fall under the rule of a human monarch. Monarchy is an idolatrous substitute for Yahweh's suzerainty.

In examining Hos 8:1–7 earlier, we saw God permitting the monarchy begrudgingly—only as a concession with strict provisos. Hosea rebuked Israel for wresting kingship from God and for violating God's conditions for allowing it.

---

5. Sparks, *Ethnicity and Identity*, 144.

If Israel was to have kings, God was to appoint them (Deut 17:15a; cf. 1 Sam 10:19–24; 12:1, 13). Hosea claims, however, that the opposite has happened. He quotes God saying, "They made kings, but not through me; they set up princes, but without my knowledge" (Hos 8:4). Hosea withdraws his support of the contemporary king for just cause, pronouncing God's removal of him (Hos 13:11).

Hosea's judgment scarcely tolerates the principle of dynastic succession. The political assumptions of Hosea's theology do not fit contemporary, monarchic norms. Royal dynasties self-perpetuate. External, sacral authority does not dictate the appointment and removal of hereditary kings.

In contrast to Hosea's statist milieu, priests in segmentary societies often do regulate political leadership. Hosea's assumptions fit this bygone Hebrew world. Societies with no monarch have leaders such as clan heads, field commanders, and tribal chiefs. These traditional political leaders often depend on the sacral support and ritual collaboration of priests for effectiveness. In some cases, priests are a society's primary chief-makers.

The political power of priests among the Tallensi people of northern Ghana provides a good example.[6] To be sure, *tendaanas* (earth custodians) do not actually select chiefs. The office of chieftaincy (*na'am*) falls by custom to most heads of maximal lineages. This is natural, given the segmentary organization of Tallensi society. Priests do control the final phase of all chiefs' installations, however.

In the installation ceremony, the priests receive the new chief and present him to their Earth shrines. Since the mystical powers of the chief require the blessing of the Earth, the priestly earth custodians control his effectiveness. After his installation, a chief cannot even go hunting or fishing without a priest's blessing. Only collaboration between chiefs and priests can ensure the general welfare of Tallensi society.

The hereditary priests (*igurramen*) among the Moroccan Berbers play an even more central role in the election of tribal chiefs.[7] The Berbers of the central High Atlas reject permanent, concentrated political power. They elect their chiefs (*imgharen*) through negotiation. They allocate them no levy, resources, or personnel. And they allow them to serve only one-year terms. Among the Berbers, all chiefs are thus merely regular tribesmen enjoining transient authority and serving lame-duck terms.

---

6. Meyer Fortes, "The Political System of the Tallensi of the Northern Territories of the Gold Coast," in *African Political Systems* (ed. M. Fortes and E. E. Evans-Pritchard; London: Oxford University Press, 1940), 255, 260.

7. Ernest Gellner, *Saints of the Atlas* (London: Weidenfeld & Nicholson, 1969), 78–84, 91.

There is normally no chief coordinating the activities of multiple Berber tribes. The Berbers activate this type of topmost chieftaincy only in the face of a grave military crisis or other overwhelming need.

The Berber priests lend sacral authorization and ratification to the process of selecting a chief (*amghar*).[8] They actively supervise elections of chiefs among the lay tribes. *Igurramen* mediate tribal negotiations at the heart of the process. Frequently, they even steer the course of the negotiations, using persuasion and pressure. The priests take pride in the fact that final tribal decisions often go to their preferred candidates. At times, they casually boast that they appoint their kinfolk's chiefs for them.

HOSEA'S DEPENDENCE ON LITURGICAL TRADITIONS

This sampling of Hosea's language and social assumptions suggests that he thinks like a tribal priest. We might expect such a traditional priest to be familiar with the liturgical traditions of Israel's ancient worship places. A next logical step, therefore, is to scour Hosea in search of liturgical concepts and language.

In fact, Hosea does use liturgical language. Many of his prophetic warnings, for example, threaten a reversal of normal worship experiences.

The Israelites expected their worship to renew God's special election of them as "my people" (see Pss 14:4; 78:1; 80:4; cf. Ps 124:1–2). In contrast, because of their apostasy, God declares at Hos 1:9 that "You are not my people, and I am not your God."

Whereas the people expected their sacrifices to please God, Hos 5:6 declares that God will ignore them instead. "With their flocks and herds they shall go to seek the LORD, but they will not find him; he has withdrawn from them."

Vigils awaiting God's renewed presence at dawn were a common worship practice in ancient Israel (cf. Pss 30:5; 46:5; 143:8; Ezek 8:16; cf. Hos 6:3). The threat of Hos 10:15 that God will cut off the Israelite king "at dawn" thus shockingly reverses Israel's liturgical assumptions.

Hosea does not use liturgical language just to reverse the people's expectations. He also uses it in trying to help the people return to God. Consider Hos 5:15, for example. The verse offers divine rapprochement to Israel, despite their offences against traditional land rights (5:10), and

---

8. Ibid., 85–87.

despite their covenants with foreign nations (5:13). God's offer of reconciliation, however, hinges conspicuously on cultic penitence.

God is waiting specifically for the people to "acknowledge their guilt and seek my face." This language about "seeking the face" (בקש פנה) of God refers explicitly to a liturgical act at a sacred shrine (Pss 24:6; 27:8; 105:4; 1 Chr 16:11; 2 Chr 7:14). Siegfried Wagner writes, "The phrase 'seeking the face of a deity' always refers to a comprehensible cultic rite at the holy places (temple, sanctuary), where it would have been possible to 'seek God' directly or mediately."[9] Hosea uses another, shortened form of the phrase in precisely this way at 5:6.

The people's attempt to respond to God's offer (Hos 6:1–3) is insufficient (Hos 6:4–6). Their response has a liturgical form completely in line with what God and Hosea want to see, but it lacks true commitment and unequivocal content (see v. 4b).

Beyond using general liturgical expressions, Hosea also leans on the specific words and concepts of north Israelite psalms. Tellingly, the psalms in question are the Psalms of Asaph. These are the very psalms (Pss 50; 73–83) that I have been at pains to connect with Hosea's Sinai theological stream of tradition.

Scholars such as Hans-Joachim Kraus, Martin J. Buss, Harry P. Nasuti, Graham I. Davies, and Michael D. Goulder have conclusively established the provenance of the Asaphite psalms. It lies in pre-722 B.C.E., north-Israelite cultic worship of Yahweh.[10] Note, for example, how Ps 80:2 requests God's aid for specifically northern tribes: Ephraim, Benjamin, and Manasseh.

Given the similarity in theology, geography, and dating between the Psalms of Asaph and the prophecies of Hosea, we might have anticipated that Hosea would be directly indebted to them. For example, Hosea speaks of Israel as Yahweh's own special people (Hos 6:11; 11:7), and so do Pss 80:4; 81:8, 11, 13. Hosea understands the special relationship between the people and God as a "covenant" (ברית; Hos 6:7; 8:1), as do Pss 50:5, 16; 74:20; 78:10, 37. The Psalms of Asaph even seem to inform Hosea's language about the ethical content of the Sinai covenant. Hosea

---

9. Siegfried Wagner, "בקש," *TDOT* 2:237; cf. Cook, "Lineage Roots," 156; Graham I. Davies, *Hosea* (NCBC; Grand Rapids: Eerdmans, 1992), 159.

10. Hans-Joachim Kraus, *Pss 60–150: A Continental Commentary* (trans. H. Oswald; CC; Minneapolis: Fortress, 1989); Martin J. Buss, "The Psalms of Asaph and Korah," *JBL* 82 (1963): 382–92; Harry P. Nasuti, *Tradition-History and the Psalms of Asaph* (SBLMS 88; Atlanta: Scholars Press, 1988); Graham I. Davies, *Hosea* (OTG; Sheffield: JSOT Press, 1993), 67–78; idem, *Hosea* (NCBC), 29–34; Michael D. Goulder, *The Psalms of Asaph and the Pentateuch: Studies in the Psalter, III* (JSOTSup 233; Sheffield: Sheffield Academic Press, 1996).

4:2 and Ps 50:18–20 share the same basic list of moral ordinances,[11] clearly the same list that forms part of the Decalogue.

The parallels in phraseology and idiom between Hosea and the Psalms of Asaph are often too close to be coincidental. Hosea 5:2 and Ps 50:17 share a description that Israel has sunk deep into wickedness, exposing themselves to divine "chastisement" (מוסר). In both Hos 5:14 and Ps 50:22 God threatens to "tear" (טרף) Israel to pieces, and "there will be none to deliver" (אין מציל). Hosea 13:2 and Ps 78:17 use an identical idiom to speak of Israel "sinning still more" (יוספו לחטא) against God. And, to cite yet another example, Hos 8:13 and 9:9 use the same language as Ps 79:8 to speak of God "remembering" (זכר) the people's "iniquities" (עון).

We have already seen (in texts such as Hos 2:8–9 and 9:2) how significantly God's dominion over nature and fertility figures in Hosea. Scholars have suggested that Hosea is innovating here—actually advancing Israel's conception of Yahweh. They argue that not until Hosea did Israel move beyond the polytheistic view that Yahweh was a specialized god, limited to acts of history such as redemption.[12] The Psalms of Asaph contravene this proposal, proving Hosea relies on theological traditions, not evolutionary breakthroughs.

As Graham Davies argues, the building blocks of Hosea's prophecy are the old cultic traditions of Israel. "The exodus and associated traditions played an important part here…. But so, it seems, did the perception of Yahweh as the true giver of the fertility of the land."[13]

Psalms 78, 80, and 81, not an evolutionary leap, informed Hosea of God's sovereignty over earth's fertility. In Ps 81:16 God declares God's ability and desire to provide Israel's food. "I would feed you with the finest of the wheat, and with honey from the rock I would satisfy you." Psalm 78:23–27 preserves the same traditional understanding. God controls the clouds of the sky and the doors of heaven. God chooses to provide Israel food in abundance.

The juxtaposition of Ps 81:9 and 10 emphasizes that no other deity besides Yahweh should receive credit for Canaan's fertility. These same verses also make clear that Yahweh is no specialized deity, but sovereign over both history and fertility. The relevant section of the psalm reads:

---

11. Walter Beyerlin, *Die Kulttraditionen Israels in der Verkündigung des Propheten Micha* (FRLANT 72; Göttingen: Vandenhoeck & Ruprecht, 1959), 42–43; Matin J. Buss, *The Prophetic Word of Hosea: A Morphological Study* (BZAW 111; Berlin: Töpelmann, 1969), 100–101; Nasuti, *Psalms of Asaph*, 61; Goulder, *Psalms of Asaph*, 50, 294, 296.

12. See, e.g., Holt, *Prophesying the Past*, 115.

13. Davies, *Hosea* (OTG), 76.

[8] Hear, O my people, while I admonish you;
   O Israel, if you would but listen to me!
[9] There shall be no strange god among you;
   you shall not bow down to a foreign god.
[10] I am the LORD your God,
   who brought you up out of the land of Egypt.
   Open your mouth wide and I will fill it.

To drive home Yahweh's control of fertility, Hosea even uses fertility language to describe Israel's historical relationship with God. This metaphorical style also traces to the Psalms of Asaph.

Hosea 10:1 metaphorically describes the Israelites as a luxuriant vine, yielding abundant fruit on God's land. According to Hos 2:23, God promises that at a time of future salvation, "I will sow [the people] for myself in the land." Similarly, Hos 14:5–7 depicts Israel's future renewal using images of vigorous agricultural growth. The same metaphors and images appear in Ps 80:8–16, a psalm of Asaph contemporary with Hosea.[14] The psalm pictures God planting Israel as a vine. It takes deep root and fills the land of Canaan, covering the mountains with its shadow.

Despite Hosea's appreciative use of liturgical traditions and psalmic images, imagining Hosea as a priest may still seem difficult. One might object that an Israelite priest would not attack other clerics as Hosea does (e.g., Hos 4:4–10; 6:9). A priest would not proclaim God's rejection of sacrificial offerings (e.g., Hos 5:6; 6:6; 8:13).

Such objections might have some force, if I was arguing that Hosea was an official priest of the centralized cult of his time. That is not the case. The evidence is leading to another conclusion. Hosea must have represented a traditional priestly lineage and ritual system that was currently in conflict with the contemporary state cult and its worship practices. Hosea rejects the integrity and sincerity of the contemporary cult, not priestly ritual and sacrifices in principle.[15]

---

14. Nasuti, *Psalms of Asaph,* 98–99; Davies, *Hosea* (NCBC), 234, 306–7; Goulder, *Psalms of Asaph,* 143.

15. Buss states, "It has been said that the prophets oppose not cult as such but only the particular cult they observe. It is indeed true that they borrow technical priestly terminology [e.g., רצה in Hos 8:13] to indicate nonacceptance of sacrifices in a way that would be applicable to an individual situation" (*Prophetic Word,* 105). Also see Franz Hesse, "Amos 5:4–6, 14f.," *ZAW* 68 (1956): 12; Ronald E. Clements, *Prophecy and Covenant* (SBT 43; London: SCM, 1968), 93–102. Commentators often remark that 1 Sam 15:22 pictures Samuel, himself a priest, prioritizing obedience over sacrifice in the mode of Hos 6:6 (e.g., Mays, *Hosea,* 98; Henry McKeating, *Amos, Hosea, Micah* [CBC; London: Cambridge University Press, 1971], 111).

Jeremiah, a Levitical priest from a later period than Hosea, provides a helpful comparison. Though a Levite himself (Jer 1:1),[16] Jeremiah frequently attacked the contemporary priests of his time (e.g., Jer 1:18; 2:8, 26; 4:9; 5:31; 6:13; 8:1, 10; 13:13; 14:18).

Malachi, another Levitical priest from an even later time,[17] also attacked sacrificial worship. In Mal 1:10, God prefers no worship to contemptible worship. Malachi's indictments do not reject sacrifice per se, however. In Mal 3:3–4, he looks forward to a time when "the tribute of Judah and Jerusalem will be pleasing to the LORD, as in the days of old."

The exact relationship of the Psalms of Asaph to the apostate cult of the northern kingdom remains a puzzle. This is particularly true for Asaphite texts, such as Pss 80 and 83, which date to Hosea's own times. Hosea experienced the northern worship sites as thoroughly corrupt (e.g., Hos 4:8; 10:5, 8; 13:2). If their apostasy is as deep-seated as Hosea says, could they have continued to celebrate the Sinai theology of the Asaph psalms through the fall of the northern kingdom?

Several possible scenarios present themselves. Although some Asaphite psalms appeared in writing only during the time of Hosea and later, like sacred lyrics in general, they nevertheless used older, traditional language and theology. The apostate cult of Hosea's era may have blithely repeated liturgical language that had genuine power in earlier times.

Editors can update traditional psalms without seriously heeding their message. Worshipers can easily mouth words without taking them to heart. Alternatively, some faithful, traditional Asaphites may have continued to function as a minority group of Levites within the state cult contemporary with Hosea.[18] Such a group might have had enough

---

16. See, e.g., Roland de Vaux, *Ancient Israel: Its Life and Institutions* (trans. J. McHugh; New York: McGraw-Hill, 1961), 376; Aelred Cody, *A History of Old Testament Priesthood* (AnBib 35; Rome: Pontifical Biblical Institute, 1969), 141; Paul D. Hanson, *The Dawn of Apocalyptic* (Philadelphia: Fortress, 1975), 224; Robert R. Wilson, *Prophecy and Society in Ancient Israel* (Philadelphia: Fortress, 1980), 233–35, 245–46; Joseph Blenkinsopp, *A History of Prophecy in Israel* (Philadelphia: Westminster, 1983), 162; Richard Elliott Friedman, *Who Wrote the Bible?* (New York: Harper & Row, 1987), 125–27.

17. Blenkinsopp, *Prophecy*, 242; Carol Bechtel (Reynolds), "Malachi and the Priesthood" (Ph.D. diss., Yale University, 1993).

18. I noted in chapter 6 that Judg 18:30 remarks about Levites remaining in office at Dan throughout the history of the northern kingdom. Further, 1 Kgs 12:32 notably refrains from complaining about non-Levitical priests at the shrine at Dan. Jeroboam I's removal of the Levites from the state sanctuaries may thus have been only partial. See Wolff, "Heimat," 244–45; Cody, *Priesthood*, 111.

influence to keep some Asaphite traditions alive in northern worship. We may owe the Asaphite psalms of Hosea's time to Asaphite "moles."

A third possibility is more hypothetical. I suggest below that some disenfranchised priests in the northern kingdom maintained peripheral, sectarian communities of worship. Such base communities, at sites such as Shechem, may have harbored and generated Asaphite psalms at Hosea's time.

HOSEA'S POSITIVE VIEW OF THE WORSHIP SHRINES OF ISRAEL'S PAST

Hosea's reliance on liturgical traditions indirectly shows that he valued Israel's traditional, tribal worship. It is difficult to confirm this directly from Hosea's own words, since his prophetic message naturally focuses on how corrupt Israel's worship had become in his own, state-era times. Nevertheless, select passages within Hosea betray the prophet's positive view of the worship shrines of Israel's past. Hosea 12:2–6 is one such text. It reads as follows:

> [2] The LORD has an indictment against [Israel],
> > and will punish Jacob according to his ways,
> > and repay him according to his deeds.
> [3] In the womb he tried to supplant his brother,
> > and in his manhood he strove with God.
> [4] He strove with the angel and prevailed,
> > he wept and sought his favor;
> he met him at Bethel,
> > and there he would speak with us.
> [5] The LORD the God of hosts,
> > the LORD is his name!
> [6] But as for you, return to your God,
> > hold fast to loyalty and justice,
> > and wait continually for your God.

The passage reminds the people of their unique history with God. Their ancestor Jacob struggled to find God, and even had to leave God's land temporarily. As he fled the land, nevertheless, Jacob told God at Bethel that he hoped to "return" (שׁוּב) in safety (Gen 28:21a [E]). Eventually he did come back to Canaan, where he purged his entourage of "foreign gods" and worshipped God at Bethel (Gen 35:1–8 [E]).

Hosea calls the Israel of his day to a similar return (שׁוּב; 12:6) to God and to God's worship. As Else K. Holt concludes, "Jacob should serve as an example of a conversion that is to be imitated by Israel: Jacob deceived his brother, fought with God and won, but afterwards begged for mercy and was found and spoken to at Bethel."[19]

The specific form that the conversion of the people must take is an embrace of God's covenant obligations. In a manner similar to Mic 6:8, Hos 12:6 summarizes those obligations using Hosea's keywords "loyalty" (חסד; Hos 2:19; 4:1; 6:4, 6; 10:12) and "justice" (משפט; Hos 2:19; 5:1). "Hold fast to loyalty and justice, and wait continually for your God."

Graham Davies incisively argues that the covenantal summary of 12:6 mirrors the priestly instruction that traditionally took place at worship shrines such as Bethel. The terms "loyalty" and "justice" appear together in the preexilic Ps 101:1.[20] More significantly, the idea of "waiting" for God is common in the psalms (e.g., Pss 25:3, 5, 21; 27:14; 37:9, 34; 40:1; 69:7; 130:5), as are expressions of "continual" devotion (e.g., Pss 16:8; 25:15; 34:1; 35:27; 40:16; 73:23).

Davies aptly draws the following conclusion: "The possibility therefore exists that these two lines [of 12:6] at least were taken up by Hosea from some form of cultic instruction. That this is the case seems to be confirmed if we go back to v. 4, where the exhortation [of 12:6] is located specifically in the encounter with God at Bethel, which is here for once (contrast 4:15; 10:5) given its real name by Hosea."[21]

Indeed, 12:4 explicitly affirms the Bethel shrine and its teaching program of a preceding era. Hosea thus condemns his audience as he lauds a history of proper worship at Bethel. This history traces back to Jacob's original discovery of Bethel and to his later dealings with God there (cf. the E strand at Gen 28:10–22 and 35:1–8).

Hosea shares with the Sinai texts of the E strand a set of traditions about Jacob's relation to the site. According to these historical traditions, Israel's ancestor had a surprise encounter with God at Bethel. Quite by accident, Jacob learned that it was an authentically holy worship site of Yahweh.[22] Since his argument presupposes these traditions, Hosea must assume that his audience also has some familiarity with them.

---

19. Holt, *Prophesying the Past*, 39.

20. Michael Goulder notes that "with the full Asaph psalmody, Davies could have cited Ps 50:5 for Israel as a people of חסד, and Ps 82 [vv. 2, 3] for God's demand for משפט" (*Psalms of Asaph*, 212).

21. Davies, *Hosea* (OTG), 72; cf. idem, *Hosea* (NCBC), 277–78. Cody makes a similar statement, writing that Hosea "condemns the calves of monarchical, non-Levitical Bethel (8:5f.; 10:5; 13:2), which he calls Beth-aven in pejorative contexts (4:15; 5:8; 10:5), but in 12:5 he hearkens back to the days of *ancient* Bethel, called now by its proper name" (*Priesthood*, 124).

22. Verse 5 confirms Hosea's view that Bethel was originally a true Yahweh shrine. Redaction may have inserted the verse to remove all ambiguity. See Holt, *Prophesying the Past*, 42.

The final words of 12:4 state that God spoke to Jacob at Bethel and also continued to speak there to Israel through the ongoing shrine at the site. Look closely at the verse. The actual Hebrew reads, "And there [שָׁם] he would speak [ongoing action] with us [עִמָּנוּ; first-person plural]."

Many English versions of 12:4 try to produce a smoother-sounding translation by emending the Masoretic, Hebrew text. They read "with him [Jacob]" instead of "with us" (e.g., NRSV, NAB, REB, NIV). It is better to retain the Hebrew meaning, however, since it is perfectly intelligible (cf. NJB; NASB).

Israelites did not tell stories about the origins of their shrines out of antiquarian interest. They preserved them because they were relevant for their own times. In the Israelite sanctuary traditions about the founding of Bethel (Bethel's *hieros logos*), Jacob represents and embodies the later people of Israel as a whole.

Hosea promotes the sanctuary tradition precisely because it had this ongoing relevance for all Israelites. Jacob's experiences are supposed to be formative for later Israel.[23] According to Davies, Hosea's basic argument is that "the Israel of his day (and indeed for a long time past) has failed to match the pattern of behavior that was prescribed in the traditions of their great ... shrine."[24]

Hosea's positive picture of Bethel's history in Hos 12:2–6 is remarkable. Elsewhere in the book, the prophet generally condemns the formerly holy site. He refers to it not by its proper name, Beth-el ("house of God"), but by a derisive Hebrew pun, "Beth-aven" ("house of wickedness"; Hos 4:15; 5:8; 10:5; cf. 10:8).

Hosea's call to the people to "return" in Hos 12:6 thus is a summons back to the true liturgical worship that once took place at Bethel, which preceded the cult that Hosea refers to as Beth-aven.[25]

Hosea associates this true worship at Bethel with prestate, premonarchic times. King Jeroboam I initiated the apostate, Beth-aven cult in establishing the northern kingdom as an independent state entity (1 Kgs 12:26–33; 13:33–34).

23. Davies, *Hosea* (OTG), 72–73; Holt, *Prophesying the Past*, 39.
24. Davies, *Hosea* (OTG), 72.
25. Holt, *Prophesying the Past*, 43, 46.

AN INSIDER CONFLICT OVER THE CONTEMPORARY CULT

HOSEA'S INSIDER KNOWLEDGE OF THE LEVITICAL ROLE

Hosea advocated Israel's traditional worship and descended genealogically from the priests originally in charge of that worship. Hosea knows far too many technical details about running a proper shrine in Israel to be a mere outside critic. He attacks the contemporary state priests of his time with the expertise of an insider at the shrines.

Hosea's assault on the priests of Jeroboam's state cult in Hos 4:4–11a best reveals his own priestly pedigree.

> [4] Yet let no one contend,
>> and let none accuse,
>> for with you is my contention, O priest.
> [5] You shall stumble by day;
>> the prophet also shall stumble with you by night,
>> and I will destroy your [kinfolk].
> [6] My people are destroyed for lack of knowledge;
>> because you have rejected knowledge,
>> I reject you from being a priest to me.
> And since you have forgotten the law of your God,
>> I also will forget your children.
> [7] The more they increased,
>> the more they sinned against me;
>> they changed their glory into shame.
> [8] They feed on the sin of my people;
>> they are greedy for their iniquity.
> [9] And it shall be like priest, like people;
>> I will punish them for their ways,
>> and repay them for their deeds.
> [10] They shall eat, but not be satisfied;
>> they shall play the whore, but not multiply;
> because they have forsaken the LORD
>> to devote themselves to[11] whoredom.

Hosea's confrontation with the priests of the state shrines occurs in the midst of a divine lawsuit against Israel for breach of the Sinai covenant. Because there is no covenant faithfulness or knowledge of God's covenantal stipulations (4:1–2), Israel is languishing (4:3). Since the Sinai covenant encompasses both the people and the land of Israel, the Israelites and nature itself suffer and mourn.

Hosea turns to Israel's priestly officials in 4:4, and puts the responsibility for this disaster squarely on their shoulders. Whereas Micah held the "heads" of society answerable for enforcing the covenant (Mic 3:1),

Hosea holds society's priests responsible (cf. also Hos 5:1).[26] His indictment is no generalized caricature but an expert, technical appraisal. The text voices the knowledge of a cultic insider in applying detailed criteria in evaluating the performance of Yahwistic priests. As Wolff argues, Hosea describes the guilt of the contemporary cult in terms of a detailed, alternative program of cultic service of God.[27]

Hosea's detailed criteria for proper ritual service of God differ sharply from the practices of the contemporary, state priesthood. According to Hosea's traditional norms, a proper priestly service would announce Yahweh's exclusive suzerainty over the land's fertility (4:10–11a). Further, a proper regulation of Israel's sacrifices would not increase the priest's material gain but rebuild the people's relationship with God. (Verse 8 indicates that the contemporary priests were interested in sacrificial offerings not as atonement for the people's sin but as a means for growing wealthy by seizing the offerings that the people brought.[28]) Above all, according to Hosea's criteria, true priests would faithfully instruct the people in the "knowledge" (דעת) of Yahweh's "torah" (תורה) stipulations (4:6).[29]

In detailing the priests' malpractice and their coming punishment by God, Hosea uses a striking amount of genealogical language. Verse 7 uses such language, for example, to describe the contemporary growth of the state priesthood. The priests have been very successful at reproduction, at proliferating their family line. As elsewhere in the book (Hos 8:11; 10:1; 13:6; cf. Deut 8:12–14), Hosea links this type of prosperity with the dangers of satiety and apostasy. The state priests have succumbed to these dangers.

The punishment that God will mete out to the priests because of their apostasy is also genealogical. In 4:5, God threatens to destroy their kinfolk

---

26. For the comparison of Hosea and Micah, see Beyerlin, *Kulttraditionen Israels*, 52–53. See also E. W. Nicholson, *Deuteronomy and Tradition* (Oxford: Basil Blackwell, 1967), 64. I adopt some such emendation of 4:4 as that in the NRSV. Cf. H. W. Wolff, *Hosea* (trans. G. Stansell; Hermeneia; Philadelphia: Fortress, 1974), 70 n. b; Mays, *Hosea*, 65 n. b.

27. Wolff, "Heimat," 245. Cf. Wilson, *Prophecy and Society*, 230, and Aelred Cody's statement: "Even though Hosea condemns wicked priests and exterior, formalized cult (4:4–14; 6:6; 8:11f.), he shows himself to be in favor of the kind of *da'at* and *mišpāṭ* and *tôrâ* characteristic of good priests by the very fact that he condemns priests for their failure to give them to the people (4:6; 5:11; 6:5f.; 8:12)" (*Priesthood*, 123–24).

28. Scholars have questioned whether Israel's traditional sacrifices aimed to atone for people's sins, but Hos 4:8; 8:11; and Mic 6:7 clearly presuppose that sacrifices were propitiatory. Cf. Bruce C. Birch, *Hosea, Joel, and Amos* (Westminster Bible Companion; Louisville: Westminster John Knox, 1997), 52.

29. Cf. Wolff, "Heimat," 244–46; idem, *Hosea*, 79, 81–82.

(reading אמה ["tribe," "people"] instead of אם ["mother"]).[30] In 4:6 God contemplates forgetting their descendants (בנים).

In these verses, Hosea clearly assumes the importance of lineage continuity among Yahweh's ritual functionaries. His threats against Israel's contemporary priests assume they should care about issues of patrilineal descent.

It is significant that Hosea stresses matters of lineage, and that he implies that his priestly adversaries in the state cult should take more of an interest in the topic. Hosea's assumptions about the importance of genealogical lineage in priesthood align him squarely with the traditional priests of a prestate society. We saw in chapter 6 that in dual-system societies, like that of Hosea's time, lineage-based priesthoods often place genealogical restrictions on their membership, whereas state-based priesthoods do not. Moreover, in nonstate societies, like that of Hosea's forebears, ritual specialists are often much more interested in genealogical matters than laypeople are.

There is no lineage requirement in the priestly lodges of urban Morocco, for example. The centralized society of the Moroccan cities and towns has devalued such genealogical concerns. In contrast, patrilineal descent virtually defines membership in the priestly lodges of Morocco's rural, tribal peoples.[31]

Because they organize their social life based on a segmentary genealogy, all traditional Berbers of the tribal areas of Morocco must know about their lineages. The priests are much more fastidious about this than the laypeople are, however. Berber laypeople generally have only enough knowledge about lineage to understand the competing genealogical segments of their society. The memory for genealogy of the Berber priests far transcends this practical knowledge. Berber priests keep track of many family ancestors, only a few of which define existing groups in Berber society.[32]

I noted in chapter 3 that the authors of the Psalms of Asaph were Levites, and we have now seen that Hosea had a special affinity for these psalms. This suggests, indirectly, that Hosea's specific priestly lineage was Levitical.

Over the years, on other grounds, various significant voices in biblical scholarship have argued precisely this theory. Bernard Duhm first

---

30. Wilhelm Rudolph, *Hosea* (KAT 13/1; Gutersloh: Mohn, 1966), 97; cf. Mays, *Hosea*, 66 n. c. Graham Davies discusses evidence supporting this emendation in cognates in Arabic and the Mari texts (*Hosea* [NCBC], 119).
31. Gellner, *Saints of the Atlas*, 8–9.
32. Ibid., 40.

advanced it in 1875. More scholars are familiar with it through the work of Hans Walter Wolff. In recent years, scholars such as Robert R. Wilson and Graham I. Davies have powerfully espoused it in various forms.

Duhm's early research found that Hosea "could himself have been one of the few Levitical priests who functioned in the northern kingdom and that precisely this experience would provide the most suitable background for Hosea's polemic."[33] Wolff revived this thesis in 1956, arguing more broadly that Hosea belonged to a disenfranchised, dissident circle of prophets and Levites that opposed the Israelite state and its official priesthood.

Wolff summarizes his view in his Hermeneia commentary: "Hosea presents a clear picture of the true priest in Israel, which was presumably kept alive in the Levitical circles of his own time (4:6; 6:6; 8:12). These circles probably had a close connection with the prophetic groups."[34]

Duhm and Wolff identified Hosea with peripheral Levites of the northern kingdom based on several lines of evidence. Wolff, for example, saw significant implications for Hosea's social identity in preceding scholarly work on the book of Deuteronomy. Deuteronomy is a later manifestation of Hosea's theological tradition, and scholars such as Adam Welch, Albrecht Alt, and Gerhard von Rad had traced this tradition to the northern kingdom and its Levitical circles.[35] In the passage at hand, Hosea's specific criteria for proper priestly service similarly point towards identifying Hosea with the Levites.

In 4:6 Hosea states bluntly that a lack of knowledge is what is destroying the Israelite people. Hosea's priestly adversaries bear the

---

33. Bernhard Duhm, *Die Theologie der Propheten als Grundlage für die innere Entwicklungsgeschichte der israelitischen Religion* (Bonn: Marcus, 1875), 130–31. I am quoting a translated citation of Duhm by Graham Davies (*Hosea* [OTG], 69).

34. Wolff, *Hosea*, xxii–xxiii; cf. pp. 79–81, 121–22, 144; idem, "Heimat," 243–50. As Blenkinsopp notes, "Wolff does not say that Hosea himself was a Levite, but, given his arguments, it is difficult to see how that possibility could be excluded" (*Prophecy*, 99).

35. Wolff, "Heimat," 248–49. Wolff provides the bibliography in nn. 64 and 65. Von Rad in particular connected Deuteronomy with the Levites. Wolff agrees, noting that Deuteronomy especially favors the Levites and gives them a new chance as re-enfranchised priests in Jerusalem. See also my bibliographic overviews and discussion in chapter 3. For additional brief sketches of this history of interpreting Deuteronomy, see S. Dean McBride Jr., "Deuteronomium," *TRE* 8:537; Konstantin Zobel, *Prophetie und Deuteronomium: Die Rezeption prophetischer Theologie durch das Deuteronomium* (BZAW 199; Berlin: de Gruyter, 1992), 4–6. I agree with Zobel (5 n. 17), against A. Alt ("Die Heimat des Deuteronomiums," in *Kleine Schriften zur Geschichte des Volkes Israel* [ed. M. Noth; 3 vols.; Munich: Beck, 1953], 2:271–74), that Deuteronomy was not composed in the northern kingdom. Composed in the south, it was merely influenced strongly by minority theological traditions of the north. Southern brands of Sinai tradition, including those of Micah, also fed its formation.

responsibility. They have "rejected knowledge" and "forgotten the torah." According to significant biblical cross-references, Levites in particular would apply this criterion in evaluating priestly performance.

Levites understood priesthood to center on responsibility for instructing the people. Priests teach the people the rules of the torah and their application in everyday life. Thus, Wolff is correct that in espousing torah instruction, Hosea sounds exactly like a Levite: It is clearly "Levitical groups whose key terms he takes up with, e.g., תורה ['torah'/'instruction'], משפט ['justice'], ברית ['covenant'], but above all, with the characteristic, comprehensive דעת אלהים ['knowledge of God']."[36]

For the strong innerbiblical link between the Levites and instruction in the covenant, see Deut 17:9–12, 18; 31:9, 25–26; 33:10; Jer 2:8; 2 Kgs 17:27–28; and Mal 2:6–7. S. Dean McBride Jr., who has researched the history of the Levites in detail, finds Deut 17:9–12 a key text showing their lineage particularly responsible for handing down, interpreting, and implementing covenantal law in Israel. He states, "Levitical competence in judicial affairs seems here to be associated with transmission and authoritative application of Mosaic law (*the law that they interpret*)."[37]

Similarly, with reference to Deut 33:9b–10 (Moses' blessing of Levi), which he dates to the eighth century, Aelred Cody states: "The text . . . is valuable for showing that the Levites were associated with fidelity to the Covenant, with the handing-down of customary laws and of instruction based on the Covenant."[38] One should also note that the literature of Chronicles portrays the Levites as teachers (2 Chr 15:3; 17:7–9; 19:8; 35:3; cf. Neh 8:7–8).

Hosea's Polemic against the Calf Images

Hosea's belligerence toward the calf images of official, northern worship is a further sign that he was a Levite. The calf images at the northern

---

36. Wolff, "Heimat," 246; cf. Cody, *Priesthood,* 123. See also Wolff, "Heimat," 249; idem, *Hosea,* 79–80; Mays, *Hosea,* 69; Robert B. Robinson, "The Levites in the Pre-Monarchic Period," *Studia Biblica et Theologica* 8 (1978): 20; Norman K. Gottwald, *The Tribes of Yahweh: A Sociology of the Religion of Liberated Israel 1250–1050 B.C.E.* (Maryknoll, N.Y.: Orbis, 1979), 320; S. Dean McBride Jr., "Deuteronomy: Introduction and Annotations," in *The HarperCollins Study Bible: New Revised Standard Version, with the Apocryphal/Deuterocanonical Books* (ed. W. Meeks; New York: HarperCollins, 1993), 268.

37. McBride, "Deuteronomy: Introduction and Annotations," 295.

38. Cody, *Priesthood,* 120. Cody's discussion on pp. 116–18 about the relationship between torah and priests is also helpful.

shrines of Dan and Bethel were a particularly heavy chip on the northern Levites' shoulders, their own "pet peeve."

King Jeroboam I, the first monarch of the northern kingdom, alienated the Levites from the old, tribal shrine at Bethel when he first set up those calves long before Hosea's time. I argued in chapter 6 for the essential historicity of Jeroboam's disenfranchisement of the Levites. The cross-cultural evidence showed that new sacral power, including new worship practices and new priests, are frequent forces helping a lineage-based society regroup as a centralized, monarchic state.

According to 1 Kgs 12:31–32, Jeroboam "made houses on high places, and appointed priests from among all the people, who were not Levites. Jeroboam ... offered sacrifices on the altar; so he did in Bethel, sacrificing to the calves that he had made. And he placed in Bethel the priests of the high places that he had made." We read further, in 2 Chr 11:14–15, that "Jeroboam and his sons ... prevented them [the Levites] from serving as priests of the LORD, and ... appointed his own priests for the high places, and for the goat-demons, and for the calves that he had made."

In 2 Chr 13:9, a prophet directly confronts Jeroboam about his dismissal of the Levites: "Have you not driven out the priests of the LORD, the ... Levites, and made priests for yourselves like the peoples of other lands? Whoever comes to be consecrated with a young bull or seven rams becomes a priest of what are no gods."

We looked closely at the anticalf polemic of Hos 8:1–7 and 13:1–3 in chapter 4.[39] Hosea does not accept the monarchy's line that the calf image of the Bethel shrine was a mere pedestal for Yahweh. In actual practice, the people are venerating the image itself. They even have a ritual of physically kissing the calf (Hos 13:2; cf. 1 Kgs 19:18).

Hosea's objection to their homage is clear. He lumps kings and calves together as false stand-ins for God (Hos 8:4–5). He calls the calf image an "idol" (עצב; Hos 13:2). And, he makes arguments to convince his audience that "It is not a god" (Hos 8:6).

Some in Hosea's audience saw the calf as an icon of Yahweh, worthy of homage. Others went farther astray, understanding the calf as a Canaanite god of power and fertility. The Hebrew term "calf" can also mean "young bull." In Canaanite tradition, "bull" was a title of the high-god, El ("Bull El"). It was also the roaring thundercloud upon which the fertility god, Hadad/Baal, rode.

---

39. I did not have a chance to examine the similar polemic of Hos 10:1–8.

Jeroboam doubtless took advantage of the ambiguity of the bull symbol when he used it in his new, state shrines. He could pass the image off to worshipers of Yahweh as a pedestal or throne platform. At the same time, he knew that using the symbol of the bull in state worship would help integrate the Canaanite population remaining in the land into his new, northern kingdom.

In chapter 4 we uncovered the dependence of Hosea's calf polemic on Sinai language and tradition. His charge that the calf images are "the work of artisans" (Hos 8:6; 13:2), for example, uses a characteristic idiom of Sinai texts (e.g., Deut 27:15; Jer 10:3, 9). I did not yet push behind Hosea's theology to its social roots in that discussion and would like to do so now.

A bit of detective work reveals Hosea's specific posture. It confirms his connection with the old, prestate Levitical lineage of priests. In the same breath that he mocks the "calf of Beth-aven," Hosea speaks of the calf's priests as illicit "idolatrous priests" (כמרים; Hos 10:5), a Hebrew term of opprobrium.

Hosea's choice of this derogatory term for priests is no accident. It depicts Jeroboam's cultic renovation of Bethel as a unique double apostasy. For Hosea, the flipside of Jeroboam's setting up the calf at Bethel was his alienating of the Levites, the authentic priestly lineage of the shrine (1 Kgs 12:31–32). Hosea sees the calf at Bethel as a symbol of Levitical exclusion. His complaint against the Bethel calf is not merely a general problem with icons and idols but the specific battle cry of a Levite.

What is more, Hosea sounds just like the Levites of Deuteronomy in his general orientation in attacking the northern calves. His program to rid northern worship of them is an obvious, immediate precursor of Deuteronomy's theological position. Deuteronomy upholds a worship of Yahweh specifically oriented toward Sinai theology, intolerant of fertility gods (such as bull deities), based on an abhorrence of images and icons, and opposed to monarchic involvement in liturgy. *Levites*, not puppets of the monarchy, administer such worship. Aelred Cody gives a cogent summary of the Levitical ideal:

> The Levites in the period of the divided monarchy had particular reason to oppose the [calf] cult in Bethel because priests of their tribe were excluded from it, but they had more idealistic reasons for opposing it, too. Conservative, attached to the old-style Yahwism and its traditional sacral institutions, they were opposed to what seemed in their eyes ... to be the idolatrous air of infidelity surrounding the worship at Bethel, and they were proud to contrast this with their own fidelity to what they thought was the purer Yahwism of olden times.... The Deuteronomic antithesis is perceptible here: on the one hand ... Levitical priests, and

fidelity to covenant law; on the other, sanctuaries like Bethel..., priests who were not Levites, and infidelity to covenant law (by making images, for example).[40]

Hosea and Exodus 32

Hosea's calf attacks are the polemics of a Levite. The evidence goes beyond the similarity of the attacks to the Levitical ideal of worship in Deuteronomy. There is a narrative in the Pentateuch—in Exodus—that mirrors Hosea's stance and overtly identifies its partisans. This remarkable story confirms Hosea's calf battle to be a skirmish in a larger, Levite-sponsored war. The text is Exod 32, the well-known story of the golden calf.[41]

The story concerns an outrageous sin in the wilderness at the foot of Mount Sinai, after the escape from Egypt under Moses. Its narrators, who live much later than the narrative setting of the episode, look back to memories of the wilderness period partly to support their current struggles. They tell the story in Exod 32, updated in not-so-subtle ways, as part of their own contemporary war of words. They believe themselves involved in a priestly conflict that will surely result in disaster for some priests and triumph for others, just as in Exodus.

Like the polemic of Hosea, Exod 32 attacks calf worship. Indeed, the passage condemns more than the singular incident of calf worship at Moses' time, as a look at the text itself shows. Let us begin with 32:1–8:

When the people saw that Moses delayed to come down from the mountain, the people gathered around Aaron, and said to him, "Come, make gods for us, who shall go before us; as for this Moses, the man who brought us up out of the land of Egypt, we do not know what has become of him." Aaron said to them, "Take off the gold rings that are on the ears of your wives, your sons, and your daughters, and bring them to me." So all the people took off the gold rings from their ears, and brought them to Aaron. He took the gold from them, formed it in a mold, and cast an image of a calf; and they said, "These are your gods, O Israel, who

---

40. Cody, *Priesthood*, 155. Cody is writing specifically about Exod 32:25–29. I shall turn to this text shortly.

41. For previous treatments of Exod 32 and its polemic against the monarchic cult at Bethel, see: Wolff, "Heimat," 244–45; Cody, *Priesthood*, 146–56; Frank Moore Cross, *Canaanite Myth and Hebrew Epic: Essays in the History of the Religion of Israel* (Cambridge: Harvard University Press, 1973), 73–75, 198–200; Alan W. Jenks, *The Elohist and North Israelite Traditions* (SBLMS 22; Missoula, Mont.: Scholars Press, 1977), 50–52; Friedman, *Who Wrote the Bible*, 70–74.

brought you up out of the land of Egypt!" When Aaron saw this, he built an altar before it; and Aaron made proclamation and said, "Tomorrow shall be a holiday to Yahweh." They rose early the next day, and offered burnt offerings and brought sacrifices of well-being; and the people sat down to eat and drink, and rose up to revel. The LORD said to Moses, "Go down at once! Your people, whom you brought up out of the land of Egypt, have acted perversely; they have been quick to turn aside from the way that I commanded them; they have cast for themselves an image of a calf, and have worshiped it and sacrificed to it.

Source critics identify most of Exod 32 as part of the E strand,[42] dating to the ninth century, after Jeroboam's cultic innovations. Its writers advocated the same Sinai traditions that made those innovations so repugnant to Hosea. Given these facts, it is doubtful that Exod 32 could speak of a "golden calf" without burning with anger over what had become of the worship at Bethel.

Indeed, the Exodus passage shares specific polemical features with Hosea that demonstrate their common focus on the aberrant, state-sponsored worship at Bethel.

Exodus 32 speaks of the bull image as a "calf" (עגל). The term is a diminutive name, meaning a small, young bull. This seems less a neutral rehearsal of history than an insulting jab at contemporary (post-Jeroboam) bull worship. Not surprisingly, Hosea uses the same Hebrew term (see 8:5–6; 10:5; and 13:2). Hosea and E apparently both invoke a shared, pejorative nickname to slur Bethel's bull image. Psalm 106:20 reveals that a more dignified term for the image was available, שׁוֹר ("bull," "ox"). The Ugaritic texts proudly use this term to speak of their high god, "Bull El" (ṯr ʾil). Ezekiel 1:10 actually approves of the term as a description of the cherubim supporting Yahweh's divine throne.

Like Hosea, Exod 32 heaps disapproval on official state priests. Following King Solomon's elevation of Aaron's priestly line at the Jerusalem temple, the traditional figure of Aaron symbolized Israel's central, power-holding priests. Aaron's disgrace in the golden-calf episode thus

---

42. The passage forms a logical sequel to E's account of the ratification of the covenant atop the holy mountain in Exod 24:1–15a, 18b. Further, Joshua has the role of Moses' special assistant (32:17–18), just as he has in Exod 17:8–16; 24:13; and 33:11 (all E). Again, the narrative prefers the divine name "Elohim" over that of "Yahweh" at points such as 32:16. Moreover, the passage shares phraseology with other E texts at places such as 32:7 (cf. Exod 3:10). Finally, the passage uses unusual words, such as the Hebrew term translated "losers" (32:18), as is E's style. For discussion, see S. R. Driver, *An Introduction to the Literature of the Old Testament* (New York: Scribner's, 1910), 126; Aage Bentzen, *Introduction to the Old Testament* (2 vols.; 4th ed.; Copenhagen: Gad, 1958), 2:30; Jenks, *Elohist*, 50.

casts a dark shadow over monarchical priests in general.[43] Hosea and Exod 32 join in spurning Aaron and his ilk, while sparing other authority figures any overt criticism. They share a common affinity for Moses and similar leaders of traditional theological integrity (Exod 32:11, 19, 21, 26; Hos 12:13–14).

Both Hos 13:4 (cf. Asaphite Ps 81:10) and Exod 32 emphasize that Yahweh alone is Israel's God, who brought the people up from Egypt. This is a lesson that their contemporary, monarchic-period audiences needed to learn. Verse 4 of the E narrative makes the point indirectly, by putting the diametrically opposite claim in the mouths of the aberrant calf worshippers. E's relevant lesson is clear. Only foolish, apostate idolaters would proclaim to Israel that Jeroboam's calf image of Bethel "brought you up from the land of Egypt."

The people's pronouncement about the calf's saving accomplishments in Exod 32:4 is odd. Since they made the calf long after the events of the exodus, would they really have made claims for the newly forged calf with these particular words? The words make better sense as a subtle attack on Jeroboam's speech inaugurating Bethel's new cult program.

After making his two golden calves, Jeroboam proclaims, "It is too much for you to go up to Jerusalem [at festival time]; behold your gods, O Israel, that brought you up from the land of Egypt" (1 Kgs 12:28). The quotes in Exod 32 and 1 Kgs 12 are identical; their connection must be intentional. The narrators of Exod 32 are specifically lambasting Jeroboam's state-based cultic program.

Exodus 32:4 repays even closer scrutiny. Aaron and the people have forged one golden calf, yet in this verse they turn to it and proclaim "*these* (אלה) are your gods," "*they* brought you up" (העלוך). The Hebrew speaks of the image in the plural. The NRSV renders the people's words correctly; yet, these words do not make sense in the context of the exodus from Egypt. We can only understand them as E's direct quote of Jeroboam's words, which he pronounced in setting up two calves—one at Dan and one at Bethel.[44]

---

43. I am following Wolff, "Heimat," 245. One should not overinterpret Exod 32. It need not imply that actual descendants of Aaron ministered at Bethel. Jeroboam's ritual functionaries apparently had no priestly blood at all. The improbable idea that the priests of Bethel were Aaronides goes back at least to H. Oort, "Die Aäroniden," *ThT* 18 (1884): 289–335. Also see R. H. Kennett, "The Origin of the Aaronite Priesthood," *JTS* 6 (1905): 161–86; Francis S. North, "Aaron's Rise in Prestige," *ZAW* 66 (1954): 191–99; S. Lehming, "Versuch zu Ex. XXXII," *VT* 10 (1960): 16–50; Cross, *Canaanite Myth and Hebrew Epic*, 73–74, 198–99.

44. It is legitimate to wonder whether the quotation of Jeroboam's words in 1 Kgs 12 would really have been known to the first readers of the E narrative. Advanced readers will

Fascinatingly, Hosea shares this literary technique of E. Hosea focuses on the one calf image at Bethel: the Assyrian army probably destroyed the other calf shrine at Dan early in Hosea's career. However, Hosea refers to Bethel's calf in the plural (as "calves") at Hos 10:5 and 13:2 as well as possibly at 8:5. Like E, he must be thinking of Jeroboam's original installation of two calf images in Israel.

It is no doubt easier to understand Hosea's straightforward, prophetic attack on Jeroboam's state cult than to appreciate the indirect, narrative-based polemic of the E story. The evidence that Exod 32 has the same polemical intent as Hosea is unassailable, however. Richard Elliott Friedman sums up this evidence in a literary tour de force:

> Why does Aaron say "A holiday to *Yahweh* tomorrow" when he is presenting the calf as a rival to Yahweh? Because the calf is not in fact a rival god. The calf, or young bull, is only the throne platform or symbol of the deity, not a deity itself. Why is the calf *treated* as a god in the story? Presumably because the story is polemical; the writer means to cast the golden calves of the kingdom of Israel in the worst light possible.... Why do the people say *"These* are your gods, Israel..." when there is only one calf? Why do they say "... that brought you up from the land of Egypt" when the calf was not made until they were out of Egypt? The answer seems to lie in the account of King Jeroboam in the book of 1 Kings. It states there that when Jeroboam made his two golden calves he declared to his people, "Here are your gods, Israel, that brought you up from the land of Egypt."[45]

There is a social-scientific payoff for the time I have invested in showing that Hosea and Exod 32 fight the same battle. Exodus 32 practically identifies the battle's partisans, confirming Hosea's social identity.

These partisans are major protagonists in the narrative along with Moses. Verses 25–29 read:

> When Moses saw that the people were running wild (for Aaron had let them run wild, to the derision of their enemies), then Moses stood in the gate of the camp, and said, "Who is on the LORD's side? Come to me!" And all the sons of Levi gathered around him. He said to them, "Thus says the LORD, the God of Israel, 'Put your sword on your side, each of

---

remember that the work of history writing of which 1 Kgs 12 forms a part probably dates two centuries after E. Obviously, my argument assumes that 1 Kgs 12:28 preserves a traditional pronouncement of Jeroboam, which would already have been familiar to E's readers. The separate writers of Exod 32 and 1 Kgs 12 must both be referencing well-known words of Jeroboam, which he pronounced in inaugurating the new, state-based worship at Bethel.

45. Friedman, *Who Wrote the Bible*, 72–73.

you! Go back and forth from gate to gate throughout the camp, and each of you kill your brother, your friend, and your neighbor.' " The sons of Levi did as Moses commanded, and about three thousand of the people fell on that day. Moses said, "Today you have ordained yourselves for the service of the LORD, each one at the cost of a son or a brother, and so have brought a blessing on yourselves this day."

Just as the Levites are the heroes of the story, Hosea and the authors of Exod 32 are Levites. Part of their goal in telling the story of the golden calf is to commend themselves to their contemporary audience. Their claim is that the Levites were faithful to the Sinai covenant from the time of the Sinai experience itself. They stood by Moses in defending it, and followed his orders even though it meant turning against their own kinfolk (cf. Deut 33:8–10, Moses' blessing of Levi). They are Israel's legitimate priestly lineage. Their ordination traces all the way back to their faithful service during the wilderness period.

It is impossible to prove that the Levites were the actual allies of a historical Moses at the foot of Mount Sinai. Social-scientific evidence corroborates their reaction to Jeroboam's use of new sacral images at Bethel, however. This reaction fits a typical pattern of response to new, centralizing practices of worship in society, which I outlined in chapter 6.

Monarchic social systems try to concentrate ritual potency in new, central worship symbols. Traditional priests decry this development, and try to turn back the clock to a time when lineage-based priests received deference in matters of worship. Levites such as Hosea were naturally inclined to repristinate the past, since their lifestyle and their Sinai theology belonged to an outmoded way of life.

It is not surprising that an image of the bull—a symbol cross-culturally of virility, the roaring thundercloud, rain, and fertility—should be at the center of a conflict between traditional and monarchic priesthoods. As kingship arises in an agrarian society, a primary goal of new, centralized worship is often to alleviate insecurity and anxiety around farming and fertility. In the face of concerns over a variable climate and the advent of new capital for land-grabbing, an agrarian populace may willingly abandon a familiar lineage of priests to embrace centrally administered clerics. As the anthropologist Robert Netting states, "In these circumstances, a claim to control the rains or promote fertility with annual ceremonies may take on an impressiveness and power to convince."[46]

---

46. Robert McC. Netting, "Sacred Power and Centralization: Aspects of Political Adaptation in Africa," in *Population Growth* (ed. B. J. Spooner; Cambridge: Massachusetts Institute of Technology, 1972), 236.

Priestly Struggle and Physical Violence

We have now seen some clear evidence of polemical warfare between the Levites and state priests of Hosea's time. Further evidence in Hosea shows the battles in this war went beyond verbal disputes. The war of words sometimes turned violent.

One text in Hosea that speaks of violence against Hosea and the Levites is Hos 9:7b–9. The passage reads:

> [7b] Israel cries,
> "The prophet is a fool,
>   the man of the spirit is mad!"
> Because of your great iniquity,
>   your hostility is great.
> [8] The prophet is a sentinel for my God over Ephraim,
> yet a fowler's snare is on all his ways,
>   and hostility in the house of his God.
> [9] They have deeply corrupted themselves
>   as in the days of Gibeah;
> he will remember their iniquity,
>   he will punish their sins.

The scene behind this text is a verbal dispute between Hosea and his audience. The occasion requires Hosea to defend his prophetic predecessors and himself. He argues that he and his forebears are like city watch-keepers, warning the people on God's behalf of approaching judgment (9:8; cf. Hos 5:8; 8:1; Jer 6:17). The shouts of his audience, who declare all prophets to be fools and lunatics (9:7), provoke the defensive reply.

As H. W. Wolff writes, "Hosea's forerunners allowed persecutors to target them as imbecilic blatherers.... Public opinion in the northern kingdom held the prophets to be muddle headed."[47] From Hosea's response, we see that their contempt included violent hostility.

Hosea's description of the obstacles confronting him and his prophetic group illuminates the violence of his contemporary social scene. Twice he accuses his hearers of "hostility," "persecution" (מַשְׂטֵמָה, 9:7b, 8). In the tradition of Elijah's opponents, their drive to muzzle Hosea's circle poses a deadly threat (1 Kgs 19:10, 14).

Fascinatingly, Hosea claims that his circle encounters this hostility specifically in the "house of God" (9:8). Conceivably, "house of God" simply refers to the whole land of Israel as H. W. Wolff suggests.[48] In

---

47. Wolff, "Heimat," 237; cf. Davies, *Hosea* (NCBC), 221.
48. Wolff, "Heimat," 238; cf. Mays, *Hosea*, 131.

light of the ongoing struggle of the Levites with official priestly opponents, however, a reference to an actual shrine—such as the Bethel
shrine—is just as likely. Verse 4 uses the phrase "house of Yahweh" in
just this way.

Hosea and the Levites must have returned to their old shrine periodically to complain and to prophesy. Doubtless, they encountered
persecution on these occasions from the new occupants of their old posts.
It may be due to the contemporary syncretistic and Canaanite worship at
the Bethel shrine that Hosea emphasizes that, originally and authentically, Bethel is "the house of *his* God."[49]

In 9:9, Hosea cryptically compares his present experience of persecution to old, corrupt days "of Gibeah." I have noted previously that
Hosea's references to Gibeah (cf. 10:9) are ambiguous. Since Gibeah was
the headquarters of Saul's monarchy (1 Sam 10:26; 11:4; 15:34–35), he may
in part intend his mentions of Gibeah to allude to Israel's ill-advised
embrace of kingship. Another powerful association of Gibeah seems
more relevant in the present context, however. We know from Judg 19
that Gibeah was the ancient scene of a gross and cruel attack against a
Levite's family. The brunt of the attack fell particularly on the Levite's
concubine, who was raped and killed.

In dredging up the disturbing story of the horrific abuse of a Levite's
concubine (the story of Judg 19), Hosea again points us toward the social
identity of his support circle. Wolff writes, "The allusion here is not to the
Saul narrative but to the Benjaminite scandal of Gibeah, a misdeed that
had befallen a roving Levite. The allusion is well made merely for that
reason, because that Levite suffered the same brutal public attack that the
prophets [of Hosea's circle] also experience."[50]

Hosea's inner circle consists of his Levitical kinfolk. Alienated to the
periphery of state society, this circle now shares the same hard lot of their
ancient, roving ancestor and his concubine.

A second passage in Hosea provides further information about the
violent persecution suffered by Hosea's Levitical support group. Hosea
6:7–10 reads:

---

49. Davies states, "Those commentators (e.g., Wolff, Rudolph, Mays) who find such a
designation ['the house of his God'] for the corrupt sanctuary impossible on Hosea's lips
miss the point: it is clear (cf. 8:2; 9:4) that worship had not ceased to be offered to Yahweh in
the sanctuaries, and so Hosea could if it suited him (as here) use **his God's** traditional claims
to reinforce his accusation" (*Hosea* [NCBC], 222). Cf. also the comments of James M. Ward,
Hosea: A Theological Commentary (New York: Harper & Row, 1966), 166.

50. Wolff, "Heimat," 246; cf. Davies, *Hosea* (NCBC), 223.

> [7] But at Adam they transgressed the covenant;
>   there they dealt faithlessly with me.
> [8] Gilead is a city of evildoers,
>   tracked with blood.
> [9] As robbers lie in wait for someone,
>   so the priests are banded together;
> they murder on the road to Shechem,
>   they commit a monstrous crime.
> [10] In the house of Israel I have seen a horrible thing;
>   Ephraim's whoredom is there, Israel is defiled.

The passage is a veritable catalog of treachery, which decries several incidents of transgression by Israel. It is hard, however, to pin down the specifics of these incidents. The reference to faithlessness at "Adam" in 6:7, for example, could refer either to apostasy far back in the Judges period or to some very recent act of political intrigue (see ch. 4).

The incident of murder on the road to Shechem (6:9) is equally opaque. It clearly has to do with priestly violence, however, so it is worth our while to probe for more insight on Hosea's social background.

Enough details appear in 6:9 to reconstruct a probable scenario as to what went on near Shechem. Note the verse's exact wording. Its indictment is not against the city of Shechem itself.[51] In fact, nowhere in his prophecy does Hosea attack the city. Far from being critical, Hosea sides with those whom the city attracts, the victims of ambush "on the road to Shechem."

Hosea's support of Shechem likely relates to the traditional ties of the site with the Sinai covenant (Deut 27; Josh 8:30–35; Josh 24). These ties extend far back into Israel's premonarchic era.

Might the victimized travelers to Shechem be proponents of Sinai traditions and rituals that persist there? If so, they may be Hosea's own colleagues and Levitical kinfolk. Joshua 21:21 lists Shechem as a Levitical city.

The strange claim that "a band of priests" perpetrates the violence near Shechem now becomes intelligible. Elsewhere in Hosea, the opponents of Sinai traditions, like those of Shechem, are the official state priests of the monarchic shrines.

The implications are clear. Verse 9 likely reflects the hostility of state priests toward Hosea's circle that we saw in Hos 9:8. Here, however, the persecution has expanded beyond the state shrines to the home territory of Levitical opposition itself. State priests "lie in wait" for Shechem's Levites.

---

51. Contrast, e.g., Nicholson, *Deuteronomy and Tradition*, 63, 74.

H. W. Wolff first proposed this interpretation.[52] He saw in Hos 6:7–10 an incident of brutal assault against the Levitical opposition party at its own home base.

A fascinating example from the cross-cultural evidence illuminates the violence between priestly groups of Hosea's time (Hos 6:9; 9:8). Mirroring Hosea's circumstances, a peripheral lodge of priests among the Moroccan Berbers came into conflict with their tribe's main priestly lodge around the turn of the twentieth century.[53]

The conflict began when the main lodge broke a long-standing agreement that Berber priests would not indulge in dancing. The priests of the less powerful Temga lodge strongly objected.

Priestly ideology in Berber society precludes violence. Like the ritual functionaries of other traditional societies, Berber priests are supposed to be peacemakers and guardians of sacred refuges. Nevertheless, priestly rivalry erupted into a violent feud at this point in Berber history. The *igurramen* actually fought each other physically in a miniature war, "The War of the Dance." Beyond polemics, the violence of the "war" resulted in casualties. Informants reported to ethnographers that at least seven priests died in the conflict.

Unlike Hosea's conflict, the "War of the Dance" took place between authentic priestly lineages within a purely segmentary society. If priestly violence is possible in this social setting, however, a violent feud between priests is all the more conceivable in Hosea's setting. In such a milieu with competing social systems, one priestly house can attack another without killing close relatives, cousins, and brothers. The violent state-based priests of Hosea's time were not the immediate kinfolk of their enemies within Hosea's lineage-based priestly circle.

HOSEA'S ROOTS IN A VILLAGE-ERA, LINEAGE-BASED PRIESTHOOD

SHECHEM AS A PREMONARCHIC SITE OF COVENANT RITUAL

Study of Hos 6:9 has suggested that Hosea and the Levites had a base of opposition at Shechem, doubtless based on the venerable role of

---

52. Wolff, "Heimat," 249 n. 70; cf. idem, *Hosea*, 122; Davies, *Hosea* (NCBC), 174–76. James Mays echoes Wolff: "Perhaps after the establishment of Jeroboam's state cult it [Shechem] continued to be a threatening competitor to the official shrines at Bethel and Dan, a hotbed of religious dissent against the state's cultic programme. Did the priests of the state cult go to the length of plotting for pilgrims to Shechem to be waylaid?" (*Hosea*, 101).

53. Gellner, *Saints of the Atlas*, 147, 248–49.

Shechem in biblical history and tradition. Shechem had ancient, prestate associations with the Sinai covenant and its liturgical celebration and renewal. According to the biblical books of Joshua and Judges, the Israelites worshiped and sacrificed at Shechem (Josh 24) before moving the ark of the covenant to locations such as Bethel (Judg 20:18, 26–28).

According to Josh 24, Joshua gathered the tribes of Israel to Shechem to renew the Sinai covenant at the end of the conquest of the land. He had rehearsed the covenant there before, according to Josh 8:30–35. At Shechem, the Levites had assisted him in sacrificing burnt offerings to Yahweh and reciting the covenant before the Israelites set out to accomplish the bulk of the conquest. The ceremony was in obedience to a command of Moses, which Deut 11 now records.

According to Deut 11:29–30, Moses ordered the people to recite the blessings and curses of the Sinai covenant at Mounts Ebal and Gerizim, near Shechem. This would properly begin their conquest of the land. Deuteronomy 27 elaborates on the procedure. As in Josh 8, the text puts special emphasis on the role of Levites. Verse 14 describes them as the special leaders of Shechem's covenant renewal ceremonies.

Deuteronomy and Joshua are recounting events of the conquest and settlement period, but a tradition of periodic covenant ceremonies at Shechem probably influenced their accounts.[54] The compilers and editors of Deuteronomy and Joshua aimed to centralize Israel's worship in the southern capital, Jerusalem. Only a strong traditional association of Shechem with covenant renewal ceremonies would have moved them to lend a northern site such prominence.

Joshua 24:26 confirms this inference. The verse speaks of Joshua preserving a copy of the covenant at a sanctuary at Shechem. Presumably, this was for ongoing liturgical use at the site.

For a time at least, regular covenant ceremonies must have occurred at the shrine of Shechem. It may have been the preeminent shrine of several Israelite kin groups, before their focus shifted to worship at Bethel and Shiloh. The emphasis on Levites in Deut 27:9, 14 and Josh 8:33 is significant. It suggests that in early times they were the priests of Shechem, or at least were strongly influential there.[55] Jeroboam expelled the Levites from Bethel, but they probably felt safe at their old base of Shechem.

---

54. Adam C. Welch, *The Code of Deuteronomy: A New Theory of Its Origin* (London: Clarke, 1924), 183–85; Gerhard von Rad, *Studies in Deuteronomy* (trans. D. Stalker; SBT 9; Chicago: Regnery, 1953), 41, 68; idem, *Deuteronomy* (trans. D. Barton; OTL; Philadelphia: Westminster, 1966), 26, 86, 166–67; Martin Noth, *The History of Israel* (2d ed.; New York: Harper & Row, 1960), 91–93; Nicholson, *Deuteronomy and Tradition*, 60–61; Cody, *Priesthood*, 51 n. 49, 127; Sparks, *Ethnicity and Identity*, 157.

55. Cody, *Priesthood*, 51 n. 49, 127.

Earlier biblical texts confirm Shechem's ancient associations with covenant-based worship. Take verse 2 of Asaphite Ps 76, for example, and its reference to "Salem." "Salem" is the name of a town and valley in Shechem's vicinity.[56] If this is the locale at issue, Ps 76 contains a pre-Deuteronomic reference to the area of Shechem as a site of old Israelite tribal ritual.

Editing within Hezekiah's and Josiah's reform movements has obscured the evidence of Ps 76 by giving verse 2 a Judean coloring. In its current, Judean form, "Salem" is a parallel term to "Zion" in 76:2 and clearly signifies "(Jeru)salem." Since "Zion" is presumably a secondary addition to an originally northern psalm, however, the name "Salem" at first must have signified not Jerusalem but Shechem. (Northern psalms do not celebrate the southern capital.)

An intriguing dual reference to Salem and Shechem in the E strand adds weight to this reconstruction of the original form of Ps 76. Though the major English versions obscure the fact, Gen 33:18 (E) can be translated: "And Jacob came to Salem, the city of Shechem."[57] This translation requires no emendation of the Hebrew. It is a live alternative to the more usual rendering, "Jacob came *safely* to the city of Shechem." ("Safely" and "Salem" are homonyms in Hebrew.)

Whether or not Ps 76:2 originally spoke of Shechem, the E source in Gen 33:18–20 manifestly does, and it confirms the fact of traditional tribal worship at a shrine there. The E narrative in Gen 33 describes Jacob, the ancestor of the Israelites, traveling to Shechem and founding a place of worship there.

A minimal conclusion is this: Gen 33:18–20, probably along with Ps 76:2, corroborates the memories of later Deuteronomistic texts in Joshua and Deuteronomy about an early Israelite shrine at Shechem. Shechem was an ancient, premonarchic worship site of Yahweh, where Levites and Sinai theology held sway. Via Hos 6:9, we have arrived at one key social root of Hosea and his biblical Yahwism.

The episode about Jacob in E states that upon arriving at Shechem, the ancestor erected a sacrificial altar to God. Psalm 76:2 also speaks of an ancient sacral institution at Shechem, namely a priestly "tabernacle" (סֻכּוֹ). Service at the priestly institutions of altar and tent shrine must originally have been a major part of the cultic-ritualistic duties of the Levites at Shechem.

---

56. See the lengthy excursus on Salem in Goulder, *Psalms of Asaph*, 86–88. Cf. Jdt 4:4; John 3:23.

57. See the interpretation of Gen 33:18 in *Jub.* 30:1. I am relying here on Goulder, *Psalms of Asaph*, 86–87.

We do not know whether Hosea and the Levites actually kept Shechem's priestly institutions functioning in the eighth century. It seems safer to suppose that the circle maintained a nonsacrificial, dissident community of worship there. Kenton Sparks correctly recognizes that Hosea's group may have worked to preserve covenantal themes without performing large-scale, covenantal ceremonies. He states, "One does not need a working covenant renewal ceremony to have a covenant idea. One needs only a tradition about covenant."[58]

The Hosea community at Shechem persisted despite official opposition, even welcoming pilgrims. They doubtless hoped some day to elevate Shechem to its former, premonarchic status as a tribal site of sacrifice and covenant instruction. Meanwhile, they probably worked on producing poetic worship materials, such as new Asaph psalms.

TURNING BACK THE CLOCK TO PRESTATE WORSHIP

Another direct reference to the prestate social roots of Hosea's Sinai theology occurs in Hos 12:7–10. The passage is a prophetic announcement of judgment, in which God threatens to forcibly reverse the course of Israel's history. The text reads:

[7] A trader, in whose hands are false balances,
    he loves to oppress.
[8] Ephraim has said, "Ah, I am rich,
    I have gained wealth for myself;
in all of my gain
    no offense has been found in me
    that would be sin."
[9] I am the LORD your God
    from the land of Egypt;
I will make you live in tents again,
    as in the days of the מוֹעֵד ["assembly," see below].
[10] I spoke to the prophets;
    it was I who multiplied visions,
    and through the prophets I will bring destruction.

The passage views Israel's social and economic development not as progress but as degeneration. The prophet decries—not celebrates—the economic and political prosperity that societal change and centralization has brought. In his view, Israel's societal centralization and new wealth

---

58. Sparks, *Ethnicity and Identity*, 157.

has led only to satiety, covenant apostasy, and oppression of the poor. As a result, God is determined to undo this degeneration by destroying Israel's state system and returning the people to a bygone era, to the "tents again" (12:9). God and Hosea want to turn back the clock (cf. Hos 2:14).[59]

Whether this text preserves authentic memories of presettlement "wanderings" of the Israelites is hard to know. What is safe to say is that it recollects the semisedentary, "pioneer" lifestyle of the early Israelites that I sketched in chapter 6. What is more, it associates an institution of the Sinai covenant with that old lifestyle. The days of the tents were also the days of the מועד ("assembly," 12:9).

Hosea is not romanticizing the wilderness or Israel's village era. He is no champion of nomadic ideals. Rather, he is advocating a sacral institution that happens to have traditional ties to the social forms of preurban, precentralization times. His assumption is that repristination of an earlier era in Israel will recreate conditions amenable to this Sinai institution.

Hosea, like Micah, highlights the Sinai institution of the covenant assembly. Both refer to the institution using the elusive, ancient term, מועד ("assembly," 12:9). For both Micah and Hosea, the term refers to some aspect, mode, or representative element of the comprehensive covenant congregation of Israel. Hosea is not an elder, and does not likely refer to the specific elders' institution with which Micah was familiar. In his case, a priestly mode or manifestation of the assembly would be much more appropriate.

As a Levite, Hosea's focus is liturgy and cultic worship. In a cultic-liturgical mode of operation, the covenant assembly would bring to the fore such ancient instruments or institutions as altars, tabernacles, and festivals. With the term "assembly," Hosea must refer to one of two such instruments. He may mean the priestly tabernacle—the אהל מועד, as in Exod 28:43. More likely, the NRSV is right that Hosea expects God to resurrect Israel's old-style "appointed festival." Hosea recalls that in old Israel, the people experienced immediate encounters with God at periodic *festal assemblies* of the tribes. God will encounter Israel anew in this way.

In either case, Hosea's covenant assembly does not convene under the jurisdiction of elders as it does in Micah's memory. It does not meet for purposes such as land distribution, organization for war, or deliberation over intertribal disputes. Rather, it convenes in an alternate mode, for sacrificial worship. In this mode, the assembly is under the jurisdiction of Levitical priests.

---

59. Wolff, "Heimat," 239.

Taking Hosea's term "assembly" (מועד) as the priestly tabernacle would fit nicely with the reference to a tabernacle at Shechem in Asaphite Ps 76:2 (see the discussion above). The idea of a festal assembly, however, fits in better with Hosea's references to sacred festivals elsewhere in the book. (The term מועד occurs in both Hos 2:11 and 9:5.) This interpretation is also in keeping with the cross-cultural evidence, in which traditional priests preside over the collective sacrificial gatherings of segmentary societies. Sometimes tribal peoples send delegates to a major, collective festival held annually or periodically at a single location. At other times, coordinated local ritual ceremonies count as a tribes-wide assembly.

A reference to the Feast of Booths is especially likely at Hos 12:9. The rituals of this festival in particular involved dwelling temporarily in tents. This exercise of worship reenacted Israel's traditional experience in the wilderness before the settlement of the land. Scripture considers the feast archaic, recalling its celebration in the village era before the rise of the monarchy (Judg 21:19).

There is a final, fascinating piece of evidence in our passage. The same verse, 12:9, that speaks of Israel's covenant assembly also presents a notable pronouncement of God. "I am the LORD your God from the land of Egypt." The pronouncement looks like a representative liturgical fragment or cultic teaching of Hosea's covenant institution. It is tempting to view it as part of the instruction at the premonarchic Feast of Booths.

The same words, which are about God's suzerainty over Israel since the exodus, occur elsewhere in Sinai texts at Hos 13:4; Deut 5:6–7; and Asaphite Ps 81:9–10. The psalm especially helps confirm the words' place in festal worship. Liturgical functionaries, such as Levites, delivered such pronouncements of the psalms as oracles on God's behalf.

As H. W. Wolff notes, the content of 12:9a is exactly the covenant instruction that the state priests of Hosea's time do *not* cultivate (Hos 4:6; 6:6). Such instruction constitutes the "knowledge of God" (דעת אלהים) that faithful Levites dutifully teach and transmit.[60] Hosea must understand the prestate Feast of Booths as a key institutional setting of this teaching. Before the rise of the monarchy, the feast was an institution where his ancient Levitical forebears could freely promote their Sinai beliefs.

---

60. Wolff, "Heimat," 247.

The Levites' Prestate "Charter"

We have retraced Hosea's brand of Sinai theology into the murky past. Old Israel's covenant assembly, in its cultic mode, harbored Hosea's Levitical forebears and their stream of tradition. The assembly authorized the sacred role of the Levites in ministering the Sinai covenant. In fact, it gave the Levites the images and symbols with which they conceptualized this role.

The language of the Levites' ancient "charter" reflects the general operations of the covenant assembly. One can examine the so-called Levitical charter with rare clarity in the text of Ps 16.[61] The relevant section, 16:4–6, reads:

> [4] Those who choose another god multiply their sorrows;
>   their drink offerings of blood I will not pour out
>   or take their names upon my lips.
> [5] The LORD is my chosen portion and my cup;
>   you hold my lot.
> [6] The boundary lines have fallen for me in pleasant places;
>   I have a goodly heritage.

Psalm 16 is a prayer song of trust in God. The speaker hopes for protection and preservation based on a special relationship with God, which 16:4–6 outlines. Taken literally, 16:4–6 can only be the words of a Levite. Other worshipers may have prayed these words in a metaphorical sense, but the metaphors derive from the real, concrete lifestyle of Levites. A glance at the specifics of the verses confirms this.

The Levites had the duty of performing the ritual duties of v. 4. Further, they were the ones among Israel's tribes who had Yahweh as their special "portion" (חלק, 16:5; cf. Deut 10:9). Indeed, God and God's sacred offerings were their sole "heritage" (נחלה, v. 6; cf. Josh 13:14).

Thus, H.-J. Kraus aptly characterizes the psalm: "A priest threatened by death is, in his avowal of the Levitical prerogatives that apply to him..., certain that Yahweh sustains his life and guards against death."[62]

The terminology of 16:5–6 comes straight from the traditional functions of the covenant assembly. Its jurisdiction over the distribution of land through sacral lottery is particularly evident. Since the operations of the old land lottery color the Levites' very charter, we can be sure of their

---

61. Gottwald, *Tribes of Yahweh*, 320, 333; Hans-Joachim Kraus, *Psalms 1–59: A Commentary* (trans. H. C. Oswald; Minneapolis: Augsburg, 1988), 235–41.
62. Kraus, *Psalms 1–59*, 241.

ancient attachment to the assembly. The Levites were the assembly's priestly ministers.

Verse 5 of the psalm uses terms such as "lot" (גורל) and "portion" (חלק). This is the language of Josh 18:6, 10 and 19:51, where a lottery parcels up the holy land at the door of the tent of meeting. Verse 6 combines the terms "boundary line" (חבל) and "heritage" (נחלה). This is a rare idiom, found elsewhere only in Sinai texts such as Asaphite Ps 78:55; Deut 32:9; and Josh 17:14; 19:9. The idiom is another way of referring to sacral land allotment. Israel surveyed the land with measuring lines before distributing it by divine lot.

When the Levites' charter declares Yahweh to be the tribe's chosen "portion" (16:5) and special "heritage" (16:6), it stakes an economic claim. Lacking the territorial farmland that the other tribes had, the Levites depended for their sustenance on a share of the revenues of Israel's shrines. Worshipers on pilgrimage to the shrines donated offerings and parts of their sacrifices in support of the sites' officiants (cf., e.g., Deut 18:1–8). As Kraus states, "The נחלה ['heritage'/'inheritance'] in the widest sense is the means of livelihood bestowed by Yahweh."[63]

The Levites' experience of alienation under monarchic centralization was no mere spiritual insult. It involved the loss of their livelihood bestowed by Yahweh. Hosea's Levitical colleagues suffered expulsion from Bethel and its traditional revenues. The state priests had pilgrims murdered on their way to the Levite base at Shechem, again depriving the Levites of possible gifts. No wonder the tribe so vehemently denounced the state-based worship of "Beth-aven." They were fighting for their very means of sustenance.

Future research may uncover additional information about the Levites' roles within the premonarchic covenant assembly, their charter by the assembly, and their traditional livelihood. Given the goals of my present project, there is no need to press further at this time.

In this chapter, I hope merely to have done sufficient sleuthing to establish the roots of Hosea's Sinai theology in prestate, lineage-based lifestyles and institutions. As with our study of Micah, investigation of Hosea demonstrates that biblical Yahwism was no late, evolutionary development. Sinai tradition has an ancient, venerable pedigree.

---

63. Ibid., 238.

9

CONCLUSION

I HAVE SOUGHT TO UNEARTH THE EARLY SOCIAL PROVENIENCE OF BIBLICAL Yahwism, to establish its ancient and venerable pedigree. Biblical Yahwism proved susceptible to interpretive "excavation," and offered us "artifactual" evidence of its archaic social roots. This brand of ancient Israelite religion did not evolve as a religious breakthrough in the sixth century at the time of the exile. Indeed, it predates King Josiah's seventh-century reign, when its proponents released the book of Deuteronomy.

Scholarly conjectures about a gradual, evolutionary emergence of monotheism and a late development of Deuteronomism are wrongheaded.

SUMMARY AND SYNTHESIS

I first identified biblical Yahwism as a stream of theological tradition, which I designated "Sinai" theology for convenience. Sinai theology is more than the ideology of a political faction in ancient Israel. Across many centuries, various Israelite groups with multiple agendas pre-served and passed along its substance. Rather than taking Sinai theology as the ideological product of these groups, it is better to view things the other way around. Sinai tradition created and molded its proponents' religious perspectives.

The proponents of Sinai theology produced a great assortment of writings, for which I have been using the shorthand term "Sinai texts." These include prose narratives, legal texts, psalms, and prophetic oracles. Their religious perspective eventually won a dominating role in the final shaping of the Hebrew Bible. This is not to claim a religious homogeneity for the Bible or to suggest it has a single theological center. Present day interpreters are correct to stress that an irreducible plurality characterizes the Bible's theological viewpoints.

Preceding scholars have long noted the shared perspective and language of Sinai texts such as Hosea, Deuteronomy, and Jeremiah. Building on the work of others, the present study extended the standard list of members of this textual family to include the Psalms of Asaph and the book of Micah. Consistent use of this new understanding was instrumental in uncovering new connections between biblical texts and new insights into their organic growth out of a tradition stream.

Based on the family resemblances between the Sinai texts of the Bible, I sketched several of their shared, core theological tenets in chapter 2. These core beliefs and values came to expression over time in diverse, changing ways. A *stream* of tradition is not stagnant. Nevertheless, drawing on a common store of idioms, expressions, and motifs, the varied biblical proponents of Sinai tradition unmistakably advocate a distinct theology.

According to the Sinai partisans, Israel owed sole allegiance to a single divine manor-lord, Yahweh, who gave Israel the divine manor-land to hold. Yahweh simply required that the people share the land justly and formally recognize its bounty as God's provision for their livelihood. A disciplined life on the land would foster strong bonds of community among the Israelites—with each other and with Yahweh. It would promote each person's full humanity.

The partisans of Sinai theology lived in both the northern and southern kingdoms, where they played a variety of social roles. They were minority groups at the periphery of society, however; and they remained so at least until the great Sinai-oriented reforms of King Hezekiah and King Josiah.

A diverse coalition of groups from differing geographical and social locations helped catalyze the great reforms. Beyond granting official recognition to their theology, the reforming kings also incorporated some of their members within official palace and temple circles. In chapter 3 I surveyed the evidence for how minority groups helped push Sinai theology to the center of Judean society in late monarchic times.

The eighth-century prophecies of Micah and Hosea provide excellent examples from both north and south of the vitality of Sinai theology before the great reforms moved it to a place of dominance. I made a strong case for this in chapters 4 and 5 through close interpretive work with texts from both prophets.

Micah and Hosea bear evidence of more than just the vitality of Sinai traditions in the eighth century, the period before it captured Judah's political center. Both prophetic books hint of an archaic heritage. To exploit these clues, a social-scientific model accounting for the unique milieu and heritage of these prophets was required.

I developed such a model in chapter 6, suggesting that Israelite society of the first millennium was a dual-system, agrarian monarchy. It developed as a monarchic state out of an earlier acephalous, segmentary organization. Its new centralized societal system could not immediately replace the earlier village system, so the two social systems coexisted for centuries in tension and conflict.

Tensions and conflicts were inevitable given the many differences between a village system and a state system of society, including significant political and economic differences. The former system relies for social stability on checks and balances between parallel segments of society. The latter system has a centralized, top-down administrative organization.

Village economics involves mixed, subsistence farming with risk spreading, ideally under the umbrella of a kinship network safeguarding each farmer's efforts. State economics involves monarchic interference in farming efforts, agricultural specialization, and extraction of farmers' agricultural surpluses as taxes and rent.

Military, cultic, and judicial differences also separate a village system from a state system of societal organization. The former system relies on a tribal militia for military defense; the latter system has a professional standing army. Various family lines of priests run the worship of the former type of society; the monarchy sponsors an official cadre of state priests in the latter type. A village society relies on the voluntary, part-time efforts of elders to resolve legal disputes; judicial matters are the responsibility of fulltime, hierarchically organized professionals in a state society.

The dual-system society of Israel's monarchic period naturally contained many factions, each with its own set of religious perspectives. This conforms to the social-scientific observation of *subcultural diversity* in complex societies. It should caution us against imagining a single "Israelite religion" during monarchic times. In particular, the cross-cultural research of this book contravenes viewing Israel's religious history in terms of any single-line evolution from Canaanite polytheism to biblical monotheism.

Archaeological finds related to polytheistic worship at the time of Micah and Hosea, or even long before, tell us about the religion of some groups within Israel—even about the religion of a majority of Israelites. Given a variety of social factions within Israel, each of which carried and transmitted its own store of religious traditions, however, archaeological artifacts of polytheism in Israel are not evidence that biblical Yahwism only emerged at the time of Micah and Hosea or later.

A dual-system, agrarian monarchy typically contains a variety of action blocs, including both urban and rural bases of political power. These power bases interrelate in a multiplicity of ways. For example, rural power blocs may have covert allies in the royal court. Conversely, a monarchy may co-opt and win over rural traditionalists to cosmopolitan, elitist ways.

Honor and wealth are found in both urban and rural action blocs. The growth of monarchy does not immediately dissipate the traditional prestige and affluence of rural elders and clan heads. A landed gentry remains in the countryside alongside dirt farmers.

A diverse mix of old and new priesthoods further complicates the social picture of a dual-system, agrarian monarchy. Old-style, lineage priesthoods resist the efforts of social scientists to pigeon hole them. Tribal priests identify with, and interpenetrate, the whole of a society, independent of geographic, political, and economic borders and strictures.

All of these complications make the task of tracing the social roots of biblical Yahwism an intricate one. The ancient groups that bore the traditions of Sinai theology resist artificial, political and ideological classification.

If nothing else, our study signals a stop to the easy distinctions that scholars suggest between, for example, official and popular religion, northern and southern religion, or oppressor and oppressed religion.

The social-scientific evidence further suggests that ties to the land played a larger role in the thinking of the traditional bearers of Israel's covenantal theology than often assumed. In many segmentary societies, communal relationships are inseparable from relationships to the land. Relationships with the land and with the gods are similarly intertwined.

Cross-culturally, land is often crucial to the thinking of traditional elders and priests. Elders guide the way their people inherit and use land. They ensure that land remains perpetually within the kin group. Priests preserve the people's traditions about the sacredness of land. They ensure the people direct sacrifices to the gods as their rightful commissions from their tenants. The emphasis on land in the theologies of Micah and Hosea points to their social roots.

I tested the social-scientific model of chapter 6 on the biblical texts of Hosea and Micah in chapters 7 and 8. As the testing proceeded, our Sinai prophets increasingly appeared to fit best in the older of Israel's two overlapping systems. This was the societal arrangement of Israel in its premonarchic era, when it lacked a centralized administration and organized itself on genealogical categories.

Micah and Hosea were members of factions that arose out of Israelite society's traditional lineage-based groupings. Their values and traditions have their roots in past ways of life. These values and customs appear as holdovers—vestiges—in these figures' prophecies.

This social-scientific evidence means these prophets were not innovators. They did not accomplish breakthroughs within a supposed ascent of Israel toward monotheism. Rather, Micah and Hosea were preservers of a stream of theological tradition emphasizing allegiance to Yahweh as Israel's sole manor-lord. This is not to discount their courageous, creative advocacy of renewal programs in their times.

Micah and Hosea operated amid confusion and conflict as Israel's original segmentary society regrouped and entrenched itself as a centralized monarchy. As inheritors of roles from the preceding, prestate era, they found themselves in considerable tension with their more progressive contemporaries.

The cross-cultural evidence shows that conflict over centralization within a society engenders and polarizes societal factions. In the case of Micah and Hosea, it left them as alienated minorities—members of a dwindling breed. They helped form a rear line of a whole phalanx of predecessors. Along with these forebears, they strove to preserve both Sinai traditions and a village-oriented lifestyle. In their period, however, this lifestyle was beginning to look outmoded.

My case for the ancient pedigree of biblical Yahwism does not rest on the evidence of archaic texts, such as the poem in Judg 5. It rests on the evidence of traditional social assumptions in the Sinai theology of the classical prophets, Micah and Hosea. Micah and Hosea can only express their Sinai convictions in language bound up with norms and customs of an older, prestate way of life.

Many remnants of this village-based, lineage-based lifestyle long survived in Israel, but they clearly did so in the face of an ever stronger, centralized organization of society that increasingly rendered older assumptions and institutions peripheral, impractical, or irrelevant. By Micah and Hosea's times, it sounded practically irrelevant to hear them referring to a twelve-tribe confederation, to the institution of land apportionment among clans, and to ad hoc military leadership by judges. But they do make these references.

Although at society's periphery in the eighth century, our prophets represented old prestige and honor. They were not paupers or peasants fomenting revolution, hoping to grab power for the first time. It is more accurate to view them as activist-traditionalists working to turn back the clock, defending old ideas with new vigor and imagination. For them, these old ideas were all about proper service of God and defense of neighbor.

Not all landed gentry become land-grabbers, even when new state systems allow for it. Even more than the poor, they may cling to traditional values and norms in the midst of radical social change. In a dual-system society, some rural aristocrats may retain both traditional authority and traditional religious beliefs. Micah was such a landed aristocrat, a clan head within traditional Israel's social structure. It was his social duty to protest the degradation of his kith and kin.

In this same milieu, old priesthoods have to fight for their traditional authority. Efforts to centralize a society alter or overturn traditional rituals and the traditional organization of shrines. New, state-oriented rites and new ritual functionaries, who neglect old norms, rise to power. This alienates and disenfranchises traditional priests.

Investigation reveals that Hosea was a traditional, lineage-based priest, whose forebears lost power as society centralized. His ancestors were Levitical officials at Israel's traditional shrines at Shechem, Bethel, and Shiloh. Despite his ancestry, he faced the hostility and physical persecution of the official, state priests of his time.

Our study leads us back behind Micah and Hosea to their forebears among old Israel's elders and Levites. Faithful parties within these circles helped bear the Sinai theological stream of tradition.

Deuteronomy 31:9 correctly identifies the two major ancient groups who treasured and handed down the Sinai covenant. The text recounts how Moses provided for the covenant's preservation at the end of his life: "Then Moses wrote down this law, and gave it to the priests, the sons of Levi, who carried the ark of the covenant of the LORD, and to all the elders of Israel."

As the social-scientific model suggested, the traditional bearers of Sinai theology focused great concern on their country folk's use of the land of their God, Yahweh. They believed God granted the land to Israel as a permanent "inheritance," ensured the land's bounty as provision for the people's livelihoods. King Solomon's prayer in 1 Kgs 8:36 assumes the authority of Israel's God over both Israel's tenure on the land and the people's enjoyment of the land's fertility. He petitions God to "grant rain on your land, which you have given to your people as an inheritance."

The administration and equitable distribution of Israel's land was the special bailiwick of the elders. This group of Sinai *tradents* ensured that Israel's kin groups and households retained perpetual title to their farmlands. Their priestly allies, for their part, focused on acknowledging and worshiping God for providing the land's bounty. These Levites directed the people's sacrifices to Yahweh alone as Israel's divine manor-lord, and instructed the people about Yahweh's suzerainty—at harvest festivals, for example.

Sinai *tradents* among the elders and Levites also unified their kinfolk in God's land. The elders of diverse kin groups promoted unity by joining forces at times—coordinating their efforts on behalf of the whole people, sharing risks across clan lines.

The Levites similarly fostered covenant unity. They divided themselves between Israel's various tribes as a unifying sodality. They coordinated sacred ceremonies and festivals shared in common by the tribes, symbolizing and enacting their unity as Yahweh's kinfolk.

The unity of the Israelites became especially necessary at times of crisis. At these junctures, both elders and Levites helped raise a commander or judge to temporary power. Sinai norms aimed to regulate this process. Within these norms, the elders would negotiate the selection of one of their number as a leader making use of a sacred lottery. The Levites would certify Yahweh's choice of this person to lead the people, and would often specially anoint the figure. Both groups would act as witnesses of a covenant between the leader, the people, and God.

Elders and Levites functioned within a prestate institution in their roles as bearers of the covenant. The biblical texts designate this institution with a set of terms that best translate as "assembly of Yahweh." The assembly represented the people of Israel as a sacred congregation of God. It granted sacral legitimacy to the preexisting roles in society of select elders and Levites. Given our limited evidence, it is impossible to judge how widely this ancient covenantal institution was recognized in Israelite tribal society as a whole.

Yahweh's assembly encompassed smaller, administrative instruments and had at least two modes of operation. In its liturgical mode, the Levites convened it for sacred festivals or oracular consultations of God in times of crisis. In its alternative mode as the bailiwick of the lay tribes, lineage heads convened it as an administrative instrument. In this mode, the assembly performed functions ranging from the adjudication of land disputes to the mustering of the tribes for warfare.

The lines demarcating the two modes of the assembly were fluid. Although the elders' mode of the assembly was an instrument of the lay tribes, it was a sacral institution nonetheless. Conversely, the Levites involved themselves not only in ritual matters but also in administrative and judicial affairs. They provided the people with a court of appeal for legal cases the elders could not successfully arbitrate. They intervened as peacemakers in clashes between large sections of society.

In the biblical stories of the exodus and wilderness wanderings, two wilderness tents symbolize the two modes of the assembly of Yahweh. One tent, associated with the Levites, stood within the wilderness camp and contained the ark of the covenant. A second tent, associated with the elders, stood outside of the camp.

The biblical images of these tents help distinguish and categorize the differing modes of operation of the assembly of Yahweh. They contain little information about the actual social forms and features of the institution in prestate Israel, however.

To gain sound insight in this area, we need the illumination of the cross-cultural, comparative evidence to help us visualize the various modes of the assembly of Yahweh and how they may have convened in a dispersed and localized manner.

Sinai loyalists most likely held regional convocations of the sacral assembly, which they understood to be local manifestations of a tribes-wide institution. Specific, concrete operations and mechanisms of the assembly made its full tribal scope obvious.

The assembly's wide inclusiveness had distinct advantages, both political and spiritual. Interrelating as one kinfolk of Yahweh, the people could broadly spread economic and military risks. They could extend the reach of their communal networks, whose covenantal bonds advanced the welfare and humanity of all society's members.

Elders and Levites managed the assembly to make the most of its collective nature. The Levites coordinated the sacral calendar and the rituals of the assembly, interlocking localized worship into a larger whole. When local groups faced unmanageable risks or when arbitration efforts failed at local levels, the elders convened the assembly for action at a higher social level, which incorporated more branched clusters of the whole people.

POLARIZATION OF FACTIONS OVER TIME

As the traditional, localized authority figures of a segmentary society come to terms with changing times, they have a range of reactions. Competing, overlapping systems of polity pull them in conflicting directions. This pull may split some traditionally peaceable colleagues into hostile factions.

Leading family lines, represented by their elders, had special political power and moral authority in old Israel. Each Israelite tribe had several such dominant lineages. Even before the rise of the monarchy in Israel, they must have lived together with some degree of tension and competition. When a dual-system society arose, tensions no doubt increased and groups became more self-differentiated.

With the rise of the monarchy, some powerful families linked themselves to the royal court. Others resisted the attempt of monarchic society to subsume them. Micah's immediate supporters were members of the latter, conservative type of dominant lineage.

Figure 1 schematizes the relationship of Micah and his forebears to their colleagues and counterparts among Israel's dominant family lines. While figure 1 relates to Israel's elders, figure 2 relates to priests. A range of priesthoods, representing different maximal lineages, vied for power in premonarchic Israel. With the development of monarchic states in both north and south, much greater tension arose between them. Both northern and southern royal dynasties granted official patronage to particular priestly houses, polarizing the opposition of competing groups.

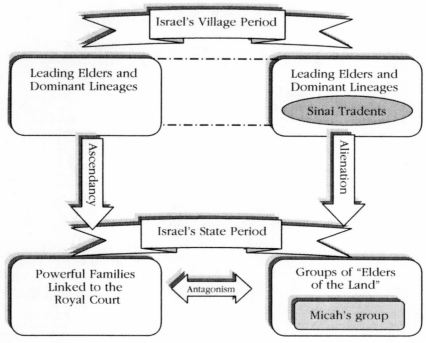

Figure 1

The first northern monarch, King Jeroboam I, created royal cult officials *de novo.* He consecrated priests lacking any genealogical credentials.
In the southern kingdom, Judah, a traditional priestly lineage, the sons of
Aaron, ascended to official state power. King Solomon expelled Abiathar,
Jerusalem's chief priest from the Levites of Shiloh, thus vesting sole
patronage in Zadok and his Aaronide line. In both cases, north and south,
developments worked against the power and prestige of the Levites'
priestly house.

Despite an authentic genealogical pedigree, the Levites thus experienced disenfranchisement in both the northern and the southern
kingdoms. Hosea drew his supporters from a circle of these conservative,
disenfranchised Levites. Figure 2 schematizes the relationship of Hosea
and his forebears to their priestly colleagues and counterparts in both
village-era and state-era Israel.

The diagrams are useful, since they summarize the results of our
investigations. The present study can be viewed as an exercise in filling
out these schemas, working backwards in time from bottom to top. The

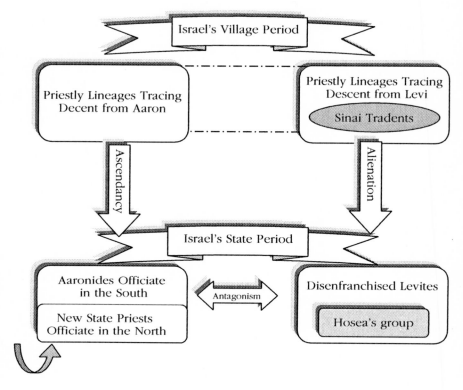

Figure 2

process allowed me to reconstruct the top sections of the charts—biblical Yahwism's social roots.

I started by sketching the scenarios at the bottom of each diagram. The bottom rectangles represent social dynamics in Israel's monarchic period. In examining these dynamics first, I began this study on a firm basis. Many biblical texts derive immediately from the monarchic period, and they supply reliable data about monarchic society. Biblical books such as Micah and Hosea provide a particularly stable witness about Israel's monarchic social milieu. The prophecies of these books contain the actual polemics of eighth-century figures, in their own words.

The social dynamics of Israel's state era had a prehistory. Using tools from biblical studies and the social sciences, I traced this history to its origins in Israel's village period. For that period, I was able to reconstruct the scenarios at the top of each of the two diagrams. The scenarios— describing prestate, village Israel—are a more speculative aspect of the diagrams. Nevertheless, we must presuppose such scenarios as a necessary background to the social tensions of Micah and Hosea's era.

Both diagrams clearly indicate the provenience of the bearers of Sinai tradition within the social scene of Israel's village era. These traditionists were groups lodged within the rectangles at the upper right of each diagram. I have marked these groups with gray circles.

The primary goal of this study, one might say, was to establish the existence of my gray circles, confirming the archaic social roots of the Sinai tradition stream. I have drawn the above diagrams with only enough complexity and detail to make this basic point. Future work will readily fill out more structural facets of these diagrams.

The diagrams could include further distinctions between groups of Levites. For example, some scholars have argued that the subgroup of Levites tracing descent from the Elides of Shiloh performed a particularly significant role in preserving Sinai theology.

In addition, the Aaronide line of priests deserves more attention. For example, this lineage contains a descent group of priests known as the Zadokites. Zadokite priests contributed several key biblical books to the canon of Scripture. Much future work remains in delineating the social-scientific dynamics of the biblical traditions and the biblical texts.

BIBLIOGRAPHY

Aharoni, Yohanan. *The Land of the Bible: A Historical Geography.* Translated by A. F. Rainey. 2d ed. London: Burns & Oates, 1979.

Ahmed, Akbar S. *Social and Economic Change in the Tribal Areas 1972–1976.* London: Oxford, 1977.

Albright, William F. "The Judicial Reform of Jehoshaphat." Pages 61–82 in *Alexander Marx Jubilee Volume.* New York: The Jewish Theological Seminary of America, 1950.

Allen, Leslie C. *The Books of Joel, Obadiah, Jonah, and Micah.* NICOT. Grand Rapids: Eerdmans, 1976.

Alt, Albrecht. "Die Heimat des Deuteronomiums." Pages 250–75 in vol. 2 of *Kleine Schriften zur Geschichte des Volkes Israel.* Edited by M. Noth. 3 vols. Munich: Beck, 1953.

———. "Micha 2,1–5: ΓΗΣ ΑΝΑΔΑΣΜΟΣ in Juda." Pages 373–81 in vol. 3 of *Kleine Schriften zur Geschichte des Volkes Israel.* Edited by M. Noth. 3 vols. Munich: Beck, 1959.

Arnaud, Daniel. *Emar VI.1–3: Textes sumériens et accadiens.* Paris: Éditions Recherche sur les Civilisations, 1985, 1986.

Avner, Uzzi. "Ancient Cult Sites in the Negev and Sinai Deserts." *TA* 11–12 (1984–85): 115–31.

———. "*Masseboth* Sites in the Negev and Sinai and Their Significance." Pages 166–81 in *Second International Congress on Biblical Archaeology in Jerusalem.* Jerusalem: Israel Exploration Society, 1990.

Ayisi, Eric O. *An Introduction to the Study of African Culture.* 2d ed. London: Heinemann, 1979.

Baltzer, Klaus. *The Covenant Formulary: In Old Testament, Jewish, and Early Christian Writings.* Translated by D. Green. Philadelphia: Fortress, 1971.

Barr, James. "Some Semantic Notes on the Covenant." Pages 37–38 in *Beiträge zur Alttestamentlichen Theologie: Festschrift für Walther Zimmerli zum 70. Geburtstag.* Edited by H. Donner, R. Hanhart, and R. Smend. Göttingen: Vandenhoeck & Ruprecht, 1977.

Beidelman, T. O. "Nuer Priests and Prophets: Charisma, Authority, and Power among the Nuer." Pages 375–415 in *The Translation of Culture: Essays to E. E. Evans-Pritchard.* Edited by T. O. Beidelman. London: Tavistock, 1971.

Bendor, Sonia. *The Social Structure of Ancient Israel: The Institution of the Family (Beit ʾab) From the Settlement to the End of the Monarchy.* Jerusalem Biblical Studies 7. Jerusalem: Simor, 1996.

Bentzen, Aage. *Introduction to the Old Testament.* 4th ed. 2 vols. Copenhagen: Gad, 1958.

———. *Die Josianische Reform und ihre Voraussetzungen.* Copenhagen: Haase, 1926.

Beyerlin, Walter. *Die Kulttraditionen Israels in der Verkündigung des Propheten Micha.* FRLANT 72. Göttingen: Vandenhoeck & Ruprecht, 1959.

———. *Origins and History of the Oldest Sinaitic Traditions.* Oxford: Blackwell, 1965.

Biebuyck, Daniel P. "Land Tenure, Introduction." *IESS* 8:562–67.

Birch, Bruce C. *Hosea, Joel, and Amos.* Westminster Bible Companion. Louisville: Westminster John Knox, 1997.

Blenkinsopp, Joseph. *A History of Prophecy in Israel.* Philadelphia: Westminster, 1983.

Bloch-Smith, Elizabeth. "Burials (Israelite)." *ABD* 1:785–89.

Block, Daniel I. *The Gods of the Nations: Studies in Ancient Near Eastern National Theology.* 2d ed. Grand Rapids: Baker, 2000. Originally published Winona Lake, Ind.: Eisenbrauns, 1988.

Bordreuil, P., F. Israel, and D. Pardee. "King's Command and Widow's Plea: Two New Hebrew Ostraca of the Biblical Period." *Near Eastern Archaeology* 61/1 (1998): 2–13.

Borowski, Oded. *Daily Life in Biblical Times.* SBLABS 5. Atlanta: Society of Biblical Literature, 2003.

———. "Hezekiah's Reforms and the Revolt against Assyria." *BA* 58/3 (1995): 148–55.

Brekelmans, Chr. H. W. "Die sogennannten deuteronomistischen Elemente in Genesis bis Numeri: Ein Beitrag zur Vorgeschichte des Deuteronomiums." Pages 90–96 in *Congress Volume: Geneva, 1965.* Edited by G. W. Anderson, P. A. H. De Boer, and G. R. Castellino. VTSup 15. Leiden: Brill, 1966.

Broshi, Magen. "The Expansion of Jerusalem in the Reigns of Hezekiah and Manasseh." *IEJ* 24 (1974): 21–26.

Brown, Sydney L. *The Book of Hosea.* London: Methuen, 1932.

Brueggemann, Walter A. "'Vine and Fig Tree': A Case Study in Imagination and Criticism." *CBQ* 43 (1981): 188–204.

Bunimovitz, Shlomo, and Zvi Lederman. "Beth-Shemesh: Culture Conflict on Judah's Frontier." *BAR* 23/1 (1997): 42–49, 75–77.

Burkitt, F. Crawford. "Micah 6 and 7 a Northern Prophecy." *JBL* 45 (1926): 159–61.

Buss, Martin J. *The Prophetic Word of Hosea: A Morphological Study.* BZAW 111. Berlin: Töpelmann, 1969.

———. "The Psalms of Asaph and Korah." *JBL* 82 (1963): 382–92.

Cagni, Luigi. *The Poem of Erra.* Sources from the Ancient Near East 1/3. Malibu: Undena, 1973.

Campbell, Anthony F., and Mark A. O'Brien. *Sources of the Pentateuch: Texts, Introductions, Annotations.* Minneapolis: Fortress, 1993.

Cassuto, Umberto. *A Commentary on the Book of Exodus.* Translated by I. Abrahams. Jerusalem: Magnes, 1967.

Chaney, Marvin L. "Whose Sour Grapes? The Addressees of Isaiah 5:1–7 in the Light of Political Economy." Pages 105–22 in *The Social World of the Hebrew*

Bible: Twenty-Five Years of the Social Sciences in the Academy. Edited by R. A. Simkins and S. L. Cook. *Semeia* 87 (1999).

Chavalas, Mark W., ed. *Emar: The History, Religion, and Culture of a Syrian Town in the Late Bronze Age.* Bethesda, Md.: CDL Press, 1996.

Childs, Brevard S. *The Book of Exodus: A Critical Theological Commentary.* OTL. Philadelphia: Westminster, 1974.

———. *Introduction to the Old Testament as Scripture.* Philadelphia: Fortress, 1979.

———. *Memory and Tradition in Israel.* SBT 37. London: SCM, 1962.

Christensen, James Boyd. "The Adaptive Functions of Fanti Priesthood." Pages 257– 78 in *Continuity and Change in African Cultures.* Edited by William R. Bascom and Melville J. Herskovits. Chicago: University of Chicago Press, 1959.

Clements, Ronald E. *Prophecy and Covenant.* SBT 43. London: SCM, 1968.

Cody, Aelred. *A History of Old Testament Priesthood.* AnBib 35. Rome: Pontifical Biblical Institute, 1969.

Cogan, Mordechai, and Hayim Tadmor. *II Kings: A New Translation with Introduction and Commentary.* AB 11. Garden City, N.Y.: Doubleday, 1988.

Cohen, Martin A. "The Role of the Shilonite Priesthood in the United Monarchy of Ancient Israel." *HUCA* 36 (1965): 59–98.

Cohen, Rudolf, and Yigal Yisrael. "Smashing the Idols: Piecing Together an Edomite Shrine in Judah." *BAR* 22/4 (1996): 40–51, 65.

Coogan, Michael David. "Canaanite Origins and Lineage: Reflections on the Religion of Ancient Israel." Pages 115–24 in *Ancient Israelite Religion: Essays in Honor of Frank Moore Cross.* Edited by Patrick D. Miller, Paul D. Hanson, and S. D. McBride. Philadelphia: Fortress, 1987.

Cook, Stephen L. "The Lineage Roots of Hosea's Yahwism." Pages 145–62 in *The Social World of the Hebrew Bible: Twenty-Five Years of the Social Sciences in the Academy.* Edited by R. A. Simkins and S. L. Cook. *Semeia* 87 (1999).

———. "Micah's Deuteronomistic Redaction and the Deuteronomists' Identity." Pages 216–31 in *Those Elusive Deuteronomists: The Phenomenon of Pan-Deuteronomism.* Edited by L. Schearing and S. McKenzie. JSOTSup 268. Sheffield: Sheffield Academic Press, 1999.

———. "The Tradition of Mosaic Judges: Past Approaches and New Directions." Pages 286–315 in *On the Way to Nineveh: Studies in Honor of George M. Landes.* Edited by S. L. Cook and S. Winter. American Schools of Oriental Research Books 4. Atlanta: Scholars Press, 1999.

Coote, Robert B., and Keith W. Whitelam. *The Emergence of Early Israel in Historical Perspective.* SWBA 5. Sheffield: Almond, 1987.

Craigie, Peter C. "El Brt.El Dn (RS 24.278, 14–15)." *UF* 5 (1973): 278–79.

Cross, Frank M. *Canaanite Myth and Hebrew Epic.* Cambridge: Harvard University Press, 1973.

———. "Kinship and Covenant in Ancient Israel." Pages 3–21 in *From Epic to Canon: History and Literature in Ancient Israel.* Baltimore: The Johns Hopkins University Press, 1998.

———. "The Priestly Tabernacle." Pages 201–28 in vol. 1 of *The Biblical Archaeologist Reader.* Edited by G. E. Wright and D. N. Freedman. Garden City, N.Y.: Doubleday, 1961.

Davies, Graham I. *Hosea.* NCBC. Grand Rapids: Eerdmans, 1992.

———. *Hosea.* OTG. Sheffield: JSOT Press, 1993.

Davies, Philip R. *In Search of "Ancient Israel."* JSOTSup 148. Sheffield: JSOT Press, 1992.

Day, John. "Asherah in the Hebrew Bible and Northwest Semitic Literature." *JBL* 105 (1986): 385–408.

———. "Pre-Deuteronomic Allusions to the Covenant in Hosea and Psalm LXXVIII." *VT* 36 (1986): 1–12.

Dearman, John Andrew. *Property Rights in the Eighth-Century Prophets: The Conflict and Its Background.* SBLDS 106. Atlanta: Scholars Press, 1988.

Dever, William G. *What Did the Biblical Writers Know and When Did They Know It? What Archaeology Can Tell Us about the Reality of Ancient Israel.* Grand Rapids: Eerdmans, 2001.

Diringer, David. "Early Hebrew Inscriptions." Pages 331–39 in *Lachish III (Tell ed-Duweir): The Iron Age.* Edited by O. Tufnell. London: Oxford University Press, 1953.

Dozeman, Thomas B. "The Song of the Sea and Salvation History." Pages 94–113 in *On the Way to Nineveh: Studies in Honor of George M. Landes.* Edited by S. L. Cook and S. C. Winter. American Schools of Oriental Research Books 4. Atlanta: Scholars Press, 1999.

Driver, Samuel R. *A Critical and Exegetical Commentary on Deuteronomy.* ICC. Edinburgh: T&T Clark, 1895.

———. *An Introduction to the Literature of the Old Testament.* New York: Scribner's, 1910.

Duhm, Bernhard. *Israels Propheten.* 2d ed. Tübingen: Mohr, 1922.

———. *Die Theologie der Propheten als Grundlage für die innere Entwicklungsgeschichte der israelitischen Religion.* Bonn: Marcus, 1875.

Dus, Jan. "Weiteres zum nordisraelitischen Psalm Micha 7,7–20." *ZDMG* 115 (1965): 14–22.

Dutcher-Walls, Patricia. *Narrative Art, Political Rhetoric: The Case of Athaliah and Joash.* JSOTSup 209. Sheffield: Sheffield Academic Press, 1996.

———. "The Social Location of the Deuteronomists: A Sociological Study of Factional Politics in Late Pre-Exilic Judah." *JSOT* 52 (1991): 77–94.

Eggan, Fred. "Kinship: Introduction." *IESS* 8:390–401.

Eissfeldt, Otto. *Der Gott Karmel.* SPAW. Berlin: Akademie, 1953.

———. *Molk als Opferbegriff im Punischen und Hebräischen und das ende des Gottes Moloch.* Beiträge zur Religionsgeschichte des Altertums 3. Halle: Niemeyer, 1935.

———. "Ein Psalm aus Nord-Israel: Micha 7, 7–20." *ZDMG* 112 (1962): 259–68.

Elliger, Karl. "Die Heimat des Propheten Micha." Pages 9–71 in *Kleine Schriften zum Alten Testament.* Edited by Hartmut Gese and Otto Kaiser. Munich: Kaiser, 1966.

Emerton, John A. "New Light on Israelite Religion: The Implications of the Inscriptions from Kuntillet 'Ajrud." *ZAW* 94 (1982): 2–20.

Evans-Pritchard, E. E. *Nuer Religion.* London: Oxford, 1962.

———. "The Nuer of the Southern Sudan." Pages 272–96 in *African Political Systems.* Edited by M. Fortes and E. E. Evans-Pritchard. London: Oxford, 1940.

Faust, Avraham. "Burnished Pottery and Gender Hierarchy in Iron Age Israelite Society." *Journal of Mediterranean Archaeology* 15/1 (2002): 53–73.

———. "Differences in Family Structure between Cities and Villages in Iron Age II." *TA* 26/2 (1999): 233–52.

———. "Ethnic Complexity in Northern Israel during Iron Age II." *PEQ* 132 (2000): 2–27.

———. "The Rural Community in Ancient Israel during Iron Age II." *BASOR* 317 (2000): 17–39.

———. "Socioeconomic Stratification in an Israelite City: Hazor VI as a Test Case." *Levant* 31 (1999): 179–90.

Finkelstein, Israel. *The Archaeology of the Israelite Settlement.* Jerusalem: Israel Exploration Society, 1988.

———. "State Formation in Israel and Judah: A Contrast in Context, a Contrast in Trajectory." *Near Eastern Archaeology* 62 (1999): 35–52.

Finkelstein, Israel, and Neil Asher Silberman. *The Bible Unearthed: Archaeology's New Vision of Ancient Israel and the Origin of Its Sacred Texts.* New York: Free Press, 2001.

Flanagan, James W. *David's Social Drama: A Hologram of Israel's Early Iron Age.* SWBA 7. Sheffield: Almond, 1988.

Fleming, Daniel E. *The Installation of Baal's High Priestess at Emar: A Window on Ancient Syrian Religion.* HSS 42. Atlanta: Scholars Press, 1992.

———. "More Help from Syria: Introducing Emar to Biblical Study." *BA* 58/3 (1995): 139–47.

Fohrer, Georg. *History of Israelite Religion.* Translated by D. Green. New York: Abingdon, 1972.

Fortes, Meyer. "The Political System of the Tallensi of the Northern Territories of the Gold Coast." Pages 238–71 in *African Political Systems.* Edited by M. Fortes and E. E. Evans-Pritchard. London: Oxford, 1940.

Fortes, Meyer, and E. E. Evans-Pritchard. "Introduction." Pages 1–23 in *African Political Systems.* Edited by M. Fortes and E. E. Evans-Pritchard. London: Oxford, 1940.

Foster, Benjamin R. *From Distant Days: Myths, Tales, and Poetry of Ancient Mesopotamia.* Bethesda, Md.: CDL, 1995.

Fraser, David A., and Tony Campolo. *Sociology through the Eyes of Faith.* San Francisco: HarperCollins, 1992.

Fretheim, Terence E. "Elohist." *IDBSup*, 259–63.

Frick, Frank S. *The Formation of the State in Ancient Israel: A Survey of Models and Theories.* SWBA 4. Sheffield: Almond, 1985.

Friedman, Richard Elliott. *Who Wrote the Bible?* New York: Harper & Row, 1987.

Gellner, Ernest. *Saints of the Atlas.* London: Weidenfeld & Nicholson, 1969.

Gelston, Anthony. "A Note on Psalm LXXIV 8." *VT* 34 (1984): 82–87.

Gerbrandt, Gerald E. *Kingship according to the Deuteronomistic History.* SBLDS 87. Atlanta: Scholars Press, 1986.

Gibson, John C. L. *Hebrew and Moabite Inscriptions.* Vol. 1 of *Textbook of Syrian Semitic Inscriptions.* Oxford: Clarendon, 1973.

Ginsberg, Harold Louis. "Dqdwqym bšnyn ʿšr." *ErIsr* 3 (1954): 83–84.

Gluckman, Max. "The Kingdom of the Zulu of South Africa." Pages 25–55 in *African Political Systems*. Edited by M. Fortes and E. E. Evans-Pritchard. London: Oxford, 1940.

———. "Political Institutions." Pp. 66–80 in *The Institutions of Primitive Society: A Series of Broadcast Talks*. Edited by E. E. Evans-Pritchard et al. Glencoe, Ill.: Free Press, 1954.

Gnuse, Robert K. "Calf, Cult, and King: The Unity of Hosea 8:1–13." *BZ* 26 (1982): 83–92.

———. "New Directions in Biblical Theology: The Impact of Contemporary Scholarship in the Hebrew Bible." *JAAR* 62 (1994): 893–918.

———. *No Other Gods: Emergent Monotheism in Israel*. JSOTSup 241. Sheffield: Sheffield Academic Press, 1997.

Godelier, Maurice. *Perspectives in Marxist Anthropology*. Cambridge: Cambridge University Press, 1977.

Golka, Friedemann W. *The Leopard's Spots: Biblical and African Wisdom in Proverbs*. Edinburgh: T&T Clark, 1993.

Goody, Jack. "Kinship: Descent Groups." *IESS* 8:401–8.

Gottwald, Norman K. *The Hebrew Bible: A Socio-literary Introduction*. Philadelphia: Fortress, 1985.

———. *The Politics of Ancient Israel*. Library of Ancient Israel. Louisville: Westminster John Knox, 2001.

———. *The Tribes of Yahweh: A Sociology of the Religion of Liberated Israel, 1250–1050 B.C.E.* Maryknoll, N.Y.: Orbis, 1979.

Goulder, Michael D. *The Psalms of Asaph and the Pentateuch: Studies in the Psalter, III*. JSOTSup 233. Sheffield: JSOT Press, 1996.

Gray, George Buchanan. *A Critical and Exegetical Commentary on Numbers*. ICC 4. New York: T&T Clark, 1903.

Habel, Norman C. *The Land is Mine: Six Biblical Land Ideologies*. OBT. Minneapolis: Fortress, 1995.

Halpern, Baruch. "Brisker Pipes than Poetry: The Development of Israelite Monotheism." Pages 77–115 in *Judaic Perspectives on Ancient Israel*. Edited by Jacob Neusner, Baruch A. Levine, and Ernest S. Frerichs. Philadelphia: Fortress, 1987.

———. "The Centralization Formula in Deuteronomy." *VT* 31 (1981): 20–38.

———. *The Constitution of the Monarchy in Israel*. HSM 25. Chico, Calif.: Scholars Press, 1981.

———. "Jerusalem and the Lineages in the Seventh Century BCE: Kinship and the Rise of Individual Moral Liability." Pages 11–107 in *Law and Ideology in Monarchic Israel*. Edited by B. Halpern and D. W. Hobson. JSOTSup 124. Sheffield: Sheffield Academic Press, 1991.

———. "The Resourceful Israelite Historian: The Song of Deborah and Israelite Historiography." *HTR* 76 (1983): 379–401.

Halpern, Baruch, and David Vanderhooft. "The Editions of Kings in the 7th–6th Centuries B.C.E." *HUCA* 62 (1991): 179–244.

Hamilton, Victor P. "Marriage (OT and ANE)." *ABD* 4:559–69.

Hammond, Peter B. "Economic Change and Mossi Acculturation." Pages 238–56 in *Continuity and Change in African Cultures*. Edited by William R. Bascom and Melville J. Herskovits. Chicago: University of Chicago Press, 1959.

Hanson, Paul D. *The Dawn of Apocalyptic: The Historical and Sociological Roots of Jewish Apocalyptic Eschatology*. Philadelphia: Fortress, 1975.

Haran, Menahem. *Temples and Temple Service in Ancient Israel: An Inquiry into Biblical Cult Phenomena and the Historical Setting of the Priestly School*. Winona Lake, Ind.: Eisenbrauns, 1985.

Harvey, Julien. *Le Plaidoyer prophétique contre Israël après la rupture de l'Alliance, Studia 22*. Paris: Desclée de Brouwer; Montreal: Bellarmin, 1967.

Hasel, Michael G. "Israel in the Merneptah Stela." *BASOR* 296 (1994): 45–61.

Healey, Joseph P. "Am ha'arez." *ABD* 1:168–69.

Herzog, Ze'ev. *Archaeology of the City: Urban Planning in Ancient Israel and Its Social Implications*. Tel Aviv: Yass Archaeology Press, Institute of Archaeology, Tel Aviv University, 1997.

Hesse, Brian, and Paula Wapnish. "Can Pig Remains Be Used for Ethnic Diagnosis in the Ancient Near East?" Pages 238–70 in *The Archaeology of Israel: Constructing the Past, Interpreting the Present*. Edited by Neil A. Silberman and David B. Small. JSOTSup 237. Sheffield: Sheffield Academic Press, 1997.

Hesse, Franz. "Amos 5:4–6, 14f." *ZAW* 68 (1956): 1–17.

Hillers, Delbert R. *A Commentary on the Book of the Prophet Micah*. Hermeneia. Philadelphia: Fortress, 1984.

———. *Treaty-Curses and the Old Testament Prophets*. BibOr 16. Rome: Pontifical Biblical Institute, 1964.

Holladay, John S., Jr. "Chapter 22. The Kingdoms of Israel and Judah: Political and Economic Centralization in the Iron IIA-B (ca. 1000–750 BCE)." Pages 368–98 in *The Archaeology of Society in the Holy Land*. Edited by Thomas E. Levy. New York: Facts on File, 1995.

Holt, Else Kragelund. *Prophesying the Past: The Use of Israel's History in the Book of Hosea*. JSOTSup 194. Sheffield: Sheffield Academic Press, 1995.

Hoonacker, Albin van. *Les douze petits prophètes*. EBib. Paris: Gabalda, 1908.

Hopkins, David C. *The Highlands of Canaan: Agricultural Life in the Early Iron Age*. SWBA 3. Sheffield: Almond, 1985.

Horn, Siegfried H. "The Divided Monarchy: The Kingdoms of Judah and Israel." Pages 109–49 in *Ancient Israel: A Short History from Abraham to the Roman Destruction of the Temple*. Edited by H. Shanks. Englewood Cliffs, N.J.: Prentice-Hall, 1988.

Hubbard, Robert L., Jr. *The Book of Ruth*. NICOT. Grand Rapids: Eerdmans, 1988.

Huffmon, Herbert B. "The Covenant Lawsuit in the Prophets." *JBL* 78 (1959): 285–95.

———. "The Treaty Background of Hebrew Yadaᶜ." *BASOR* 181 (1966): 31–37.

Isaacs, H. "Basic Group Identity." Pages 29–52 in *Ethnicity: Theory and Experience*. Edited by N. Glazer and D. P. Moynihan. Cambridge: Harvard University Press, 1975.

Janssen, Enno. *Juda in der Exilszeit: Ein Beitrag zur Frage der Entstehung des Judentums*. FRLANT 69. Göttingen: Vandenhoeck & Ruprecht, 1956.

Jenks, Alan W. "Elohist." *ABD* 2:478–82.

———. *The Elohist and North Israelite Traditions*. SBLMS 22. Missoula, Mont.: Scholars Press, 1977.

Jepsen, Alfred. "Kleine Beiträge zum Zwölfprophetenbuch." *ZAW* 56 (1938): 96–99.

Jones, Christopher P. *Kinship Diplomacy in the Ancient World*. Cambridge: Harvard University Press, 1999.

Kallai, Zechariah. "Judah and Israel—A Study in Israelite Historiography." *IEJ* 28 (1978): 251–61.

Kaufmann, Yehezkel. *The Religion of Israel from Its Beginnings to the Babylonian Exile*. Translated by M. Greenberg. Chicago: University of Chicago Press, 1960.

Kennett, Robert H. "The Origin of the Aaronite Priesthood." *JTS* 6 (1905): 161–86.

Kessler, Rainer. *Staat und Gesellschaft im vorexilischen Juda vom 8. Jahrhundert bis zum Exil*. VTSup 47. Leiden: Brill, 1992.

King, Philip J., and Lawrence E. Stager. *Life in Biblical Israel*. Library of Ancient Israel. Louisville: Westminster John Knox, 2001.

Knierim, Rolf. "Exodus 18 und die Neuordnung der mosäischen Gerichtsbarkeit." *ZAW* 73 (1961): 146–71.

Knohl, Israel. *The Sanctuary of Silence: The Priestly Torah and the Holiness School*. Minneapolis: Fortress, 1995.

Knoppers, Gary N. "Jehoshaphat's Judiciary and the 'Scroll of YHWH's Torah.'" *JBL* 113 (1994): 59–80.

Koch, Klaus. *The Growth of the Biblical Tradition: The Form-Critical Method*. Translated by S. M. Cupitt. London: Black, 1969.

Köhler, Ludwig. *Hebrew Man*. Translated by P. Ackroyd. New York: Abingdon, 1956.

Kraus, Hans-Joachim. *Psalms 1–59: A Continental Commentary*. Translated by H. C. Oswald. Minneapolis: Fortress, 1993.

———. *Psalms 60–150: A Continental Commentary*. Translated by H. C. Oswald. Minneapolis: Fortress, 1989.

Kuenen, Abraham. *De Profeten en de Profetie onder Israël: Historisch-Dogmatisch Studie*. 2 vols. in one. Leiden: Engels, 1875.

———. *The Religion of Israel to the Fall of the Jewish State*. Translated by A. H. May. Edinburgh: Williams & Norgate, 1874.

Kutsch, Ernst. *Verheissung und Gesetz: Untersuchungen zum sogenannten "Bund" im Alten Testament*. BZAW 131. Berlin: de Gruyter, 1973.

Lambert, Wilfred G. "Enmeduranki and Related Matters." *JCS* 21 (1967): 128–31.

Lamphear, John. "Aspects of Turkana Leadership during the Era of Primary Resistance." *Journal of African History* 17 (1976): 225–43.

Lang, Bernhard. *Monotheism and the Prophetic Minority: An Essay in Biblical History and Sociology*. SWBA 1. Sheffield: Almond, 1983.

Lehming, Sigo. "Versuch zu Ex. XXXII." *VT* 10 (1960): 16–50.

Lemche, Niels Peter. *Ancient Israel: A New History of Israelite Society*. The Biblical Seminar 5. Sheffield: JSOT Press, 1988.

———. "Is It Still Possible to Write a History of Ancient Israel?" *SJOT* 8 (1994): 165–90.

Levenson, Jon D. *Sinai and Zion: An Entry into the Jewish Bible*. San Francisco: Harper & Row, 1987.

Levenson, Jon D., and Baruch Halpern. "The Political Import of David's Marriages." *JBL* 99 (1980): 507–18.

Lewis, Theodore J. "The Identity and Function of El/Baal Berith." *JBL* 115 (1996): 401–23.

Lienhardt, Godfrey. *Divinity and Experience: The Religion of the Dinka.* Oxford: Clarendon, 1961.

———. "The Western Dinka." Pages 97–135 in *Tribes without Rulers: Studies in African Segmentary Systems.* Edited by J. Middleton and D. Tait. London: Routledge & Kegan Paul, 1958.

Lindars, Barnabas. *Judges 1–5.* Edinburgh: T&T Clark, 1975.

Lindblom, Johannes. *Micha, Literarisch Untersucht.* Åbo: Åbo Akademi, 1929.

Lipiński, Edward. "Recherches Ugaritiques: (RS 16, 264; 15, 117; 24, 278)." *Syria* 50 (1973): 35–51.

Lowery, Richard H. *The Reforming Kings: Cults and Society in First Temple Judah.* JSOTSup 120. Sheffield: JSOT Press, 1991.

Malamat, Abraham. "*Ummātum* in Old Babylonian Texts and Its Ugaritic and Biblical Counterparts." *UF* 11 (1979): 527–36.

Matthews, Victor H., and Don C. Benjamin. *Social World of Ancient Israel 1250–587 B.C.E.* Peabody, Mass.: Hendrickson, 1993.

Mayes, Andrew D. H. *Israel in the Period of the Judges.* SBT 2/29. London: SCM, 1974.

———. *Deuteronomy.* NCBC. Grand Rapids: Eerdmans, 1979.

Mays, James L. *Hosea: A Commentary.* OTL. Philadelphia: Westminster, 1969.

———. *Micah: A Commentary.* OTL. Philadelphia: Westminster, 1976.

Mazar, Benjamin. *The Early Biblical Period.* Jerusalem: Israel Exploration Society, 1986.

McBride, S. Dean, Jr. "Deuteronomium." *TRE* 8:530–43.

———. "Deuteronomy: Introduction and Annotations." Pages 266–325 in *The HarperCollins Study Bible: New Revised Standard Version, with the Apocryphal/ Deuterocanonical Books.* Edited by W. Meeks. New York: HarperCollins, 1993.

McCarthy, Dennis J. *Old Testament Covenant: A Survey of Current Opinions.* Atlanta: John Knox, 1972.

———. *Treaty and Covenant.* AnBib 21A. Rome: Pontifical Biblical Institute, 1968.

McKeating, Henry. *Amos, Hosea, Micah.* CBC. London: Cambridge University Press, 1971.

McKenzie, Donald A. "Judicial Procedure at the Town Gate." *VT* 14 (1964): 100–104.

McNutt, Paula. *Reconstructing the Society of Ancient Israel.* Library of Ancient Israel. Louisville: Westminster John Knox, 1999.

Menchú, Rigoberta. *I, Rigoberta Menchú: An Indian Woman in Guatemala.* Edited by Elisabeth Burgos-Debray. Translated by Ann Wright. London: Verso, 1984.

Mendenhall, George E. *Law and Covenant in Israel and the Ancient Near East.* Pittsburgh: Biblical Colloquium, 1955.

———. "Social Organization in Early Israel." Pages 132–51 in *Magnalia Dei: The Mighty Acts of God.* Edited by F. M. Cross, W. E. Lemke, and P. D. Miller Jr. Garden City, N.Y.: Doubleday, 1976.

———. "The Suzerainty Treaty Structure: Thirty Years Later." Pages 85–100 in *Religion and Law: Biblical-Judaic and Islamic Perspectives.* Edited by E. B. Firmage, B. G. Weiss, and J. W. Welch. Winona Lake, Ind.: Eisenbrauns, 1990.

————. *The Tenth Generation: The Origins of the Biblical Tradition*. Baltimore: Johns Hopkins University Press, 1973.

Mendenhall, George E., and Gary A. Herion. "Covenant." *ABD* 1:1179–1202.

Messenger, John C., Jr. "The Role of Proverbs in a Nigerian Judicial System." *Southwestern Journal of Anthropology* 15 (1959): 64–73.

Mettinger, Tryggve N. D. *No Graven Image? Israelite Aniconism in Its Ancient Near Eastern Context*. ConBOT 42. Stockholm: Almqvist & Wiksell, 1995.

————. *Solomonic State Officials: A Study of the Civil Government Officials of the Israelite Monarchy*. ConBOT 5. Lund: Gleerup, 1971.

Meyers, Carol. *Discovering Eve: Ancient Israelite Women in Context*. Oxford: Oxford University Press, 1988.

————. "The Family in Early Israel." Pages 1–47 in *Families in Ancient Israel*. The Family, Religion, and Culture. Louisville: Westminster John Knox, 1997.

Middleton, John. "The Political System of the Lugbara of the Nile-Congo Divide." Pages 203–29 in *Tribes without Rulers: Studies in African Segmentary Systems*. Edited by J. Middleton and D. Tait. London: Routledge & Kegan Paul, 1958.

————. "Prophets and Rainmakers: The Agents of Social Change among the Lugbara." Pages 179–201 in *The Translation of Culture: Essays to E. E. Evans-Pritchard*. Edited by T. O. Beidelman. London: Tavistock, 1971.

Middleton, John, and David Tait. "Introduction." Pages 1–31 in *Tribes without Rulers: Studies in African Segmentary Systems*. Edited by J. Middleton and D. Tait. London: Routledge & Kegan Paul, 1958.

Milgrom, Jacob. *Numbers: The Traditional Hebrew Text with the New JPS Translation*. JPSTC. Philadelphia: The Jewish Publication Society, 1990.

Miller, Patrick D. *The Religion of Ancient Israel*. Library of Ancient Israel. Louisville: Westminster John Knox, 2000.

Miller, Patrick D., Paul D. Hanson, and S. Dean McBride, eds. *Ancient Israelite Religion: Essays in Honor of Frank Moore Cross*. Philadelphia: Fortress, 1987.

Miller, Robert D., II. "Identifying Earliest Israel." *BASOR* 333 (2004): 55–68

Moerman, Michael. "Being Lue: Uses and Abuses of Ethnic Identification." Pages 153–69 in *Essays on the Problem of Tribe*. Edited by June Helm. Proceedings of the Annual Spring Meeting of the American Ethnological Society, 1967. Seattle: University of Washington, 1968.

Moor, Johannes C. de. *The Rise of Yahwism: The Roots of Israelite Monotheism*. Leuven: Uitgeverij Peeters, 1990, 1997.

Moran, William L. "The Ancient Near Eastern Background of the Love of God in Deuteronomy." *CBQ* 25 (1963): 77–87.

Mosala, Itumeleng J. *Biblical Hermeneutics and Black Theology in South Africa*. Grand Rapids: Eerdmans, 1989.

Muilenburg, James. "The Form and Structure of the Covenantal Formulations." *VT* 9 (1959): 347–65.

Nasuti, Harry P. *Tradition History and the Psalms of Asaph*. SBLDS 88. Atlanta: Scholars Press, 1988.

Ndoro, Dorcas Chanya. "Biblical Inheritance: An African Interpretation—Today." MTS thesis, Virginia Theological Seminary, Alexandria, Va., 1997.

Nelson, Richard D. *The Double Redaction of the Deuteronomistic History*. JSOTSup 18. Sheffield: JSOT Press, 1981.

Netting, Robert McC. "Sacred Power and Centralization: Aspects of Political Adaptation in Africa." Pages 219–44 in *Population Growth*. Edited by B. J. Spooner. Cambridge: Massachusetts Institute of Technology, 1972.

———. *Smallholders, Householders: Farm Families and the Ecology of Intensive, Sustainable Agriculture.* Stanford, Calif.: Stanford University Press, 1993.

Newman, Murray L. *The People of the Covenant: A Study of Israel from Moses to the Monarchy.* Nashville: Abingdon, 1962.

Nicholson, Ernest W. *Deuteronomy and Tradition.* Oxford: Basil Blackwell, 1967.

———. "The Meaning of the Expression 'am ha'arez in the Old Testament." *JSS* 10 (1965): 59–66.

Niditch, Susan. *Ancient Israelite Religion.* New York: Oxford University Press, 1997.

Nogalski, James. *Literary Precursors to the Book of the Twelve.* BZAW 217. Berlin: de Gruyter, 1993.

North, Francis S. "Aaron's Rise in Prestige." *ZAW* 66 (1954): 191–99.

Noth, Martin. *The Deuteronomistic History.* JSOTSup 15. Sheffield: JSOT Press, 1981.

———. *The History of Israel.* 2d ed. New York: Harper & Row, 1960.

Oberg, K. "The Kingdom of Ankole in Uganda." Pages 121–62 in *African Political Systems*. Edited by M. Fortes and E. E. Evans-Pritchard. London: Oxford University Press, 1940.

Oden, Robert A., Jr. "The Place of Covenant in the Religion of Israel." Pages 429–47 in *Ancient Israelite Religion: Essays in Honor of Frank Moore Cross*. Edited by Patrick D. Miller, Paul D. Hanson, S. D. McBride. Philadelphia: Fortress, 1987.

Ollenburger, Ben C. *Zion The City of the Great King: A Theological Symbol of the Jerusalem Cult.* JSOTSup 41. Sheffield: JSOT Press, 1987.

Olyan, Saul M. *Asherah and the Cult of Yahweh in Israel.* SBLMS 34. Atlanta: Scholars Press, 1988.

———. *Rites and Rank: Hierarchy in Biblical Representations of Cult.* Princeton: Princeton University Press, 2000.

———. "Zadok's Origins and the Tribal Politics of David." *JBL* 101 (1982): 177–93.

Oort, H. "Die Aäroniden." *ThT* 18 (1884): 289–335.

Park, George K. "Kinga Priests: The Politics of Pestilence." Pages 229–37 in *Political Anthropology*. Edited by M. Swartz, V. Turner, and A. Tuden. Chicago: Aldine, 1966.

Parrinder, Geoffrey. *West African Religion: A Study of the Beliefs and Practices of Akan, Ewe, Yoruba, Ibo, and Kindred Peoples.* London: Epworth, 1961.

Pedersen, Johannes. *Israel: Its Life and Culture.* 2 vols. London: Oxford, 1947.

Peristiany, J. G. "Law." Pages 39–49 in *The Institutions of Primitive Society: A Series of Broadcast Talks*. Edited by E. E. Evans-Pritchard et al. Glencoe, Ill.: Free Press, 1954.

Perlitt, Lothar. *Bundestheologie im Alten Testament.* WMANT 36. Neukirchen: Neukirchen-Vluyn, 1969.

Petersen, David L. *The Roles of Israel's Prophets.* JSOTSup 17. Sheffield: JSOT, 1981.

Pleins, J. David. *Social Visions of the Hebrew Bible: A Theological Introduction.* Louisville: Westminster John Knox, 2001.

Polk, Timothy. "The Levites in the Davidic-Solomonic Empire." *Studia Biblica et Theologica* 9 (1979): 3–22.

90 THE SOCIAL ROOTS OF BIBLICAL YAHWISM

ritchard, James B., ed. *Ancient Near Eastern Texts Relating to the Old Testament*. 3d ed. Princeton: Princeton University Press, 1969.
Rad, Gerhard von. *Deuteronomy*. Translated by D. Barton. OTL. Philadelphia: Westminster, 1966.
———. "The Form-Critical Problem of the Hexateuch." Pages 1–78 in *The Problem of the Hexateuch and Other Essays*. Translated by E. T. Dicken. Edinburgh: Oliver & Boyd, 1966.
———. "The Promised Land and Yahweh's Land in the Hexateuch." Pages 79–93 in *The Problem of the Hexateuch and Other Essays*. Translated by E. T. Dicken. Edinburgh: Oliver & Boyd, 1966.
———. *Studies in Deuteronomy*. Translated by D. Stalker. SBT 9. Chicago: Regnery, 1953.
Radcliffe-Brown, A. R. "Preface." Pages xi–xxiii in *African Political Systems*. Edited by M. Fortes and E. E. Evans-Pritchard. London: Oxford University Press, 1940.
Rainey, Anson F. "Reply to D. Edelman." *BAR* 18/2 (1992): 73–74.
Rast, Walter E. *Tradition History and the Old Testament*. GBS. Philadelphia: Fortress, 1972.
Ratnagar, Shereen. "Ideology and the Nature of Political Consolidation and Expansion: An Archaeological Case." Pages 170–86 in *Ideology and the Formation of Early States*. Edited by H. J. M. Claessen and J. G. Oosten. Studies in Human Society 2. Leiden: Brill, 1996.
Reicke, Bo. "Liturgical Traditions in Micah 7." *HTR* 60 (1967): 349–67.
Reviv, Hanoch. *The Elders in Ancient Israel: A Study of a Biblical Institution*. Jerusalem: Magnes, 1989.
Richards, Audrey I. "The Political System of the Bemba Tribe—North-Eastern Rhodesia." Pages 83–120 in *African Political Systems*. Edited by M. Fortes and E. E. Evans-Pritchard. London: Oxford University Press, 1940.
Riggs, F. W., ed. *Ethnicity: Concepts and Terms Used in Ethnicity Research*. International Conceptual Encyclopedia for the Social Sciences 1. Honolulu: COCTA, 1985.
Robinson, Robert B. "The Levites in the Pre-Monarchic Period." *Studia Biblica et Theologica* 8 (1978): 3–24.
Rogerson, John, and Philip Davies. *The Old Testament World*. Englewood Cliffs, N.J.: Prentice-Hall, 1989.
Routledge, Bruce E. "Learning to Love the King: Urbanism and the State in Iron Age Moab." Pages 130–44 in *Urbanism in Antiquity: From Mesopotamia to Crete*. Edited by Walter E. Aufrecht, Neil A. Mirau, and Steven W. Gauley. JSOTSup 244. Sheffield: Sheffield Academic Press, 1997.
———. "The Politics of Mesha: Segmented Identities and State Formation in Iron Age Moab." *JESHO* 43 (2000): 221–56.
Rowley, Harold H. "Hezekiah's Reform and Rebellion." *BJRL* 44 (1962): 395–431.
Rudolph, Wilhelm. *Hosea*. KAT 13/1. Gutersloh: Mohn, 1966.
Schapera, I. "The Political Organization of the Ngwato of Bechuanaland Protectorate." Pages 56–82 in *African Political Systems*. Edited by M. Fortes and E. E. Evans-Pritchard. London: Oxford, 1940.
Schniedewind, William. "The Problem with Kings: Recent Study of the Deuteronomistic History." *RelSRev* 22/1 (1996): 22–27.

Seitz, Christopher R. *Theology in Conflict: Reactions to the Exile in the Book of Jeremiah.* BZAW 176. Berlin: de Gruyter, 1989.

Smith, Mark S. *The Early History of God: Yahweh and the Other Deities in Ancient Israel.* San Francisco: Harper & Row, 1990.

———. *The Origins of Biblical Monotheism: Israel's Polytheistic Background and the Ugaritic Texts.* New York: Oxford University Press, 2001.

Smith, Morton. *Palestinian Parties and Politics That Shaped the Old Testament.* New York: Columbia University Press, 1971.

Snell, Daniel C. "Taxes and Taxation." *ABD* 6:338–40.

Soggin, J. Alberto. "Der Judäische ʿam-haʾareṣ und das Königtum in Juda: Ein Beitrag zum Studium der Deuteronomistischen Geschichtsschreibung." *VT* 13 (1963): 187–95.

Sparks, Kenton L. *Ethnicity and Identity in Ancient Israel: Prolegomena to the Study of Ethnic Sentiments and Their Expression in the Hebrew Bible.* Winona Lake, Ind.: Eisenbrauns, 1998.

Sperling, S. David. "An Arslan Tash Incantation: Interpretations and Implications." *HUCA* 53 (1982): 1–10.

Stager, Lawrence E. "The Archaeology of the Family in Ancient Israel." *BASOR* 260 (1985): 1–35.

Steck, Odil Hannes. "Theological Streams of Tradition." Pages 183–214 in *Tradition and Theology in the Old Testament.* Edited by D. Knight. Philadelphia: Fortress, 1977.

Steinberg, Naomi. "The Deuteronomic Law Code and the Politics of State Centralization." Pages 161–70 in *The Bible and the Politics of Exegesis: Essays in Honor of Norman K. Gottwald on His Sixty-Fifth Birthday.* Edited by D. Jobling, P. L. Day, and G. T. Sheppard. Cleveland: Pilgrim, 1991.

Tadmor, Hayim. "Traditional Institutions and the Monarchy: Social and Political Tensions in the Time of David and Solomon." Pages 239–57 in *Studies in the Period of David and Solomon and Other Essays.* Edited by T. Ishida. Tokyo: Yamakawa-Shuppansha, 1982.

Tate, Marvin E. *Psalms 51–100.* WBC 20. Dallas: Word, 1990.

Thompson, Thomas L. *Early History of the Israelite People: From the Written and Archaeological Sources.* SHANE 4. Leiden: Brill, 1992.

———. *The Mythic Past: Biblical Archaeology and the Myth of Israel.* New York: Basic Books, 1999.

Tuden, Arthur. "Leadership and the Decision-Making Process." Pages 275–83 in *Political Anthropology.* Edited by M. Swartz, V. Turner, and A. Tuden. Chicago: Aldine, 1966.

Valeri, Valerio. *Kingship and Sacrifice: Ritual and Society in Ancient Hawaii.* Translated by P. Wissing. Chicago: University of Chicago Press, 1985.

Vaux, Roland de. *Ancient Israel: Its Life and Institutions.* 2 vols. New York: McGraw-Hill, 1961.

Wagner, Günter. "The Political Organization of the Bantu of Kavirondo." Pages 196–236 in *African Political Systems.* Edited by M. Fortes and E. E. Evans-Pritchard. London: Oxford University Press, 1940.

Ward, James M. *Hosea: A Theological Commentary.* New York: Harper & Row, 1966.

Weinfeld, Moshe. *Deuteronomy 1–11*. AB 5. New York: Doubleday, 1991.

———. *Deuteronomy and the Deuteronomic School*. Oxford: Clarendon, 1972.

———. "The Emergence of the Deuteronomic Movement: The Historical Antecedents." Pages 76–98 in *Das Deuteronomium: Entstehung, Gestalt und Botschaft*.
Edited by N. Lohfink. BETL 68. Leuven: Leuven University Press, 1985.

Welch, Adam C. *The Code of Deuteronomy: A New Theory of Its Origin*. London:
Clarke, 1924.

Wellhausen, Julius. *Israelitische und Jüdische Geschichte*. 9th ed. Berlin: de Gruyter,
1958.

———. *Prolegomena to the History of Ancient Israel*. Translated by W. Robertson
Smith. New York: Meridan Books, 1957. Reprint of a translation of *Prolegomena zur Geschichte Israels*. 2d ed. Berlin: Reimer, 1883.

Willis, John T. "A Reapplied Prophetic Hope Oracle." Pages 64–76 in *Studies on
Prophecy*. Edited by G. W. Anderson et al. VTSup 26. Leiden: Brill, 1974.

Willis, Timothy M. "Elders in Pre-exilic Israelite Society." Ph.D. diss., Harvard
University, 1990.

———. *The Elders of the City: A Study of the Elders-Laws in Deuteronomy*. SBLMS 55.
Atlanta: Society of Biblical Literature, 2001.

Wilson, Robert R. "1 and 2 Kings: Introduction and Annotations." Pages 509–604
in *The HarperCollins Study Bible: New Revised Standard Version with the
Apocryphal/Deuterocanonical Books*. Edited by W. A. Meeks. San Francisco:
HarperSanFrancisco, 1993.

———. "Enforcing the Covenant: The Mechanisms of Judicial Authority in Early
Israel." Pages 39–69 in *The Quest for the Kingdom of God: Studies in Honor of
George E. Mendenhall*. Edited by H. B. Huffmon et al. Winona Lake, Ind.:
Eisenbrauns, 1983.

———. *Genealogy and History in the Biblical World*. Yale Near Eastern Researches 7.
New Haven: Yale, 1977.

———. "Israel's Judicial System in the Preexilic Period." *JQR* 74 (1983): 229–48.

———. *Prophecy and Society in Ancient Israel*. Philadelphia: Fortress, 1980.

———. *Sociological Approaches to the Old Testament*. GBS. Philadelphia: Fortress,
1984.

Wolf, Eric R. *Europe and the People Without History*. Berkeley and Los Angeles: University of California Press, 1982.

Wolff, Hans Walter. *Hosea*. Translated by G. Stansell. Hermeneia. Philadelphia:
Fortress, 1974.

———. "Hoseas Geistige Heimat." Pages 232–50 in *Gesammelte Studien zum Alten
Testament*. Munich: Kaiser, 1964 [orig. 1956].

———. *Micah: A Commentary*. Translated by G. Stansell. CC. Minneapolis: Augsburg, 1990.

———. "Micah the Moreshite—The Prophet and His Background." Pages 77–84
in *Israelite Wisdom: Theological and Literary Essays in Honor of Samuel Terrien*.
Edited by J. Gammie et al. Missoula, Mont.: Scholars Press for Union Theological Seminary, New York, 1978.

———. "Wie verstand Micha von Moreschet sein prophetisches Amt?" Pages
403–17 in *Congress Volume: Göttingen, 1977*. Edited by James A. Emerton,
William L. Holladay, and Andre Lemaire. VTSup 29. Leiden: Brill, 1978.

Woude, Adam S. van der. "Deutero-Micha: Ein Prophet aus Nord-Israel?" *NedTT* 25 (1971): 365–78.

———. "Micah IV 1–5: An Instance of the Pseudo-Prophets Quoting Isaiah." Pages 396–402 in *Symbolae biblicae et Mesopotamicae Francisco Mario Theodoro de Liagre Böhl dedicatae.* Edited by M. A. Beek, A. A. Kampman, C. Nijland, and J. Ryckmans. Leiden: Brill, 1973.

———. "Micah in Dispute with the Pseudo-Prophets." *VT* 19 (1969): 244–60.

Wright, Christopher J. H. *God's People in God's Land: Family, Land, and Property in the Old Testament.* Grand Rapids: Eerdmans, 1990.

———. "Jubilee, Year of." *ABD* 3:1025–30.

Wright, G. Ernest. "The Lawsuit of God: A Form-Critical Study of Deuteronomy 32." Pages 26–67 in *Israel's Prophetic Heritage: Essays in Honor of James Muilenburg.* Edited by B. W. Anderson and W. Harrelson. London: SCM, 1962.

———. "The Present State of Biblical Archaeology." Pages 89–90 in *The Study of the Bible Today and Tomorrow.* Edited by H. Willoughby. Chicago: University of Chicago Press, 1947.

Würthwein, Ernst. *Der 'amm ha'arez im Alten Testament.* BWANT 17. Stuttgart: Kohlhammer, 1936.

Yoffee, Norman. "The Decline and Rise of Mesopotamian Civilization: An Ethnoarchaeological Perspective on the Evolution of Social Complexity." *American Antiquity* 44 (1979): 5–35.

Yurco, Frank. "3,200-Year-Old Picture of Israelites Found in Egypt." *BAR* 16/5 (1990): 20–38.

———. "Merneptah's Palestine Campaign." *JSSEA* 8 (1978): 70.

Zobel, Konstantin. *Prophetie und Deuteronomium: Die Rezeption prophetischer Theologie durch das Deuteronomium.* BZAW 199. Berlin: de Gruyter, 1992.

SCRIPTURE AND ANCIENT SOURCES INDEX

(selected)

AUTHOR INDEX

SUBJECT INDEX

stipulations of covenant *See* covenant: instruction
stone slabs *See* standing stones
stratification (socioeconomic) 81–82, 85, 95, 146 n. 1, 149–51, 155–56, 176, 200–203, 206, 225, 228
stream of tradition *See* tradition stream
subcultural diversity 11, 269
succession of monarchs 47, 110, 116, 124–25, 149, 210–11, 213 n. 28, 214, 226, 235
syncretism 7, 11, 36, 45, 49–51, 257
Syro-Ephraimite war 80, 232

taxation 40–41, 43, 48, 107, 136, 143–44, 148, 154, 178, 269
Tell Beit Mirsim 146 n. 1, 150 n. 4
Tell el-Far'ah (north) 151 n. 5
Tell en-Nasbeh 146 n. 1
temple *See* Jerusalem: temple
tempered rule 32, 40–44, 48–49, 106–19, 122, 124–25, 138–39, 143, 152, 210, 225–26, 234–35, 249–50, 257
terracing 158 n. 18
theophany 22, 93–94, 129–31, 132 n. 7
tombs *See* burial
torah *See* covenant: instruction
trade 151, 165, 175 n. 56, 177, 262
tradents 16, 205, 213, 230, 272, 275–76
tradition stream 12, 16, 18–19, 24, 29–30, 37, 45, 49, 62 n. 39, 63, 68, 77–79, 81, 84, 91, 93 n. 30, 94, 97,

tradition stream *(continued)*
99–100, 103–4, 106–7, 113, 116, 120, 127, 132, 139, 144, 153 n. 7, 195, 204, 213–14, 217–18, 224, 229, 231, 237, 265, 267–68, 271–2, 277
tribal society *See* segmentary society
tribe 20, 31, 41, 57, 81, 84, 100–101, 117, 129, 135, 147, 152, 155, 159, 161–62, 164, 166, 168, 179, 183, 191, 193, 220–21, 226–27, 229, 232, 236, 246, 260–61, 263–64, 266, 271–74

Ugarit 27, 29, 33, 88, 252

vassal treaties 24, 26–27, 38–40, 74, 76 n. 15, 77, 86 n. 25, 95–96, 101, 192. *See also* covenant
vestiges *See* repristination

weather 33–34, 39, 79, 129–30, 179–80, 186, 192, 206, 255, 272
widow's plea ostracon 32–33, 154–55
wilderness 2 n. 1, 19, 25, 36–37, 79, 89–90, 129, 212, 221–24, 251–55, 263–64, 273

Zadok 125, 148, 181, 275, 277
Zedekiah 207 n. 18
Zion tradition 19, 43, 65, 69, 75, 85, 103, 105–6, 114 n. 57, 116–18, 120, 121–22, 124–26, 132–34, 137–38, 140–43, 198